D0407735

WEBSTER'S

GUIDE TO

ABBREVIATIONS

Webster's
GUIDE
TO
ABBREVIATIONS

A Merriam-Webster ®

M E R R I A M - W E B S T E R   I N C.

Springfield, Massachusetts

A GENUINE MERRIAM-WEBSTER

The name *Webster* alone is no guarantee of excellence. It is used by a number of publishers and may serve mainly to mislead an unwary buyer.

A Merriam-Webster® is the registered trademark you should look for when you consider the purchase of dictionaries or other fine reference books. It carries the reputation of a company that has been publishing since 1831 and is your assurance of quality and authority.

Library of Congress Cataloging in Publication
Main entry under title:

Webster's guide to abbreviations.

1. Abbreviations, English—Dictionaries.
I. Merriam-Webster, Inc.
PE1693.W4   1985   423'.1   85-15286
ISBN 0-87779-072-8

MADE IN THE UNITED STATES OF AMERICA

56WAK919089

CONTENTS

PREFACE

Webster's Guide to Abbreviations is a product of Merriam-Webster Inc., publishers of Merriam-Webster® dictionaries and reference books. Although it is a completely new book, and our first to be devoted entirely to abbreviations, it is, nevertheless, very much like other Merriam-Webster® books in being based on actual usage as recorded in this company's citation files of over 13 million examples of English words used in context. Webster's Guide to Abbreviations is not meant to be an exhaustive listing of all the abbreviations that may be used in English. Rather it is meant to present information about abbreviations that are found most often in general use, especially those that are apt to appear in one's daily reading and work activities.

The book is divided into two parts. In the first section of the book, the headwords are abbreviations, acronyms, initialisms, and symbols; they are followed by the words or phrases they stand for. The second section of the book is intended to help the user who seeks an acceptable abbreviation for a particular word or phrase. It lists the words and phrases found in the first section in alphabetical order and follows each with its abbreviation.

In some cases, we have included combinations of letters (such as *SOS*) or of letters and numbers (such as *4-F*) which resemble abbreviations, strictly so called, but for which no word or phrase is being abbreviated. In these cases, entries in the first section take the form of a headword followed by a short explanatory phrase.

    4-F unfit for military service

    SOS a recognized signal of distress

In the second section, these entries are alphabetized by a key word or phrase that serves as the headword.

    distress signal **SOS**

    unfit for military service **4-F**

Phrases beginning with *a, an,* or *the* have been alphabetized in the second section according to the second word in the phrase. Thus, the phrase *an hour and a half* is alphabetized as *hour and*

In most cases, abbreviations in the first section are followed by the English word or phrase they stand for, even if the abbreviation is actually derived from a foreign word or phrase. In such entries, the expansion is followed by an etymology in square brackets that gives the derivation.

a.m. before noon [L *ante meridiem*]

In these etymologies, the following abbreviations have been used.

F	French	LL	Late Latin
Ger	German	ML	Medieval Latin
Gk	Greek	NL	New Latin
IrGael	Irish Gaelic	Port	Portuguese
It	Italian	Russ	Russian
L	Latin	Sp	Spanish

Entries of this type in the second section are placed alphabetically at the English version only and do not include etymologies.

One exception to the pattern described above concerns some international sports associations with French names that are best known by their initials. In these cases, the French name rather than its English equivalent has been given in both the first and the second section. If there is any part of the French name whose meaning cannot be made out easily, an explanatory note has been added to the end of the entry.

FIRA Fédération Internationale
de Rugby Amateur

FINA Fédération Internationale
de Natation Amateur (swimming)

The contemporary styling of abbreviations is to a large extent inconsistent and arbitrary, and no set of rules can hope to encompass all of the possible variations, exceptions, and peculiarities actually encountered. The styling of abbreviations in print—whether capitalized or lowercased, closed up or spaced, punctuated or unpunctuated—depends most often on the writer's, editor's, or publisher's preference or on the context in which the abbreviation is found.

All is not confusion, however, and general patterns can be discerned. Some abbreviations (such as *a.k.a., e.g., etc., i.e.,* and *viz.*) have a strong tradition of punctuation, while others (such as *NATO, NASA, NOW, OPEC,* and *SALT*) that are pronounced as words tend to be all-capitalized and unpunctuated. A period follows most abbreviations that are formed by omitting all but the first few letters of a word (such as *bull.* for *bulletin* and *bro.* for *brother*) or that are formed by omitting letters from the middle of the word (such as *agcy.* for *agency* or *Mr.* for *Mister*). Punctuation is almost never used with symbols (such as the symbols for chemical elements) or with abbreviations for metric measurements. When an abbreviation appears in a table, such as a transportation schedule or a sports box score, it is usually unpunctuated. The trend today among many writers is to omit punctuation from nearly all abbreviations; however, as indicated above, for some kinds of abbreviations, the punctuated styling is still more common.

In most cases, the styling shown for an abbreviation in this book is the one that our citations indicate to be the most common. However, because the styling of abbreviations is so inconsistent, some arbitrary guidelines were followed in editing this book in order to present the information in a manner as internally consistent as possible. For example, all academic degrees are entered with only the initial letter of each abbreviated word capitalized and with a period following each abbreviated word.

Webster's Guide to Abbreviations includes nearly all of the abbreviations entered in other Merriam-Webster® publications, the largest number coming from Webster's Third New International Dictionary and Webster's Ninth New Collegiate Dictionary. It also includes many other abbreviations attested in our citation file but not entered in any of our other publications. One result of this inclusiveness, clearly evident in the second section, is that in many cases we have entered more than one abbreviation for a given word or phrase. In such cases, one must simply choose the abbreviation that is most appropriate to the context in which one is writing. In choosing one abbreviation over another one should always remember that the paramount concern is that it be easily understood by the people who encounter it.

Webster's Guide to Abbreviations, like other Merriam-Webster® publications, is the result of a collective effort. Dr. Frederick C. Mish, Editorial Director, contributed to the development of the plan for this book. John M. Morse, Manager of Editorial Operations and Planning, not only made major contributions during the initial stages of the book but also lent support and gave invaluable suggestions throughout the editing. Thomas L. Coopee, Comptroller, devised the computer program which made possible a speedier editing process. Several people were involved during the data-entry stage: Ardelia Thomas and Barbara A. Winkler under the direction of Gloria J. Afflitto; also, Carolyn O. Cushman, Dolores A. Goncalves, Theresa M. Klewin, and Linda M. Toro. Kara L. Puskey, Editorial Assistant, was responsible for most of the proofreading. Robert D. Copeland, Editorial Production Coordinator, helped with the computer programming and directed the book through its typesetting stages.

Kathleen M. Doherty
Editor

A

a alternate captain; are; at [L *ad*]; atto-; before noon [L *ante meridiem*]; goals against; to [L *ad*]

a. about; absent; absolute; absorbency; absorbent; academician; academy; acceleration; accepted; accommodation; acetum; acid; acidity; acre; act; actin; acting; active; activity; adjective; adjutant; administration; adult; after; afternoon; age; aged; air; aircraft; airplane; allergist; allergy; alpha; alto; amateur; amphibian; amphibious; amplitude; anna; anode; anonymous; ante; anterior; approved; aqua; area; army; artery; article; artillery; asked; associate; association; asymmetric; asymmetry; at; atom; atomic; atomic weight; author; automobile; fast — used of a clock [F *avancé*, past part. of *avancer* to be fast]; in the year [L *anno*]; year [L *annus*]

A ace; adenine; airman; ampere; ana; angstrom unit; answer; arctic; argon; assist; mass number

A. American; Australian

aa ana

a.a. always afloat

AA acting appointment; administrative assistant; Alcoholics Anonymous; ana; antiaircraft; athletic association; atomic absorption; author's alterations

A.A. achievement age; approximate absolute; Associate in Arts; automobile association

AAA Agricultural Adjustment Administration; Amateur Athletic Association; American Automobile Association; antiaircraft artillery; approved as amended

AAAL American Academy of Arts and Letters

AAAS American Association for the Advancement of Science

A.A.C. in the year before Christ [L *anno ante Christum*]

AACJC American

Association of Community and Junior Colleges

AACSL American Association for the Comparative Study of Law

AAF absorbic acid factor

AAFP American Academy of Family Physicians

AAL anterior axillary line

AAM air-to-air missile

A & M agricultural and mechanical

A. and M. ancient and modern

A & P anterior and posterior; auscultation and percussion

A & R artists and repertory

A & W alive and well

AAP affirmative action plan; American Academy of Pediatrics; Association of American Publishers

a.a.r. against all risks

AARP American Association of Retired Persons

A.A.S. Associate in Applied Science

AASCU American Association of State Colleges and Universities

AAU Amateur Athletic Union

AAUP American Association of University Professors

AAUW American Association of University Women

ab. abort; abortion; about; abstract

Ab. abbot

AB able-bodied seaman; aid to blind; airbase; airborne; airman basic; Alberta; at bats

A.B. Bachelor of Arts [NL *artium baccalaureus*]

ABA Amateur Boxing Association; American Badminton Association; American Bankers Association; American Bar Association; American Basketball Association; American Booksellers Association

abb. abbey

Abb. abbess; abbot

abbr. abbreviated; abbreviation

abbrev. abbreviated; abbreviation

ABC A Better Chance; advanced booking charter; American Bowling Congress; American Broadcasting Company; atomic, biological, and chemical; Audit Bureau of Circulations; Australian Broadcasting Company

ABCD accelerated business collection and delivery

abd. abdomen; abdominal

ABD all but dissertation

abdom. abdomen; abdominal

ab init. from the beginning [L *ab initio*]

abl. ablative

ABL Amateur Bicycling League; Automated Biological Laboratory

ABLA Amateur Bicycle League of America

ABM antiballistic missile

abn. airborne

Abp. archbishop

abr. abridged; abridger; abridgment

abs. absent; absolute; absolutely; abstract

ABS able-bodied seaman; acrylonitrile-butadiene-styrene; acute brain syndrome; American Bible Society

abs. re. the defendant being absent [NL *absente reo*]

abstr. abstract; abstracted

abt. about

ABT American Ballet Theatre

ABTA American Board of Trial Advocates

abv. above

ac. account; acre; acute; alicyclic; money of account

a.c. before meals [L *ante cibos*]

Ac actinium; altocumulus

AC adult contemporary; air corps; aircraftsman; alternating current; area code; army corps; athletic club; author's correction; automobile club; aviation cadet

A.C. after Christ; before Christ [L *ante Christum*]; in the year of Christ [L *anno Christi*]

A/C absolute ceiling; account current; air-conditioning

ACA American Camping Association; American Canoe Association; American Casting Association

acad. academic; academy

AC and U Association of Colleges and Universities

acc. acceptance; accepted; accompanied; accompaniment; accordant; according; account; accountant;

accusative

ACC Atlantic Coast Conference; automatic color control

acce. acceptance

accel accelerando

accomp. accompaniment

accpt. accompaniment

accrd. accrued

accred. accredited

acct. account; accountant

accus. accusative

ACCUS Automobile Competition Committee for the United States

A.C.D. adjourn in contemplation of dismissal

ACDA Arms Control and Disarmament Agency

ACE American Council on Education

acft. aircraft

AcG factor V [accelerator globulin]

ACh acetylcholine

AChE acetylcholinesterase

ack. acknowledge; acknowledgment

ackgt. acknowledgment

ACLU American Civil Liberties Union

ACNM American College of Nurse-Midwives

ACOG American College of Obstetricians and Gynecologists

ACP American College of Physicians

acpt. acceptance

ACS American Cancer Society; American Chemical Society; American College of Surgeons; antireticular cytotoxic serum; autograph card signed

ACSW Academy of Certified Social Workers

act. action; active; actor; actual; actuary

ACT American College Test; American College Testing; Association of Classroom Teachers

A.C.T. Australian Capital Territory

actg. acting; actuating

ACTH adrenocorticotropic hormone

ACTL American College of Trial Lawyers

ACU American Conservative Union; American Cycling Union; Association of Cricket Umpires

ACV actual cash value; air-cushion vehicle

ACW aircraftswoman; alternating continuous wave

ad advantage;

advertisement; advertising

ad. adapted; administration; administrative; adult; adverb

AD active duty; air-dried; alternate days; Alzheimer's disease; archduke; assembly district; assistant director; associate director; athletic director; autograph document; average deviation

A.D. before the day [L *ante diem*]; in the year of our Lord [L *anno domini*]

A/d after date

A/D analog to digital

ADA American Dental Association; American Dietetic Association; Americans for Democratic Action; assistant district attorney; average daily attendance

adag adagio

adapt. adaptation; adapted by

ADC Aid to Dependent Children; aide-de-camp; Air Defense Command; analog-to-digital converter; assistant division commander

add. add [L *adde*]; addendum; addition; additional; address; adduction; adductor; let it be added [L *addatur*]; let them be added [L *addantur*]

ADD American Dialect Dictionary

addn. addition

addnl. additional

ADF automatic direction finder

ad fin. at the end [L *ad finem*]; to the end [L *ad finem*]

ADG average daily gain

ADH antidiuretic hormone

ad inf. to infinity [L *ad infinitum*]

ad init. at the beginning [L *ad initium*]

ad int. for the intervening time [L *ad interim*]

ADIZ air defense identification zone

adj. adjacent; adjective; adjourned; adjudged; adjunct; adjustable; adjusted; adjustment

Adj. adjutant

Adjt. adjutant

ADL activities of daily living; Anti-Defamation League

ad lib. at pleasure [NL *ad*

libitum]

ad loc. at the place [L *ad locum*]; to the place [L *ad locum*]

adm. administration; administrative; administrator; admit

Adm. admiral; admiralty

ADM admiral

admin. administration

admix. administratrix

Adml. admiral

admor. administrator

admr. administrator

admrx. administratrix

adms. administrator

admstr. administrator

admx. administratrix

ADP adenosine diphosphate; automatic data processing

ADR American depositary receipt; asset depreciation range

ad s. at the suit of [L *ad sectam*]

ADS autograph document signed

ad sat. to saturation [L *ad saturandum*]

ad us. exter. for external use [L *ad usum externum*]

adv. advance; advent; adverb; adverbial; adverbially; adversus; advertisement;

advertising; advice; advise; advisory; against [L *adversum*]

Adv. advocate

ad val. according to value [L *ad valorem*]

advg. advertising

advt. advertisement

advtg. advantage; advertising

ae. aged [L *aetatis*]; of age [L *aetatis*]

A.E. account executive; Aeronautical Engineer; Agricultural Engineer

AEC Atomic Energy Commission

Ae.E. Aeronautical Engineer

AEF American Expeditionary Force

a.e.g. all edges gilt

aeq. equal [L *aequalis*]

aero. aeronautical; aeronautics

AES atomic emission spectroscopy

aet. aged [L *aetatis*]; of age [L *aetatis*]

aetat. aged [L *aetatis*]; of age [L *aetatis*]

a.f. at the end [L *ad finem*]; done in faith [L *actum fide*]; to the end [L *ad finem*]

Af affix

Af. afghani; Afghanistan

AF admiral of the fleet; air force; audio frequency; auricular fibrillation

AFA Amateur Fencing Association; Amateur Football Alliance; Amateur Football Association

AFAM Ancient Free and Accepted Masons

AFB acid-fast bacillus; air force base

AFC American Football Conference; American Foxhound Club; Association Football Club; automatic flight control; automatic frequency control

AFCA American Football Coaches Association

AFDC Aid to Families with Dependent Children

aff. affairs; affectionate; affirmative

affly. affectionately

afft. affidavit

A/1C airman first class

AFL American Federation of Labor; American Football League

AFLA Amateur Fencers League of America; American Foreign Law Association

AFL-CIO American Federation of Labor and Congress of Industrial Organizations

AFM American Federation of Musicians

Afr. Africa; African

AFSCME American Federation of State, County, and Municipal Employees

aft. afternoon

AFT American Federation of Teachers; automatic fine tuning

AFTRA American Federation of Television and Radio Artists

ag agricultural; agriculture

Ag August; silver [L *argentum*]

AG accountant general; adjutant general; agent-general; attorney general; corporation [Ger *Aktiengesellschaft*]

AGA Amateur Gymnastics Association

AGC advanced graduate certificate; automatic gain control

agcy. agency

agd. agreed

agg. aggregate

agglut. agglutination

AGI adjusted gross income

agit. a. us. shake before using [L *agita ante usum*]

agit. bene shake well [L *agita bene*]

agn. again

AGO adjutant general's office

AGP average goals against per period

agr. agricultural; agriculture

agri. agriculture

agric. agricultural; agriculture

agrl. agricultural

agron. agronomist; agronomy

agst. against

agt. against; agent; agreement

Ah ampere-hour

AH arts and humanities

A.H. in the year of the hegira [ML *anno hegirae*]

AHA American Hospital Association

AHAUS Amateur Hockey Association of the United States

AHCA American Hockey Coaches Association

AHF antihemophilic factor; factor VIII [antihemophilic factor]

AHG antihemophilic globulin; antihuman globulin

AHL American Hockey League

AHRA American Hot Rod Association

AHST Alaska Hawaii standard time

a.i. for the intervening time [L *ad interim*]

AI active ingredient; airborne intercept; aircraft interception; Amnesty International; artificial insemination; artificial intelligence

AIA American Institute of Architects

AIAW Association of Intercollegiate Athletics for Women

AIB American Institute of Banking

AIBA Association Internationale de Boxe Amateur (boxing)

AICPA American Institute of Certified Public Accountants

AID Agency for International Development; artificial insemination by donor

AIDS acquired immunodeficiency syndrome

AIH   artificial insemination by husband

AIM   American Indian Movement

AINL   Association of Immigration and Nationality Lawyers

AJ   ankle jerk; associate justice

AJBC   American Junior Bowling Congress

AK   above knee; Alaska

a.k.a.   also known as

AKC   American Kennel Club

al.   alias; alley

a.l.   all lengths

Al   aluminum

AL   air letter; Alabama; American League; American Legion; autograph letter

A.L.   in the year of light [L *anno lucis*]

Ala.   Alabama

ALA   American Library Association; aminolevulinic acid; Automobile Legal Association

Alas.   Alaska

alb.   albumin

Alb.   Albania; Albanian

Alba.   Alberta

ALBA   American Lawn Bowling Association

alc.   alcohol

ALCM   air-launched cruise missile

ald.   alderman

aldm.   alderman

alg.   algebra

ALG   antilymphocyte globulin; antilymphocytic globulin

ALI   American Law Institute

ALJ   administrative law judge

alk.   alkaline

alky.   alkalinity

ALL   acute lymphoblastic leukemia

allo   allegro

allow.   allowance

ALP   American Labor Party

ALS   amyotrophic lateral sclerosis; antilymphocyte serum; antilymphocytic serum; autograph letter signed

ALSA   American Law Student Association

alt   alto

alt.   alter; alteration; alternate; alternating; alternative; altitude

Alta.   Alberta

alter.   alteration

alt. hor.   every two hours [L *alternis horis*]

altn. alteration; alternate

ALU arithmetic logic unit

alum. aluminum; alumna; alumnus

alv. alveolar

alw. allowance; allowance race

am. ammeter; ammunition; amplitude

a.m. before noon [L *ante meridiem*]

Am americium

Am. America; American

AM air marshal; Air Medal; airmail; amplitude modulation; associate member

A.M. Ave Maria; in the year of the world [L *anno mundi*]; Master of Arts [ML *artium magister*]

AMA against medical advice; American Medical Association; American Motorcyclist Association

amb. ambassador; ambulance; ambulatory

A.M.D.G. to the greater glory of God [L *ad majorem Dei gloriam*]

amdt. amendment

AmE American English

AME African Methodist Episcopal

Amer. America; American

AmerInd American Indian

Ameslan American Sign Language

Amex American Stock Exchange

amg. among

AMG allied military government

AMI acute myocardial infarction

amn. ammunition

Amn. airman

amp amperage; ampere

amp. ampul; amputation

AMP adenosine monophosphate

amph. amphibian; amphibious

amp-hr ampere-hour

Ams autographed manuscript

AMS Agricultural Marketing Service

AMsS autographed manuscript signed

amt. amount

a.m.u. atomic mass unit

AMVETS American Veterans of World War II, Korea, Vietnam

an. animate; anonymous; in the year [L *anno*]; year [L *annus*]

a.n. above-named

AN airman (navy); army-navy

A.N. arrival notice
ANA Administration for Native Americans; American Newspaper Association; American Nurses Association
anag. anagram
anal. analogous; analogy; analysis; analytic; analyze
anat. anatomic; anatomical; anatomy
anc. ancient
anct. ancient
and andante
ang. angular
Ang. Angola
Angl. Anglican
anhyd. anhydrous
anl. animal; anneal
ann. annals; annealed; annual; annuity; years [L *anni*]
anon. anonymous; anonymously
anor. another
ANOVA anaylsis of variance
anr. another
ans. answer; answered
ANS autograph note signed; autonomic nervous system
ANSI American National Standards Institute
ant. antenna; anticipated; antiquarian; antiquity; antonym
Ant. Antarctica; Antrim
anth. anthology
anthro. anthropologist; anthropology
anthrop. anthropological; anthropology
antiq. antiquarian; antiquary
ANTU alpha-naphthylthiourea
ANZAC Australia and New Zealand Army Corps
ANZUK Australia, New Zealand, United Kingdom
ANZUS Australia, New Zealand, United States
a.o. among others; and others
AO area of operation
A/O account of
AOB alcohol on breath
AOL absent over leave
AONB area of outstanding natural beauty
aor. aorist
AOTA American Occupational Therapy Association
ap. according to [L *apud*]; apostle; apothecaries'; in the works of [L *apud*]
Ap. April
AP above proof; account paid; accounts payable; action potential;

additional premium;
Advanced Placement;
advanced post; advice of
payment; airplane;
airplane pilot; air
position; alkaline
phosphatase; American
plan; anteroposterior;
antipersonnel; aortic
pressure; armor-piercing;
assessment paid;
Associated Press; assumed
position

A.P. anterior pituitary;
arithmetic progression; as
purchased; author's proof

A/P authority to pay;
authority to purchase

APA American Paddleball
Association

APB all points bulletin

APBA American Power
Boat Association

APC armored personnel
carrier; aspirin,
phenacetin, caffeine;
autographed presentation
copy

APF animal protein factor

API air position indicator;
American Petroleum
Institute

APL A Programming
Language

apo. apogee

APO Army post office

Apoc. Apocalypse;
Apocrypha

apos. apostrophe

app. apparatus; apparent;
apparently; appeal;
appellate; appended;
appendix; applied;
appointed; appraised;
apprentice; approximately

appd. approved

appl. appeal; applicable;
applied

appln. application

appmt. appointment

appnt. appointment

appoint. appointment

appr. apprentice; approved

appro. approbation;
approval

approx. approximate;
approximately

appt. appoint; appointed;
appointment

apptd. appointed

appx. appendix

Apr. April

APR annual percentage
rate

apt. apartment; aptitude

APTA American Platform
Tennis Association

apx. appendix

aq. aqueous; water [L
aqua]

AQ accomplishment
quotient; achievement

quotient

aq. bull. boiling water [L *aqua bulliens*]

aq. dest. distilled water [NL *aqua destillata*]

aq. ferv. warm water [L *aqua fervens*]

aq. font. spring water [L *aqua fontana*]

ar area; aromatic

ar. arrival; arrive

Ar argon; aryl

Ar. Arabic

AR accounts receivable; analyzed reagent; argentum; Arkansas; army regulation; automatic rifle; autonomous republic

A.R. acknowledgement of receipt; all rail; all risks; annual return; in the year of the reign [L *anno regni*]

Arab. Arabian; Arabic

arb arbitrager; arbitrageur

arb. arbitration; arbitrator

arbtrn. arbitration

ARC American Red Cross

ARCA Automobile Racing Club of America

arccos arccosine

arccot arccotangent

arccse arccosecant

arch. archaic; archery; archipelago; architect; architectural; architecture; archive

Arch. archbishop

Archbp. archbishop

Archd. archdeacon; archduke

archeol. archeology

archit. architecture

archt. architect

arcsec arcsecant

arcsin arcsine

arctan arctangent

ARD acute respiratory disease

ARDC American Race Drivers Club

arg. argent; in arguing [L *arguendo*]

Arg. Argentina; Argyll

arith. arithmetic; arithmetical

Ariz. Arizona

Ark. Arkansas

ARL American Roque League

arm. armament; armature

Arm. Armagh; Armenia; Armenian

ARM adjustable rate mortgage

armd. armored

ARO after receipt of order

ARP air-raid precautions

arr. arranged; arrangement; arranger; arrival; arrive

A.R.R. in the year of the king's reign [L *anno regni regis*]; in the year of the queen's reign [L *anno regni regnae*]

ARRC American Road Race of Champions

arrgt. arrangement

ARRT American Registered Respiratory Therapist; American Registry of Radiological Technologists

ars. arsenal

art. article; artificial; artillery; artist

ART Accredited Record Technician

ARTCC air route traffic control center

arty. artillery

arv. arrive

ARV American Revised Version

ARVN Army of the Republic of Vietnam (South Vietnam)

ARW air raid warden

as. astigmatism

As altostratus; arsenic

AS administrative support; airspeed; alongside; American Samoa; Anglo-Saxon; aortic stenosis; applied science; apprentice seaman; arteriosclerosis; at sight

A.S. air service; Associate in Science; in the year of redemption [ML *anno salutis*]

A/S account sales; after sight; antisubmarine

ASA acetylsalicylic acid; Amateur Softball Association; American Standards Association; Army Security Agency

ASAP as soon as possible

ASAT anti-satellite

asb. asbestos

ASC altered states of consciousness

ASCAP American Society of Composers, Authors, and Publishers

ASCII American Standard Code for Information Interchange

ASCP American Society of Clinical Pathologists

ASCU Association of State Colleges and Universities

ASCVD arteriosclerotic cardiovascular disease

ASE American Stock Exchange

ASEAN Association of Southeast Asian Nations

A.S.E.T. Associate in Engineering Technology

asg. assigned; assignment

asgd. assigned
asgmt. assignment
ASHD arteriosclerotic heart disease
ASI airspeed indicator
A.S.I. American Safety Institute
a.s.l. above sea level
ASL American Shuffleboard League; American Sign Language; American Soccer League
asm. assembly
ASME American Society of Mechanical Engineers
ASN Army service number
ASP American Selling Price; Anglo-Saxon Protestant
ASPAC Asian and Pacific Council
ASPCA American Society for the Prevention of Cruelty to Animals
ASR airport surveillance radar; air-sea rescue
ass. assembly; assistant; association
assce. assurance
assd. assessed; assigned; assured
assigt. assignment
assmt. assessment
assn. association
assoc. associate; associated; association

ASSR Autonomous Soviet Socialist Republic
asst. assistant
asstd. assented; associated; assorted
assy. assembly
Assyr. Assyrian
AST Atlantic standard time
ASTM American Society for Testing and Materials
as tol. as tolerated
ASTP Army specialized training program
astrol. astrologer; astrology
astron. astronomer; astronomy
ASUUS Amateur Skating Union of the United States
ASV American Standard Version
ASW antisubmarine warfare
at. atmosphere; atmospheric; atomic; attorney
At astatine
AT ampere-turn; antitank; assay ton; assertiveness training; automatic transmission
A.T. air temperature; airtight; American terms
ATA Amateur

Trapshooting Association
ATC air traffic control
atdt. attendant
ATF Bureau of Alcohol, Tobacco, and Firearms
ATGSB Admissions Test for Graduate Study in Business
Atl. Atlantic
ATL antitrust law
ATLA American Trial Lawyers Association
atm. atmosphere; atmospheric
ATM automated teller machine; automatic teller machine
at. no. atomic number
ATP adenosine triphosphate; Admissions Testing Program; Association of Tennis Professionals
ATS at the suit of
att. attaché; attached; attempts; attention; attorney
att. gen. attorney general
attn. attention
attrib. attributive; attributively
atty. attorney
atty. gen. attorney general
ATV all-terrain vehicle
at. wt. atomic weight
au antitoxin unit

a.u. according to custom [L *ad usum*]
Au gold [L *aurum*]
AU angstrom unit
A.U. almost uncirculated; astronomical unit
A.U.C. from the year of the founding of the city (of Rome) [L *ab urbe condita*]; in the year from the founding of the city (of Rome) [L *anno urbis conditae*]
aud. audible; audit; auditor
aug. augmentative; augmented
Aug. August
a.u.n. free from marking [L *absque ulla nota*]
aur. aurum
Aus. Austria; Austrian
AUS Army of the United States
Austral. Australia; Australian
auth. authentic; author; authoress; authorities; authority; authorized
auto. automatic
aux. auxiliary
auxil. auxiliary
av. avenue; average; aviation; avoirdupois
a.v. he/she lived (a given number of) years [L *annos*

vixit]

AV arteriovenous; atrioventricular; audiovisual; Authorized Version; average variability

A/V according to the value [L *ad valorem*]

AVC automatic volume control

avdp. avoirdupois

ave. avenue

AVE automatic volume expansion

avg. average

AVMA American Veterinary Medical Association

avn. aviation

avoir. avoirdupois

a.w. all widths

AW above water; aircraft warning; all water; articles of war; automatic weapon

A/W actual weight

AWACS airborne warning and control system

AWG American wire gauge

AWL absent with leave

AWOL absent without leave

AWSA American Water Ski Association

ax. axiom; axis

AYC American Youth Congress

AYD American Youth for Democracy

AYH American Youth Hostels

Ayr. Ayrshire

az. azure

Az azimuth

AZ Arizona

B

b basso; bel

b. bachelor; bacillus; back; backward edge; bag; bale; ball; ban; band; bar; barge; barometric; base; bass; bat; bath; battery; battle; bay; bearing; before; behavior; bid; billion; black; blend; blessed [L *beata* (fem.), *beatus* (masc.)]; blinkers; blue; boatswain; boils at; bond; book; born; bottom; bowled; bowled out; bowler; brass; breadth; breezing; brick; broadcast; broken; brother; brotherhood; bulletin; butut; bye

B bachelor; baht; balboa; bar; Baumé; bench [ML

bancus]; bid; bishop; bitch; bolivar; bomber; bond; born; boron; brightness; British thermal unit; bulb; magnetic induction

B. baron; Bible; British

ba. bath

Ba barium

BA batting average; blood alcohol; bronchial asthma

B.A. Bachelor of Arts; Buenos Aires

B.A.A. Bachelor of Applied Arts

BAAB British Amateur Athletic Board

B.A.A.E. Bachelor of Aeronautical and Astronautical Engineering

bac. bachelor [ML *baccalaureus*]

BAC blood alcohol concentration

bach. bachelor

back. backwardation

bact. bacteria; bacterial; bacteriological; bacteriology; bacterium

BaE barium enema

BAE barium enema

B.A.E. Bachelor of Aeronautical Engineering; Bachelor of Agricultural Engineering; Bachelor of Architectural Engineering; Bachelor of

Art Education; Bachelor of Arts in Education

B.A.Ed. Bachelor of Arts in Education

B.Ae.E. Bachelor of Aeronautical Engineering

B.A.E.E. Bachelor of Arts in Elementary Education

bag. baggage

B.Ag. Bachelor of Agriculture

bal. balance

BAL Basic Assembly Language; blood alcohol level; dimercaprol [British Anti-Lewisite]

Balt. Baltimore

Balto. Baltimore

B.A.M. Bachelor of Applied Mathematics; Bachelor of Arts in Music

B & B bed-and-breakfast

B and D bondage and discipline

B & E breaking and entering

B and L building and loan

B and S brandy and soda

b and w bread and water

B & W black and white

bankr. bankruptcy

Bap. Baptist

Bapt. Baptist

bar. bark; barometer; barometric; barque; barrel

Bar. Baruch

B.Ar. Bachelor of Architecture

BAR Browning automatic rifle

barr. barrister

Bart. baronet

bas. basso

BAS basic airspeed

B.A.S. Bachelor of Applied Science; Bachelor of Arts and Sciences

BASIC Beginner's All-purpose Symbolic Instruction Code

baso. basophil

BAT basic air temperature

B.A.T. Bachelor of Arts in Teaching

batn. battalion

batt. battalion; batten; battery; battle

Bav. Bavaria; Bavarian

BB B'nai B'rith; base on balls; bats both right-handed and left-handed; battleship; best of breed; blue book

BB. blessed

B.B. bail bond; ball bearing; bankbook; bearer bond; bill book; break bulk

B.B.A. Bachelor of Business Administration

bbb bed, breakfast, and bath

BBB Better Business Bureau; bundle branch block

BBC British Broadcasting Corporation

B.B.E. Bachelor of Business Education

bbl. barrel; barrels

BBT basal body temperature

bc thorough bass [It *basso continuo*]

BC bail court; bankruptcy cases; battery commander; bicycle club; boat club; bowling club; British Columbia; broadcast

B.C. Bachelor of Commerce; before Christ; board of control; borough council; British Columbia

BCA Billiard Congress of America

B.Can.L. Bachelor of Canon Law

BCC body-centered cubic

BCD bad conduct discharge; binary-coded decimal

B.C.E. Bachelor of Chemical Engineering; Bachelor of Civil Engineering; Before the Christian Era; Before the Common Era

bcf billion cubic feet

BCF British Cycling Federation

BCG bacillus Calmette-Guérin; ballistocardiogram; bromocresol green

bch. bunch

B.Ch. Bachelor of Chemistry

B.Ch.E. Bachelor of Chemical Engineering

BCL broadcast listener

B.C.L. Bachelor of Canon Law; Bachelor of Civil Law; Bachelor of Commercial Law

bcn. beacon

B.C.S. Bachelor of Chemical Science; Bachelor of Commercial Science

BCSE Board of Civil Service Examiners

bd. band; board; bond; bound; boundary; brindled; bundle

b.d. twice a day [L *bis die*]

b/d barrels per day

BD back dividend; bank draft; bills discounted; bomb disposal

B.D. Bachelor of Divinity

B/D bondage/domination; brought down

B.D.A. Bachelor of Domestic Arts; Bachelor of Dramatic Art

bde. brigade

bd.ft. board foot

bdg. binding

b.d.i. both dates included; both days inclusive

bdl. bundle

bdle. bundle

BDOS basic disk operating system

bdr. bombardier; brigadier

bdrm. bedroom

bdry. boundary

BDS bomb disposal squad

bdy. boundary

Be beryllium

Bé Baumé

BE band elimination; barium enema; below elbow; bill of entry; bill of exchange; board of education

B.E. Bachelor of Education; Bachelor of Engineering; Buddhist Era

BEA Bureau of Economic Analysis

BEC Bureau of Employees' Compensation

B.Ed. Bachelor of Education

Beds. Bedfordshire

B.E.E. Bachelor of Electrical Engineering

bef. before

BEF British Expeditionary Force

beg. begin; beginning

bel. below

Belg. Belgian; Belgium

B.E.M. Bachelor of Engineering of Mines; British Empire Medal

B.Engr. Bachelor of Engineering

B.Eng.S. Bachelor of Engineering Science

BEOG Basic Educational Opportunity Grant

Berks. Berkshire

Berw. Berwick

B.E.S. Bachelor of Engineering Science

bet. between

bev. beverage

BeV billion electron volts

bf. brief

b.f. board foot; boldface

BF beat frequency

B.F. Bachelor of Forestry; boyfriend

B/F brought forward

B.F.A. Bachelor of Fine Arts

BFO beat frequency oscillator

BFOQ bona fide occupational qualification

BFP biologic false-positive

bg. background; bag; beige; being

BG bonded goods; brigadier general

B.G. background; bluegrass

B.Gen. brigadier general

bght. bought

B.G.S. Bachelor of General Studies

bgt. bought

BH base hospital; bill of health; Brinell hardness

BHA butylated hydroxyanisole

BHC benzene hexachloride

bhd. bulkhead

B.H.L. Bachelor of Hebrew Letters; Bachelor of Hebrew Literature

BHN Brinell hardness number

bhp brake horsepower

bhp. bishop

bhpric. bishopric

BHT butylated hydroxytoluene

bi bisexual

Bi bismuth

BIA Braille Institute of America; Bureau of Indian Affairs

B.I.A. Bachelor of Industrial Administration; Bachelor of Industrial Arts

bib. biblical; drink [L *bibe*]

Bib. Bible

bibl. biblical; bibliography

bibliog. bibliographer; bibliography

b.i.d. twice a day [L *bis in die*]

B.I.D. Bachelor of Industrial Design

B.I.E. Bachelor of Industrial Engineering

BIG best in group

bil billion

bili. bilirubin

BIM best in match

bio. biography

biochem. biochemistry

biog. biographer; biographical; biography

biol. biologic; biological; biologist; biology

BIOS basic input/output system

BIOT British Indian Ocean Territory

bis. bissextile

BIS Bank for International Settlement; best in show

BJ biceps jerk

B.J. Bachelor of Journalism

bk. backwardation; balk; bank; bark; black; block; book; brake; brook

Bk berkelium

BK below knee

bkcy. bankruptcy

bkg. banking; bookkeeping; breakage

bkgd. background

Bklyn. Brooklyn

bkp. bookplate

bkpg. bookkeeping

bkpr. bookkeeper

bkpt. bankrupt

bkry. bakery

bks. backstrip; barracks

bkt. basket; bracket

bl. bale; barrel; black; block; blue

Bl. Blessed

BL baseline; bats left; bats left-handed; black letter; breadth-length; breech-loading; building line

B.L. Bachelor of Law; Bachelor of Laws; Bachelor of Letters

B/L bill of lading

blc. balance

bld. blond; blood

bldg. building

Bldg.E. building engineer

bldr. builder

B.Lit. Bachelor of Letters [ML *baccalaureus litterarum*]; Bachelor of Literature [ML *baccalaureus litterarum*]

B.Litt. Bachelor of Letters [ML *baccalaureus litterarum*]; Bachelor of Literature [ML *baccalaureus litterarum*]

blk. black; blank; block; bulk

blkd. bulkhead

B.LL. Bachelor of Laws

BLM Bureau of Land Management

blr. boiler

BLR breech-loading rifle

BLS Bureau of Labor Statistics

B.L.S. Bachelor of Liberal Studies; Bachelor of Library Science

blst. ballast

blt. built

BLT bacon, lettuce, and tomato

blvd. boulevard

bm. beam

b.m. board measure

BM basal metabolism; bill of material; bishop and martyr; bowel movement; brigade major; bronze medal; burgomaster

B.M. Bachelor of Medicine; Bachelor of Music; bench mark; British Museum; of blessed memory [L *beatae memoriae*]

BMD ballistic missile defense

B.M.E. Bachelor of Mechanical Engineering; Bachelor of Mining

Engineering; Bachelor of Music Education

B.M.Ed. Bachelor of Music Education

BMEP brake mean effective pressure

BMEWS ballistic missile early warning system

BMI Broadcast Music Incorporated

BMOC big man on campus

BMR basal metabolic rate

B.M.S. Bachelor of Marine Science

B.M.T. Bachelor of Medical Technology

B.M.V. Blessed Mary the Virgin [LL *Beata Maria Virgo*]

BMX bicycle motocross

bn. battalion; beacon; been

Bn. baron; battalion

BN Bureau of Narcotics

B.N. Bachelor of Nursing; bank note

BNA Basle Nomina Anotomica

bnd. band; bound

BNDD Bureau of Narcotics and Dangerous Drugs

B.N.S. Bachelor of Naval Science

Bnss. baroness

BO back order; blackout; branch office; broker's

order; brought over; buyer's option

B.O. body odor; box office

BOB best of breed

BOD biochemical oxygen demand; biological oxygen demand

BOF basic oxygen furnace

B of E board of education

B of H board of health

B of T board of trade

bom. bombardier

BOM business office must

BOMFOG brotherhood of man, fatherhood of God

BOPD barrels of oil per day

BOQ bachelor officers' quarters

bor. borough

bot. botanical; botanist; botany; bottle; bottom; bought

BOT board of trade

botan. botanical

bp baptized; birthplace; boiling point

b.p. the public good [L *bonum publicum*]

Bp. bishop

BP band pass; batting practice; beautiful people; before present; before the present; below proof; blood pressure; blueprint; bonus points; British

Pharmacopoeia

B.P. Bachelor of Pharmacy

B/P bill of parcels; bills payable

BPA basic pressure altitude

BPB bank post bill

bpd barrels per day

B.P.E. Bachelor of Petroleum Engineering; Bachelor of Physical Education

B.Ph. Bachelor of Philosophy

BPH benign prostatic hypertrophy

B.Phil. Bachelor of Philosophy

bpi bits per inch; bytes per inch

bpl. birthplace

bpm bottles per minute

BPOE Benevolent and Protective Order of Elks

bps bits per second; bytes per second

BPT best practicable technology

BPW board of public works

bq. barque

b.q. may he/she rest well [L *bene quiescat*]

bque. barque

br. branch; brand; brass; bridge; brief; brig;

brigade; broché; bronze; brother; brown; brush
Br bromine
Br. Britain; British
BR bank rate; bats right; bats right-handed; bedroom; bill of rights; builder's risk
B.R. British Railways
B/R bills receivable
Braz. Brazil; Brazilian
brd. board; braid
BrE British English
BRE business reply envelope
B.R.E. Bachelor of Religious Education
Breck. Brecknockshire
brf. brief
brg. bearing; bridge
brig. brigade; brigadier
Brig.Gen. brigadier general
Brit. Britain; British
brl. barrel
BRL Babe Ruth League
brlp. burlap
brm. barometer
brmc. barometric
brn. brown
bro. bronze; brother; brothers
bros. brothers
BRP bathroom privileges
brs. brass
brt. brought

brz. bronze
b.s. bullshit
BS balance sheet; bottom settlings; bowel sounds; breath sounds
B.S. Bachelor of Science; bishop suffragan; British standard
B/S bill of sale; bill of store
BSA Boy Scouts of America
B.S.A. Bachelor of Science in Agriculture
B.S.A.A. Bachelor of Science in Applied Arts
B.S.A.E. Bachelor of Science in Aeronautical Engineering; Bachelor of Science in Agricultural Engineering; Bachelor of Science in Architectural Engineering
B.S.Ag. Bachelor of Science in Agriculture
B.S.Arch. Bachelor of Science in Architecture
B.S.B. Bachelor of Science in Business
bsc. basic
B.Sc. Bachelor of Science
BSC binary synchronous communication
B.S.Ch. Bachelor of Science in Chemistry
B.Sc.N. Bachelor of

Science in Nursing
B.S.E. Bachelor of Science
in Education
B.S.Ec. Bachelor of
Science in Economics
B.S.Econ. Bachelor of
Science in Economics
B.S.Ed. Bachelor of
Science in Education
B.S.E.E. Bachelor of
Science in Electrical
Engineering; Bachelor of
Science in Elementary
Education
B.S.E.T. Bachelor of
Science in Engineering
Technology
B.S.For. Bachelor of
Science in Forestry
B.S.F.S. Bachelor of
Science in Foreign Service
bsh. bushel
BSI British Standards
Institution
B.S. in L.E. Bachelor of
Science in Law
Enforcement
BSJA British Show
Jumping Association
bskt. basket
B.S.L. Bachelor of Sacred
Literature; Bachelor of
Science in Languages;
Bachelor of Science in
Law; Bachelor of Science
in Linguistics

B.S.L.S. Bachelor of
Science in Library Science
B.S.M.E. Bachelor of
Science in Mechanical
Engineering
bsmt. basement
B.S.N. Bachelor of Science
in Nursing
B.S.N.A. Bachelor of
Science in Nursing
Administration
B.S.N.E. Bachelor of
Science in Nursing
Education
B.S.Ph. Bachelor of
Science in Pharmacy
B.S.P.H. Bachelor of
Science in Public Health
B.S.Phar. Bachelor of
Science in Pharmacy
B.S.P.H.N. Bachelor of
Science in Public Health
Nursing
B.S.P.T. Bachelor of
Science in Physical
Therapy
B/St bill of sight
BST blood serological test;
British standard time
bt. beat; bent; boat;
bought; brevet
Bt Bacillus thuringiensis
Bt. baronet
BT basic training;
bedtime; berth terms;
brain tumor

B.T. board of trade
BTA board of tax appeals; butylated hydrozyanisole
BTAM basic telecommunications access method
btn. battalion
btr. better
btry. battery
Btu British thermal unit
BTU board of trade unit
Btuh British thermal units per hour
btwn. between
bty. battery
bu. blue; bulletin; bureau; bushel
BU brilliant uncirculated
Bucks. Buckinghamshire
BUdR bromodeoxyruidine
bufly. butterfly
Bulg. Bulgaria; Bulgarian
bull. bulletin
BUN blood urea nitrogen
bur. bureau; buried
Bur. Burma
bus. business
BV book value
B.V. Blessed Virgin
BVD bovine virus diarrhea
B.V.I. British Virgin Islands
B.V.M. Blessed Virgin Mary
BW bacteriological

warfare; biological warfare; black and white; blood Wassermann; board of works; body weight; bonded warehouse; bread and water
bwd. backward
BWD bacillary white diarrhea
BWG Birmingham wire gauge
B.W.I. British West Indies
BWR boiling water reactor
BWV Bach-Werke-Verzeichnis
bx. box
Bx biopsy
BX base exchange
bxd. boxed
by billion years
BYO bring your own
BYOB bring your own booze; bring your own bottle
byp. bypass
Byr billion years
Bz benzoyl

C

c calm; candle; cedi; centi-; cloudy; common meter; common time; continental; contralto; coulomb; curie;

velocity of light; 4/4 —
used after the clef sign on
a musical staff

c. canceled; canoe; canon;
cape; captain; caput;
carat; cargo; case; castle;
cathode; caught; caught
out; cause; cent; cental;
centavo; center; centime;
centimeter; century;
cervical; chairman;
chancellor; chancery;
chapter; chief; child;
church; circa; circiter;
circuit; circum; clearance;
clonus; closure; cobalt;
codex; coefficient; cognate;
cold; college; colon; color;
colt; combat; commander;
companion; condemned;
conductor; confessor;
confidential; congregation;
congress; conservative;
constable; consul; contact;
contraction; copper; copy;
copyright; cord; cordoba;
corps; correct; cost; count;
coupon; court; cousin;
created; crowned; cubic;
cup; currency; current;
cycle; cylinder; with [L
cum]

C calorie; capacitance;
capacity; carbon; catcher;
Celsius; centigrade;
charge conjugation;
circumference; clockwise;
cocaine; complement;
conclusion; consonant;
gallon [L *congius*];
hundred [L *centum*]

C. Canadian; Catholic;
contra

ca centare; with the bow
[It *coll'arco*]

ca. cable; candle; case;
cathode; circa

c.a. English horn [F *cor
anglais*]

Ca calcium

Ca. California

CA California; cancer;
carcinoma; cardiac arrest;
chronological age; coast
artillery; controller of
accounts; court of appeal;
credit account

C.A. Central America;
chartered accountant;
chief accountant; claim
agent; cold air;
commercial agent; cost
accountant; council
accepted; crown agent

C/A capital account;
current account

cab. cabin; cabinet; cable

CAB Citizens' Advice
Bureau; Civil Aeronautics
Board

cabnt. cabinet

CAC cardiac accelerator

center

cad. cadenza; cadet

CAD computer-assisted design; computer-aided design; coronary artery disease

CADD computer-aided design and drafting

CAE computer-aided engineering

CAF clerical, administrative, and fiscal

C.A.F. cost, assurance, and freight

CAFE corporate average fuel economy

C.A.G.S. Certificate of Advanced Graduate Study

CAI computer-aided instruction; computer-assisted instruction; confused artificial insemination

cal. calando; calendar; calends; caliber; calibrate; calorie; small calorie

Cal. California; large calorie

calc. calculate; calculated; calculating

Calif. California

cam. camouflage

CAM computer-aided manufacturing

CAMAC combinatorial and algebraic machine

aided computation

Cambs. Cambridgeshire

can. canal; canceled; cancellation; canon; canto; cantoris

Can. Canada; Canadian

Canad. Canada; Canadian

canc. canceled

cancln. cancellation

C & D construction and development

C. & D. collection and delivery

C. & F. cost and freight

C. & I. cost and insurance

c. & l.c. capitals and lower case

c. & s.c. capital and small capitals

C & W country and western

Cant. Canticle of Canticles; Cantonese

CAO chief administrative officer

cap. capacity; capital; capitalize; capitalized; capitulum; captain; caput; let him/her take [L *capiat*]

CAP Civil Air Patrol

Capcom capsule communicator

cap. moll. soft capsule [L *capsula mollis*]

caps. capitals; capsule

Capt. captain

capy. capacity
car. carat; cargo
Car. Carlow
CAR civil air regulation;
computer-assisted
retrieval
Card. cardinal
CARE Cooperative for
American Relief to
Everywhere
carp. carpenter
carr. carriers
CAR-RT carrier route
CART Championship Auto
Racing Teams
cas. casing; castle;
casualty
CAS calibrated air speed;
collision avoidance system
C.A.S. Certificate of
Advanced Study
CASC Canadian
Automobile Sports Club
cat. catalog; catalyst;
cataplasm; catechism
CAT clear-air turbulence;
college ability test;
computerized axial
tomography
cath. cathartic; cathedral;
catheter; cathode
Cath. Catholic
CATV community
antenna television
caus. causative
cav. cavalier; cavalry;

caveat; cavity
c.a.v. the court wishes to
consider [L *curia advisari
vult*]
CAV constant angular
velocity
CAVU ceiling and
visibility unlimited
cb centibar; with the bass
[It *col basso*]
Cb columbium;
cumulonimbus
CB cashbook; center back;
chief baron; citizens band;
confined to barracks;
construction battalion;
cornerback; currency bond
C.B. Bachelor of Surgery
[L *chirurgiae
baccalaureus*]; common
bench; Companion of the
Order of the Bath;
contrabass
cbal. counterbalance
CBC Canadian
Broadcasting Corporation;
complete blood count;
contraband control
CBD central business
district; closed bladder
drainage; common bile
duct
C.B.D. cash before
delivery
C.B.E. Commander of the
Order of the British

Empire

CBF cerebral blood flow

CBI Caribbean Basin Initiative; China, Burma, India; computer-based instruction; Cumulative Book Index

cbn. carbine

CBOE Chicago Board Options Exchange

CBR chemical, bacteriological, and radiological; chemical, biological, and radiological; cost-benefit ratio

cbt. cabinet

CBT Chicago Board of Trade

CBU cluster bomb unit

CBW chemical and biological warfare

CBX computerized branch exchange

cby. carboy

cc carbon copy; cubic centimeter

cc. centuries; chapters; copies

Cc cirrocumulus

CC cash credit; cashier's check; chamber of commerce; chess club; chief clerk; chief complaint; chief counsel; circuit court; city council; civil cases; civil code; civil commotion; combat command; commission certified; common carrier; common council; community college; company commander; confined to camp; connecting carrier; contra credit; council of churches; counterclockwise; country club; county council; county court; cricket club; criminal cases; critical condition; cubic contents; current complaint; current cost; cycling club

C.C. continuation clause; crown cases; crown colony

CCA chick cell agglutinating; circuit court of appeals

CCAT Cooperative College Ability Test

CCC Civilian Conservation Corps

CCD charge-coupled device; Confraternity of Christian Doctrine

CCF Chinese communist forces; Cooperative Commonwealth Federation (of Canada)

CCI chronic coronary insufficiency

CCK cholecystokinin

cckw. counterclockwise

CCLS court of claims

CCLSR court of claims reports

CCP Chinese Communist Party; console command processor; court of common pleas

CCPA court of customs and patent appeals

CCRN Cardiac Care Registered Nurse; Critical Care Registered Nurse

CCS casualty clearing station; combined chiefs of staff

CCT chocolate-coated tablet

CCU cardiac care unit; coronary care unit; critical care unit

CCW counterclockwise

cd candela; candle; with the right hand [It *colla destra*]

cd. canned; card; cataloged; command; commissioned; condemned; cord; could

Cd cadmium; coefficient of drag

CD cash discount; certificate of deposit; chief of division; Civil Defense; coast defense; commercial dock; communicable

disease; completely denatured; confidential document; congressional district; constant drainage; consular declaration; contagious disease; convulsive disorder; curative dose

C.D. cum dividend; current density; diplomatic corps [F *corps diplomatique*]

C/D carried down

CDBG Community Development Block Grant

CDC calculated date of confinement; Centers for Disease Control

CDD certificate of disability for discharge

cde. code

cdg. commanding

cdl. cardinal

Cdn. Canadian

CDP Certificate in Data Processing

Cdr. commander

CDR commander

CDRE commodore

CdS cadmium sulfide

CDS cash on delivery service

CDT central daylight time; commandant

c.e. let the buyer beware [L *caveat emptor*]

Ce cerium

CE cardiac enlargement; counterespionage; customs and excise; International Society of Christian Endeavor

C.E. Chemical Engineer; Christian Era; Civil Engineer; Common Era; consumption entry; Corps of Engineers

CEA carcinoembryonic antigen; College English Association; Council of Economic Advisors

CED capacitance electronic disc; Committee for Economic Development

cel celluloid

Cel. Celsius

Cels. Celsius

cem. cement; cemetery

CEM channel electron multiplier

CEMF counter electromotive force

cen. central

cent. cental; center; centiare; centigrade; centime; central; centum; century

CENTO Central Treaty Organization

CEO chief executive officer

CEP circular error probable

CEQ Council on Environmental Quality

CER conditioned emotional response

CERN European Center for Nuclear Research [F *Conseil Européen pour la Recherche Nucléaire*]

cert. certificate; certification; certified; certify; certiorari

cerv. cervical

CES central excitatory state

CET computerized emission tomogram

CETA Comprehensive Employment and Training Act

CETI communication with extraterrestrial intelligence

CEU continuing education unit

cf. calf; compare [L *confer*]

c.f. centrifugal force; complement fixation

Cf californium

CF cannot find; center field; center forward; corresponding fellow; cystic fibrosis

C.F. cost and freight; plainchant [ML *cantus firmus*]

C/F carried forward

CFA Chartered Financial Analyst; College Football

Association
CFC chlorofluorocarbon
cfh cubic feet per hour
CFI Certified Flight Instructor; chief flying instructor
C.F.I. cost, freight, and insurance
CFL Canadian Football League
cfm cubic feet per minute
CFM chlorofluoromethane
CFO canceling former order
C.F.P. Certified Financial Planner
cfs cubic feet per second
CFT complement fixation test
C.F.Z. contiguous fisheries zone
cg centigram
c.g. center of gravity
CG captain general; chorionic gonadotropin; coast guard; combat group; commanding general; commissary general; complete games; comptroller general; consul general
CGA Certified General Accountant
C.G.A. cargo's proportion of general average
cge. carriage

CGI computer-generated imagery
cgo. cargo; contango
cgs centimeter-gram-second
CGS chief of general staff
CGT General Confederation of Labor [F *Confédération Générale du Travail*]
ch chain
ch. chairman; chaldron; champion; chancellor; chancery; chapter; check; checkered; chervonets; chest; chestnut; chief; child; children; choice; choir organ; choke; chromogenic; chronic; church
Ch. chaplain
CH center halfback; central heating; clearinghouse; compass heading; customhouse
C.H. case-hardened; Companion of Honour; courthouse
chan. channel
chanc. chancellor; chancery
chap. chapter
Chap. chaplain
char. character; characteristic; charity; charter

Ch.B. Bachelor of Surgery
[L *chirurgiae baccalaureus*]
CHB center halfback
chd. chaldron; chord
CHD childhood disease;
coronary heart disease
ChE cholinesterase
Ch.E. Chemical Engineer
chem. chemical; chemist;
chemistry
Ches. Cheshire
chev. chevalier; chevron
chf. chief
CHF congestive heart
failure
chg. change; charge
chgd. changed; charged
Chin. Chinese
chk. check
chl chloroform
CHL Central Hockey
League
chm. chairman; checkmate
chmn. chairman
CHO carbohydrate
chol. cholesterol
chp. championship
chq. cheque
chr. chronic
chron. chronicle;
chronological; chronology
Chron. Chronicles
chstnt. chestnut
chtr. charter
CHU centigrade heat unit
chwdn. churchwarden

chy. chimney
Ci cirrus; curie
CI chemotherapeutic
index; chief inspector;
counterintelligence
C.I. cast iron; cephalic
index; color index;
consular invoice
C/I certificate of insurance
Cía. company [Sp
compañia]
CIA Central Intelligence
Agency; Certified Internal
Auditor
CIAA Central
Intercollegiate Athletic
Association; Coordinator
of Inter-American Affairs
cib. food [L *cibus*]; meal [L
cibus]
CIC Commander in Chief
CICU coronary intensive
care unit
CID Criminal
Investigation Department;
Criminal Investigation
Detachment; Criminal
Investigation Division;
cubic inch displacement
Cie. company [F
compagnie]
c.i.f. cost, insurance, and
freight
CIF central information
file
c.i.f. & c. cost, insurance,

freight, and commission

c.i.f. & e. cost, insurance, freight, and exchange

c.i.f. & i. cost, insurance, freight, and interest

CIM computer-integrated manufacturing

C in C Commander in Chief

Cinn. Cinncinnati

CIO Congress of Industrial Organizations

CIP Cataloging in Publication

cir. circa; circle; circuit; circular; circulation; circumference

circ. circa; circle; circuit; circular; circulation; circumference

cit. citation; cited; citizen; citrate

civ. civil; civilian

C.J. chief judge; chief justice

ck. cake; cask; chalk; check; cook; countersink

CK creatine kinase

CKD completely knocked down

ckw. clockwise

cl centiliter; close

cl. claim; claiming; class; classical; classification; clause; clavicle; clearance; clergyman; clerk; clinic;

closet; closure; cloth; clove; clutch; coil

Cl chlorine

Cl. chloride

CL chest and left arm; civil liberties; connecting line; corpus luteum; critical list

C.L. carload; carload lot; center line; civil law; common law

C/L cash letter

CLA Certified Laboratory Assistant; College Language Association

clar. clarinet

C.L.B. Bachelor of Civil Law

cld. called; cleared

C.L.D. cost laid down; Doctor of Civil Law

CLEP College Level Examination Program

Clev. Cleveland

clg. ceiling

CLI cost of living index

clin. clinical

clk. clerk; clock

clkg. calking

CLL chronic lymphocytic leukemia

clm. claiming race

clmg. claiming

clo. clothing

CLO cod-liver oil

clr. clear; clearance; color

clt. claimant; collateral
CLU Certified Life Underwriter; Chartered Life Underwriter
CLV constant linear velocity
cm centimeter
cm. cumulative
c.m. by reason of death [L *causa mortis*]; circular mil
Cm curium
CM circular measure; circular muscle; corresponding member; countermark; countermarked; court-martial
C.M. center matched; Certificated Master; Certificated Mistress; common meter; Congregation of the Mission; Master of Surgery [L *chirurgiae magister*]
CMA Certified Medical Assistant; court of military appeals
CMA-A Certified Medical Assistant-Administrative
CMA-AC Certified Medical Assistant-Administrative & Clinical
CMA-C Certified Medical Assistant-Clinical
cmd. command

C.M.D. common meter double
cmdg. commanding
Cmdr. commander
Cmdre. commodore
CME continuing medical education
CMEA Council for Mutual Economic Assistance
CMET Certified Medical Electroencephalographic Technician; Certified Medical Electroencephalographic Technologist
C.M.G. Companion of the Order of St. Michael and St. George
CMHC community mental health center
cml. commercial
CMOS complementary metal oxide semiconductor
CMR court of military review
C.M.Sgt. chief master sergeant
CMV cytomegalovirus
cn. canon; consolidated
CN case of need; chloroacetophenone; circular note; compass north
C/N consignment note; cover note; credit note
CNC computer numerical

control
CNG compressed natural gas
CNM Certified Nurse Midwife
CNO chief of naval operations
CNP continuous negative pressure
cnr. corner
CNS central nervous system
c/o care of; complains of
co. colon; company; container; coral; county
Co cobalt; coenzyme
Co. Colorado
CO carbon monoxide; cardiac output; carried over; Colorado; commanding officer; commissioner for oaths; communications officer; conscientious objector; cut out
C.O. colonial office
C/O cash order; certificate of origin
COBOL Common Business Oriented Language
COC cathodal opening contraction
cochl. spoonful [L *cochleare*]
COCl cathodal opening clonus

cod. codex
c.o.d. cash on delivery; collect on delivery
COD chemical oxygen demand
codd. codices
codl. codicil
COE cab-over-engine
coef. coefficient
coeff. coefficient
C. of B. confirmation of balance
C. of C. chamber of commerce
C. of M. Certificate of Merit
C. of S. chief of section; chief of staff
cog. cognate
COH carbohydrate
col. collated; collateral; colleague; collect; collected; collective; collector; college; collegiate; colloquial; colloquialism; colonial; colony; colophon; color; colored; column; counsel
Col. Colombia; colonel; Colorado; Colossians
COL colonel; cost of living
COLA cost-of-living adjustment
coll. collated; collateral; colleague; collect; collected; collection;

collective; collector;
college; collegiate;
colloidal; colloquial;
colloquialism; collyrium

collat. collateral

colloq. colloquial

collut. mouthwash [L *collutorium*]

coln. column

colo. colophon

Colo. Colorado

colog cologarithm

com. comedy; comic;
comma; commander;
comment; commerce;
commercial;
commissioner; committee;
common; commoner;
commonwealth;
communication;
communist; community;
completions

COM computer output
microfilm; computer
output microfilmer

C.O.M. customer's own
material

comb. combination;
combined; combining;
combustion

comd. command;
commander; commanding;
commissioned

comdg. commanding

comdr. commander

comdt. commandant

COMECON Council for
Mutual Economic
Assistance

comint communications
intelligence

coml. commercial

comm. command;
commandant; commander;
commanding;
commentary; commerce;
commercial; commission;
commissioned;
commissioner; committee;
common; commoner;
commonwealth; commune;
communication;
communist; community

commn. commission

commo. commodore

commr. commissioner

commy. commissary

comp. companion;
company; comparative;
compare; compass;
compensation;
compilation; compiled;
compiler; complement;
complete; complier;
composed; composer;
composite; composition;
compositor; compound;
compounded [L
compositus];
comprehensive;
comprising; comptroller

compar. comparative

compd. compound
compl. completely
compt. compartment; comptroller
compy. company
comr. commissioner
coms. commissioner
con confidence
con. against [L *contra*]; concerto; conclusion; conic; connecting; connection; consol; consolidated; consort [L *conjux*]; consul; continued; contra
conc. concentrate; concentrated; concentration; concentric; concerning; concrete; council [L *concilium*]
conch. conchology
conchol. conchology
concn. concentration
cond. condensed; condenser; condition; conditional; conditioner; conduct; conducted; conductivity; conductor
condr. conductor
cond. ref. conditioned reflex
cond. resp. conditioned response
conf. compare [L *confer*]; confederation; conference; confessor; confidential
Confed. Confederate

cong. congenital; congregation; congress; congressional; gallon [L *congius*]
conj. conjugation; conjunction; conjunctive
conn. connected; connection; connotation; connotative
Conn. Connecticut
cons. consecrated; conservative; consigned; consignment; consol; consolidated; consonant; constable; constitution; construction; consul; consulting; keep [L *conserva*]
consgt. consignment
consol. consolidated
consperg. dust [L *consperge*]; sprinkle [L *consperge*]
const. constant; constituent; constitution; constitutional; construction
constl. constitutional
constr. construction
cont. containing; contemporary; contents; continent; continental; continue; continued; continuous; contract; contrary; control
contbd. contraband

contbg. contributing
contbn. contribution
contbr. contributor
contd. continued
conter. rub together [L *contere*]
contg. containing
contl. continental; control
contn. continuation
contr contralto
contr. contract; contraction; contractor; contrary; control; controller
contrib. contribution; contributor
conv. convalescent; convenient; convent; convention; conventional; conversation; converted; converter; convertible; convict; convocation
coord. coordination
cop. copper; copulative; copy; copyright
Cop. Coptic
COPD chronic obstructive pulmonary disease
COPE chronic obstructive pulmonary emphysema; Committee on Political Education
copr. copyright
Copt. Coptic
cor. corner; cornet; coroner; coronet; corpus; correct; corrected; correction; correlative; correspondence; correspondent; corresponding; corrigendum; corrugated; corrupt; corruption
Cor. Corinthians
CoR Congo red
CORE Congress of Racial Equality
Corn. Cornish; Cornwall
corp. corporate; corporation
corr. correct; corrected; correction; correlative; correspondence; correspondent; corresponding; corrigendum; corrugated; corrupt; corruption
Corr. Fell. corresponding fellow
CORT Certified Operating Room Technician
cos cosine
cos. companies; consul; consulship; counties
COS chief of section; chief of staff
C.O.S. cash on shipment
cosec cosecant
cot cotangent
COTA Certified Occupational Therapy Assistant

coul coulomb

coun. council; counsel

COWPS Council on Wage and Price Stability

coy. company

cp with the solo part [It *colla parte*]

cp. centipoise; compare; coupon

c.p. candlepower

CP Cape Province; capillary pressure; carriage paid; cerebral palsy; charge-conjugation/parity; civil power; civil procedure; clerk of the peace; command post; common pleas; common prayer; Communist Party; constant pressure; continental plan; cor pulmonale; court of probate; cover point

C.P. center of pressure; charter party; chemically pure; code of procedure; Congregation of the Passion

C/P custom of port

CPA Certified Public Accountant; Chartered Public Accountant

CPAP continuous positive airway pressure

CPB competitive protein binding; Corporation for Public Broadcasting

CPC chronic passive congestion; crafts, protective, custodial

C.P.C. & N. certificate of public convenience and necessity

CPCU Chartered Property and Casualty Underwriter

cpd. compound

c.p.d. charterers pay dues

CPD common pleas division; contact potential difference

cpe. coupe

CPE College Proficiency Examination; cytopathogenic effects

CPFF cost plus fixed fee

CPI constitutional psychopathic inferiority; consumer price index

CPK creatine phosphokinase

cpl. complete; compline

Cpl. corporal

cpm counts per minute; cycles per minute

CPM common particular meter; cost per thousand; critical path method

CP/M Control Program/Microcomputers

CPO Certified Prosthetist-Orthotist; chief petty officer

CPOM master chief petty officer

CPOS senior chief petty officer

cpr. copper

CPR cardiopulmonary resuscitation

cps characters per second; cycles per second

CPS cards per second; Certified Professional Secretary; Civilian Public Service; constitutional psychopathic state

CPSC Consumer Product Safety Commission; Consumer Product Safety Corporation

cpt. captain; counterpoint

Cpt. captain

CPT captain

cptr. carpenter

CPU central processing unit

CPV canine parvo virus

CPVC chlorinated polyvinyl chloride

CPZ chlorpromazine

CQ call to quarters; charge of quarters; commercial quality; conceptual quotient

CQT College Qualification Test

cr crescendo

cr. center; circular; commander; councillor; crate; cream; creased; created; credit; creditor; creed; creek; crew; crochet; crown; cruiser; cruzeiro

Cr chromium; creatinine

CR cardiorespiratory; cathode ray; chest and right arm; civil rights; clot retraction; conditioned reflex; conditioned response; consciousness-raising; creditable record; critical ratio; crossroad; currency regulation

C.R. carrier's risk; class rate; commodity rate; company's risk; Costa Rica; current rate

C/R change of rating

CRC Civil Rights Commission; cyclic redundancy check

CRD chronic respiratory disease

CREEP Committee to Reelect the President

cresc crescendo

crim. criminal

crim. con. criminal conversation

criminol. criminologist; criminology

crit. critical; criticism;

criticized
CRM cross reacting material
CRNA Certified Registered Nurse Anesthetist
CRO cathode-ray oscilloscope
croc. crocodile
CrP creatine phosphate
CRP C-reactive protein
CRS Congressional Research Service
crt. court; crate
CRT cathode-ray tube; complex reaction time
CRTT Certified Respiratory Therapy Technician
cryst. crystalline; crystallized
cs centistoke; cesarean section; corticosteroid; current strength
c/s cycles per second
cs with the left hand [It *colla sinistra*]
cs. case; cases; census; consul
Cs cesium; cirrostratus; consciousness
CS chief of staff; chlorobenzamalonitrile; Christian Science practitioner; Civil Service; conditioned stimulus;

cooperative society; county seat; court of sessions; current series
C.S. capital stock
CSA Canadian Standards Association; Community Services Administration
C.S.A. Confederate States of America
CSB chemical stimulation of the brain
csc cosecant
CSC Civil Service Commission
C.S.C. Congregation of the Holy Cross [L *Congregation Sanctae Crucis*]
C.S.E. Certificate of Secondary Education
CSF cerebrospinal fluid
csg. casing
CSI Commission Sportive Internationale; Construction Specifications Institute
csk. cask; countersink
CSM cerebrospinal meningitis; command sergeant major; command service module; corn-soya-milk
C-Span Cable Satellite Public Affairs Network
CSR Certified Shorthand Reporter; Chartered

Stenographic Reporter

C.SS.R. Congregation of the Most Holy Redeemer [L *Congregatio Sanctissimi Redemptoris*]

CST central standard time; convulsive shock therapy

cstg. casting

CSW Certified Social Worker

ct. carat; carton; caught; cent; centum; circuit; count; county; court; current

CT cable transfer; central time; Certificated Teacher; Certified Teacher; Certified Technician; circulation time; coated tablet; code telegram; combat team; commercial traveler; computed tomography; computerized axial tomography; computerized tomography; Connecticut; current transformer

C.T. compressed tablet

c.t.a. with the will annexed [L *cum testamento annexo*]

CTC centralized traffic control; chlortetracycline

CTCLS court of claims

ctf. certificate

ctg. cartage

ctge. cartage

ctl. cental

CTL constructive total loss

ctmo. centesimo; centimo

ctn cotangent

ctn. carton

cto. concerto

c.t.o. canceled to order

c. to c. center to center

C. to S. carting to shipside

ctr. center; counter

CTR control; controlled thermonuclear reactor; currency transaction report

CTRL control

cts. cents

CTS clear to send

Ctss. countess

cttee. committee

CTU centigrade thermal unit

ctvo. centavo

cty. county

cu. cubic; cumulative

Cu copper [L *cuprum*]; cumulus

CU clinical unit; close-up

CUC chronic ulcerative colitis

cult. culture

cum. cumulative

Cumb. Cumbria

c.u.p. copper unit of pressure

cur. curative; currency; current

curt. current

cust. customer

cv with the voice [It *colla voce*]

cv. convertible; cultivar

c.v. chief value

CV cardiovascular; curriculum vitae

C.V. common version

CVA cerebrovascular accident; Columbia Valley Authority

CVP central venous pressure

CVR cardiovascular renal; cardiovascular respiratory; cerebrovascular resistance

CVS clean voided specimen

cvt. convertible

CW chemical warfare; child welfare; churchwarden; clockwise; continuous wave; crutch walking

C.W. cold water; commercial weight

CWA Communications Workers of America

CWO chief warrant officer; commissioned warrant officer

C.W.O. cash with order

cwt. hundredweight [L *centum* + weight]

cx. convex

cy. capacity; county; currency; cycle

Cy cyanogen

CY calendar year

cyc. cyclopedia

cycl. cyclopedia

cyl. cylinder

cyn. cyanide

CYO Catholic Youth Organization

cytol. cytological; cytology

CZ Canal Zone

D

d deci-; deuteron; dyne; penny nail [L *denarius* penny]

d. dam; dame; damn; date; daughter; day; deacon; dead; dean; deceased; deciduous; deep; defeated; degree; dele; delete; density; depart; department; departure; deputy; deserted; deserter; developed; deviation; dexter; diameter; died; differential; dime; dimensional; dinar; director; discharged;

disease; disqualified; distance; dividend; division; divorced; dog; dollar; dominus; dorsal; dose; double; dowager; drachma; draw; drive; driving; drizzling; duration; pence [L *denarii*]; penny [L *denarius*]

D D day; defense; deuterium; diopter; duodecimo

D. data; Democrat; Democratic; derivative; doctor; dollar; duchess; duchy; duke; Dutch

d.b. dirty book; double biased; double-breasted

da deka-

da. daughter; day

DA delayed action; Department of the Army; deposit account; Dictionary of Americanisms; direct action; documents attached; don't answer; ducktail [duck's ass]

D.A. district attorney; Doctor of Arts

D/A days after acceptance; digital to analog; documents against acceptance; documents for acceptance

DAB Dictionary of American Biography

DAC digital-to-analog converter

DAD deputy assistant director

DAE Dictionary of American English

dag dekagram

DAH Dictionary of American History

dal dekaliter

dam dekameter

dam. damaged

Dan. Daniel; Danish

D & C dilation and curettage

D and D drunk and disorderly

D & H dressed and headed

D & M dressed and matched

D. and P. developing and printing

DAR Daughters of the American Revolution

DAS delivered alongside ship

dat. dative

DAT delayed action tablet; Differential Aptitude Test

dau. daughter

DAV Disabled American Veterans

db decibel

db. debenture

dB decibel

DB data base; delayed broadcast

D.B. daybook; Domesday Book

d/b/a doing business as

D.B.A. Doctor of Business Administration

DBCP dibromochloropropane

D.B.E. Dame Commander of the Order of the British Empire

d.b.h. diameter at breast height

dbk. drawback

dbl. double

dble. double

DBMS data base management system

d.b.n. of the goods not administered [L *de bonis non*]

DBS direct broadcast satellite

d.c. double crochet; from the beginning [It *da capo*]

DC decimal classification; defense counsel; deputy chief; deviation clause; diagnostic center; direct current; district court; District of Columbia; double column

D.C. District of Columbia; Doctor of Chiropractic

DCB Dictionary of Canadian Biography

D.Ch.E. Doctor of Chemical Engineering

D.C.I. Director of the Central Intelligence Agency

D.C.L. Doctor of Canon Law; Doctor of Civil Law; Doctor of Commercial Law

D.C.M. Doctor of Comparative Medicine

D.Cn.L. Doctor of Canon Law

D.Comp.L. Doctor of Comparative Law

dd. dated; delivered

d.d. he/she gave as a gift [L *dono dedit*]

DD day's date; delayed delivery; delivered at docks; demand draft; deputy director; destroyer; dishonorable discharge; due date

D.D. Doctor of Divinity

D/D days after date; days after delivery

DDA demand deposit accounting; digital differential analyzer

DDC Dewey Decimal Classification

DDD dichlorodiphenyl-dichloroethane; direct distance dialing

D.D.D. he/she gave and dedicated as a gift [L *dono dedit dedicavit*]; he/she gives, devotes, and dedicates [L *dat, dicat, dedicat*]

DDE dichlorodiphenyl-dichloroethylene

DDP distributed data processing

D.D.S. Doctor of Dental Science; Doctor of Dental Surgery

D.D.Sc. Doctor of Dental Science

DDT dichlorodiphenyl-trichloroethane; dynamic debugging tool

DDVP dimethyl-dichlorovinylphosphate

DE deckle edged; defensive end; Delaware; destroyer escort; double entry

D.E. Doctor of Engineering

dea. deacon

DEA Drug Enforcement Administration

deb. debenture

dec decimeter; decrescendo

dec. decade; decani; deceased; decimal; declaration; declared; declension; declination; decompose; decorated; decorative; decrease

Dec. December

decd. deceased; declared; decreased

ded. dedicated; dedication

D.Ed. Doctor of Education

def. defecation; defendant; defense; deferred; deficient; deficit; defined; definite; definition

deft. defendant

deg. degeneration; degree

del. delegate; delegation; delete; deliver; delivery; delusion; he/she drew it [L *delineavit*]

Del. Delaware

deld. delivered

delin. he/she drew it [L *delineavit*]

dely. delivery

dem. demonstrative; demurrage; demy

Dem. Democrat; Democratic

demj. demijohn

den. denotation; denotative

Den. Denmark

D.Eng. Doctor of Engineering

dent. dental; dentist; dentistry

dep. depart; department; departure; deponent; deposed; deposit; depot; deputy

depr. depreciation;

depression
dept. department;
deponent; deputy
der. derivation; derivative;
derived
Derbys. Derbyshire
deriv. derivation;
derivative
derm. dermatologist;
dermatology
des. deserted; deserter;
desertion; design;
designed; desired
DES diethylstilbesterol
desc. descendant
desp. despatch
destn. destination
det. detached; detachment;
detail; detective;
determine; determiner
detd. determined
detn. detention;
determination
Deut. Deuteronomy
dev. develop; developer;
development; deviation
devel. development
Devon. Devonshire
DEW distant early
warning
d.f. dead freight; degree of
freedom
DF damage free; Defender
of the Faith [ML *Defensor
Fidei*]; direction finder;
direction finding

D.F. Doctor of Forestry
D.F.A. Doctor of Fine Arts
DFC Distinguished Flying
Cross
DFDT difluorodiphenyl-
trichloroethane
DFM Distinguished Flying
Medal
DFP diisopropyl
fluorophosphate
dft. defendant; draft
dftg. drafting
dg decigram
DG degaussing
D.G. by the grace of God
[LL *Dei gratia*];
directional gyro; director
general; thanks to God
[LL *Deo gratias*]
dgt. daughter
DH dead heat; designated
hitter
D.H. Doctor of Humanities
D.H.A. Doctor of Hospital
Administration
D.H.Adm. Doctor of
Hospital Administration
D.H.L. Doctor of Hebrew
Letters; Doctor of Hebrew
Literature
Di didymium
DI deterioration index;
diabetes insipidus; drill
instructor
dia. diameter; diathermy
DIA Defense Intelligence

Agency

diag. diagonal; diagram

dial. dialect; dialectal; dialectic; dialectical; dialectics; dialogue

diam. diameter

dict. dictaphone; dictation; dictator; dictionary

dif. difference

DIF data interchange format

diff. difference; different; differential

dig. digest

dil. dilute; dilution

dilat. dilatation

dim diminuendo

dim. dimension; diminished; diminutive; half [L *dimidium*]

dimin diminuendo

din. dinar

dip. diploma

DIP dual in-line package

diph. diphtheria

dipl. diploma; diplomacy; diplomat; diplomatic

dir. director

dis. disabled; discharge; discharged; disciple; discipline; disconnect; discontinued; discount; diseased; distance; distribute

disc. discharged; disconnect; discontinue;

discontinued; discount; discovered

DISC domestic international sales corporation

disch. discharge; discharged

disct. discount

disp. dispatch; dispatcher; dispensary; dispenser

diss. dissertation

dissd. dissolved

dist. distance; distilled; distinguished; district

dist. atty. district attorney

distn. distillation

distr. distribute; distribution; distributive; distributor

div. divergence; diversion; divide; divided; dividend; divine; divinity; division; divorced; separate [It *divisi*]

divd. dividend

DIY do-it-yourself

d.j. dust jacket

DJ disc jockey

D.J. district judge; Doctor of Jurisprudence; Dow Jones

DJIA Dow-Jones Industrial Average

D.J.S. Doctor of Juridical Science

D.Jur. Doctor of

Jurisprudence

D.Jur.Sc. Doctor of Juridical Science

dk. dark; deck; dock; duck

dkg dekagram

dkl dekaliter

dkm dekameter

dks dekastere

dkt. docket

dl deciliter

DL danger list; day letter; demand loan; dominical letter

D.L. Doctor of Law

dld. delivered

D.Lit. Doctor of Letters [L *doctor litterarum*]; Doctor of Literature [L *doctor litterarum*]

D.Litt. Doctor of Letters [L *doctor litterarum*]; Doctor of Literature [L *doctor litterarum*]

d.l.o. dispatch loading only

D.L.O. dead letter office

D.L.S. Doctor of Library Science

dlvy. delivery

dly. daily; delivery

dm decimeter

dm. drum

DM dam; deutsche mark; diabetes mellitus; diastolic murmur

D.M. right hand [It *destra mano*]

DMA direct memory access

D.M.A. Doctor of Musical Arts

D.M.D. Doctor of Dental Medicine [NL *dentariae medicinae doctor*]; Doctor of Medical Dentistry

DME distance measuring equipment

D.M.E. Doctor of Mechanical Engineering

DMF decayed, missing, and filled teeth

D.M.L. Doctor of Modern Languages

DMS data management system

D.M.Sc. Doctor of Medical Science

DMSO dimethylsulfoxide

DMT dimethyl terephthalate; dimethyltryptamine

DMV department of motor vehicles

DMZ demilitarized zone

dn. down; dun

DNA deoxyribonucleic acid

DNase deoxyribonuclease

DNB Dictionary of National Biography; dinitrobenzene

DNC Democratic National Committee

DND Department of

National Defence

DNF did not finish

DNOC dinitro-ortho-cresol

DNP did not play

D.N.Sc. Doctor of Nursing Science

dnus. dominus

do. ditto

DO defense order; delivery order; diamine oxidase; district officer; duty officer

D.O. Doctor of Osteopathic Medicine and Surgery; Doctor of Osteopathy

D.O.A. dead on arrival

doc. doctor; document

DOD Department of Defense

DOE Department of Energy

dol soft [It *dolce*]

dol. dollar

dom. domestic; dominant; dominion; dominus

DOM dimethoxy methyl

D.O.M. to God, the best and greatest [ML *Deo optimo maximo*]

Dom. Rep. Dominican Republic

Don. Donegal

D.O.P. developing-out-paper

dopa dihydroxyphenylalanine

Dors. Dorset

dos. dosage

DOS disk operating system

DOT Department of Transportation

doz. dozen

d.p. direct port

DP data processing; displaced person; double play; durable press; duty paid

D.P. degree of polymerization; Doctor of Podiatry; documents for payment; domestic prelate; double pole

DPA diphenylamine

DPB deposit passbook

D.P.D.T. double pole, double throw

D.P.E. Doctor of Physical Education

D.Ph. Doctor of Philosophy

DPH department of public health

D.P.H. Doctor of Public Health

D.Phil. Doctor of Philosophy

dpl. diploma

DPL diplomat; diplomatic

D.P.M. Doctor of Podiatric Medicine

DPN diphosphopyridine nucleotide

D.P.S.T. double pole,

single throw

dpt. department; deponent; depth

DPT diphtheria, pertussis, tetanus

dpty. deputy

DPU duel processing unit

DPW department of public works

DQ deterioration quotient; developmental quotient; disqualified

D.Q. direct question

dr. debit; debtor; drachma; dram; drawer; drawing; drawn; dressing; drum

Dr. doctor; drive

DR dead reckoning; delivery room; deposit receipt; differential rate; dining room; district registry; dock receipt

dram. dramatic; dramatist

DRAM direct random access memory

D.R.E. director of religious education; Doctor of Religious Education

drg. drawing

Dr.Jur. Doctor of Law [L *doctor juris*]

Dr.LL. Doctor of Laws

Dr.P.H. Doctor of Public Health

ds decistere

ds. double stitch

d.s. document signed; from the sign [It *dal segno*]

DS dead air space; Department of State; deputy sheriff; dilute strength; dioptric strength; double strength; Down's syndrome

D.S. detached service; Doctor of Science

D/S days after sight

D.Sc. Doctor of Science

DSC Distinguished Service Cross

D.S.C. Doctor of Surgical Chiropody

D.Sc.D. Doctor of Science in Dentistry

DSD dry sterile dressing

DSK Dvorak Simplified Keyboard

DSN deep space network

DSO Distinguished Service Order

d.s.p. died without issue [L *decessit sine prole*]

D.S.P. Doctor of Surgical Podiatry

DSR dynamic spatial reconstructor

D.S.S. Doctor of Holy Scripture [L *doctor sacrae scripturae*]

D.S.Sc. Doctor of Social Science

DST daylight saving time

D.S.T. Doctor of Sacred Theology

dstn. destination

dstspn. dessertspoon

D.S.W. Doctor of Social Welfare

DT daylight time; defensive tackle

D.T. Doctor of Theology; double throw; double time

DTE data terminal equipment

D.Th. Doctor of Theology

DTP diphtheria, tetanus, pertussis

d.t.'s delerium tremens

du. dual

Du. duke; Dutch

DU diagnosis undetermined

Dub. Dublin

DUI driving under the influence

Dumf. Gal. Dumfries and Galloway

duo duodecimo

dup. duplex; duplicate

dupl. duplicate

Dur. Durham

d.v. double vibration

DV dilute volume; distinguished visitor

D.V. Douay Version; God willing [L *Deo volente*]

D.V.M. Doctor of Veterinary Medicine

dvr. driver

d.w. deadweight; dust wrapper

D.W. delayed weather; distilled water

D/W dock warrant

dwc deadweight capacity

dwg. drawing; dwelling

DWI died without issue; driving while intoxicated

dwt deadweight ton

dwt. pennyweight [L *denarius* + weight]

Dx diagnosis

DX distance

dy. delivery; duty

Dy deputy; dysprosium

dynam. dynamics

dz. dozen

D.Z. drop zone

E

e earnings

e. earth; east; easterly; eastern; edge; eldest; ell; empty; end; energy; erg; error; excellent

E east; einsteinium; electric field; electromotive force; emmetropia; enema; energy; enzyme; evidence; experimenter; eye

E.   English
ea.   each
EA   enemy aircraft
E.A.   economic advisor; educational age
EAC   East African Community
ead.   the same [L *eadem*]
E. and O.E.   errors and omissions excepted
E. and P.   extraordinary and plenipotentiary
EAON   except as otherwise noted
earn.   earnings
EAROM   electrically alterable read-only memory
EB   Epstein-Barr
E.B.   eastbound
EBCDIC   extended binary coded decimal interchange code
ec.   economics
Ec.   Ecuador
EC   East Caribbean; east central; error corrected; established church; European Community
ECAC   Eastern Collegiate Athletic Conference
eccl.   ecclesiastic; ecclesiastical; ecclesiology
Eccles.   Ecclesiastes
Ecclus.   Ecclesiasticus
ECE   extended coverage endorsement
ECF   extracelluar fluid
ECG   electrocardiogram
ech.   echelon
ecl.   eclectic; eclogue
ECL   emitter coupled logic
ECM   electronic countermeasures; European Common Market
ECO   electron-coupled oscillator; engineering change order
ecol.   ecological; ecology
E-COM   electronic computer-originated mail
econ.   economic; economics; economist; economy
ECSC   European Coal and Steel Community
ECT   electroconvulsive therapy
ECU   European Currency Unit
Ecua.   Ecuador
ed.   edited; edition; editor; educated; education
ED   effective dose; election district; erythema dose; ex dividend; extra duty
EDA   Economic Development Administration
Ed.B.   Bachelor of Education
EDB   ethylene dibromide

EDC expected date of confinement

Ed.D. Doctor of Education

EDD English Dialect Dictionary

EDL edition deluxe

Ed.M. Master of Education

edn. edition; education

ednl. educational

EDP electronic data processing

EDR electrodermal response

Ed.S. Specialist in Education

EDT eastern daylight time

EDTA ethylenediamine-tetraacetic acid

educ. educated; education; educational

EE envoy extraordinary

E.E. electrical engineer; errors excepted

EEC European Economic Community

EEE eastern equine encephalomyelitis

EEG electroencephalogram; electroencephalograph

EENT eye, ear, nose, and throat

EEO equal employment opportunity

EEOC Equal Employment Opportunity Commission

EEPROM electrically erasable programmable read-only memory

EER energy efficiency ratio

EEROM electrically erasable read-only memory

EEZ exclusive economic zone

E.F. English finish; expeditionary force; extra fine; extremely fine

eff. effect; effective; efficiency; efficient

EFO earnings from operations

EFT electronic funds transfer

EFTA European Free Trade Association

EFTS electronic funds transfer system

e.g. for example [L *exempli gratia*]

Eg. Egypt; Egyptian

E.G. edge grain

Egypt. Egyptian

EHBF extrahepatic blood flow

EHF extremely high frequency

EHL Eastern Hockey League

EHP effective horsepower; electric horsepower

EHT extra high tension
EHV extra high voltage
E.I. East Indies;
endorsement irregular
EIA Energy Information
Administration
EIES Electronic
Information Exchange
System
EKG electrocardiogram
[Ger *elektrokardiogramm*];
electrocardiograph
el. eldest; elected; electric;
electricity; element;
elevated; elevation
eld. elder; eldest
elec. electric; electrical;
electrician; electricity;
electrified; electuary
elect. electric; electrical;
electrician; electricity;
electrified; electuary
elem. element; elementary
elev. elevation
ELF extremely low
frequency
el. fo. elephant folio
elix. elixir
Eliz. Elizabethan
El Salv. El Salvador
ELSS extravehicular life
support system
ELT emergency locator
transmitter
em. emanation; eminence
Em emanation

EM electron microscope;
end matched; enlisted
man
E.M. bishop and martyr [L
episcopus et martyr]; earl
marshall; electromagnetic;
Engineer of Mines
emb. embankment;
embargo; embark;
embarkation; embassy;
embossed; embroidered;
embryo; embryology
embr. embroidered;
embryo; embryology
embryol. embryology
emer. emergency;
emeritus
emf electromotive force
EMG electromyogram;
electromyograph;
electromyography
EMI electromagnetic
interference
EMIC emergency
maternity and infant care
emp. emperor; empire;
employment; empress
EMP electromagnetic
pulse
EMR educable mentally
retarded
EMT emergency medical
technician
emu electromagnetic unit
EMU European Monetary
Union

emul. emulsion

en. enemy

EN exception noted

enc. enclosed; enclosure; encyclopedia

encl. enclosed; enclosure

ency. encyclopedia

encyc. encyclopedia

end. endorsed; endorsement

ENE east-northeast

eng. engine; engineer; engineering; engraved; engraver; engraving

Eng. England; English

ENG electronic news gathering

engg. engineering

engin. engineering

engr. engineer; engraved; engraver; engraving

ENIAC Electronic Numerical Integrator and Calculator

enl. enlarged; enlisted; enlistment

Ens. ensign

ENS ensign

ent. entered; entertainment; entomology; entrance

ENT ear, nose, and throat

entd. entered

entom. entomological; entomology

entomol. entomological; entomology

env. envelope; envoy

e.o. ex officio

EO executive officer; executive order

E.O. errors and omissions

EOE equal opportunity employer

E.O.E. errors and omissions excepted

EOF end of file

EOG electrooculogram

E.O.G. educational opportunity grant

EOHP except as otherwise herein provided

EOM end of month

EOP employee ownership plan

EOR enhanced oil recovery

eos. eosinophil

eosin. eosinophil

ep. epistle

e.p. electroplate; endpaper; endpoint; in passing [F *en passant*]

Ep. bishop [LL *episcopus*]

EP European plan; extended play

E.P. estimated position; evening prayer; excess profits; extreme pressure

EPA Environmental Protection Agency

EPC editor's presentation

copy
EPCOT Experimental Prototype Community of Tomorrow
EPD excess profits duty
Eph. Ephesians
Ephes. Ephesians
epil. epilepsy; epileptic; epilogue
Epis. Episcopal
Episc. Episcopal
epit. epitaph; epitome
epith. epithelial; epithelium
EPN ethylparanitrophenyl
E.P.N.S. electroplated nickel silver
EPR electron paramagnetic resonance
EPROM electrically programmable read-only memory; erasable programmable read-only memory
EPS earnings per share
EPT excess-profits tax
eq. equal; equation; equator; equatorial; equerry; equipment; equitable; equity; equivalent
EQ educational quotient
eqpt. equipment
equip. equipment
equipt. equipment
equiv. equivalency; equivalent
Er erbium
ER earned run; emergency room; endoplasmic reticulum; equivalent roentgen; extended release
ERA earned run average; Economic Regulatory Administration; Equal Rights Amendment
ERDA Energy Research and Development Administration
ERG electroretinogram
ERISA Employee Retirement Income Security Act
erm. ermine
ERPF effective renal plasma flow
erron. erroneous
ERT estrogen replacement theory
es electrostatic
Es einsteinium
ES engine-sized; executive secretary; extra series
ESA Employment Standards Administration
ESB electrical stimulation of the brain
ESCA electron spectroscopy for chemical analysis
Esd. Esdras
ESE east-southeast

ESF erythropoietic stimulating factor

Esk. Eskimo

ESL English as a second language

ESN educationally subnormal

ESOL English for students of other languages

ESOP employee stock ownership plan

esp with expression [It *espressivo*]

esp. especial; especially

ESP extrasensory perception

Esq. esquire

Esqr. esquire

Esqre. esquire

ESR electron spin resonance; erythrocyte sedimentation rate

ess. essence

est Erhard Seminars Training

est. establishment; estate; estimated; estuary

EST eastern standard time; electroshock therapy

estab. establish; establishment

estbd. established

estd. established; estimated

este. estate

Esth. Esther

esu electrostatic unit

E.S.U. English-Speaking Union

ESV earth satellite vehicle; experimental safety vehicle

Et ethyl

ET eastern time; Easter term; educational therapy; elapsed time; electrical transcription; electric telegraph; ephemeris time

ETA Employment and Training Administration; estimated time of arrival

et al. and elsewhere [L *et alibi*]; and others [L *et alii, et aliae,* or *et alia*]

etc. et cetera

ETD estimated time of departure

eth. ether; ethical; ethics

Eth. Ethiopia

ethnol. ethnologist; ethnology

ETI extraterrestrial intelligence

ETO European theater of operations

ETS expiration of term of service

et seq. and the following one [L *et sequens*]; and the following ones [L *et sequentes* or *et sequentia*]

et ux. and wife [L *et uxor*]

ETV educational
television

ety. etymology

eu entropy unit

Eu europium

EUA European Unit of
Account

Eur. Europe; European

Euratom European
Atomic Energy
Community

EUV extreme ultraviolet

ev. evangelical

eV electron volt

EV electric vehicle

EVA extravehicular
activity

eval. evaluate; evaluation;
evaluator

evap. evaporate

evg. evening

evng. evening

EW electronic warfare;
enlisted woman

ex. examined; example;
excellent; exception;
exchange; excluding;
excursion; executed;
executive; exempt;
exercise; exhibit; export;
express; extra; extract

Ex. Exodus

exam. examination;
examiner

exc. excellent; except;
excepted; exception;

exchange; exciter; excuse;
he/she engraved it [L
excudit]

Exc. Excellency

exch. exchange;
exchanged; exchequer

excl. exclamation; exclude;
excluding; exclusive

excpt. exception

exd. examined

ex div. ex dividend

exec. executed; execution;
executive; executor

ex. gr. for example [L
exempli gratia]

exhbn. exhibition

Eximbank Export-Import
Bank

exmr. examiner

Exod. Exodus

exor. executor

exp. expansion; expense;
experience; experiment;
experimental; expiration;
expired; explosive;
exponent; exponential;
export; exported;
exposure; express; on
behalf [L *ex parte*]

expdn. expedition

exper. experience;
experienced; experiment;
experimental

expn. expiration;
exposition

expt. experiment; expert;

export
exptl. experimental
exptr. exporter
expy. expressway
exr. executor
ex rel. by the information of [L *ex relatione*]; by the relation of [L *ex relatione*]
exrx. executrix
ext. extended; extension; exterior; external; externally; extinct; extinguisher; extra; extract; extreme; extremely; extremity
extg. extracting
extl. external
extr. extruded; extrusion
exx. examples; executrix
Ez. Ezra
Ezech. Ezechiel
Ezek. Ezekiel
Ezr. Ezra

F

f farad; femto-; fermi; fluidounce; focal length; forte; frequency
f. and the following one; brother [L *frater*]; failure; family; farthing; father; fathom; fawn; feast; female; feminine; fibrous; fiction; field; fighter; filly; finance; financial; fine; finish; fire; firm; fixed; flat; fleet; florin; flower; fluid; fluidness; fog; folio; foot; for; force; forma; formed; formula; forward; foul; fragile; fragmentation; franc; from; fuel; full; function; furlong; he/she made it [L *fecit*]; let it be done [L *fiat*]; let it be made [L *fiat*]; make [L *fac*]; son [L *filius*]
F Fahrenheit; fair; false; faraday; fellow; filial; filial generation; fluorine; focal length; luminous flux
F. France; French; friar; Friday
FA felonious assault; field goal attempt; fielding average; financial advisor; first aid; forage acre; free alongside; free of all average
F.A. field artillery; football association; freight agent
F/A free astray
FAA Federal Aviation Administration; free of all average
FAAP Fellow of the American Academy of Pediatrics

fab. fabricated

fac. facsimile; factor; factory; faculty

FAC forward air controller

FACA Fellow of the American College of Anesthesiologists; Fellow of the American College of Apothecaries

FACC Fellow of the American College of Cardiology

FACD Fellow of the American College of Dentists

FACOG Fellow of the American College of Obstetricians and Gynecologists

FACP Fellow of the American College of Physicians

FACR Fellow of the American College of Radiologists

FACS Fellow of the American College of Surgeons

FAD flavin adenine dinucleotide; free air delivered

FADM fleet admiral

FAF flyaway factor

Fah. Fahrenheit

Fahr. Fahrenheit

fam. family; famous

FAM foreign airmail

FAMA Fellow of the American Medical Association

f. and a. fore and aft

f. & d. freight and demurrage

F. & F. furniture and fixtures

F & G folded and gathered

FAO Food and Agriculture Organization of the United Nations

FAP first-aid post

FAPA Fellow of the American Psychological Association

FAPHA Fellow of the American Public Health Association

FAQ fair average quality; free at quay

far. farthing

FAS firsts and seconds; Foreign Agricultural Service

F.A.S. free alongside

FASB Federal Accounting Standards Board

fasc. fascicle

fath. fathom

fav. favorite

FB fire brigade; flying boat; foreign body; fullback

F.B. freight bill

FBA Federal Bar Association

FBI Federal Bureau of Investigation

FBM foot board measure

fbr fast breeder reactor

FBS forward-based systems

fc. franc

f.c. bequest in trust [L *fideicommissum*]; follow copy; footcandle

FC fielder's choice; fire control; fire controlman; flood control; food control

F.C. football club; free church

FCA Farm Credit Administration

f.c. & s. free of capture and seizure

fcap. foolscap

FCAP Fellow of the College of American Pathologists

FCC Federal Communications Commission; first-class certificate

FCCP Fellow of the American College of Chest Physicians

fcg. facing

FCGP Fellow of the College of General Practitioners

FCIC Federal Crop Insurance Corporation

fco delivered free [It *franco*]; postage free [It *franco*]

fcp. foolscap

FCP final common pathway

FCPS Fellow of the College of Physicians and Surgeons

fcst. forecast

fcty. factory

fcy. fancy

fd. field; forced; ford; found; fund

f.d. focal distance; free delivery; free discharge; free dispatch; free dock

F.D. Defender of the Faith [L *Fidei Defensor*]; fire department; first day

FDA Food and Drug Administration

FDC fire direction center; fleur de coin

F.D.C. first-day cover

F.D.D. free of charge [F *franc de droits*]

fdg. funding

FDIC Federal Deposit Insurance Corporation

fdn. foundation

fdry. foundry

Fe iron [L *ferrum*]

Feb. February

fec. he/she made it [L *fecit*]

FEC Federal Election Commission

fed. federal; federated; federation

fedl. federal

fedn. federation

FEI Fédération Equestrienne Internationale

fem. female; feminine; femur

FEMA Federal Emergency Management Agency

FEP fore edges painted

FEPA Fair Employment Practices Act

FEPC Fair Employment Practices Commission

FERA Federal Emergency Relief Administration

Ferm. Fermanagh

FET Federal Excise Tax; field effect transistor

ff fortissimo

ff. and the following ones; folios; they made it [L *fecerunt*]

f.f. fixed focus

FF brothers [L *fratres*]; first family; folded flat; freight forwarder; French fried; full-fashioned; thick fog

f.f.a. free from alongside; free from average

FFA for further assignment; free fatty acid; free foreign agency; Future Farmers of America

F.F.A. foreign freight agent

FFB Federal Financing Bank

fff as loud as possible [It *fortississimo*]

FFI free from infection

FFT for further transfer

FFV First Families of Virginia

ffy. faithfully

FG field goal; fine grain; friction glaze; fuel gas; fully good

F.G. flat grain

F.G.A. foreign general agent; foreign general average; free of general average

fgn. foreign

fgt. freight

f.h. make a draught [L *fiat haustus*]

F.H. fire hydrant

FHA Federal Housing Administration

FHAA Field Hockey Association of America

FHLBB Federal Home Loan Bank Board

f.i. for instance

F.I. Falkland Islands

FIA full interest admitted

fib. fibrillation

f.i.b. free into barge; free into bunker

FIBA Fédération Internationale de Basketball Amateur

FIBI Fédération Internationale de Bobsleigh et de Tobogganing

FIC Federal Information Centers

FICA Federal Insurance Contributions Act

FICD Fellow of the International College of Dentists

FICS Fellow of the International College of Surgeons

fict. earthen [L *fictilis*]; fiction; fictitious

fid. fidelity; fiduciary

FIDE Fédération Internationale des Echecs (chess)

FIDO Fog Investigation Dispersal Operations

FIE Fédération Internationale de d'Escrime (fencing)

fi. fa. fieri facias

FIFA Fédération Internationale de Football Association (soccer)

FIFO first in, first out

fig. figurative; figuratively; figure

FIG Fédération Internationale de Gymnastique

FIGMO forget it, I've got my orders

FIH Fédération Internationale de Handball; Fédération Internationale de Hockey

FIJ Fédération Internationale de Judo

fil. filament; fillet; fillister; filter

FIL Fédération Internationale de Luge

FIM Fédération Internationale Motorcycliste

fin. finance; financial; finis; finish; finished

Fin. Finland; Finnish

FINA Fédération Internationale de Natation Amateur (swimming)

Finn. Finnish

fin. sec. financial secretary

FIO free in and out

fir. firkin

FIRA Fédération Internationale de Rugby Amateur

fis. fiscal

FIS Fédération Internationale de Ski

FISA Fédération Internationale des Societes d'Aviron (rowing)

fisc. fiscal

f.i.t. free in truck; free of income tax

FIT Federal Income Tax; foreign independent travel; foreign individual travel

FITA Fédération Internationale de Tir à l'Arc (archery)

FITT Fédération Internationale de Tennis de Table

FIVB Fédération Internationale de Volleyball

f.i.w. free in wagon

Fk. fork

fl. flange; flanker; flash; flashing; flood; floor; florin; flour; flourished [L *floruit*]; flowers [L *flores*]; fluid; flush; flute

fL foot-lambert

FL false reading [L *falsa lectio*]; flag lieutenant; flight lieutenant; Florida; focal length; foreign language

Fla. Florida

fld. field; fluid

fl. dr. fluidram

Flem. Flemish

flex. flexible

FLEX Federal Licensing Examination

flg. flange; flooring

Flint. Flintshire

Flints. Flintshire

FLIP Flexible Loan Insurance Program

FLIR forward-looking infrared

FLN National Liberation Front [F *Front de Libération Nationale*]

flou. flourished [L *floruit*]

fl. oz. fluidounce

FLQ Front de Libération du Québec

flr. floor; florin

Fls falls

FLSA Fair Labor Standards Act

flt. fleet; flight; float

fltg. floating; flotage

flx. flexible

fm. farm; fathom; form; from

Fm Fermium

FM fan marker; field manual; field marshall; flavin mononucleotide; foreign mission; foundation member;

frequency modulation

F.M. face measurement; fine measurement

FMB Federal Maritime Board

FMCS Federal Mediation and Conciliation Service

FMG foreign medical graduate

FmHA Farmers Home Administration

FMN flavin mononucleotide

fmr. former

fn. footnote; fusion

fnd. found

fndd. founded

fndg. founding

fndn. foundation

fndr. founder

FNLA Angolan National Liberation Front [Port *Frente Nacional de Libertação da Angola*]

FNMA Federal National Mortgage Association

FNS Food and Nutrition Service

fo. folio

f.o. for orders; free overside; full out

FO field officer; field order; finance officer; firm offer; flag officer; flight officer; flying officer; foreign office; forward observer;

fuel oil; full organ

f.o.b. free on board

FOBS fractional orbital bombardment system

f.o.c. free of charge; free on car

f.o.d. free of damage

FOE Fraternal Order of Eagles

F.O.I.A. Freedom of Information Act

f.o.k. free of knots

fol. folio; following

foll. following

f.o.q. free on quay

for. foreign; forel; forensic; forest; forestry

FOR free on rail

fort. fortification; fortified

FORTRAN formula translation

forz forzando

FOS free on steamer

FOSDIC Film Optical Sensing Device for Input to Computers

FOT free on truck

found. foundation

4-F unfit for military service

4-H head, heart, hands, and health

4WD four-wheel drive

f.o.w. first open water; free on wagon

fp freezing point; loud,

then soft [It *fortepiano*]

f.p. fireplace

F.P. field punishment; fine paper; fireplug; flash point; floating policy; footpound; freight and passenger; fully paid

FPA Foreign Press Association

F.P.A. free of particular average

FPC Federal Power Commission; fish protein concentrate; for private circulation

fpm feet per minute

FPO field post office; fleet post office

fprf. fireproof

fps feet per second; footpound second; frames per second

fqcy. frequency

fqt. frequent

fr. fragment; frame; franc; frequent; from; front; fruit

Fr francium

Fr. brother [L *frater*]; father; France; French; friar; Friday

FR fire resistent; fire retardant; full rate

F.R. freight release

FRA Federal Railroad Administration

frag. fragment

f.r. and c.c. free of riot and civil commotion

FRB Federal Reserve Board

freq. frequency; frequent; frequentative; frequently

FRG Federal Republic of Germany

Fri. Friday

frl. fractional

frm. frame; framing; from

f.r.o.f. fire risk on freight

front. frontispiece

frpl. fireplace

FRS Federal Reserve System; Fellow of the Royal Society (British)

FRSC Fellow of the Royal Society, Canada

frt. freight

frwy. freeway

Fry ferry

f/s factor of safety

fs. facsimile

f.s. feet per second; please forward [F *faire suivre*]

FS field service; final statement; financial secretary; foreign service

FSA Farm Security Administration

F.S.C. Brothers of the Christian Schools [L *Fratres Scholarum Christianarum*]

FSH follicle-stimulating

hormone
FSLIC Federal Savings and Loan Insurance Corporation
FSM free speech movement
FSO foreign service officer
FSP food stamp program
fspc. frontispiece
fst. fast
ft. feet; foot; forint; fort; fortification; fortified; let it be done [L *fiat*]; let it be made [L *fiat*]
f.t. full terms
FT free throw
FTC Federal Trade Commission
ftd. fortified
FTE full-time equivalent
fth. fathom
fthm. fathom
FTI federal tax included
FTIR Fourier transform infrared
ft-lb foot-pound
ftr. fighter; fitter
FTS Federal Telecommunications System
FUBAR fouled up beyond all recognition
fund. fundamental
FUO fever of undetermined origin
fur. furlong; furlough; further
furn. furnished; furniture
fus. fuselage; fusilier
fut. future
f.v. on the back of the page [L *folio verso*]; on the back page of [L *folio verso*]
FVT Family Viewing Time
F.W. freshwater
f.w.b. four-wheel brake
fwd front-wheel drive
fwd. foreword; forward
f.w.d. freshwater damage
FWD four-wheel drive
fwdd. forwarded
FWE finished with engines
fwhm full width at half maximum
F.W.I. French West Indies
fx. foxed
FX foreign exchange
fy. ferry
FY fiscal year
FYI for your information
fz forzando

G

g acceleration of gravity; gauss; gilbert; gravity
g. game; garage; gauge; gelding; gender; general; genitive; gilt; glider;

gloom; goal; goalie; gold; good; government; grain; gram; grand; great; green; grid; groschen; gross; group; guard; guardian; guide; left [F *gauche*]

G conductance; General (movie rating); German; giga-; gourde; Greenwich time; guilder; gulden; gulf

ga. gauge

Ga gallium

Ga. Georgia

GA Gamblers Anonymous; general agent; general assembly; general assistance; general of the army; Georgia; graduate assistant

G.A. general average

GAAP generally accepted accounting principles

GaAs gallium arsenide

GABA gamma-aminobutyric acid

Gael. Gaelic

GAI guaranteed annual income

gal. gallery; galley; gallon

Gal. Galatians

galv. galvanic; galvanism; galvanized

gam. gamut

GAO General Accounting Office

GAPA ground-to-air pilotless aircraft

gar. garage

GAR Grand Army of the Republic

GARP Global Atmospheric Research Program

GAS general adaptation syndrome; Government of American Samoa

GAT Greenwich apparent time

GATT General Agreement of Tariffs and Trade

GAW guaranteed annual wage

gaz. gazette; gazetteer

GB gallbladder; games behind; gold bond; gunboat

G.B. Great Britain; guidebook

G.B.E. Dame Grand Cross Order of the British Empire; Knight Grand Cross Order of the British Empire

GBF Great Books Foundation

g.b.h. girth breast height

GC gas chromatograph; gas chromatography; gigacycle; gonococcus

G.C. general circular; general counsel; George Cross; grand commander;

grand cross; great circle; group captain; gun control

GCA general claim agent; ground-controlled approach

G.C.B. Knight Grand Cross of the Order of the Bath

GCD greatest common divisor

GCF greatest common factor

GCI ground-controlled interception

GCL ground-controlled landing; Guild of Catholic Lawyers

GCM general court-martial

GCT Greenwich civil time

gd. good; ground; guard

g.d. granddaughter

Gd gadolinium

GD general delivery; general duty; good delivery

G.D. grand duchess; grand duchy; grand duke

gde. gourde

gdn. garden; guardian

GDP gross domestic product

GDR German Democratic Republic

gds. goods

gdsm. guardsman

g.e. gilt edges

Ge germanium

GE gastroenterology; gilt edges

GED general equivalency diploma

G.E.D. general educational development

gel. gelatinous

GEM ground-effect machine; growing equity mortgage

gen. gender; general; generation; generator; generic; genetics; genitive; genus

Gen. Genesis

Gen.A.F. general of the air force

genl. general

geog. geographic; geographical; geography

geol. geologic; geological; geology

geom. geometric; geometrical; geometry

ger. gerund; gerundial; gerundive

Ger. German; Germany

GeV giga-electron-volt

GFA general freight average; good fair average

GFCI ground fault circuit interrupter

GFE government furnished equipment

GFI ground fault

interrupter

GG gamma globulin

G.G. governor general; great gross

GGPA graduate grade-point average

GH growth hormone

GHA Greenwich hour angle

GHQ general headquarters

GHz gigahertz

gi. gill

GI galvanized iron; gastrointestinal; general issue; government issue

GIA Gemological Institute of America

Gib. Gibraltar

Gibr. Gibraltar

GIGO garbage in, garbage out

gir. girder

GIT Group Inclusive Tour

GJ grand jury

Gk. Greek

GK goalkeeper

gl. gill; glass; glaze; gloria; gloss; glossary

GL Gothic letter; grid leak; gunlaying

G.L. Graduate in Law; Grand Lodge; ground level

GLC gas-liquid chromatographic; gas-liquid chromatography

GLCM ground-launched cruise missile

gld. guilder

GLM graduated length method

glos. glossary

Glos. Gloucestershire

gloss. glossary

glt. gilt

gm gram

GM Geiger-Müller; general merchandise; general mortgage; gold medal; Greenwich meridian; guided missile; gunmetal

G.M. general manager; grand master

GM & S general medicine and surgery

GMAT Graduate Management Admissions Test

Gmc. Germanic

GME gilt marble edges

GMST Greenwich mean sidereal time

GMT Greenwich mean time

GMV gram-molecular volume

GMW gram-molecular weight

gn guinea

gn. general; green; gun

GN golden number;

Graduate Nurse
gnd. ground
GNI gross national income
GNMA Government National Mortgage Association
GNP gross national product
gnr. gunner
Gn.R.H. gonadotropin releasing hormone
G.O. general obligation; general office; general officer; general order; grand organ; great organ
G.O.C. general officer commanding
GOCO government-owned, contractor-operated
GOE gas, oxygen, and ether
GOES geostationary operational environmental satellite
GOM grand old man
GOP Grand Old Party (Republican)
Goth. Gothic
gov. government; governmental; governor
govt. government
gox gaseous oxygen
gp. group
GP general pause; general practice; general practitioner; geographic

position; glide path; grand prix; great primer
G.P. general paralysis; general paresis; general purpose; geometric progression; Glory be to the Father [L *Gloria Patria*]
GPA general passenger agent; grade-point average
gpd gallons per day
gph gallons per hour
GPI general paralysis of the insane; ground position indicator
GPM gallons per minute; geopotential meter; Graduated Payment Mortgage
GPO general post office; Government Printing Office
gps gallons per second
GQ general quarters
gr. grade; grain; gram; grammar; grammatical; grand; graphite; gravity; gray; great; grind; groschen; gross; group
Gr. Greece; Greek
GR general reconnaissance
G.R. general reserve; gentleman rider; grooved roofing
grad. gradient; graduate;

graduated
gram. grammar;
grammatical
Gramp. Grampian
GRAS generally
recognized as safe
grav. gravid; gravity
graz graceful [It *grazioso*]
Gr.Br. Great Britain
grd. grind; ground;
guaranteed
GRE Graduate Record
Examination
GRI guaranteed
retirement income
G.R.I. Graduate Realtors
Institute
grm. germ; germination
grn. green
gro. gross; group
GRP glass-reinforced
plastic; glass-reinforced
polyester
GR-S government rubber
styrene
G.R.U. Soviet Army
Intelligence [Russ *Glavnoe
Razvedivatelnoe
Upravlenie*]
gr. wt. gross weight
gs gauss
g.s. grandson
GS general schedule;
general semantics;
general service; general
staff; general support;

gold standard;
government service;
grammar school; ground
speed
G.S. general secretary;
general sessions; general
superintendent
GSA General Services
Administration; Girl
Scouts of America
GSC general staff corps
GSH glutathione
GSO general staff officer
GSP Generalized System
of Preferences
GSR galvanic skin
response
GSSG glutathione
GST Greenwich sidereal
time
GSV guided space vehicle
gt. drop [L *gutta*]; gilt;
great
g.t. gilt top
GT grand touring car
G.T. gross ton
GTA grand theft auto
G.T.A. graduate teaching
assistant
Gt.Br. Great Britain
Gt.Brit. Great Britain
GTC good till canceled;
good till countermanded
gtd. guaranteed
GTE gilt top edge
GTM general traffic

manager; good this month

GTO gate turn off

GTP guanosine triphosphate

Gtr. Man. Greater Manchester

gtt. drops [L *guttae*]

GTW good this week

gu. guarantee; guaranteed; guinea; gules

GU genitourinary; Guam

guar. guarantee; guaranteed; guarantor; guaranty

Guat. Guatemala

guid. guidance

GUTS grand unification theories

gutt. drop [L *gutta*]; drops [L *guttae*]; guttural

GVH graft versus host

gvl. gravel

GVW gross vehicle weight

GW gigawatt

Gwyn. Gwynedd

gy. gray

gyn. gynecologic; gynecological; gynecologist; gynecology

gynecol. gynecologic; gynecological; gynecologist; gynecology

Gy.Sgt. gunnery sergeant

GZ ground zero

H

h hecto-; henry; Planck's constant

h. film [Ger *hauch*]; hail; haler; half; hall; handily; harbor; hardness; haze; headquarters; heat; height; heir [L *heres*]; helicopter; heller; hence; heroin; high; holy; home; honor; horizon; horizontal; horn; horse; hot; hour; house; humidity; hundred; husband; hydrant

H enthalpy; Hamiltonian; hard; henry; heroin; hit; Hubble constant; hydrogen; intensity of magnetic field

ha hectare

h.a. in this year [L *hoc anno*]; of this year [L *huius anni*]

HA hour angle

H.A. heavy artillery; high-angle; horse artillery; hot air

HAA heavy antiaircraft

hab. habitat

Hab. Habakkuk

HAB high-altitude bombing

hab. corp. habeas corpus

Hag. Haggai

handbk. handbook

H & J hyphenation and justification

Hants Hampshire

har. harbor

hav haversine

haz. hazard

Hb hemoglobin

HB halfback; hard black; heavy bomber; House bill

H.B. His Beatitude; His Blessedness

HBM Her Britannic Majesty; His Britannic Majesty

HBO Home Box Office; hyperbaric oxygenation

Hbr. harbor

h.c. for the sake of honor [L *honoris causa*]

HC half calf; half chest; hand control; hard copy; high capacity; high commissioner; high-compression; hockey club; Holy Communion; hot and cold; House of Commons; hydrocarbon

H.C. held covered; High Church; hold covered; House of Commons; house of correction

hcap. handicap

HCB hexachlorobenzene

HCF highest common factor

HCFA Health Care Financing Administration

HCG human chorionic gonadotropin

HCL high cost of living

hcp. handicap

hct. hematocrit

hd. hand; head; hogshead

HD Hansen's disease; harbor defense; hearing distance; heavy-duty; high density; high detergent; home defense; horse-drawn; Huntington's disease

hdbk. handbook

hdkf. handkerchief

hdl. handle; headline

HDL high-density lipoprotein

HDLC high-level data link control

hdlg. handling

HDPE high-density polyethylene

hdqrs. headquarters

HDS Human Development Services

HDTV high definition television

hdw. hardware

hdwd. hardwood

hdwe. hardware

hdwre. hardware

h.e. that is [L *hoc est*]; this

is [L *hic est*]
He helium
HE high efficiency
H.E. Her Excellency; high explosive; His Eminence; His Excellency
Heb. Hebrew; Hebrews
HEH Her Exalted Highness; His Exalted Highness
HEI high explosive incendiary
HEP hydroelectric power
her. heir [L *heres*]; heraldic; heraldry
Heref./Worcs. Hereford and Worcester
Herts. Hertfordshire
HETP hexaethyl tetraphosphate
HEU hydroelectric unit
HEW Department of Health, Education, and Welfare
hex. hexachord; hexagon; hexagonal
hf. half
Hf hafnium
HF height finding; high frequency
H.F. home fleet; home forces
HFC high-frequency current
HFM hold for money
hg. hectogram; heliogram

Hg mercury [NL *hydrargyrum*, lit., water silver]
HG High German
H.G. Her Grace; His Grace; home guard
Hgb hemoglobin
HGH human growth hormone
hgm hectogram
hgt. height
hgwy. highway
hh hands high
H.H. Her Highness; His Highness; His Holiness
H.H.A. home health aide
hhd. hogshead
H.H.D. Doctor of Humanities [NL *humanitatum doctor*]
HHFA Housing and Home Finance Agency
HHG household goods
HHP household pet
HHS Department of Health and Human Services
HI Hawaii; hemagglutination inhibition; humidity index
H.I. high intensity
HID high intensity discharge
HIH Her Imperial Highness; His Imperial Highness

HILAC heavy ion linear accelerator

HIM Her Imperial Majesty; His Imperial Majesty

Hind. Hindi; Hindustani

his. history

hist. historian; historical; history

Hitt. Hittite

H.J. here lies [L *hic jacet*]

HJR House joint resolution

h.j.s. here lies buried [L *hic jacet sepultus*]

H.K. Hong Kong; House of Keys (Isle of Man)

hkf. handkerchief

hl hectoliter

h.l. in this place [L *hoc loco*]; of this place [L *hujus loci*]

HL height-length; horizontal line

H.L. House of Lords

HLA human leukocyte antigen

hld. hold

HLF Heart and Lung Foundation

hlqn. harlequin

HLS holograph letter signed; laid in this place [L *hoc loco situs*]

hlt. halt

hm hectometer

h.m. headmaster; headmistress; in this month [L *hoc mense*]; of this month [L *hujus mensis*]

HM half morocco; handmade; harbor master; heavy mobile; Her Majesty; Her Majesty's; His Majesty; His Majesty's

H.M. harmonic mean; Home Missions

HMAS Her Majesty's Australian ship; His Majesty's Australian ship

HMBS Her Majesty's British ship; His Majesty's British ship

HMC Her Majesty's Customs; His Majesty's Customs

HMCS Her Majesty's Canadian ship; His Majesty's Canadian ship

hmd. humid

HMD hyaline membrane disease; hydraulic mean depth

HMF Her Majesty's Forces; His Majesty's Forces

HMG heavy machine gun; Her Majesty's Government; His Majesty's Government; human menopausal gonadotrophin

hmlt. hamlet

HMMWV high mobility multi-purpose wheeled vehicle

HMO health maintenance organization

h.m.p. he/she erected this monument [L *hoc monumentum posuit*]

HMP handmade paper

HMS Her Majesty's Service; Her Majesty's ship; His Majesty's Service; His Majesty's ship

HMSO Her Majesty's Stationery office; His Majesty's Stationery office

hnd. hand; hundred

hndbk. handbook

HNIS Human Nutrition Information Service

HNS Holy Name Society

hny. honey

ho. house

Ho holmium

H.O. head office; holy day of obligation; home office; hostilities only

hol. hollow

hom. homiletics; homily

hon. honor; honorable; honorary; honored

Hon. Honduras

honble. honorable

Hond. Honduras

hony. honorary

HOP high oxygen pressure

HOPE Health Opportunity for People Everywhere

hor. horizon; horizontal; horological; horology

horol. horology

hort. horticultural; horticulture

Hos. Hosea

hosp. hospital

HOV high-occupancy vehicle

how. howitzer

hp horsepower

h.p. half pay; handpainted

HP handmade paper; high-pass; high power; hollow point; horizontal parallax; house physician

H.P. high pressure; high priest; hire purchase; hot pressed; House of Parliament

HPA high-power amplifier

HPF highest possible frequency; high power field

HPGC heading per gyrocompass

h.p.h. horsepower-hour

HPI history of present illness

HPLC high performance

liquid chromatograph;
high performance liquid
chromatography
HPNS high-pressure
nervous syndrome
HPO highway post office
hps. harpsichord
HPV human powered
vehicle
h.q. look for this [L *hoc
quaere*]; see this [L *hoc
quaere*]
HQ headquarters
hr. here; hour
Hr. Herr
HR high resistance; home
run
H.R. home rule; House of
Representatives
HRA Health Resources
Administration
hrd. hard
hrdwre. hardware
H.Res. House resolution
HRH Her Royal Highness;
His Royal Highness
HRI height-range
indicator
HRIP here rests in peace
[L *hic requiescit in pace*]
HRMS high-resolution
mass spectrometry
HRSA Health Resources
and Services
Administration
hrt. heart

Hrt. Hertfordshire
hrtwd. heartwood
hrzn. horizon
h.s. at bedtime [L *hora
somni*]; in this sense [L
hoc sensu]
HS hemstitched; high
speed; honorary secretary
H.S. here is buried [L *hic
sepultus* or *hic situs*]; high
school; house surgeon
HSA human serum
albumin
hse. house
HSE here is buried [L *hic
sepultus est* or *hic situs
est*]
hsg. housing
HSGT high-speed ground
transport
HSH Her Serene
Highness; His Serene
Highness
HSL high-speed launch
HSM Her Serene Majesty;
His Serene Majesty
HST Hawaiian standard
time; hypersonic transport
HSV herpes simplex virus
ht. heat; height
h.t. at this time [L *hoc
tempore*]; high tension;
under this title [L *hoc
titulo*]
HT half time; halftone;
hardtop; Hawaii time;

herd test

HTA heavier than air

htg. heating

HTGR high-temperature gas-cooled reactor

HTH high-test hypochlorite

HTR high-temperature reactor

Hts. heights

HUAC House Un-American Activities Committee

HUD Department of Housing and Urban Development

hum. humanities [NL *humaniora*]; humor; humorous

Humber. Humberside

HUMINT human intelligence

hun. hundred

Hung. Hungarian; Hungary

hv have

HV high-voltage

H.V. high velocity

HVAC heating, ventilation, and air conditioning

HVL half-value layer

hvy. heavy

hw. how

HW hit wicket

H.W. high water; hot water

HWL high-water line

HWM high-water mark

hwy. highway

hy. heavy

Hy. henry

hyb. hybrid

hyd. hydraulic; hydraulics; hydrographic; hydrography; hydrostatic; hydrostatics

hydt. hydrant

hyg. hygiene

hyp. hypothesis; hypothetical

hypoth. hypothesis; hypothetical

Hz hertz

hzy. hazy

I

---

i imaginary unit; positive square root of minus one

i. emperor [L *imperator*]; empress [L *imperatrix*]; imperial; incendiary; incomplete; independent; indicated; indicative; industrial; infantry; infield; inhibitory; initial; inner; inside; inspector; instantaneous; institute; institution; instrumental;

intelligence; intensity;
interest; international;
interstate; intransitive;
iron; island; isle; that [L
id]

I   candlepower; electric
current; iodine; moment of
inertia

I.   Indian; Iraqi; Israeli

i.a.   among other things [L
inter alia]

Ia.   Iowa

IA   impedance angle;
infected area;
international angstrom;
intra-arterial; Iowa

I.A.   Incorporated
Accountant

IAA   indoleacetic acid

IAAF   International
Amateur Athletic
Federation

IABA   International
Amateur Boxing
Association

IAC   industry advisory
committee; interview after
combat

IADB   Inter-American
Defense Board; Inter-
American Development
Bank

IAEA   International
Atomic Energy Agency

IAF   Inter-American
Foundation

IALC   instrument
approach and landing
chart

IALS   International
Association of Legal
Science

IAM   International
Association of Machinists
and Aerospace Workers

I and E   information and
education

I and P   indexed and
paged

I and R   initiative and
referendum; intelligence
and reconnaissance

I and S   inspection and
security; inspection and
survey

IAP   international airport

IAS   indicated airspeed

IAT   indicated air
temperature

IATA   International Air
Transport Association

IAU   International
Association of
Universities;
International
Astronomical Union

IAZ   inner artillery zone

ib.   in the same place [L
ibidem]

IB   incendiary bomb;
intelligence branch

I.B.   in bond; inbound;

International Baccalaureate; invoice book

IBA Independent Bar Association; indolebutyric acid; International Bar Association

IBEW International Brotherhood of Electrical Workers

ibid. in the same place [L *ibidem*]

IBM intercontinental ballistic missile

IBRD International Bank for Reconstruction and Development

IBY International Biological Year

i/c in charge

IC immediate constituent; index correction; information center; information circular; inspected and condemned; inspiratory capacity; integrated circuit; interior communications; internal combustion; internal connection

ICA International Communication Agency; International Cooperation Administration; International Cooperative Alliance

ICAO International Civil Aviation Organization

ICAS intermittent commercial and amateur service

ICBM intercontinental ballistic missile

ICC Indian Claims Commission; International Chamber of Commerce; Interstate Commerce Commission

Ice. Iceland

ICE internal-combustion engine; International Cultural Exchange

Icel. Icelandic

ICF intracellular fluid

ICFTU International Confederation of Free Trade Unions

ich. ichthyology

ichth. ichthyology

ICJ International Commission of Jurists; International Court of Justice

ICN International Council of Nurses

icon. iconography

ICP inductively coupled plasma

ICRC International Committee of the Red Cross

ICSH interstitial-cell-stimulating hormone

ICSS intracranial self-stimulation

ICT inflammation of connective tissue; insulin coma therapy

ICU intensive care unit

ICW interrupted continuous waves

id. island; the same [L *idem*]

i.d. inner diameter; inside diameter; inside dimensions; internal diameter

ID Idaho; identification; industrial design; intelligence department

IDA International Development Association

IDB industrial development bond

IDC Industrial Development Certificate

IDP inosine diphosphate; integrated data processing; international driving permit

IDR industrial development revenue bond; infantry drill regulations; international drawing rights

IDU idoxuridine

i.e. that is [L *id est*]

IE Indo-European; industrial engineer; initial equipment

I.E. inside edge

I.E.P. individualized education program

IESC International Executive Service Corps

i.f. he/she did it himself/herself [L *ipse fecit*]

IF in full; interferon; intermediate frequency

IFC International Finance Corporation

iff if and only if

IFF identification, friend or foe

IFN interferon

IFO identified flying object

IFR instrument flight rules

Ig immunoglobulin

IG inspector general

ign. ignition; unknown [L *ignotus*]

IGS imperial general staff

IGY International Geophysical Year

i.h. here lies [L *iacet hic*]; inside height

IH infectious hepatitis

IHC Jesus [part transliteration of Gk IHΣ, abbreviation for IHΣOYΣ Jesus]

IHD International Hydrological Decade

IHF Institute of High
Fidelity
i.h.p. indicated horse-
power
IHP indicated horsepower
IHS Jesus [part
transliteration of Gk IHΣ,
abbreviation for IHΣOYΣ
Jesus]
IHSA iodinated human
serum albumin
I/I indorsement irregular;
inventory and inspection
IIE Institute of Industrial
Engineers
il. illustrated; illustration;
illustrator
i.l. inside length
Il illinium
IL Illinois; including
loading; inside left
I.L. interline
ILA International Law
Association; International
Longshoremen's
Association
ILAA International Legal
Aid Association
ILGWU International
Ladies' Garment Workers'
Union
ill. illuminated;
illumination; illustrated;
illustration; illustrator;
most illustrious [L
illustrissimus]

Ill. Illinois
illus. illustrated;
illustration; illustrator
illust. illustrated;
illustration; illustrator
ilmo. most illustrious [L
illustrissimo]
i.l.o. in lieu of
ILO International Labor
Organization
ILP Independent Labour
Party
ILS instrument landing
system
im. immature
i.m. intramuscular;
intramuscularly
IM imperial measure;
individual medley; inner
markov; intermodulation
distortion; intramural
I.M. Isle of Man
IMCO Inter-Governmental
Maritime Consultative
Organization
imdtly. immediately
IMF International
Monetary Fund
imit. imitation; imitative
IMM International
Monetary Market
immun. immunity;
immunization
immunol. immunology
immy. immediately
imp. emperor [L

imperator]; empress [L
imperatrix]; imperative;
imperfect; imperial;
implement; import;
important; imported;
importer; impression;
imprimatur; imprint;
improved; improvement;
in the first place [L
imprimis]
IMP inosinic acid;
International Match
Point; interplanetary
monitoring platform
imperf. imperfect;
imperforate
impf. imperfect
impl. imperial; implement
impr. improved;
improvement
impt. important
imptr. importer
impv. imperative
impx. empress [L
imperatrix]
in. inch; inlet
In indium
IN Indiana
INA international normal
atmosphere
inbd. inboard
inc. engraved [L *incisus*];
inclosure; included;
including; inclusive;
income; incoming;
incomplete; incorporated;

incorporation; increase;
incumbent
ince. insurance
inch. inchoative
incl. inclosure; included;
including; inclusive
incld. included
incln. inclusion
incog. incognito
incr. increase; increased;
increasing
ind. independence;
independent; index;
indexed; indicated;
indicative; indicator;
indigo; indirect; induction;
industrial; industry
Ind. Indian; Indiana
IND investigational new
drug
Ind.E. industrial engineer
indef. indefinite
indemy. indemnity
indic. indicated;
indicative; indicator
indiv. individual
indn. indication
Indon. Indonesia;
Indonesian
indre. indenture
indsl. industrial
indus. industrial; industry
inf. infantry; inferior;
infield; infielder;
infinitive; infinity;
infirmary; informant;

information; infra;
infused; infusion

INF intermediate-range
nuclear force

infin. infinitive

infl. inflammable;
inflorescence; influence;
influenced

info. information

INH isoniazid
[iso-nicotinic acid
hydrazide]

INI intranuclear inclusion

inj. inject; injection

inn. inning

inorg. inorganic

INP International News
Photo

inq. inquire

in. req. information
requested

INRI Jesus of Nazareth,
King of the Jews [L *Iesus
Nazarenus Rex
Iudaeorum*]

ins. inches; inscribed;
inside; inspected;
inspector; insular;
insulated; insulation;
insurance

INS Immigration and
Naturalization Service

insc. inscribed

insce. insurance

insol. insoluble

insp. inspector

Insp. Gen. inspector
general

inst. installment; instant;
instantaneous; institute;
institution; institutional;
instruction; instructor;
instrument; instrumental

instl. installation

instmt. instrument

instn. institution;
instruction

instr. instruction;
instructor; instrument;
instrumental

instrn. instruction

int. intelligence; intercept;
interest; interim; interior;
interjection; interleaved;
intermediate; internal;
international; interpreter;
intersection; interval;
interview; intransitive

int. al. among other
persons [L *inter alios*];
among other things [L
inter alia]

INTELPOST
International Electronic
Post

Intelsat International
Telecommunications
Satellite

inter. intermediate;
interrogative

interj. interjection

Interpol International

Criminal Police
Organization
interpr. interpreter
interrog. interrogative
intg. interrogate;
interrogator
intl. international
intmd. intermediate
intmt. intermittent
intn. intention
intnl. international
intpr. interpreter
intr. intransitive;
introduced; introducing;
introduction; introductory
in trans. in transit [L *in
transitu*]
intrans. intransitive
introd. introduction
intsv. intensive
inv. he/she designed [L
invenit]; he/she devised [L
invenit]; he/she invented
[L *invenit*]; invented;
invention; inventor;
inventory; investment;
invitation; invoice
invert. invertebrate
invest. investment
invt. he/she designed [L
invenit]; he/she devised [L
invenit]; he/she invented
[L *invenit*]; inventory
Io ionium
IO in order; information
officer; inspecting order;

intelligence officer
I/O input/output
IOC initial operating
capability; International
Olympic Committee
IOM interoffice memo
I.O.M. Isle of Man
IOOF Independent Order
of Odd Fellows
IORM Improved Order of
Red Men
IOU I owe you
I.O.W. Isle of Wight
i.p. installment paid
IP ice point; India paper;
initial point; innings
pitched; intermediate
pressure
IPA including particular
average; indicated
pressure altitude;
individual practice
association; intermediate
power amplifier;
International Phonetic
Alphabet
IPD individual package
delivery
ipf. imperfect
IPI in the regions of
unbelievers [L *in partibus
infidelium*]
ipm inches per minute
IPP India paper proofs
IPPF International
Planned Parenthood

Federation

ipr inches per revolution

ips inches per second

IPS iron pipe size

IPSA Independent Postal System of America

IPT indexed, paged, and titled

IPTS International Practical Temperature Scale

ipv. imperative; improve

IPW interrogation prisoner of war

i.q. the same as [L *idem quod*]

IQ intelligence quotient

IQED that which is to be proved [L *id quod erat demonstrandum*]

IQSY International Quiet Sun Year

Ir iridium

Ir. Irish

IR information retrieval; infrared; insoluble residue; intelligence ratio; interim report; interrogator-responder

I.R. Inland Revenue; Internal Revenue

IRA individual retirement account

I.R.A. Irish Republican Army

IRB industrial revenue

bond

IRBM intermediate range ballistic missile

IRC International Red Cross; irregular route carrier

Ire. Ireland

IRE Institute of Radio Engineers

irid. iridescent

I.R.O. Inland Revenue Officer; Internal Revenue Officer

irr. irredeemable; irregular

irred. irredeemable

irreg. irregular

IRS Internal Revenue Service

IRU international radium unit

is. island; isle

Is. Isaiah

IS interservice

I.S. intermediate school; interstate

Isa. Isaiah

ISAM indexed sequential-access method

ISBN International Standard Book Number

ISC interstate commerce

ISD international subscriber dialing

ISDN integrated-services digital networks

i.s.g. imperial standard gallon

isl. island

ISO incentive stock option; International Standards Organization

isoln. isolation

Isr. Israel; Israeli

iss. issue

ISSN International Standard Serial Number

IST insulin shock therapy

isth. isthmus

ISV International Scientific Vocabulary

ISWG imperial standard wire gauge

it. item

i.t. in transit [L *in transitu*]

It. Italian; Italy

IT immediate transportation; immunity test; income tax; information technology; internal thread; international tolerance

ITA initial teaching alphabet

ital. italic; italicized

Ital. Italian

ITC Inclusive Tour Charter; investment tax credit

itin. itinerary

ITO International Trade Organization

ITU International Telecommunication Union; International Typographical Union

ITV Independent Television; instructional television

IU immunizing unit

I.U. international unit

IUCD intrauterine contraceptive device

IUD intrauterine device

i.v. increased valve; initial velocity; invoice value; under the word [L *in verbo* or *in voce*]

IV intravenous; intravenously; iodine value

i.w. inside width

IW isotopic weight

I.W. Isle of Wight

IWW Industrial Workers of the World

J

j. jack; join; journal; journalism; judge [L *judex*]; junior; justice; juvenile; law [L *jus*]

J angular momentum; January; joule; July;

June; mechanical equivalent of heat; radiant intensity

Ja January

Ja. January

JA joint agent; judge advocate; Junior Achievement

J/A joint account

JAG Judge Advocate General

Jam. Jamaica

Jan. January

JAN joint army-navy

j. & w.o. jettison and washing overboard

Jap. Japan; Japanese

Jas. James

JATO jet-assisted takeoff

Jav. Javanese

JB joint board; joint bond; junction box

J.B. Bachelor of Laws [L *jurum baccalaureus*]

JBS John Birch Society

jc. junction

JC junior college; juvenile court

J.C. Jesus Christ; jurisconsult [L *jurisconsultus*]; justice clerk

JCAH Joint Commission on Accreditation of Hospitals

J.Can.B. Bachelor of

Canon Law [L *juris canna baccalaureus*]

J.Can.D. Doctor of Canon Law [L *juris canna doctor*]

JCB junior college of business

J.C.B. Bachelor of Canon Law [NL *juris canonos baccalaureus*]; Bachelor of Civil Law [L *juris civilis baccalaureus*]

JCC junior chamber of commerce

J.C.D. Doctor of Canon Law [NL *juris canonos doctor*]; Doctor of Civil Law [L *juris civilis doctor*]

J.C.L. Licentiate in Canon Law [NL *juris canonici licentiatus*]

J.C.M. Master of Civil Law [L *juris civilis magister*]

JCR junior common room

JCS Joint Chiefs of Staff

jct. junction

jctn. junction

jd. joined

JD justice department; juvenile delinquent

J.D. Doctor of Jurisprudence [L *juris doctor*]; Doctor of Law [L *juris doctor*]; Doctor of Laws [L *jurum doctor*]; Julian day; junior deacon;

junior dean; jury duty
Je. June
JEA joint export agent
Jer. Jeremiah; Jeremias
jg junior grade
JHS Jesus [part transliteration of Gk IHΣ, abbreviation for IHΣOYΣ Jesus]
J.H.S. junior high school
JIC joint industrial council; joint intelligence committee
JIT job instruction training
JJ judges; justices
jl. journal
Jl. Joel; July
J.M. Master of Laws [L *juris magister*]
JMA junior military aviator
J.M.J. Jesus, Mary, Joseph
JMT job methods training
jn. join; junction
Jn. John
jnc. junction
j.n.d. just noticeable difference
jnl. journal
jnlst. journalist
Jno. John
jnr. junior
jnt. joint
Jo. Joel

JO junior officer
JOBS Job Opportunities in the Business Sector
joc. jocose; jocular
JOC joint operations center
Josh. Joshua
jour. journal; journey; journeyman
JP Japan paper; jet propellant; jet-propelled; jet propulsion
J.P. justice of the peace
Jpn. Japan; Japanese
JPP Japan paper proofs
jr. journal; juror
Jr. junior
JR joint resolution
JRC Junior Red Cross
JROTC Junior Reserve Officers' Training Corps
JS joint support
JSC joint-stock company
jt. joint
JTC junior training corps
jtly. jointly
Ju. June
Juco junior college
jud. judge; judgment; judicature; judicial; judiciary
Jud. Judith
Judg. Judges
judgt. judgment
Jul. July
jun. junior

Jun. June
junc. junction
Junr. Junior
jur. juridical; jurist
juris. jurisprudence
jurisp. jurisprudence
Jur.M. Master of
Jurisprudence [L *juris
magister*]
jus. justice
juss. jussive
just. justice
juv. juvenile; young [L
juvenis]
JV Japanese vellum;
junior varsity
JVP Japanese vellum
proofs
J.W. junior warden
jwlr. jeweler
Jy. July

K

k kilo-; kilogram; thousand
[F *kilo-*]
k. calends [L *kalendae*];
cathode [Ger *kathode*];
keel; keg; key; kicker;
kindergarten; kitchen;
knight; knit; knot; kopeck;
kurus
K absolute zero; constant;
karat; kelvin; kilobyte;
king; kosher; kwacha;
kyat; potassium [NL
kalium]; strikeout
ka cathode [Ger *kathode*]
K.A. king of arms
kal. calends [L *kalendae*]
Kan. Kansas
Kans. Kansas
kb kilobar; kilobase
KB kilobyte
K.B. King's Bench; kitchen
and bathroom; kite
balloon; Knight Bachelor
kbar kilobar
K.B.E. Knight
Commander of the Order
of the British Empire
K.B.P. kite balloon pilot
kbps kilobits per second
kc kilocycle
K.C. Kansas City; kennel
club; King's Counsel;
Knight Commander;
Knights of Columbus
kcal kilocalorie; kilogram
calorie
K.C.B. Knight
Commander of the Order
of the Bath
K.C.M.G. Knight
Commander of the Order
of St. Michael and St.
George
kc/s kilocycles per second
Kčs koruna [Czech *koruna
československà*]

K.C.S.G. Knight Commander of the Order of St. Gregory
kd. killed
KD kiln-dried
K.D. knocked down
K.D.C.L. knocked down, in carloads
K.D.F. knocked down flat
K.D.L.C.L. knocked down, in less than carloads
kdm. kingdom
K.E. kinetic energy
Ker. Kerry
keV kilo-electron volt
kg kilogram
kg. keg; king
kG kilogauss
K.G. Knight of the Order of the Garter
KGB Soviet State Security Committee [Russ *Komitet Gosudarstvennoi Bezopasnosti*]
K.G.C. Knight Grand Commander; Knight of the Grand Cross
kg-m kilogram-meter
kgps kilograms per second
K.H. Knight of the Royal Guelphic Order of Hanover
kHz kilohertz
ki. kitchen
Ki. king
KIA killed in action

kil kilderkin
kild kilderkin
Kild. Kildare
Kilk. Kilkenny
Kin. Kinross-shire
kind. kindergarten
kit. kitchen
k.j. knee jerk
kJ kilojoule
KJV King James Version
KKK Ku Klux Klan
kl kiloliter
klm kilometer
km kilometer
km. kingdom
K.M. king's messenger
kmps kilometers per second
kmw kilomegawatt
kmwh kilomegawatt-hour
kn. knot
knt. knight
KO knockout
K.O. keep off
K of C Knights of Columbus
K of P Knights of Pythias
Kor. Korea; Korean
KP kitchen police
K.P. king post; knotty pine
kPa kilopascal
kpc kiloparsec
kph kilometers per hour
kr. kreuzer
Kr krypton
Kr. krona; krone

KS　Kansas
K.S.　keep standing; King's Scholar
ksf　kips per square foot
ksi　kips per square inch
KSR　keyboard send and receive
kt　karat; kiloton
kt.　knot
Kt.　knight
k.t.l.　et cetera [Gk *kai ta loipa*]
KUB　kidney, ureter, and bladder
kv　kilovolt
kV　kilovolt
kva　kilovolt-ampere
kvah　kilovolt-ampere-hour
kvar　kilovar
kvarh　kilovar-hour
kw　kilowatt
kW　kilowatt
kwh　kilowatt-hour
kWh　kilowatt-hour
kw-hr　kilowatt-hour
KWIC　keyword in context
KWOC　keyword out of context
Ky.　Kentucky
KY　Kentucky

L

l　large; liter
l.　book [L *liber*]; in the place [L *loco*]; lady; land; landing; landplane; late; latitude; launch; law; leaf; league; learner; leather; leave; left; legitimate; length; letter; liaison; lift; light; lightening; line; liner; link; liquid; lit; little; lodge; longitude; lord; lost; low; lumen; place [L *locus*]; pound [L *libra*]
L　inductance; kinetic potential; Lagrangian; lake; lambert; large; Latin; left; lempira; leu; levorotatory; lewisite; Liberal; Limes; lira; lire; liter; lithium; long; lower; lumbar; pound [L *libra*]
L.　lady; licentiate
la.　last
La　lanthanum
La.　lane; Louisiana
LA　law agent; leading aircraftsman; lightening arrester; lighter than air; local authority; Louisiana; low altitude
L.A.　law agent; legislative

assembly; library association; local agent; Los Angeles

L/A landing account; letter of authority

LAA light antiaircraft

lab. labor

Lab. Labrador

LAC leading aircraftsman

LACW leading aircraftswoman

LAD language acquisition device

LADT local area digital transmission

lam. laminated

Lam. Lamentations

LAMPS light airborne multipurpose system

LAN local apparent noon; local area network

Lancs. Lancashire

L and D loans and discounts; loss and damage

L and R lake and rail

L and W living and well

lang. language

lap. laparotomy

laser light amplification by stimulated emission of radiation

LASH lighter aboard ship

lat. latent; lateral; latitude

Lat. Latin; Latvia

LAT local apparent time

LATA Local Access and Transport Area

latd. latitude

LATS long-acting thyroid stimulator

lav. lavatory

law. lawyer

lb letter box; pound [L *libra*]

l.b. leg bye

LB Labrador; landing barge; left on base; light bomber

L.B. local board

lbf pounds force

LBF lactobacillus bulgaricus factor

LBO leveraged buyout

LBP length between perpendiculars

lbr. labor; lumber

l.c. in the place cited [L *loco citato*]; lower case

LC label clause; lance corporal; landing craft; law courts; left center; level crossing; Library of Congress; lightly canceled; line of communication; liquid chromatography

L.C. lord chamberlain; lord chancellor

L/C letter of credit

LCAC landing craft air cushion

LCB left cornerback

LCD   least common denominator; liquid crystal display; lowest common denominator

LCDR   lieutenant commander

lce.   lance

L.C.J.   lord chief justice

lcl.   local

LCL   less than carload; less-than-carload lot

LCM   least common multiple; lowest common multiple

L.C.M.   Master of Comparative Law [NL *legis comparativae magister*]

LCpl   lance corporal

LCQ   liquid crystal quartz

LCT   local civil time

ld.   land; lead; limited; load; lord

Ld.   Lord

LD   learning disability; learning disabled; left defense; lethal dose; line of duty; local delivery; long delay; long distance

LDC   less developed country; lower dead center

LDF   Legal Defense and Educational Fund

ldg.   landing; leading; loading; lodging

LDH   lactate dehydrogenase; lactic dehydrogenase

LDL   low-density lipoprotein

LDO   limited duty officer

ldp.   ladyship; lordship

ldr.   leader

ldry.   laundry

LDS   Latter-day Saints; praise to God always [L *laus Deo semper*]

le.   lease

LE   labor exchange; law efficiency; leading edge; left end; low explosive; lupus erythematosus

lea.   league; leather; leave

LEA   local education authority

LEAA   Law Enforcement Assistance Administration

Leb.   Lebanese; Lebanon

lect.   lector; lecture; lecturer

led.   ledger

LED   light-emitting diode

LEED   low-energy electron diffraction

leg.   he/she reads [L *legit*]; legal; legate; legation; legato; legend; legislation; legislative; legislature; they read [L *legunt*]

legis.   legislation; legislative; legislature

Leics.   Leicestershire

Leit. Leitrim
LEM lunar excursion module
LES local excitatory state
LET linear energy transfer
leu leucine
lev. levant
Lev. Leviticus
Levit. Leviticus
lex. lexical; lexicon
lf. leaf; leaflet
l.f. lightface
LF ledger folio; left field; left foot; left forward; left front; lettering faded; lineal feet; load factor; lock forward; low frequency
L.F. lineal feet
LFA local freight agent
LFB left fullback
LFC low-frequency current
LFD least fatal dose
lft. leaflet
lg. large; long
LG landing ground; large grain; left guard; Low German
L.G. Life Guards
lge. large
lgr. larger; longer
lgt. light
lgth. length
LH left hand; lighthouse; lower half; luteinizing hormone
L.H. Legion of Honor [F *Légion d'honneur*]
LHA local hour angle
L.H.A. lord high admiral
LHB left halfback
L.H.C. lord high chancellor
L.H.D. Doctor of Humane Letters [L *litterarum humaniorum doctor*]; Doctor of Humanities [L *litterarum humaniorum doctor*]
LHRH luteinizing hormone-releasing hormone
L.H.T. lord high treasurer
li. link
Li lithium
L.I. light infantry; Long Island; low intensity
lib. book [L *liber*]; liberal; liberation; librarian; library; pound [L *libra*]
libn. librarian
libr. librarian
lic. license; licensed
Lic. Licentiate
LID League for Industrial Democracy
lidar light detection and ranging
Lieut. lieutenant
LIFO last in, first out
lim. limit; limited

Lim. Limerick

lin. lineal; linear; liniment

Lincs. Lincolnshire

ling. linguistic; linguistics

LIP life insurance policy

LIPS logical inferences per second

liq. liquid; liquor

lit. liter; literal; literally; literary; literature

Lit lira (Italy)

Lit.B. Bachelor of Letters [ML *litterarum baccalaureus*]; Bachelor of Literature [ML *litterarum baccalaureus*]

lit. crit. literary criticism

Lit.D. Doctor of Letters [ML *litterarum doctor*]; Doctor of Literature [ML *litterarum doctor*]

lith. lithographic; lithography

Lith. Lithuania; Lithuanian

litho. lithography

Litt.B. Bachelor of Letters [ML *litterarum baccalaureus*]; Bachelor of Literature [ML *litterarum baccalaureus*]

Litt.D. Doctor of Letters [ML *litterarum doctor*]

Litt.D. Doctor of Literature [ML *litterarum doctor*]

L.J. Lord Justice

L.JJ. Lords Justices

Lk. Luke

lkg. leakage

lkr. locker

ll. laws [L *leges*]; leaves; lines

l.l. in the place cited [L *loco laudato*]; loose leaf

LL large letter; Late Latin; Law Latin; lending library; limited liability; Low Latin; lower left

L.L. live load; lord lieutenant

LLB left linebacker

LL.B. Bachelor of Laws [NL *legum baccalaureus*]

LL.D. Doctor of Laws [NL *legum doctor*]

LLI latitude and longitude indicator

LL.JJ. Lords Justices

LL.M. Master of Laws [NL *legum magister*]

LLR line of least resistance

lm lumen

LM land mine; Legion of Merit; lunar module

L.M. long meter; lord mayor

L.M.D. long meter double

LMG light machine gun

LMN lineman

lmt. limit

LMT length, mass, time; local mean time

LMTD logarithmic mean temperature difference

ln natural logarithm

ln. lane; lien; loan

Ln lanthanide

LNC local naval commander

LND limiting nose dive

lndg. landing

lng. lining

LNG liquefied natural gas

Lo. lord

LO liaison officer; local origination; lubricating oil

LOA length over all

LOADS low altitude defense system

LOB left on base

loc. in the place [L *loco*]; local; location; locative

LOC lines of communication

LOCA loss of coolant accident

loc. cit. in the place cited [L *loco citato*]

LOD line of dance; line of direction; line of duty

L of C line of communications

log logarithm

log. logic; logistic

lon. longitude

Lond. London; Londonderry

long. longitude

Long. Longford

longl. longitudinal

LOOM Loyal Order of Moose

LOP least objectional program; line of position

loq. he/she speaks [L *loquitur*]

LORAN long-range navigation

LOS length of stay; line of scrimmage; line of sight

LOST Law of the Sea Treaty

lot. lotion

Loth. Lothian

Lou. Louth

lox liquid oxygen

lp long picot

l.p. large paper; long primer

Lp. ladyship; lordship

LP landplane; large post; linear programming; liquefied petroleum; long play; long playing; loss of pay; low pass

L.P. lord provost; low point; low pressure

LPC linear predictive coding

LPF leukocytosis-promoting factor

LPG liquefied petroleum

gas

LPGA Ladies Professional Golf Association

lpm lines per minute

LPM long particular meter

LPN Licensed Practical Nurse

LPP large paper proofs

L.P.S. lord privy seal

LPTV low power television

LPW lumens per watt

lr large ring

Lr lawrencium

LR left rear; living room; log run; long range; lower right

L.R. lock rail

L.R.C.P. Licentiate of the Royal College of Physicians

L.R.C.S. Licentiate of the Royal College of Surgeons

LRF luteinizing hormone-releasing factor

lrg. large

l.r.r.p. lowest required radiated power

LRV light rail vehicle; lunar roving vehicle

l.s. left side

LS land service; landing ship; leading seaman; letter signed; library science; listed securities; local sunset; long shot; longitudinal section; loudspeaker; low speed; lump sum

L.S. land service; legal scroll; place of the seal [L *locus sigilli*]

LSAT Law School Admission Test

l.s.c. in the place cited above [L *loco supra citato*]

LSC Legal Services Corporation

lsd. leased

LSD landing ship dock; lysergic acid diethylamide; pounds, shillings, pence [L *librae, solidi, denarii*]

LSI large-scale integrated; large-scale integration

LSM landing ship medium; letter-sorting machine

LSO landing signal officer

LSR local sunrise

LSS life-support system; lifesaving service; lifesaving station

LST landing ship, tank; local sidereal time; local standard time

lt. light

l.t. landed terms; long ton; low tension

Lt lira (Turkey)

Lt. lieutenant
LT left tackle; legal tender; letter telegram; line telegraphy; local time
LTA lighter than air
LTC lieutenant colonel
Lt.Col. lieutenant colonel
Lt.Comdr. lieutenant commander
ltd. limited
Ltd. limited
ltg. lightening
LTG lieutenant general
ltge. lighterage
Lt.Gen. lieutenant general
Lt.Gov. lieutenant governor
L.Th. Licentiate in Theology
LTH luteotropic hormone
lthr. leather
LTI light transmission index
Lt.(jg) lieutenant, junior grade
LTJG lieutenant, junior grade
LTL less than truckload
LTM long-term memory
ltng. lightening
ltr. letter; lighter
LTS launch telemetry station; launch tracking system
LTT less than truckload
lu lumen

Lu lutetium
lub. lubricant; lubricating
LUHF lowest useful high frequency
Luth. Lutheran
Lux. Luxembourg
lv legal volt
lv. lava; leave
Lv lev
LV light vessel; low voltage
L.V. licensed victualler
lve. leave
LVN Licensed Vocational Nurse
lvs. leaves
LVT landing vehicle, tracked
LW left wing
L.W. long wave; low water
LWB long wheelbase
L.W.L. length at waterline; load waterline
L.W.M. low-water mark
L.W.P. load water plane
LWR light water reactor
LWV League of Women Voters
lx lux
LXX Septuagint [fr. the Roman numeral 70]
ly langley
LZ landing zone

M

m maxwell; medium; micro-; milli-

m- meta

m. half [It *mezzo*]; hand [F *main* or It *mano*]; handful [L *manipulus*]; magistrate; magnetic; maiden; maiden over; mail; majesty; make; male; manual; mare; maritime; mark; marker; marquis; married; martyr; masculine; mass; mate; mean; measure; mechanical; medical; melts at; member; memorandum; meridian; metal; meter; metropolitan; middle; mil; mile; military; mill; million; mine; minim; minor; minute; miscellaneous; mist; mixture [L *mistura*]; model; modulus; molal; molality; molar; molarity; mole; moment; monoplane; monsoon; month; moon; morning; morphine; mortar; mortgage; mother; motor; mountain; mucoid; mud; muscle; mustard gas; muster; myopia; noon [L *meridies*]; of death [L *mortis*]; of medicine [L *medicinae*]; thousand [L *mille*]

M Mach; March; master; May; medium; mega-; mix [L *misce*]; Monday

M. monsieur

ma major; milliampere

mA milliangstrom

MA maritime administration; Massachusetts; mental age; meter angle; Middle Ages; military attaché; military aviator; mill annealed; my account

M.A. Master of Arts [ML *magister artium*]; military academy; mountain artillery

MAA master-at-arms

M.A.A. Master of Applied Arts

MAB medical advisory board

MABA meta-aminobenzoic acid

M.A.B.E. Master of Agricultural Business and Economics

mac. macadam; macerate

Mac. Maccabees

MAC maximum allowable

concentration; Military Airlift Command; model airplane club; Municiple Assistance Corporation

Macc. Maccabees

mach. machine; machinery; machining; machinist

machy. machinery

MAD magnetic airborne detector; magnetic anomaly detector; mutual assured destruction

M.A.E. Master of Arts in Education

M.A.Ed. Master of Arts in Education

mag. magazine; magnesium; magnet; magnetic; magnetism; magneto; magnitude

maglev magnetic levitation

magn. magnetic; magnetism; magneto

maint. maintenance

Maj. major

Maj.Gen. major general

Mal. Malachi

malac. malacology

M.A.L.D. Master of Arts in Law and Diplomacy

M.A.L.S. Master of Arts in Liberal Studies; Master of Arts in Library Science

MAM milliampere minute

man. handful [L *manipulus*]; manila; manual; manufacture

Man. Manitoba

M and A management and administration

M and B matched and beaded

M and D medicine and duty

M and S maintenance and supply

manf. manufacturer

mangt. management

manuf. manufacture; manufacturing

MAO monoamine oxidase

MAOI monoamine oxidase inhibitor

MAP maximum average price; medical aid post; modified American plan

MAQ money allowance for quarters

mar. marine; maritime; married

Mar. March

MAR microanalytical reagent

marc. marcato

MARC machine readable cataloging

March. marchioness

marg. margin; marginal

Marq. marquess; marquis

mart. martyr; martyrology

MARV maneuverable reentry vehicle

mas. masculine

MAS milliampere second

masc. masculine

Maser microwave amplification by stimulated emission of radiation

MASH mobile army surgical hospital

Mass. Massachusetts

mat. material; matinee; matins; maturity

MAT mechanical aptitude test; military aircraft types; Miller Analogies Test

M.A.T. Master of Arts in Teaching

math. mathematical; mathematician; mathematics

matric. matriculated; matriculation

MATS Military Air Transport Service

Matt. Matthew

MATV master antenna television

max. maximum

mb millibar

MB Manitoba; megabyte

M.B. Bachelor of Medicine; Medical Board; medium bomber; motor boat; municiple borough; munitions board

M.B.A. Master of Business Administration

mbd million barrels per day

MBD minimal brain dysfunction

M.B.E. Member of the Order of the British Empire

M.B.F. thousand board feet [L *mille* thousand]

mbl. mobile

MBM thousand feet board measure [L *mille* thousand]

MBO management by objective

Mbps megabits per second

MBS Mutual Broadcasting System

MBT mercaptobenzothiazole

mc megacycle; millicurie; millicycle

mC millicurie

Mc megacycle

MC machinery certificate; magnetic course; marine corps; marked capacity; master of ceremonies; medical corps; medico-chirurgical; metaling clause; meter-candle; metric carat; movement control; multiple contact;

my account

M.C. Master of Surgery [NL *magister chirurgiae*]; Member of Congress; Member of Council; motor contact; motorcycle

M/C marginal credit

MCAT Medical College Admission Test

M.C.D. Doctor of Comparative Medicine

Mcf thousand cubic feet [L *mille* thousand]

mcg microgram

M.Ch. Master of Surgery [NL *magister chirurgiae*]

MCH mean corpuscular hemoglobin

MCHC mean corpuscular hemoglobin concentration

mcht. merchant

mCi millicurie

MCi megacurie

MCI malleable cast iron

M.C.J. Master of Comparative Jurisprudence

MCL Marine Corps League

M.C.L. Master of Civil Law; Master of Comparative Law

MCO mill culls out

M.Comp.L. Master of Comparative Law

MCP male chauvinist pig

MCPO master chief petty officer

MCS missile control system

M.C.S. Master of Commercial Science; Master of Computer Science

MCU medium close-up

MCV mean corpuscular volume

MCW modulated continuous wave

Md mendelevium

Md. Maryland

MD managing director; Maryland; medical department; mental defective; mentally deficient; message dropping; muscular dystrophy; right hand [F *main droite* or It *mano destra*]

M.D. Doctor of Medicine [NL *medicinae doctor*]

M/D memorandum of deposit; months after date; month's date

MDD milligrams per square decimeter per day

M.Div. Master of Divinity

Mdlle. mademoiselle

Mdm. madam

Mdme. madame

mdnt. midnight

MDR minimum daily requirement

MDS main dressing station; multipoint distribution service; multipoint distribution system

M.D.S. Master of Dental Surgery

mdse. merchandise

mdt. moderate

MDT mountain daylight time

m.e. marbled edges

Me methyl

Me. Maine

ME Maine; maximum effort; metabolizable energy; Middle English; Muhammadan Era

M.E. managing editor; mechanical engineer; mechanical engineering; medical examiner; mining engineer

Mea. Meath

MEA monoethanolamine

meas. measure

mech. mechanic; mechanical; mechanics; mechanism; mechanized

med. medalist; median; mediator; medical; medicine; medieval; medium

Med. Mediterranean

M.Ed. Master of Education

MED minimal effective dose; minimum erythema dose

Med.Sc.D. Doctor of Medical Science

meg megacycle; megohm

megaflop million floating point operations per second

MEK methyl ethyl ketone

mem. member; memento; memoir; memorandum; memorial

meml. memorial

mentd. mentioned

mep mean effective pressure

mEq milliequivalent

mer. meridian; meridional

merc. mercantile; mercurial; mercury

merch. merchantable

Mersey. Merseyside

MESFET metal-semiconductor field-effect transistor

Messrs. messieurs

met. metal; metallurgical; metallurgy; metaphor; metaphorical; metaphysical; metaphysics; meteorological; meteorology; metronome; metropolitan

Met methionine

metal. metallurgical; metallurgy

metall. metallurgical; metallurgy

metaph. metaphor; metaphorical; metaphysical; metaphysics

meteor. meteorological; meteorology

meteorol. meteorology

metgl. meteorological

meth. method; methylated

Meth. Methodist

METO maximum except take-off; Middle East Treaty Organization

meV millielectron volt

MeV million electron volts

Mex. Mexican; Mexico

mf mezzo forte; millifarad

mf. manufacture

mF millifarad

MF medium frequency; microfiche; Middle French; motor freight

M.F. machine finish; Master of Forestry; mill finish

M.F.A. Master of Fine Arts

M.F.B.M. thousand feet board measure [L *mille* thousand]

mfd microfarad

mfd. manufactured

MFD minimum fatal dose

mfg. manufacturing

M.F.H. Master of Foxhounds

MFN most favored nation

MFP mean free path

mfr. manufacture; manufacturer

mg milligram

mg. margin; meaning; morning

Mg magnesium

MG left hand [F *main gauche*]; machine gun; major general; make good; military government; mill glazed

M.G. machine-glazed; mixed grain; motor generator

mgal milligal

MGB Ministry of State Security [Russ *Ministerstvo Gosudarstvennoi Bezopasnosti*]; motor gunboat

MGC machine-gun company; machine-gun corps

mgd million gallons per day

mgm milligram

mgmt. management

MGO military government officer

mgr. manager
Mgr. monseigneur; monsignor
mgrm milligram
mgt. management
M.Gy.Sgt. master gunnery sergeant
mh millihenry
MH magnetic heading; maleic hydrazide; medal of honor; mobile home
M.H. Most Honorable
M.H.A. Master of Hospital Administration
MHC major histocompatibility complex
mhcp mean horizontal candlepower
MHD magnetohydrodynamic; magnetohydrodynamics; minimum hemolytic dose
mhg mahogany
MHG Middle High German
MHSCP mean hemispherical candlepower
MHT mean high tide
MHW mean high water
MHWN mean high water neaps
MHWS mean high water springs
MHz megahertz

mi. mile; mileage; mill; minor; minute
MI malleable iron; medical inspection; metabolic index; Michigan; military intelligence; myocardial infarction
M.I. monumental inscription
MIA missing in action
Mic. Micah
MIC minimal inhibitory concentration; minimum inhibitory concentration
Mich. Michigan
MICR magnetic ink character recognition
mid. middle; midland; midnight; midshipman
MID military intelligence department; military intelligence division; minimal infective dose
Middx. Middlesex
Mid Glam. Mid Glamorgan
midn. midnight; midshipman
MIH miles in the hour
mil. mileage; military; militia; millieme; million
mill. million
mim. mimeograph
min. mineral; mineralogical; mineralogy; minim;

minimum; mining;
minister; ministry; minor;
minute
mineral. mineralogy
Minn. Minnesota
MIO minimum identifiable
odor
m.i.p. mean indicated
pressure
MIP marine insurance
policy
MIPS million instructions
per second
MIRV multiple
independently targeted
reentry vehicle
MIS management
information service;
management information
systems
misc. miscellaneous;
miscellany
miscl. miscellaneous
misn. misnumbered
miss. mission; missionary
Miss. Mississippi
missy. missionary
mist. mixture [L *mistura*]
mit. send [L *mitte*]
MIT milled in transit;
milling in transit
mixt. mixture
MJ military judge
mk. mark; markka
Mk. Mark
mkd. marked

mkm. marksman
mks meter-kilogram-
second
mkt. market
mktg. marketing
ml milliliter
ml. mail
m.l. mixed lengths
mL millilambert
M.L. Master of Law [L
magister legum]; mean
level; mine layer; mold
line; motor launch;
muzzle-loading
MLA Member of the
Legislative Assembly;
Modern Language
Association
M.Laws Master of Laws
MLB middle linebacker
mld. mild; mold; molded;
molding
MLD median lethal dose;
minimum lethal dose
mldg. molding
mldr. molder
MLF multilateral force
Mlle. mademoiselle
Mlles. mademoiselles
mlnr. milliner
MLR main line of
resistance; muzzle-loading
rifle
MLS microwave landing
system
M.L.S. Master of Library

Science

MLT mean low tide; Medical Laboratory Technician

M.L.T. Master of Law and Taxation

MLW mean low water

MLWN mean low water neaps

MLWS mean low water springs

mm millimeter

m.m. with the necessary changes having been made [NL *mutatis mutandis*]; with the respective differences having been considered [NL *mutatis mutandis*]

mM millimole

MM Majesties; martyrs [L *martyres*]; masters [L *magistri*]; messieurs; methyl methacrylate; middle marker

M.M. machinist's mate; made merchantable; Maelzel's metronome; Maryknoll Missioners; master mechanic; Master of Music; mercantile marine; merchant marine

Mme madame

mmf magnetomotive force; micromicrofarad

mmfd micromicrofarad

mmm micromillimeter

mmol millimole

mmole millimole

MMPI Minnesota Multiphasic Personality Inventory

MMT methylcyclopentadienyl manganese tricarbonyl; multiple mirror telescope

MMU manned maneuvering unit

Mn manganese

MN magnetic north; Minnesota

M.N. Master of Nursing; merchant navy

MNC multinational company; multinational corporation

mng. managing

mngr. manager

Mngr. monseigneur; monsignor

MNT mononitrotoluene

mntn. maintenance

mo. month; monthly

Mo molybdenum

MO Missouri

M.O. mail order; manually operated; mass observation; medical officer; modus operandi; money order; mustered out

mob mobile; mobilization;

mobilized
MOB money-order business
mod. model; moderate; moderato; moderator; modern; modification; modified; modify; modulator; modulo; modulus
MOD mail-order department; money-order department
modif. modification
M.O.H. Master of Otterhounds; medical officer of health
mol. molecular; molecule
MOL manned orbiting laboratory
mol.wt. molecular weight
MOM middle of month
mon. monastery; monetary; monitor; monument
Mon. Monaghan; Monday; monsieur; monsignor
mono mononucleosis; monophonic
Mons. monsieur
Mont. Montana
mop mother-of-pearl
MOP manuscript on paper; mustering-out pay
mor. morendo; morocco; mortar
MOR middle of the road

morph. morphological; morphology
mos. months
MOS metal-oxide semiconductor; military occupational specialty
MOSFET metal-oxide-semiconductor field-effect transistor
mot. motor; motorized
MOV manuscript on vellum
moy. money
mp melting point; mezzo piano
MP mail payment; military police; military policeman; motion picture; multipole
M.P. meeting point; Member of Parliament; metropolitan police; milepost; minister plenipotentiary; morning prayer; mounted police; municipal police
M/P memorandum of partnership
MPa megapascal
M.P.A. Master of Public Administration
M.P.A.A. Motion Picture Association of America
MPB missing persons bureau
MPC maximum

permissible concentration
MPD maximum
permissible dose
mpg miles per gallon
mph miles per hour
M.P.H. Master of Public
Health
mphps miles per hour per
second
mpi mean point of impact
MPL maximum
permissible level
M.P.L. Master of Patent
Law
mpm meters per minute
MPM meters per minute;
multipurpose meal
MP/M Multiprogramming
Control Program for
Microprocessors
MPO military post office
M.P.P. Member of
Provincial Parliament
M.P.P.M. Master of Public
and Private Management
mps meters per second
MPS marbled paper sides;
meters per second
MPX multiplex
mr milliroentgen
Mr. mister
MR map reference; mate's
receipt; mentally retarded;
mill run; mine-run;
mineral rubber;
missionary rector

M.R. Master of the Rolls;
minister residentiary
MRA moral rearmament
mrad milliradion
MRBM medium range
ballistic missile
MRC medical reserve
corps
MRCA multirole combat
aircraft
M.R.C.P. Member of the
Royal College of
Physicians
M.R.C.S. Member of the
Royal College of Surgeons
MRD minimum reacting
dose
mrkr. marker
mRNA messenger RNA
mrng. morning
MRO maintenance, repair,
and operation
MRP material
requirements planning
Mrs. mistress
MRS medical receiving
station
mrtm. maritime
MRV multiple reentry
vehicle
ms meso-; millisecond
Ms. miss; mistress
MS left hand [It *mano
sinistra*]; machinery
survey; mail steamer;
main switch; manuscript;

margin of safety; mass spectrometry; mean square; medium shot; medium steel; metric system; mild steel; military science; mint state; Mississippi; morphine sulfate; multiple sclerosis

M.S. Master of Science; maximum stress; minesweeper

M/S meters per second; month's after sight; month's sight; motor ship

MSAT Minnesota Scholastic Aptitude Test

msc millisecond; miscellaneous; miscellany

M.Sc. Master of Science

MSC Military Sealift Command

M.Sc.D. Doctor of Medical Science

M.S.C.E. Master of Science in Civil Engineering

M.S.C.J. Master of Science in Criminal Justice

mscp mean spherical candlepower

M.S.D. Doctor of Medical Science

msec millisecond

M.S.Ed. Master of Science in Education

M.S.E.E. Master of Science in Electrical Engineering

MSF muscle shock factor

msg. message

MSG master sergeant; monosodium glutamate

msgr. messenger

Msgr. monseigneur; monsignor

M.Sgt. master sergeant

MSH melanocyte-stimulating hormone

M.S.H. Master of Staghounds

MSI medium-scale integration

msl mean sea level

MSL mean sea level

M.S.L.S. Master of Science in Library Science

MSM thousand feet surface measure [L *mille* thousand]

M.S.M.E. Master of Science in Mechanical Engineering

msn. mission

M.S.N. Master of Science in Nursing

msngr. messenger

MSO multiple systems operator

m.s.p. dead without issue [L *mortuus sine prole*]

M.S.P.H. Master of

Science in Public Health
MSS manuscripts
M.S.S.W. Master of
Science in Social Work
mst. measurement
MST mean solar time;
mountain standard time
mstr. master; moisture
MSTS Military Sea
Transportation Service
M.S.W. Master of Social
Work
MSY maximum
sustainable yield
mt. empty; might; most;
mount; mountain
Mt. Matthew
MT machine translation;
mail transfer; mandated
territory; mean tide; mean
time; measurement ton;
mechanical transport;
Medical Technologist;
metric ton; military
training; Montana; motor
transport; mountain time
MTB motor torpedo boat
MTBE methyl tert-butyl
ether
MTC mechanical transport
corps; motor transport
corps
mtd. mounted
MTD mean temperature
difference
MTF mechanical time fuse

mtg. meeting; mortgage;
mounting
mtgd. mortgaged
mtge. mortgage
mtgee. mortgagee
mtgor. mortgagor
mth. month
M.Th. Master of Theology
MTI moving target
indicator
mtl. material; metal
MTL mean tidal level
mtn. mountain
MTN multilateral trade
negotiations
MTO Mediterranean
theater of operations
mtr. motor
MTR materials testing
reactor; multiple track
radar
mtrl. material
M.T.S. Master of
Theological Studies
M.U. maintenance unit;
mobile unit; motor union
muc. mucilage
MUF material
unaccounted for;
maximum usable
frequency
mull. mullion
mult. multiple
mun. municipal;
municipality; munitions
munic. municipal;

municipality; munitions

mus. museum; music; musical: musician

MUSA multiple-unit steerable antenna

Mus.A.D. Doctor of Musical Arts

Mus.B. Bachelor of Music

Mus.D. Doctor of Music

mut. mutilated; mutual

mv mezza voce; millivolt

mV millivolt

Mv mendelevium

MV main verb; market value; mean variation; medium voltage; methyl violet; million volts; muzzle velocity

M.V. merchant vessel; motor vessel

MVA Missouri Valley Authority

MVC manual volume control

MVD Ministry of Internal Affairs [Russ *Ministerstvo Vnutrennikh Del*]

MVFR maintain visual flight rules

MVP most valuable player

mvt. movement

mw milliwatt

m.w. mixed widths

MW megawatt; music wire

M.W. Most Worshipful; Most Worthy

MWe megawatts electric

MWG music-wire gauge

mwh megawatt-hour

MWP maximum working pressure

Mx maxwell

MX missile, experimental; motocross; multiplex

mxd. mixed

my million years; muddy; myopia

My. May

M.Y. motor yacht

myc. mycology

mycol. mycology

myg myriagram

myl myrialiter

mym myriameter

Myr million years

mythol. mythology

N

n index of refraction; nano-; novice slope

n. at night [L *nocte*]; born [L *natus*]; nail; name; nasal; national; nationalist; naval; navigate; navigating; navigation; navy; nephew; net; neuter; neutron; new; new [L *novus*]; newspaper; night; night stop; nomen;

nominative; none; noon; normal; note; noun; number; us [F *nous*]; we [F *nous*]

N knight; Negro; newton; ngultrum; nitrogen; north; northern; November

na. nadir; nail

Na sodium [NL *natrium*]

NA nautical almanac; naval academy; naval architect; naval attaché; naval aviator; no advice; nonacceptance; not applicable; not available; nurse's aide; nursing auxiliary

N.A. national academician; national academy; national association; North America; numerical aperture

N/A no account

n.a.a. not always afloat

NAA National Archery Association; neutron activation analysis

N.A.A. National Aeronautic Association

NAACP National Association for the Advancement of Colored People

NAAO National Association of Amateur Oarsmen

NAB national aircraft beacon; National Association of Broadcasters; National Association of Businessmen; naval air base; New American Bible

nac. nacelle

NAC national advisory committee; national advisory council; naval aircraftsman; non-airline carrier

NACU National Association of Colleges and Universities

NAD nicotinamide adenine dinucleotide; no appreciable disease; nothing abnormal discovered

NADA National Automobile Dealers Association

NADP nicotinamide adenine dinucleotide phosphate

Nah. Nahum

NAHL North American Hockey League

NAIA National Association of Intercollegiate Athletes

NAMH National Association for Mental Health

n.a.n. unless otherwise noted [L *nisi aliter notetur*]

NAP naval aviation pilot

nar. narrow

NAS National Academy of Sciences; naval air station

NASA National Aeronautics and Space Administration

NASCAR National Association of Stock Car Auto Racing

NASD National Association of Securities Dealers

NASDAQ National Association of Securities Dealers Automated Quotations

NASL North American Soccer League

NASTAR National Standard Race

NASW National Association of Social Workers

nat. national; nationalist; native; natural; naturalist; naturalized

natl. national

NATO North Atlantic Treaty Organization

NAUI National Association of Underwater Instructors

naut. nautical

nav. naval; navigable; navigate; navigation; navigator; navy

navr. navigator

n.b. no ball

Nb niobium

Nb. nimbus

NB naval base; newborn; no bid; northbound

N.B. mark well [L *nota bene*]; New Brunswick

NBA National Basketball Association; National Boxing Association

NBC National Basketball Committee; National Broadcasting Company

NBP normal boiling point

NBPRP National Board for the Promotion of Rifle Practice

NBRT National Board for Respiratory Therapy

NBS National Bureau of Standards

NC new charter; new crop; no change; no charge; no connection; no credit; noncollectible; North Carolina; numerical control; nurse corps

N.C. North Carolina

NCA neurocirculatory asthenia

NCAA National Collegiate

Athletic Association

NCCS National Climbing Classification System

NCE New Catholic Edition

NCFA National Club Football Association

NCI National Cancer Institute

NCJA National Collegiate Judo Association

NCO noncommissioned officer

NCS net control station

NCUP no commission until paid

NCV no commercial value

n.d. no date; not dated

Nd neodymium

ND national debt; navy department; North Dakota

N.D. no date; North Dakota

NDA National Dental Association; new drug application

N. Dak. North Dakota

NDB nondirectional beacon

NDGA nordihydroguaiaretic acid

NDT neurodevelopmental treatment

n.e. not exceeding; not to exceed

Ne neon

NE national emergency; Nebraska; new edition; New England; nonessential; northeast; northeastern

N/E no effects

NEA National Education Association; National Endowment for the Arts

Neb. Nebraska

NEB New English Bible

Nebr. Nebraska

NED New English Dictionary

neg. negative; negotiable

Neh. Nehemiah

NEH National Endowment for the Humanities

n.e.i. he/she was not found [L *non est inventus*]; not elsewhere included; not elsewhere indicated

n.e.m. not elsewhere mentioned

nem. con. no one contradicting [NL *nemine contradicente*]

nem. diss. no one dissenting [NL *nemine dissentiente*]

neol. neologism

NEP New Economic Policy

NEPA nuclear energy for propulsion of aircraft

n.e.s. not elsewhere specified

n.e.t. not earlier than

NET National Educational Television

NETFS National Educational Television Film Service

Neth. Netherlands

n. et m. night and morning [L *nocte et mane*]

neurol. neurological; neurology

neut. neuter; neutral

Nev. Nevada

New Eng. New England

nf nanofared; nonfundable; not fordable

NF National Formulary; near face; Newfoundland; no funds; nonferrous

NFAA National Field Archery Association

NFBPWC National Federation of Business and Professional Women's Clubs

NFC National Flying Club; National Football Conference

NFCAA National Fencing Coaches Association of America

nfd no fixed date

NFL National Football League

Nfld. Newfoundland

NFS not for sale

ng nanogram

NG nasogastric; national guard; nitroglycerin

N.G. New Guinea; no good; not good

NGF naval gun fire; nerve growth factor

NGk New Greek

NGO nongovernmental organization

ngt. night

NGU nongonococcal urethritis

NH never hinged; New Hampshire; nonhygroscopic

N.H. New Hampshire

NHC National Handball Club

N.H.I. National Health Insurance

NHL National Hockey League

nhp nominal horsepower

NHPAA National Horseshoe Pitchers Association of America

NHRA National Hot Rod Association

NHS National Health Service

NHTSA National Highway Traffic Safety Administration

ni. night

Ni nickel

NI naval intelligence

N.I. Northern Ireland

NID Naval Intelligence Department; Naval Intelligence Division

NIE National Institute of Education

NIFA National Intercollegiate Fencing Association

NIH National Institutes of Health; not invented here

NIMH National Institute of Mental Health

NIOSH National Institute of Occupational Safety and Health

ni. pr. unless before [L *nisi prius*]

ni. pri. unless before [L *nisi prius*]

NIRA National Industrial Recovery Act

NIT National Invitational Tournament

NIWFA National Intercollegiate Women's Fencing Association

NJ New Jersey

N.J. New Jersey

NJCAA National Junior College Athletic Association

nk. neck

NK not known

NKVD People's Commissariat of Internal Affairs [Russ *Narodnyi Komissariat Vnutrennikh Del*]

n.l. it is not clear [L *non liquet*]; it is not permitted [L *non licet*]; new line; not far [L *non longe*]

NL National League; New Latin; night letter

N.L. north latitude

NLF National Liberation Front

NLL National Lacrosse League

NLM National Library of Medicine

NLO naval liaison officer

NLRB National Labor Relations Board

n.l.t. not later than

NLT net long ton; night letter; not less than

nm nanometer

n.m. nautical mile; night and morning [L *nocte et mane*]

N/m no mark; not marked

NM New Mexico; night message

N.M. New Mexico

NMC National Maritime Council

N. Mex. New Mexico

n. mi. nautical mile

NMI no middle initial

NMLRA National Muzzle

Loading Rifle Association

NMOS N-channel metal oxide semiconductor; nonvolatile metal oxide semiconductor

NMR nuclear magnetic resonance

NMSQT National Merit Scholarship Qualifying Test

NMT not more than

nn. names; notes; nouns

n.n. bare name [NL *nomen nudum*]; new name [L *nomen novem*]

N/N not to be noted

NND new and nonofficial drugs

NNE north-northeast

NNR new and nonofficial remedies

NNW north-northwest

no. lifts not operating; north; northern; nose; number [L *numero*]

No nobelium

NO name of; natural order; naval officer; no orders; nonofficial; not out

NOAA National Oceanic and Atmospheric Administration

NOB naval operating base

N.O.E. not otherwise enumerated

N.O.H.P. not otherwise

herein provided

NOIBN not otherwise indexed by name

NOIC naval officer in charge

nol. pros. to be unwilling to prosecute [L *nolle prosequi*]

nom. nomenclature; nominal; nominative

nom. nov. new name [L *nomen novum*]

nom. nud. bare name [L *nomen nudum*]

non obs. notwithstanding [L *non obstante*]

non obst. notwithstanding [L *non obstante*]

non pros. he/she does not prosecute [LL *non prosequitur*]

non seq. non sequitur

n.o.p. not otherwise provided for

NOP not our publication

nor. normal; north; northern

Nor. Norway; Norwegian

NORAD North American Air Defense Command

Norf. Norfolk

norm. normal

NORRA National Off Road Racing Association

Northants. Northamptonshire

Norw. Norway; Norwegian
nos. numbers
NOS not otherwise specified
NOTAM notice to airmen
Notts. Nottinghamshire
nov. novelist
n.o.v. notwithstanding the verdict [L *non obstante veredicto*]
Nov. November
NOW National Organization for Women; negotiable order of withdrawal
NO$_x$ nitrogen oxide
np. neap
n.p. new paragraph; no pagination; no place; nonparticipating; unless before [L *nisi prius*]
Np neptunium
NP net proceeds; neuropsychiatric; neuropsychiatry; nickel-plated; no protest; notary public; noun phrase; Nurse Practitioner
NPA National Paddleball Association
NPD north polar distance
n.p.f. not provided for
NPL nonpersonal liability
NPN nonprotein nitrogen
NPNA no protest nonacceptance

n.p. or d. no place or date
NPR National Public Radio
NPT normal pressure and temperature; Nuclear Nonproliferation Treaty
NPV no par value
NQR nuclear quadrupole resonance
nr. near; number
n.r. net register; no risk; not to be repeated [L *non repetatur*]
NRA National Recovery Administration; National Rifle Association
n.r.a.d. no risk after discharge
NRC National Research Council; Nuclear Regulatory Commission
NREM nonrapid-eye-movement
nrml. normal
n.r.t. net register ton
ns nanosecond
ns. nose
Ns nimbostratus
NS national special; near side; new school; new series; new side; new style; nickel steel; Nova Scotia; nuclear ship; numismatic society
N.S. not specified; Nova Scotia; Our Lord [F *Notre*

Seigneur]
N/S not sufficient
NSA National Security Agency; National Shuffleboard Association; National Ski Association
NSC National Security Council
nsec nanosecond
NSF National Science Foundation; not sufficient funds
Nsg. nursing
NSIC Our Savior Jesus Christ [L *Noster Salvator Iesus Christus*]
NSJC Our Savior Jesus Christ [L *Noster Salvator Iesus (Jesus) Christus*]
NSO naval staff officer
NSP navy standard part
NSPF not specifically provided for
NSPS National Ski Patrol System
NSTA National Squash Tennis Association
nstd. nested
NSU nonspecific urethritis
N.S.W. New South Wales
nt. net; neuter; night
NT net ton; new terms; New Testament; new translation; Northern Territory; Northwest Territories

N.T. Northern Territory; Northwest Territories
NTA nitrilotriacetic acid
ntc negative temperature coefficient
ntfy. notify
NTGA National Tournament Golf Association
Nthmb. Northumberland
nthn. northern
ntm net ton mile
NTO not taken out
NTP no title page; normal temperature and pressure
NTS not to scale
NTSB National Transportation Safety Board
NTSC National Television System Committee
nt. wt. net weight
n.u. name unknown
NU national union; number unobtainable
num. number; numeral
Num. Numbers
numb. numbered
Numb. Numbers
numis. numismatic; numismatical; numismatics
NV Nevada; new version; nonvoting
NVM Nativity of the Virgin Mary; nonvolatile

matter
NVR no voltage release
NW naked weight; net
weight; northwest;
northwestern
NWC National Wrestling
Confederation
NWFL National Women's
Football League
NWG national wire gauge
n.wt. net weight
NWT Northwest
Territories
NY navy yard; new year;
New York; no year
N.Y. New York
NYA National Youth
Administration
N.Y.C. New York City
NYD not yet diagnosed
NYFE New York Futures
Exchange
NYP not yet published
NYR not yet returned
NYSE New York Stock
Exchange
N.Z. New Zealand

O

o ohm; overcast
o. best [L *optimus*]; bone
[L *os*]; eye [L *oculus*];
object; oblast; observation;
observer; ocean; off; office;
officer; official; of the
order of [L *ordinis*]; oil;
old; only; opening;
operation; order; order [L
ordo]; ordnance; oriental;
original; out; outfield;
outlet; outside edge; over;
owner
o- orth-; ortho-
O octavo; opening; ovation;
oxygen; pint [NL *octarius*]
O. Occident; Occidental;
October; Ohio
o/a on account; on or
about; open account; our
account
OA occiput anterior; old
age; osteoarthritis;
overall; Overeaters
Anonymous
OAA old-age assistance
O and C onset and course
O & M operations and
maintenance
O & O owned and operated
O and R ocean and rail
O.A.P. old age pension; old
age pensioner
OAS on active service;
Organization of American
States; Organization of
the Secret Army [F
*Organisation de l'Armée
Secrète*]
OASDI Old Age,

Survivors, and Disability
Insurance

OASI Old Age and
Survivors Insurance

OASP organic acid soluble
phosphorus

OAU Organization of
African Unity

ob. halfpenny [L *obolus*];
he/she died [L *obiit*];
obiter; oblong; oboe;
observation

o/b outboard

Ob. Obadiah

OB obstetrical;
obstetrician; obstetrics;
opening of books; order of
battle; ordered back;
outward bound

O.B. off-Broadway

Obad. Obadiah

obb. obbligato

obdt. obedient

OBE out-of-body
experience

O.B.E. Officer of the Order
of the British Empire

OB-GYN obstetrician-
gynecologist; obstetrics-
gynecology

obj. object; objection;
objective

obl. obligation; oblique;
oblong

OBL order bill of lading

obs. obscure; observation;

observatory; observed;
observer; obsolete;
obstacle; obstruction

OBS obstetrician;
obstetrics

obsd. observed

obsn. observation

obsr. observer

obstet. obstetrical;
obstetrics

obt. he/she died [L *obiit*];
obedient

obtd. obtained

obv. obverse

oc. ocean

o.c. by aid and counsel [L
ope consilio or *ope et
consilio*]; in the work cited
[L *opere citato*]; only child

OC of course; off center;
office copy; officer
candidate; officer in
charge; officer's cook;
official classification; old
charter; old crop; on
center; on course; open
charter; open cover; order
canceled; original cover;
outing club; overcharge;
oxygen consumed

O.C. officer commanding

O/C over the counter

OCA Office of Consumer
Affairs

occ. occasional;
occasionally; occulting

occas. occasionally

occn. occasion

occup. occupation; occupational

OCDM Office of Civil and Defense Mobilization

oceanog. oceanography

OCLC Online Computer Library Center

OCR optical character reader; optical character recognition

OCS Officer Candidate School; Old Church Slavonic

O.C.S.O. Order of Cistercians of the Strict Observance

oct. octavo

Oct. October

OCT ornithine carbamyl transferase

OCTV open-circuit television

o.d. every day [L *omnes dies*]

OD occupational disease; officer of the day; olive drab; on demand; on duty; optical density; ordinary seaman; ordnance datum; organization development; origin and destination; overdose

O.D. Doctor of Optometry; outside diameter; outside dimension; right eye [L *oculus dexter*]

O/D overdraft; overdrawn

odly. orderly

o.e. omissions excepted

Oe oersted

OE offensive end; Old English

OECD Organization for Economic Cooperation and Development

OED Oxford English Dictionary

OEM original equipment manufacturer

OEO Office of Economic Opportunity

OER officer efficiency report

OES Order of the Eastern Star

OF occipital-frontal; Old French; outfield; oxidizing flame

ofc. office

ofcl. official

ofcr. officer

off. offensive; offered; office; officer; official; officinal

offic. official

offr. officer

O.F.M. Order of Friars Minor

OFr Old French

O.F.S. Orange Free State

o.g. original gum
OG offensive guard; outside guard
O.G. officer of the guard
OH Ohio; open hearth; outside home; overhead
ohc overhead camshaft
OHD organic heart disease
OHG Old High German
OHI ocular hypertension indicator
OHMS On Her Majesty's Service; On His Majesty's Service
ohv overhead valve
O.I. osteogenesis imperfecta
OIC Ohio Improved Chester white
oint. ointment
OIr Old Irish
OIT Office of International Trade
OJ orange juice
OJT on-the-job training
OK all correct [fr. altered spelling *oll korrect*]; Oklahoma; outer keel
o.k.a. otherwise known as
Okla. Oklahoma
ol oleum
OL Old Latin; outside left forward
O.L. left eye [L *oculus laevus*]; occupational level; overflow level; overhead

line; overload
OL and T owners, landlords, and tenants
OLS ordinary least squares
o.m. every morning [L *omni mane*]
OM outer marker
O.M. old man; old measurement; order of merit
OMB Office of Management and Budget
OMBE Office of Minority Business Enterprise
O.M.I. Oblates of Mary Immaculate
omn. hor. every hour [L *omni hora*]
omn. man. every morning [L *omni mane*]
omn. noct. every night [L *omni nocte*]
OMPA octamethyl-pyrophosphoramide
OMS output per man shift
o.n. every night [L *omni nocte*]
ON Old Norse; Ontario
O.N. octane number
O/N order notify
ONC Ordinary National Certificate
OND Ordinary National Diploma
1b first base; single

[one-base hit]

ONI Office of Naval Intelligence

o.n.o. or nearest offer

ONP operating nursing procedure

Ont. Ontario

oo on order

O/o order of

OO ordnance office; ordnance officer

OOB off-off-Broadway; out-of-the-body

OOD officer of the deck

OOLR ophthalmology, otology, laryngology, rhinology

op. opera; operation; operative; operator; opposite; opus

OP observation plane; observation post; occiput posterior; Old Persian; old prices; open policy; operation; opposite prompt; opposite prompter; osmotic pressure; other than psychotic; out of print; outpatient; outpost; overprint; overproof

O.P. Order of Preachers [L *Ordinis Praedicaturum*]

op-amp operational amplifier

OPC outpatient clinic

op. cit. in the work cited [L *opere citato*]; the work cited from [L *opus citatum*]

OPD outpatient department

OPEC Organization of Petroleum Exporting Countries

opg. opening

oph. ophthalmic; ophthalmologic; ophthalmologist; ophthalmology; ophthalmoscope; ophthalmoscopy

opn. open race; operation; opinion

opng. opening

opp. opera; opponent; opportunity; opposed; opposite

OPP out of print at present

oppy. opportunity

opr. lifts operating; operate; operator

opt. operate; optative; optical; optician; optics; option; optional

opt. clm. optional claiming race

Opt.D. Doctor of Optometry

OPV oral polio vaccine

or. oriental; original

OR operating room; operations research; operations room; opponents' runs; Oregon; outside right forward; own recognizance

O-R oxidation-reduction

O.R. official receiver; official referee; ordered recorded; orderly room; other ranks; owner's risk

O/R on request

ora. oratorio

ORB omnidirectional radio beacon

O.R.B. owner's risk of breakage

ORC Officers' Reserve Corps; Organized Reserve Corps

O.R.C. owner's risk of chafing

orch. orchestra

ord. ordained; order; orderly; ordinal; ordinance; ordinary; ordnance

O.R.D. owner's risk of damage

Ore. Oregon

Oreg. Oregon

O.R.F. owner's risk of fire; owner's risk of freezing

org. organic; organization; organized

orgn. organization

orig. origin; original; originally; originator

Ork. Orkney

O.R.L. owner's risk of leakage

ornith. ornithology

O.R.S. owner's risk of shifting

orse. otherwise

ORT Registered Occupational Therapist

ORV off-road vehicle

O.R.W. owner's risk of becoming wet

o.s. off scene; offscreen; offstage; only son

Os osmium

OS Old Saxon; on sale; on sample; on side; operating system; ordinary seaman; out of stock; out stealing

O.S. left eye [L *oculus sinister*]; old school; old series; old side; old style; one side; on schedule; on sheet; order sheet; original series; outside; outside sentinel; outsize

O/S outstanding

O.S.A. Order of St. Augustine [L *Ordo Sancti Augustini*]

O.S. & D. over, short, and damaged

O.S.B. Order of St. Benedict [L *Ordo Sancti*

Benedicti]

osc. oscillate; oscillating; oscillator

OSC order to show cause

OSHA Occupational Safety and Health Administration

OSI open systems interconnection

Osm osmol

OSO Orbiting Solar Observatory

o.s.p. he/she died without issue [L *obiit sine prole*]

OSS Office of Strategic Services

ost. osteopathic

o.s.t. ordinary spring tides

o.t. on truck

OT Occupational Therapist; occupational therapy; offensive tackle

O.T. oiltight; Old Testament; Old Tuberculin; on time; on track; overtime

O/T old terms

OTA Office of Technology Assessment

OTB offtrack betting; open to buy

OTC officer in tactical command; officers' training camp; officers' training corps; over-the-counter; oxytetracycline

O.T.C. one-stop tour charter

otdb. outboard

OTEC ocean thermal energy conversion

OTI official test insecticide

OTR Occupational Therapist, Registered

OTS Officers' Training School

OTU operational taxonomic unit; operational training unit

O.U. both eyes [L *oculi uterque*]; each eye [L *oculus uterque*]

ov. ovum

OV oil of vitriol; over voltage

ovc overcast

ovhd. overhead

OW Old Welsh; one-way

O/W oil-in-water

OWF optimum working frequency

OXFAM Oxford Committee for Famine Relief

Oxon of Oxford [L *Oxoniensis*]; Oxford [L *Oxonia*]

Oxon. Oxfordshire

oz. ooze; ounce [obsolete It *onza* (now *oncia*)]; ounces

P

p afternoon [L *post meridiem*]; games played; matches played; momentum of a particle; petite; piano; pico-; picot; pipe; pitch; pitcher; poor skiing conditions; principal; pro; prompter; proton; purl

p. by [L *per*]; father [F *père* or L *pater*]; for [L *pro*]; holy [L *pius*]; in part [L *partim*]; pacer; page; part; participle; past; paste; pater; pence; penny; people [L *populus*]; per; perch; perimeter; period; peseta; peso; piaster; pie; pint; point; pole; port; post; postage; primary

p- para-

P paperback; paragraph; parallax; parental; parental generation; park; pass; pastor; patrol; pawn; percentile; peta; pharmacopeia; pharmacopoeia; phosphorus; phrase; plaintext; planed; plate; pleasant; polar; pope [L *papa*]; population; position; positive; posterior; power; predicate; present; president; present; priest; prince; proconsul; pulse; punter; pupil; pursuit; weight [F *poids*]

P. perforation; perishable

pa. paper; piaster

p.a. participial adjective; per annum

Pa pascal; protactinium

Pa. Pennsylvania

PA Pennsylvania; personal appearance; physician's assistant; post adjutant; power amplifier; professional association; public accountant; public address; public administration; public assistance; purchasing agent

P.A. particular average; passenger agent; pernicious anemia; prefect apostolic; press agent; press association; prothonotary apostolic

P/A power of attorney; private account

PAB parabolic-aluminized reflector

PABA para-aminobenzoic acid

PABX private automatic

branch exchange

Pac. Pacific

PAC political action committee

PA-C Physician's Assistant-Certified

p. ae. equal parts [L *partes aequales*]

PAF platelet-activating factor

PAH para-aminohippurate; para-aminohippuric acid; polycyclic aromatic hydrocarbon; polynuclear aromatic hydrocarbon

Pak. Pakistan

pal. paleontology

PAL parcel airlift; prisoner at large

paleon. paleontology

palm. palmistry

pam. pamphlet

PAM pulse-amplitude modulation

pan. paneled; panorama

Pan. Panama

PAN peroxyacetyl nitrate; polyacrylonitrile

P & C put and call

P & D pickup and delivery

p & h postage and handling

p. & i. protection and indemnity

P & L profit and loss

pap. paper; papyrus

par. paragraph; parallax; parallel; parenthesis; parish

Par. Paraguay

PAR perimeter acquisition radar; precision approach radar

para. paragraph

Para. Paraguay

parl. parliament; parliamentary

part. participating; participial; participle; particular; partner

part. aeq. equal parts [L *partes aequales*]

partn. partition

part. vic. in divided parts [L *partitis vicibus*]

PAS para aminosalicylic acid; periodic acid-Schiff

PASA para-aminosalicylic acid

pass. passage; passenger; passim; passive

pat. patent; patented; patrol; pattern

PAT point after touchdown

path. pathological; pathology

pathol. pathological; pathologist; pathology

patmkg. patternmaking

patt. pattern

PAU Pan American Union
PAX private automatic exchange
PAYE pay as you earn; pay as you enter
payr. paymaster
payt. payment
p.b. piebald
Pb lead [L *plumbum*]
PB passbook; passed ball; patrol boat; patrol bomber; phonetically balanced; power brakes
P.B. permanent bunkers; pocket book; prayer book; privately bonded
PBA permanent budget account; Professional Bowlers Association
PBB polybrominated biphenyl
PBGC Pension Benefit Guaranty Corporation
PBI protein-bound iodine
PBK Phi Beta Kappa
PBM permanent bench mark
PBS Public Broadcasting Service
PBX private branch exchange
pc parsec
pc. piece
p.c. after meals [L *post cibum*]; percent; percentage; postcard

PC Panama Canal; parliamentary cases; past commander; patent cases; patrol craft; Peace Corps; penal code; personal computer; pitch circle; pleas of the crown; plug-compatible; police commissioner; political code; post commander; practice cases; printed circuit
P.C. perpetual curate; police constable; privy council; privy councillor; Professional Corporation
P/C petty cash; price current
PCA Production Credit Association
PCB petty cashbook; polychlorinated biphenyl
pce. piece
PCE pyrometric cone equivalent
pch. porch
PCHL Pacific Coast Hockey League
pchs. purchase
pcl. parcel
PCL Pacific Coast League
PCM plug-compatible maker; plug-compatible manufacturer; pulse-code modulation
PCNB pentachloro-

nitrobenzene

PCO pest control operator

PCP pentachlorophenol; phencyclidine [phencyclidine pill]

PCPA para-chlorophenylalanine

pcpn. precipitation

Pcs preconscious

PCS permanent change of station

P.C.S. principal clerk of session

pct. percent; percentage

PCV packed cell volume; positive crankcase ventilation

PCWP pulmonary capillary wedge pressure

pd. paid; passed; pond; pound

p.d. per diem

Pd palladium

PD interpupillary distance; pitch diameter; point detonating; port of debarkation; position doubtful; postage due; postal district; prism diopter; program director; property damage

P.D. police department; port dues; postdated; potential difference; public domain

PDA predicted drift angle

PDB paradichlorobenzene

PDD past due date

PDF point detonating fuse

pdg. paradigm

PDI pilot direction indicator

pdl. poundal

PDM pulse-duration modulation

PDQ pretty damn quick

pdr. pounder; powder; powder snow

PDR Physicians' Desk Reference

PDT Pacific daylight time

PE photoelectric; physical education; physical examination; pinion end; polyethylene; port of embarkation; post exchange; Prince Edward Island; printer's error; probable error; Protestant Episcopal; pulley end

P.E. petroleum engineer; presiding elder; professional engineer

P/E price/earnings; profits/earnings

PEC photoelectric cell

ped. pedal; pedestal; pedestrian

PEEP positive end-expiratory pressure

PEG prior endorsement guaranteed

P.E.I. Prince Edward Island

pen. penetration; peninsula; penitent

PEN International Association of Poets, Playwrights, Editors, Essayists and Novelists

penin. peninsula

Penn. Pennsylvania

Penna. Pennsylvania

PEP phosphoenolpyruvate

per. perdendosi; perennial; period; person

Per. Persia; Persian

perc. percussion

perf. perfect; perforate; perforated; perforation; performance; performed; performer

perh. perhaps

peri. perigee

perm. permanent

perp. perpendicular; perpetual

per proc. by proxy [L *per procurationem*]; by the agency of [L *per procurationem*]

pers. person; personal; personally; personnel

Pers. Persia; Persian

persh. perishable

persp. perspective

pert. pertaining

PERT program evaluation and review technique

pet. petrolatum; petroleum

Pet. Peter

PET parent effectiveness training; polyethylene terephthalate; positron-emission tomography

petn. petition

PETN pentaerythritol tetranitrate

PETT positron emission transverse tomography

pf a little louder [It *piú forte*]; personal foul; pianoforte; picofarad

pf. perfect; pfennig; preferred

p.f. power factor; pro forma

PF prop forward

P.F. procurator fiscal

PFC private first class

pfce. performance

pfd. preferred

PFD personal flotation device

pfg. pfennig

PFI physical fitness index

pfte pianoforte

pfx. prefix

pg picogram

pg. page

Pg. Portugal; Portuguese

PG parental guidance (movie rating); postgraduate;

prostaglandin; proving ground

P.G. Paris granite; paying guest; public gaol

PGA Professional Golfers' Association; pteroylglutamic acid

pgm. program

PGM precision guided munitions

pgn. pigeon

PGR psychogalvanic response

pgt per gross ton

PGY postgraduate year

ph phot

ph. pharmacopoeia; phase; phone; phosphor

Ph phenyl

PH pinch hit; pinch hitter; public health; Purple Heart

PHA phytohemagglutinin; Public Housing Agency

phar. pharmaceutical; pharmacist; pharmacopoeia; pharmacy

Phar.D. Doctor of Pharmacy

pharm. pharmaceutical; pharmacist; pharmacy

Pharm.D. Doctor of Pharmacy

Ph.B. Bachelor of Philosophy [L *philosophiae baccalaureus*]

Ph.D. Doctor of Philosophy [L *philosophiae doctor*]

Ph.G. Graduate in Pharmacy

phi. philosophy

phil. philharmonic; philological; philologist; philology; philosopher; philosophical; philosophy

Phil. Philippians

Phila. Philadelphia

Philem. Philemon

philol. philological; philologist; philology

philos. philosopher; philosophy

Ph.M. Master in Pharmacy

Phm.B. Bachelor of Pharmacy

Phm.G. Graduate in Pharmacy

PHN public health nurse

pho. photographer

phon. phonetics; phonology

phono. phonograph

phot. photograph; photographer; photographic; photography

PHOTINT photographic intelligence

photog. photographic; photography

p.h.p. pump horsepower

P.H.P. packing-house

products
phr. phrase; phraseology
PHS Public Health Service
P.H.V. for this occasion [L *pro hace vice*]; for this purpose [L *pro hace vice*]; for this turn [L *pro hace vice*]
phy. ed. physical education
phys. physical; physician; physics; physiological
physiol. physiologist; physiology
pi. piaster
PI per inquiry; photo interpretation; photo interpreter; present illness; programmed instruction; protamine insulin
P.I. paper insulated; Philippine Islands; private investigator
pias. piaster
pic. picture
pict. pictorial
PID pelvic inflammatory disease
PIK payment in kind
pil. pill [L *pilula*]; pilot
pim penalities in minutes
PIN personal identification number; private identification number

PINS person in need of supervision
pinx. he/she painted it [L *pinxit*]
PIO public information office; public information officer
PIRG public interest research group
PITI principal, interest, taxes, insurance
pizz pizzicato
P.J. police justice; presiding judge; probate judge
pk. pack; park; peak; peck; pike
PK preacher's kid; psychokinesis
pkd. pdr. packed powder
pkg. package
pkge. package
pkm. packmaster
pkr. packer
pkt. packet; pocket
PKU phenylketonuria
pkwy. parkway
pky. pecky
pl. pile; place; plain; plaster; plate; platoon; plural
PL perception of light; phase line; programming language; public law; public liability
P.L. partial loss; poet

laureate; private line

P/L profit and loss

PLA People's Liberation Army; programmable logic array

PLAM price-level adjusted mortgage

plat. plateau; platform; platoon

plbg. plumbing

plbr. plumber

Plc. public limited company

PLC programmable logic controller

pleb. plebeian

plen. plenipotentiary

plf. plaintiff

PLL phase-locked loop

plmb. plumbing

plmg. plumbing

pln. plain

PLO Palestine Liberation Organization

P.L.R. Public Lending Right

pls. please

PLSS portable life-support system

plstc. plastic

plstr. plasterer

plstrer. plasterer

plt. pilot; plate

pltf. plaintiff

pltg. plating

pltry. poultry

plu. plural

pm penalty minutes; pumice

pm. premium; premolar

p.m. afternoon [L *post meridiem*]; per month

Pm promethium

PM paymaster; per thousand [L *pro mille*]; permanent magnet; police magistrate; postmaster; postmortem; purchase money; push money

P.M. past master; peculiar meter; phase modulation; Pontifex Maximus; prime minister; prize money; provost marshal

P/M put of more

PMA primary mental abilities

PMG paymaster general; postmaster general; provost marshal general

PMH production per man-hour

pmk. postmark

PML progressive multifocal leukoencephalopathy

PMMA polymethylmethacrylate

PMN polymorphonuclear neutrophilic leukocyte

PMO principal medical officer

pmol picomole

pmole picomole

PMS pregnant mare serum; premenstrual syndrome

pmt. payment

PMT photomultiplier tube

pn. position

p.n. promissory note

Pn. partition

PN please note; psychoneurotic

PNA pentose nucleic acid

PNdb perceived noise decibel

pneu. pneumatic

pneum. pneumatic

p.n.g. persona non grata

P.N.G. Papua New Guinea

pnl. panel

PNP Pediatric Nurse Practitioner

pnr. pioneer

pns. position

pntd. painted

pntr. painter

pnxt. he/she painted it [L *pinxit*]

po putout

po. poetry; point; pole

p.o. by mouth [L *per os*]; orally [L *per os*]

Po polonium

PO personnel officer; petty officer; pilot officer; postal order; purchase order

P.O. parole officer; post office; probation officer

P.O.B. post office box

p.o.c. port of call

POD payable on death

P.O.D. pay on delivery; post office department

Pod.D. Doctor of Podiatry

POE port of embarkation; port of entry

pol. polar; polish; polished; political; politician; politics

Pol. Poland; Polish

POL petroleum, oil, and lubricants

polit. political

poly. polytechnic

polytech. polytechnic

pomp pomposo

POMR problem oriented medical record

pon. pontoon

pond. by weight [L *pondere*]

pont. bishop [L *pontifex*]; pontoon

P.O.O. post office order

pop. popular; popularly; population

POP printing out paper

P.O.P. point of purchase

por. portion; portrait

POR pay on return; payable on receipt; price on request

porc. porcelain
port. portable; portfolio; portrait
Port. Portugal; Portuguese
pos. fielding position; position; positive; possession; possessive
POS point-of-sale
P.O.S.B. post office savings bank
poss. possession; possessive; possible; possibly
posslq person of the opposite sex sharing living quarters
possn. possession
post. postal
pot. potential; potentiometer; potion; pottery
POW prisoner of war
pp more softly [It *più piano*]; parts per; pianissimo; pope [L *papa*]; power play
pp. pages
p.p. by proxy [L *per procurationem*]; by the agency of [L *per procurationem*]; in his/her own person [L *propria persona*]; in his/her proper person [L *propria persona*]; past participle; picked ports; pounds

pressure
P.p. near point [L *punctum proximum*]
PP parcel post; peak to peak; pellagra preventive; personal property; Planned Parenthood; post position; postpartum
PP. Fathers [L *patres*]
P.P. parish priest; part paid; postpaid; power plant; prepaid; privately printed
p.p.a. per power of attorney
PPA phenylpropanolamine
ppb parts per billion
PPB planning, programming, budgeting
PPC picture postcard
P.P.C. to take leave [Fr *pour prendre congé*]
ppd. postpaid; prepaid
ppg picopicogram
PPG points per game; power play goals
pph. pamphlet
p.p.i. policy proof of interest
PPI plan position indicator
P.P.I. parcel post insured
ppl. participle
PPLO mycoplasma [pleuropneumonia-like organism]

ppm parts per million
PPM pulse position modulation
ppmv parts per million by volume
ppn. precipitation
PPO polypropylene oxide; preferred provider organization
ppp pianississimo
pps pulses per second
P.P.S. additional postscript [L *post postscriptum*]; parliamentary private secretary
ppt parts per thousand; parts per trillion
ppt. precipitate
pptn. precipitation
PPV pay-per-view
PQ Parti Québecois; previous question
P.Q. personality quotient; Province of Quebec
pr presbyopia
pr. pair; pounder; power; prayer; preferred; present; price; priest; primitive; prince; printed; printer; prior; private; pronoun; pronounced; pronunciation; prose; proved
p.r. in proportion [L *pro rata*]

Pr far point [L *punctum remotum*]; praseodymium; propyl
PR personal record; press release; profit rate; public relations
P.R. parliamentary report; prize ring; proportional representation; Puerto Rican; Puerto Rico; Roman people [L *populus Romanus*]
P/R payroll
prac. practical; practice; practitioners
PRC People's Republic of China; Postal Rate Commission
prchst. parachutist
prcht. parachute
preb. prebend; prebendary
prec. preceding
pred. predicate; predicative
pref. preface; prefatory; prefect; prefecture; preference; preferred; prefix
prelim. preliminary
prem. premier; premium
prep. preparation; preparatory; prepare; preposition
prepd. prepared
prepg. preparing
prepn. preparation

prereq. prerequisite

pres. present;
presentation; presidency;
president; presidential;
pressure; presumptive

Presb. Presbyterian

presdl. presidential

press. pressure

pret. preterit

prev. previous; previously

prf. proof

PRF pulse recurrence
frequency; pulse repetition
frequency

pri. primary; prison;
private

prim. primary; primate;
primitive

prin. principal;
principally; principle

princ. principal; principle

pris. prisoner

priv. private; privately;
privative

prk. park

prm. premium

p.r.n. as occasion arises [L
pro re nata]; for the
emergency [L *pro re nata*]

prntr. printer

pro. progressive; pronoun;
provost

PRO public records office;
public relations office;
public relations officer

prob. probable; probably;
probate; probation;
problem

proc. procedures;
proceedings; process;
proclamation; proctor

prod. produce; produced;
producer; product;
production

pro dos. for a dose [L *pro
dose*]

prof. profession;
professional

Prof. professor

prog. program; progress;
progressive

proj. project; projector

prol. prologue

prom. prominent;
promontory; promoted

PROM programmable
read only memory

pron. pronominal;
pronoun; pronounced;
pronunciation

prop. propeller; proper;
properly; property;
proposed; proposition;
proprietary; proprietor

pro. per. in his/her own
person [L *propria
persona*]; in his/her proper
person [L *propria persona*]

propl. proportional

propn. proportion

propr. proprietor

pro quer. for the plaintiff

[L *pro querente*]

pro rat. aet. according to age [L *pro ratione aetatis*]

pros. prosecuting; prosecutor; prosody

prot. protected; protection; protectorate

Prot. Protestant

pro tem. for the time being [L *pro tempore*]

pro us. ext. for external use [L *pro usu externo*]

prov. proverb; proverbial; provided; province; provincial; provision; provisional; provost

Prov. Proverbs

prox. in the next month [L *proximo*]

pr. p. present participle

PRR pulse recurrence rate; pulse repetition rate

prs. present

prsfdr press feeder

prsmn pressman

PRT personal rapid transit

prtr. printer

PRU photographic reconnaissance unit

ps picosecond

ps. pieces; pseudo; pseudonym

Ps. Psalms

PS phrase structure; power steering; power

supply

P.S. passenger steamer; permanent secretary; police sergeant; postscript [L *postscriptum*]; private secretary; privy seal; prompt side; public school; public stenographer

P/S public sale

Psa. Psalms

PSA public service announcement

PSAT Preliminary Scholastic Aptitude Test

psc per standard compass

PSC postal service center

P.S.C. public service commission

PSE Psychological Stress Evaluator

psec picosecond

pseud. pseudonym; pseudonymous

psf pounds per square foot

PSG platoon sergeant

psgr. passenger

psi pounds per square inch

PSI Pollution Standard Index; presentence investigation report

psia pounds per square inch absolute

psig pounds per square inch gauge

P sol partly soluble

PSRO professional

standards review
organization
P.SS. postscripts [L
postscripta]
psso pass slip stitch
over
pst. peseta
PST Pacific standard time
pstg. postage
psych. psychic; psychical;
psychological;
psychologist; psychology
psychol. psychologist;
psychology
Psy.D. Doctor of
Psychology
pt patient
pt. part; payment; peseta;
pint; point; port
p.t. past tense; postal
telegraph; post town;
private terms; pro
tempore; pupil teacher
Pt platinum
PT Pacific time; part-time;
patrol torpedo; physical
therapist; physical
therapy; physical training
P.T. Easter time [L
Paschale tempore]
pta. peseta
PTA parent-teacher
association; prior to
admission
ptbl. portable
p.t.c. postal telegraph

cable
PTC phenylthiocarbamide
ptd. painted; pointed;
printed
Pte. private
ptg. printing
PTH parathyroid hormone
Ptl. patrolman
PTM pulse-time
modulation
PTO parent-teacher
organization; Patent and
Trademark Office; please
turn over; power takeoff
ptr. painter; printer
ptrnmkr. patternmaker
pts. points
PTSD post-traumatic
stress disorder
PTT postal, telegraph,
telephone
PTV public television
pty. party
Pty. proprietary
Pu plutonium
PU pickup
pub. public; publication;
published; publisher;
publishing
publ. public; publication;
published; publisher;
publishing
PUC public utilities
commission
PUD public utility district
P.U.D. pickup and

delivery

PUFA polyunsaturated fatty acid

pulv. powder [L *pulvis*]; pulverized; pulverizer

pun. puncheon

punc. punctuation

PUO pyrexia of unknown origin

pur. purchase; purchaser; purchasing; purification; pursuit

pv par value

p.v. post village; priest vicar

PV photovoltaic; pipe ventilated; polyvinyl

PVA polyvinyl acetate; polyvinyl alcohol

PVC polyvinyl chloride; premature ventricular contraction

PVD peripheral vascular disease

PVE prosthetic valve endocarditis

PVP polyvinylpyrrolidone

pvt. private

PVT pressure, volume, temperature

PW power window; prisoner of war; psychological warfare; public works

P.W. packed weight

PWA Public Works Administration

PWBA Professional Women Bowlers Association

pwd. powder

pwr. power

PWR pressurized water reactor

pwt. pennyweight

Px pneumothorax; prognosis

PX post exchange; private exchange

P.X. please exchange

pxt. he/she painted it [L *pinxit*]

pymt. payment

PYO pick your own

pyro. pyrotechnic; pyrotechnics

PZI protamine zinc insulin

Q

q quintal

q. every [L *quaque*]; farthing [L *quadrans*]; inquire [L *quaere*]; quantity; quart; quasi; query; question; quick; quire

Q quadrillion; quality factor; quarter; quartermaster;

quarterback; quarterly;
quartile; quarto; queen;
quetzal

QA quality assurance

Q-A question and answer

Q. and A. question and
answer

QB quarterback

Q.B. Queen's Bench

QC quality control;
quartermaster corps

Q.C. Queen's Counsel

QCD quantum
chromodynamics

q.d. every day [L *quaque
die*]; four times a day [L
quater in die]

QD quarterdeck

qda quantity discount
agreement

q.e. which is [L *quod est*]

QED quantum
electrodynamics

Q.E.D. which was to be
demonstrated [L *quod erat
demonstrandum*]

Q.E.F. which was to be
done [L *quod erat
faciendum*]

Q.E.I. which was to be
found out [L *quod erat
inveniendum*]

QF quarterfinals

Q.F. quick-firing

q.h. every hour [L *quaque
hora*]

q.hr. every hour [L *quaque
hora*]

q.i.d. four times a day [L
quater in die]

ql quintal

q.l. as much as you please
[L *quantum libet*]

Qld. Queensland

qlty. quality

qm. in what manner [L
quomodo]

q.m. every morning [L
quoque matutino]

QM quartermaster

QMC quartermaster corps

QMG quartermaster
general

Qmr. quartermaster

QMS quartermaster
sergeant

qn. question; quotation

q.n. every night [L *quoque
nocte*]

QNB quinuclidinyl
benzilate

q.p. as much as you please
[L *quantum placet*]

q.pl. as much as you
please [L *quantum placet*]

qq. questions

qq. hor. every hour [L
quaque hora]

qq.v. which see [L *quae
vide*]

qr. quarter; quire

qrly. quarterly

qrtly. quarterly

q.s. as much as suffices [L *quantum sufficiat*]

QS quarter section

Q.S. quarter sessions

QSO quasi-stellar object

qt. quantity; quart

q.t. quiet

qtd. quartered

qtly. quarterly

qto. quarto

QTOL quiet takeoff and landing

qtr. quarter; quarterly

qtrs. quarters

qty. quantity

qtz. quartz

qu. quart; quarter; quarterly; quasi; queen; query; question

quad quadrilateral

quad. quadrant

qual. qualification; qualified; qualify; qualitative; quality

quant. quantitative

quar. quarter; quarterly

quasar quasi-stellar radio source

quat. four [L *quattuor*]

Que. Quebec

ques. question

quint. fifth [L *quintus*]; quintuple

quot. as often as needed [L *quoties*]; quotation

quotid. every day [L *quotidie*]

q.v. as much as you will [L *quantum vis*]; which see [L *quod vide*]

qy. query

qz. quartz

R

r correlation coefficient; racemic; real; returning; ring; roentgen

r. railroad; railway; rain; rare; rarity; ratio; rear; received; recto; rector; reddish; refrigerator; registered; reigned; rerun; reside; residence; resident; retired; right; rises; road; rod; rood; rubber; ruble; rule

R gas constant; king [L *rex*]; queen [L *regina*]; radical — used esp. of a univalent hydrocarbon radical; radio; radius; rank; Rankine; Reaumur; rebounds; reconnaissance; refraction; registered trademark — often enclosed in a circle; regular; regulating; repeat; rerun; reserves;

resistance; resistor; respiration; respondent; restricted; retree; Reynolds number; rifle; right edge; rook; rough — used in bacteriology; run; runs; rupee; Rydberg constant; slow — used of a clock [F *retarder*]

R. rabbi; range; recipe; red; republic; Republican; respond; response; riser; river; Roman; rotor; route; royal; runic

ra. range

Ra radium

RA radioactive; rate of application; rear admiral; reduction of area; regular army

R.A. right ascension; Royal Academician; Royal Academy; Very Reverend [L *Reverendus Admodum*]

R/A refer to acceptor

RAAF Royal Australian Air Force

rabb. rabbinic

RAC Royal Automobile Club

rad radian; radiation absorbed dose

rad. radial; radiant; radiator; radical; radio; radium; radius; radix

RADA Royal Academy of Dramatic Art

RADINT radar intelligence

R.Adm. rear admiral

RADM rear admiral

RAF Royal Air Force

RAL resorcylic acid lactone

rallo rallentando

RAM random access memory; reverse annuity mortgage

R & B rhythm and blues

R. & C. rail and canal

r. & c.c. riot and civil commotion

R & D research and development

R. & L. rail and lake

R. & O. rail and ocean

R & R rest and recreation; rest and recuperation; rest and rehabilitation

R and R rock and roll

R. & W. rail and water

raob radiosonde observation

rap. rapid

RAP regimental aid post; rupees, annas, pies

RAST radioallergosorbent test

RATO rocket-assisted takeoff

rb. ruble

Rb rubidium

RB relative bearing; right back; right fullback; running back

R.B. rifle brigade

RBC red blood cells; red blood count

RBE relative biological effectiveness

RBH regimental beachhead

RBI runs batted in

rbl. ruble

RBn radiobeacon

RC recruiting center; Red Cross; rehabilitation center; remote control; reply coupon; resistance-capacitance; right center; Roman Catholic; rotary combustion

R.C. reinforced concrete; release clause; relief claim

RCA Rodeo Cowboys Association

RCAF Royal Canadian Air Force

RCB right cornerback

RCC radio common carrier

RCCC Royal Caledonia Curling Club; Royal Curling Club of Canada

rcd. received; record

rcg reverberation-controlled gain

RCL ruling case law

RCM radar countermeasure; regimental court-martial

RCMM registered competitive market maker

RCMP Royal Canadian Mounted Police

rcn. reconnaissance

RCN Royal Canadian Navy

rcpt. receipt

RCPT Registered Cardiopulmonary Technologist

RCS reaction control system

rct. receipt; recruit

RCT regimental combat team

rctg. recruiting

rcvr. receiver

RCVT Registered Cardiovascular Technologist

rd rod; rutherford

rd. red; reduce; reduced; reduction; rix-dollar; road; rood; round

r.d. running days

RD reaction of degeneration; Registered Dietitian; right defense; rural delivery

R.D. refer to drawer; regional director; rural dean; rural district

RDA recommended daily

allowance; recommended
dietary allowance

RdAc radioactinum

RDC rail diesel car

R.D.C. running-down
clause; rural district
council

RDF radio direction
finder; radio direction
finding; range direction
finding; rapid deployment
force

rdg. reading; reducing;
ridge

rdm. radarman; random

RDMS Registered
Diagnostic Medical
Sonologist

rdo. radio

RDS respiratory distress
syndrome

RdTh radiothorium

rdv. rendezvous

RDX cyclonite [Research
Department explosive]

RDY royal dockyard

re. reference; regarding;
rupee

r.e. red edges;
reticuloendothelial

Re rhenium

RE rare earth; rate of
exchange; real estate;
right end; right eye; rural
electrification

R.E. radium emanation;

Right Excellent

R/E repayable to either

REA Railway Express
Agency; Rural
Electrification
Administration

reaptd. reappointed

reas. reasonable

reb. rebounds

rec. receipt; receive;
receiver; receptacle;
reception; recipe;
reclamation;
recommended; record;
recorded; recorder;
recording; recovery;
recreation

recd. received

recip. recipient; reciprocal;
reciprocate; reciprocity

recirc. recirculation

recit recitative

recm. recommend;
recommended

recp. reception

recpst. receptionist

recpt. receipt

recr. receiver

recryst. recrystallize

rec. sec. recording
secretary

rect. receipt; rectangle;
rectangular; rectified;
rectifier; rector; rectory

red. redactor; reduce;
reduced; reducer;

reducing; reduction

redox oxidation-reduction

REE rare earth element

ref. referee; reference; referred; refinery; refining; reform; reformation; reformed; reformer; refrain; refrigeration; refrigerator; refunding

refd. referred; reformed

reff. references

refl. reflex; reflexive

refr. refraction; refrigerate; refrigerating; refrigeration

refrig. refrigerating; refrigeration

reg. queen [L *regina*]; regent; regiment; region; register; registered; registrar; registration; registry; regular; regularly; regulate; regulation; regulator

regd. registered

reg. gen. general rule [L *regula generalis*]

regl. regimental

regt. regent; regiment

regtl. regimental

REIT real estate investment trust

rejd. rejoined

rel. related; relating; relative; relatively; relay;

release; released; relics [L *reliquae*]; relief; relieve; relieved; relieving; religion; religious

REL rate of energy loss

reld. relieved

relig. religion

rem. remain; remainder; remark; remit; remittance; remitted; remove

REM rapid eye movement

REMT radiological emergency medical team

rep roentgen equivalent physical

rep. repair; repeat; report; reported; reporter; representative; republic

Rep. Republican

repet. let it be repeated [L *repetatur*]

repl. replace; replacement

repr. repair; represent; representative; represented; representing; reprint; reprinted

rept. receipt; report

req. request; require; required; requisition

reqd. required

reqmt. requirement

res. resawed; research; reservation; reserve; reservoir; residence; residency; resident;

residential; residue;
resigned; resistance;
resistor; resolution; resort

resp. respective;
respectively; respiration;
respiratory; respondent;
responsible

rest. restored

restr. restaurant

ret. retain; retainer;
retaining; retard; retired;
return; returned

retd. retained; retired;
returned

retnr. retainer

retrg. retracting

retrog. retrogression;
retrogressive

rev. revenue; reverse;
reversed; review;
reviewed; revise; revised;
revision; revolution;
revolving

Rev. Revelation; reverend

Revd. reverend

revol. revolution

Rev. St. revised statutes

Rev. Stat. revised statutes

rf refunding; rinforzando;
rough finish

rf. refunding; roof

RF radio frequency;
representative fraction;
reserve force; rheumatic
fever; right field; right
foot; right forward; right

front; right fullback

R.F. range finder; rapid
fire; reducing flame

RFB right fullback

RFC radio-frequency
choke

RFD rural free delivery

RFE Radio Free Europe

rfg. refunding; roofing

R.F.G. rapid-fire gun

RFI radio-frequency
interference

rfl. refuel

rfn. rifleman

RFP request for proposal

rfr. roofer

rfz rinforzando

r.g. general rules [L
regulae generales]

RG red-green; reduction
gear; right guard

R.G. rolled gold

RGB red-green-blue

rgr. ringer

rgt. regiment

Rh rhesus; rhodium

RH relative humidity;
right halfback; right
hand; Rockwell hardness;
roundhouse

R.H. Royal Highness

rhap. rhapsody

RHB right halfback

rhd. railhead

rheo. rheostat

rhet. rhetoric

RHI range-height indicator

RHIP rank has its privileges

rhm roentgen per hour at one meter

RHQ regimental headquarters

r/hr roentgens per hour

rhs right-hand side

RI repulsion induction; Rhode Island

R.I. refractive index; reinsurance; Rhode Island

RIA radioimmunoassay

r.i.e. retirement income endowment

RIF reduction in force

rig. ridgeling

RIM reaction injection molding; resource interface module

rip ripieno

rip. ripped

R.I.P. may he/she rest in peace [L *requiescat in pace*]; may they rest in peace [L *requiescant in pace*]

rit ritardando

R.I.T. refining in transit

riten ritenuto

riv. river

R.J. road junction

rk. rock

RK radial keratotomy

R.K. run of kiln

rkt. rocket

rkva reactive kilovolt-ampere

rky. rocky

r.l. random lengths

RL rhumb line; right line; rocket launcher

R.L. reduced level

R/L radiolocation

R.L. & R. rail, lake, and rail

RLB right linebacker

RLF retrolental fibroplasia

R.L.O. returned letter office

RLQ right lower quadrant

rls. release

RLT Registered Laboratory Technician

Rltr. Realtor

rly. railway

rm. ream; room

RM radioman; reichsmark

R.M. resident magistrate; royal mail

RMA Royal Military Academy

RMC Royal Military College

RMI radio magnetic indicator

rms root-mean-square

R.M.S. Royal Mail Service; Royal Mail ship; Royal Mail steamer; Royal Mail steamship

rmt. remount

RMT Registered Medical Technologist

Rn radon

RN Registered Nurse; Reynolds number; Royal Navy

RNA ribonucleic acid

RNAase ribonuclease

RNase ribonuclease

RNC Republican National Committee

rnd. round

rng. range

rnwy. runway

RNZAF Royal New Zealand Air Force

ro. recto; road; roan; rood; ruble [F *rouble*]

RO radar operator; read only; reconnaissance officer; recruiting officer; regimental order; reverse osmosis; royal observatory; royal octavo

R.O. receiving office

ROA return on assets

ROC reserve officer candidate

R.O.C. Republic of China

ROE return on equity

R.O.G. receipt of goods

ROI return on investment

R.O.K. Republic of Korea

rom. roman; romance

r.o.m. run of mine

Rom. Roman; Romance; Romania; Romanian; Romans

ROM radiopaque contrast material; read-only memory; Register of Merit

ROP run-of-paper; run-of-press

R.O.P. record of performance; record of production

R.O.R. released on own recognizance

Ros. Roscommon

ROS read only storage

Rosc. Roscommon

rot. rotary; rotating; rotation; rotten

ROTC Reserve Officers' Training Corps

rotn. rotation

roul. roulette

ROV remotely operated vehicle

ROW right of way

rp. rappen; recipe

Rp. rupiah

RP Received Pronunciation; relief pitcher; reply paid; reprint; reprinted; reprinting; republic [L *res publica*]; rust preventive

R.P. refilling point; regius professor; return

premium; reverend father
[L *reverendus pater*]
R/P return of post
RPC reply postcard
rpf. reichspfennig
RPF relaxed pelvic floor;
renal plasma flow
rpg rebounds per game
RPG Report Program
Generator
R.Ph. Registered
Pharmacist
rpm revolutions per
minute
RPN reverse Polish
notation
RPO railway post office
RPP reply paid postcard
RPR rapid plasma reagin
rps revolutions per second
rpt. repeat; report;
reported; reporting
RPT Registered Physical
Therapist
rptd. repeated; reported;
reprinted; ruptured
RPV remotely piloted
vehicle
R.Q. respiratory quotient
rqn. requisition
rr rear
rr. very rarely [L *rarissime*]
RR railroad; recovery
room; registered
representative; right rear;
rural route

R.R. Right Reverend
RRA Registered Records
Administrator
RRC regular route carrier
RRL Registered Records
Librarian
rRNA ribosomal RNA
RRT Registered
Respiratory Therapist
r.s. right side
Rs. rupees
RS rabbinical supervision;
radio station; recruiting
service; recruiting station;
right safety; Royal Society
R.S. recording secretary;
reformed spelling; revised
statutes
R/S report of survey
R.S.F.S.R. Russian Soviet
Federated Socialist
Republic [Russ
*Rossiiskaya Sovetskaya
Federativnaya
Sotsialisticheskaya
Respublika*]
R.S.M. regimental
sergeant major
RSO regimental supply
officer
R.S.O. railway sorting
office; railway suboffice
RSV research safety
vehicle; respiratory
syncytial virus; Revised
Standard Version; Rous

sarcoma virus

RSVP Retired Senior Volunteer Program

R.S.V.P. please reply [F *répondez s'il vous plaît*]

R.S.W.C. right side up with care

rt. right; route

RT radio technician; Radiological Technologist; recreational therapy; register ton; released time; Respiration Therapist; respiratory therapist; respiratory therapy; return ticket; right tackle; room temperature; round trip; running title

R.T. reading test

R/T radio telegraphy; radiotelephone

RTA real-time analyzer; reciprocal trade agreement; renal tubular acidosis

RTC replacement training center; reserve training corps

rtd. retired; returned

rte. route

RTF resistance transfer factor

Rt. Hon. Right Honorable

RTN registered trade name

RTO radiotelephone operator; railroad transportation officer; railway transportation officer

Rt. Rev. Right Reverend

rtw ready-to-wear

rty. rarity

Ru ruthenium

RU rat unit

rub. red [L *ruber*]; rubbed; rubber

rud. rudder

RUE right upper extremity

Rum. Rumania; Rumanian

rupt. rupture

RUQ right upper quadrant

Russ. Russia; Russian

RV recreational vehicle; reentry vehicle

R.V. rendezvous; Revised Version

rva reactive volt-ampere

R.V.S.V.P. please reply at once [F *répondez vite s'il vous plaît*]

rw reverse work

r.w. random widths

RW radiological warfare; right of way; right wing

R.W. Right Worshipful; Right Worthy

rwy. railway

℞ prescription [L *recipe* take]

Rx prescription [℞]; tens of rupees

ry Rydberg

Ry. railway

S

s scruple; secondary; sine; slip; small; snow; solid; soprano; spurs; stere; subito; symmetrical

s. buried [L *sepultus*]; fellow [L *socius* or *sodalis*]; generation [L *saeculum*]; left [L *sinister*]; satang; school; scribe; seat; second; secretary; section; see; semi-; series; set; shilling; ship; side; sign; signature; signed; silver; simplex; single; singular; socialist; society; solidus; solo; solubility; son; sou; south; southerly; southern; species; spherical; staff; standard; station; statute; steamer; steel; stem; stock; straight; substantive; succeeded; sun; surplus; survey; without [L *sine*]; write on label [L *signa*]

S entropy; sacral; sacrifice; safety; sand; scalar; science; seaman; search; sentence; sharp; siemens; silicate; single; slow; small; smooth; soft; sol; south; special; speed; sphere; standard deviation of a sample; stimulus; stolen base; subject; submarine; sulfur; superb; superior; surfaced; svedberg; switch

S. sabbath; sacred; saint; Saturday; senate; September; signor; silversmith; sink; sire; southern; Sunday; surgeon

S/ sucre

sa. sable

s.a. according to art [L *secundum artem*]; under the year [L *sub anno*]; without date [L *sine anno*]

s/a subject to approval

Sa samarium

Sa. Saturday

SA salt added; Salvation Army; seaman apprentice; seasonally adjusted; second attack; semiannual; semiautomatic; sex appeal; slugging average; small arms; surface area

S.A. corporation [F *société anonyme* or Sp *sociedad anonima* or It *societa*

anonima]; South Africa;
South African; South
America; South American;
South Australia; South
Australian; stormtroopers
[Ger *Sturmabteilung*]
S-A sinoatrial
SAA small arms
ammunition
Sab. sabbath
SAB science advisory
board
S.A.B. soprano, alto,
baritone
sac. sacrifice
SAC Strategic Air
Command
SAD sugar, acetone,
diacetic acid
SADR Saharan Arab
Democratic Republic
SAE self-addressed
envelope; Society of
Automotive Engineers;
stamped addressed
envelope; standard
average European
saec. century [L *saeculum*]
saf. safety
S. Af. South Africa
SAF strategic air force
S. Afr. South Africa
SAG Screen Actors Guild
SAGE semiautomatic
ground environment
SAH subarachnoid

hemorrhage
sal. salad; salary
SALT Strategic Arms
Limitation Talks
salv. salvage
Sam. Samuel
S. Am. South America
SAM shared appreciation
mortgage; special air
mission; surface-to-air
missile
S. Amer. South America
Saml. Samuel
san. sanitary; sanitation
SAN styrene acrylonitrile
S. & C. shipper and
carrier; sized and
calendered
S and D song and dance
S. & F.A. shipping and
forwarding agent
S. & H. Sundays and
holidays
S & L savings and loan
association
S & M sadism and
masochism; sadist and
masochist
S & P Standard & Poor's
S. & S.C. sized and
supercalendered
S & T science and
technology
S. & T. supply and
transport
sanit. sanitary; sanitation

s.a.n.r. subject to approval, no risk

sap. sapwood

SAP semi-armor-piercing; soon as possible

sapon. saponification

SAR safety analysis report; search and rescue; semiautomatic rifle; Sons of the American Revolution; stock appreciation rights; synthetic-aperture radar

S.A.R. South African Republic

SAS sodium aluminum sulfate

SASE self-addressed stamped envelope

Sask. Saskatchewan

sat. satellite; saturate; saturated; saturation

Sat. Saturday

SAT Scholastic Aptitude Test; without thymonucleic acid [NL *sine acido thymonucleico*]

S.A.T. systematic assertiveness training

S.A.T.B. soprano, alto, tenor, bass

satcom communications satellite; satellite communications

satd. saturated

satg. saturating

satn. saturation

sat. sol. saturated solution

S. Aust. South Australia

sav. savings

savs. savings

SAW squad automatic weapon

sb stilb

sb. substantive

s/b should be

Sb antimony [L *stibium*]; strabismus; switchboard

SB senate bill; signal boatswain; spina bifida; splash block; standard bead; Stanford-Binet intelligence test; stolen base; stuffing box

S.B. Bachelor of Science [NL *scientiae baccalaureus*]; sales book; savings bank; separately binned; shipping board; short bill; simultaneous broadcast; small bonds; southbound; steamboat; stretcher bearer

S/B statement of billing

SBA Small Business Administration; standard beam approach

SBIC small business investment company

sbj. subjunctive

SBN Standard Book Number

SBR styrene-butadiene rubber

SBU strategic business unit

sc screen; single crochet; spring conditions

sc. he/she carved it [L *sculpsit*]; he/she engraved it [L *sculpsit*]; scale; scene; science; scientific; screw; scruple; subcutaneous; that is to say [L *scilicet*]

s.c. self-contained; single case; small capitals; subcutaneous; subcutaneously; supercalendered

Sc scandium; stratocumulus

Sc. scapula; Scots

SC same case; sanitary corps; security council; see copy; select cases; self-contained; service ceiling; ship's cook; signal corps; single comb; South Carolina; spacecraft; special circular; special constable; staff college; staff corps; submarine chaser; sugar coated; summary court; superimposed current; supply corps; supreme court; swimming club

S.C. by the decree of the Senate [L *Senatus consulto*]; salvage charges; school certificate; self-closing; single column; Sisters of Charity; South Carolina; spreading coefficient; steel casting

S/C statement of charges

Scand. Scandinavia; Scandinavian

S.C. & S. strapped, corded, and sealed

SCAT School and College Ability Test; supersonic commercial air transport

Sc.B. Bachelor of Science [NL *scientiae baccalaureus*]

SCC specialized common carrier

SCCA Sports Car Club of America

scd. schedule; screwed

Sc.D. Doctor of Science [NL *scientiae doctor*]

S.C.E. standard calomel electrode

scf standard cubic feet

sch. note [L *scholium*]; schedule; schilling; scholar; school; schoolhouse; schooner

s'chase steeplechase

sched. schedule

schl. school

schr. schooner

sci. science; scientific

SCID severe combined immune deficiency

scil. that is to say [L *scilicet*]

scl. scale

SCL student of the civil law

SCLC Southern Christian Leadership Conference

Sc.M. Master of Science [NL *scientiae magister*]

SCM summary court-martial

S.C.M. State Certified Midwife

SCORE Service Corps of Retired Executives

Scot. Scotland; Scottish

scp spherical candlepower

scp. scrip; script

SCP single-cell protein

SCPO senior chief petty officer

scr. screen; screw; screwed; scrip; script; scruple

SCR senior common room

scrip. scriptural; scripture

script. scriptural; scripture

scrn. screen

SCS Soil Conservation Service

S.C.S. superintendent of car service

sct. scout

sctd. scattered

sctr. sector

SCU special care unit

scuba self-contained underwater breathing apparatus

sculp. he/she carved it [L *sculpsit*]; he/she engraved it [L *sculpsit*]; sculptor; sculptural; sculpture

sculpt. carved [L *sculptus*]; engraved [L *sculptus*]; he/she carved it [L *sculpsit*]; he/she engraved it [L *sculpsit*]

sd short delivery

sd. said; sand; seasoned; seed; sewed; signed; sound

s.d. same day; saturation deficit; several dates; solid drawn; without date [L *sine dato*]; without day [L *sine die*]

SD second defense; semidiameter; service dress; short delay; South Dakota; special delivery; special duty; specially denatured; stage direction; standard deviation; straight duty; supply department; supply depot

S.D. Doctor of Science [NL *scientiae doctor*]; sash door; secret service [Ger

Sicherheitsdienst]; senior deacon; single deck; soft drawn; South Dakota; survival dose

S/D sea-damaged; sight draft

SDA specific dynamic action; succinic dehydrogenase activity

S. Dak. South Dakota

SDAT senile dementia of the Alzheimer's type

S.D.-B.L. sight draft, bill of lading attached

S.D.D. store door delivery

sdg. siding

sdl. saddle; seedling

SDLC synchronous data link control

SDP Social Democratic Party

sdr. sender

SDR special drawing rights

sds. sounds

SDS sodium dodecyl sulphate; Students for a Democratic Society

SDT shell-destroying tracer

s.e. second entrance; single entry

Se selenium

SE southeast; southeastern; split end; Standard English;

standard error; stock exchange; systems engineer

S.E. sanitary engineer; sanitary engineering; starch equivalent

sea. seaman

SEA Southeast Asia

SEATO Southeast Asia Treaty Organization

sec secant

sec. according to [L *secundum*]; second; secondary; secretariat; secretary; section; sector; secured; security

SEC Securities and Exchange Commission; Southeastern Conference

SECAM Color Sequence with Memory [F *Sequence de Couleurs avec Memoire*]

sech hyperbolic secant [secant + hyperbolic]

sec'l secretarial

sec. leg. according to law [L *secundum legem*]

sec. nat. naturally [L *secundum naturam*]

sec. reg. according to rule [L *secundum regulam*]

sect. section; sectional

secty. secretary

secy. secretary

sed. sedan; sediment; sedimentation

S.E.D. skin erythema dose
SEE Signing Essential English
seg. segment
sel. select; selected; selection; selector
sem. one half [L *semi* or *semis*]; semble; semen; semicolon; semimobile; seminal; seminar; seminary
Sem. Semitic
SEM scanning electron microscope; scanning electron microscopy; shared equity mortgage
semih. half an hour [L *semihora*]
sem. ves. seminal vesicle
sen without [It *senza*]
sen. senate; senator; senior
sent. sentence
sentd. sentenced
sep. sepal; separate; separated; separation
Sep. September
SEP simplified employee pension
sepd. separated
sepg. separating
sepn. separation
Sept. September
seq. it follows [L *sequitur*]; sequel; sequence; the following [L *sequens* or *sequentes* or *sequentia*]

seqq. in the following places [L *sequentibus*]; the following ones [L *sequentes* or *sequentia*]
sequ. it follows [L *sequitur*]
ser. serial; series; sermon; serve; service; serving
Ser serine
Serb. Serbian
Serg. sergeant
Sergt. sergeant
Serj. serjeant
Serjt. serjeant
serv. preserve [L *serva*]; servant; service; services
servt. servant
SES Senior Executive Service; socioeconomic status
sesquih. an hour and a half [L *sesquihora*]
sess. session
SETI Search for Extraterrestrial Intelligence
sev. several
sevl. several
sewg. sewing
sf science fiction; sforzando; soft; surface foot
s.f. toward the end [L *sub finem*]
Sf sexagesimo-quarto
SF sacrifice fly;

semifinished; shipfitter;
signal-frequency; spot-
faced; square foot; Swiss
franc

S.F. San Francisco;
semifinals; senior fellow;
sinking fund

SFC sergeant first class

sfm surface feet per
minute

sfpm surface feet per
minute

sft. shaft; soft

sftwd. softwood

sfz sforzando

sg specific gravity

sg. signed; singular;
surgeon

SG screen grid; senior
grade; sergeant; solicitor
general; surgeon general

S.G. secretary-general

sgd. signed

sgg. signatures

sgl. single

SGO squadron gunnery
officer; surgeon general's
office

SGOT serum glutamic-
oxaloacetic transminase

SGPT serum glutamic
pyruvic transminase

Sgt. sergeant

Sgt.Maj. sergeant major

SGZ surface ground zero

sh. sash; shall; share;

sheep; sheet; shilling;
shipping; shipwright;
shock; shop; short;
shoulder; show; shower;
shunt

s/h shipping/handling

Sh shell

SH sacrifice hit; scrum
half; semester hour;
serum hepatitis; ship's
heading; shorthair; social
history; somatotrophic
hormone; Southern
Hemisphere

S.H. schoolhouse; specified
hours

SHA sidereal hour angle

Shak. Shakespeare

shd. should

Shet. Shetland

SHF superhigh frequency

shg. shipping

SHG shorthanded goals

ship. shipment; shipping

shipt. shipment

shl. shell; shoal

SHL Southern Hockey
League

shld. shield; shoulder

shlp. shiplap

shltr. shelter

shlw. shallow

S.H.M. simple harmonic
motion

SHO shutouts

shp shaft horsepower

shpg. shipping
shpmt. shipment
shpt. shipment
SHQ station headquarters
shr. share
sht. sheet
shtg. shortage
shthg. sheathing
s.h.v. under this word [L *sub hac voce* or *sub hoc verbo*]
shwr. shower
si. silent
s.i. short interest
Si silicon
SI International System of Units [F *Système International d'Unités*]; Smithsonian Institution
S.I. Sandwich Islands; Staten Island (N.Y.)
sib. sibling
s.i.c. specific inductive capacity
Sic. Sicily
SIC standard industrial classification
SID sports information director; sudden infant death; sudden ionospheric disturbance
SIDS sudden infant death syndrome
sig. label [L *signa*]; let it be labeled [L *signetur*]; signal; signaler; signalman; signature; signifying
Sig. signor
SIG special interest group
sigg. signatures
sigill. seal [L *sigillum*]
SIGINT signal intelligence
sil. silence; silver
sim. similar; simile
SIMS secondary ion mass spectrometry
sin sine
sin. left hand [L *sinistra*]
sing. of each [L *singulorum*]; single; singular
sinh hyperbolic sine [sine + hyperbolic]
SIOP strategic integrated operational plan
SIP standard inspection procedure; step in place
SIS Secret Intelligence Service; Special Intelligence Service
sist. sister
sit. situation
S.I.T. spontaneous ignition temperature; stopping in transit; storage in transit
SITES Smithsonian Institution Traveling Exhibition Service
SIW self-inflicted wound
s.j. under consideration [L

sub judice]

S.J. Society of Jesus

SJC Supreme Judicial Court

S.J.D. Doctor of Juridical Science [L *scientiae juridicae doctor*]

Sjt. serjeant

sk skip

sk. sack; sick; sink; sinking; sketch

Sk skewness

SK Saskatchewan; storekeeper

Skt. Sanskrit

sl. slate; slide; slightly; slip; slow

s.l. according to law [L *secundum legem*]; in its place [L *suo loco*]; salvage loss; without place [L *sine loco*]

SL sea level; searchlight; session laws; statute law; stock length

S.L. seditious libeler; sergeant-at-law; single line; solicitor-at-law; south latitude; squadron leader; sublieutenant

S-L sound locator

S/L streamline

SLA Special Libraries Association; Symbionese Liberation Army

s.l.a.n. without place, year, or name [L *sine loco, anno, vel nomine*]

S.L. & C. shipper's load and count

S.L. & T. shipper's load and tally

SLAR side-looking airborne radar

Slav. Slavic

SLBM submarine-launched ballistic missile

slc straight-line capacitance

S.L.C. Salt Lake City

SLCM submarine-launched cruise missile

sld. sailed; sealed; sold; solder

SLE systemic lupus erythematosus

slg. sailing

Slo. Sligo

s.l.p. without lawful issue [L *sine legitima prole*]

SLP super long play

SLR single lens reflex

slsmgr. sales manager

slsmn. salesman

slt. searchlight; sleet

slv. sleeve; solvent

slw straight-line wavelength

sly sloppy

sm service mark

sm. small

s.m. surface measure

Sm samarium

SM sergeant major; signalman; silver medal; soldier's medal; standard matched; streptomycin

S.M. left hand [L *sinistra mano*]; Master of Science [NL *scientiae magister*]; senior magistrate; short meter; Society of Mary; stage manager; state militia; station master; stipendiary magistrate; surgeon major

S-M sadomasochism; sadomasochist

SMA sergeant major of the army; shape memory alloy

S.Maj. sergeant major

SMATV satellite master antenna TV

sm. cap. small capitals

SMG submachine gun

smkd. smoked

smkls. smokeless

sml. small

smls. seamless

SMO senior medical officer; squadron medical officer

s.m.p. without male issue [L *sine mascula prole*]

smry. summary

SMSA standard metropolitan statistical area

S.M.Sgt. senior master sergeant

smstrs. seamstress

SMV slow-moving vehicle

sn. sanitary; sanitation; without [L *sine*]

s.n. naturally [L *secundum naturum*]; without name [L *sine nomine*]

s.-n. side note

Sn tin [LL *stannum*]

SN serial number

S/N shipping note; signal to noise; speech to noise ratio

SNA system network architecture

snafu situation normal, all fouled up; situation normal, all fucked up

SNAP Systems for Nuclear Auxiliary Power

SNC shergottites, nakhlites, chassignites

SNCC Student Nonviolent Coordinating Committee

snd. sound

s.n.d. sap no defect

S.N.D. static no delivery

SNF skilled nursing facility

S.N.F. solids not fat

SNG substitute natural gas; synthetic natural gas

SNH skilled nursing home

SNLR services no longer

required
SNO senior naval officer; senior navigation officer
SNP soluble nucleoprotein
snr. senior
SNR signal to noise ratio
SNU solar neutrino unit
snw. snow
so. south; southern
s.o. special order
SO seller's option; senior officer; sex offender; ship's option; shipping order; shop order; shutouts; staff officer; strikeouts; supply officer
S.O. standing order; suboffice
So. Afr. South Africa; South African
SOB shortness of breath
S.O.B. Senate Office Building; son of a bitch; souls on board
sobnd. southbound
soc. social; socialist; society; sociology; socket
sociol. sociologist; sociology
socy. society
sod. sodium
SOD seller's option to double
SOF sound on film
SOFAR sound fixing and ranging

sol. soldier; solenoid; solicitor; soluble; solution
Sol. Solomon
SOL shipowner's liability; shit out of luck
soln. solution
solr. solicitor
solut. dissolved [L *solutus*]
solv. dissolve [L *solve*]
soly. solubility
Som. Somersetshire
SOM serous otitis media
son. sonata; southern
Son. Sonora
sop. soprano
SOP senior officer present; standard operating procedure; standing operating procedure
soph. sophomore
S-O-R stimulus-organism-response
sos sostenuto
s.o.s. if occasion requires [L *si opus sit*]
SOS a recognized signal of distress; services of supply; silicon-on-sapphire
SOSUS Sound Surveillance System
sou. south; southern
sov. sovereign; soviet
SOV shut-off valve
SO_x sulfur oxide
sp. space; spare; special; specialist; species; specific;

specimen; speck; speech;
speed; spell; spelled;
spelling; spinal; spine;
spirit; sponge; spoon; sport

s.p. without issue [L *sine prole*]

Sp. Spain; Spanish

SP self-propelled;
semipostal; shore patrol;
shore patrolman; shore
police; short page;
smokeless powder;
specialist; standard play;
standpipe; static pressure;
submarine patrol;
subprofessional

S.P. single phase; single
pole; small packet; small
paper; small pica; soil
pipe; starting point;
starting price; stern post;
stirrup pump; stop
payment; stretcher party;
supraprotest

s.p.a. subject to particular
average

SPA special public
assistance

SPADATS Space
Detection and Tracking
System

Span. Spanish

SPAR Semper Paratus

SPCA serum prothrombin
conversion accelerator

S.P.C.A. Society for the
Prevention of Cruelty to
Animals

S.P.C.C. Society for the
Prevention of Cruelty to
Children

spd. speed; sprayed

s.p.d. steamer pays dues

SPD silicon photodiode;
Social Democratic Party of
Germany [Ger
*Sozialdemokratische
Partei Deutschlands*]

spdl. spindle

S.P.D.T. single pole,
double throw

SPE sucrose polyester

spec. special; specialist;
species; specific;
specifically; specification;
specimen; spectacle;
spectacular; spectrum;
speculation

specif. specific;
specifically; specification

SPF sun protection factor

SPFX special effects

spg. sponge; spring

sp gr specific gravity

sph. sphere; spherical

sp. ht. specific heat

spir. spiral

spk. speckled

spkl. sprinkle

spkr. speaker; sprinkler

spl. special

s.p.l. without legitimate

issue [L *sine prole legitima*]

splty. specialty

spm strokes per minute

s.p.m. without male issue [L *sine prole mascula*]

SPM self-propelled mount; smaller profit margin

S.P.M. short particular meter

spn. specimen

SPO sea post office

spon. spontaneous

SPOT satellite positioning and tracking

spp. species

SPQR the senate and the people of Rome [L *senatus populusque romanus*]

S.P.Q.R. small profits, quick returns

spr. spring

s.p.s. without surviving issue [L *sine prole superstite*]

SPS service propulsion system; solar power satellite

S.P.S.T. single pole, single throw

spt. seaport; spirit; support

sq. sequence; squadron; square; the following [L *sequens* or *sequentes* or *sequentia*]

Sq. squire

sqd. squad

sqdn. squadron

SQMS staff quartermaster sergeant

sqn. squadron

sqq. the following ones [L *sequentes* or *sequentia*]

sqr. square

squad. squadron

SQUID superconducting quantum interference device

sr self-rectifying; small ring; steradian

sr. seer

s.r. semantic reaction; short rate

Sr strontium

Sr. senior; señor; sir; sister; sister [L *soro*]

SR saturable reactor; seaman recuit; senate resolution; sensibility reciprocal; sound ranging; special regulation; star route; stateroom; subject ratio; supplementary regulation

S.R. sedimentation rate; shipping receipt; sigma reaction; socialist-revolutionary; storage room

S-R stimulus-response

S/R service record

Sra. señora

SRA sulfo-ricinoleic acid; supplemental retirement annuity

SRAM short-range attack missile

SR & CC strikes, riots, and civil commotions

S.R. & O. statutory rules and orders

srch. search

SRF Self-Realization Fellowship

Srita. señorita

SRM speed of relative movement; Standard Reference Materials

S.R.N. state registered nurse

sRNA transfer RNA [soluble RNA]

SRO single room occupancy; standing room only

SRS slow reacting substance

Srta. señorita

ss to wit [L *scilicet*]; without mutes [It *senza sordini*]

ss. authors [L *scriptores*]; one half [L *semis*]; sections

s.s. same size; soapsuds; stainless steel; sworn statement; written above [L *supra scriptum*]

SS screw steamer; secret service; Secretary of State; selective service; semisteel; set screw; shortstop; single sideband; social science; Social Security; social service; steamship; sterile solution; strong safety; suspended sentence

SS. most holy [L *sanctissimus*]; Saints

S.S. elite guard [Ger *Schutztaffel*]; Sabbath school; Sacred Scripture; shipside; side seam; simplified spelling; slop sink; special session; staff surgeon; steel sash; Sunday school

SSA Social Security Administration

SSAA Skate Sailing Association of America

SSAN Social Security account number

S.S. & C. supersized and calendered

SSAT Secondary School Admissions Test

SSB single sideband

S.S.C. solicitor before the supreme court

SSE south-southeast

SSG staff sergeant

S.Sgt. staff sergeant

SSI small-scale integration; Supplemental Security Income

S.S.L. Licentiate of Sacred Scriptures [L *sacrae scripturae licentiatus*]

SSM squadron sergeant major; staff sergeant major; surface-to-surface missile

SSN Social Security number

ssp subspecies

SSPE subacute sclerosing panencephalitis

SSR Soviet Socialist Republic

s.s.s. layer upon layer [L *stratum super stratum*]

SSS Selective Service System; strong soap solution

S.S.S. specific soluble substance

SST supersonic transport

SSU second, Saybolt universal

SSW south-southwest

st stere; stitch; without regard to time [It *senza tempo*]

st. stain; stamped; stand; stanza; start; starting line; state; statute; steam; steel; stem; stet; stimulus; stock; stone; stotinka; straight; strait; street; strophe; stumped

s.t. short ton; steam trawler

St stratus

St. saint

ST sounding tube; space telescope; standard time; standardized test

S.T. shipping ticket; single throw; static thrust; superintendent of transportation; surface tension

sta. station; stationary; stationer; stator; statute

Sta. saint [It *santa*]

stac staccato

stacc staccato

Staffs. Staffordshire

stan. stanchion; standard

staph. staphylococcus

START Strategic Arms Reduction Talks

stat. immediately [L *statim*]; static; stationary; statistic; statistical; statistician; statuary; statue; statute

statis. statistical

staty. stationary

S.T.B. Bachelor of Sacred Theology [L *sacrae theologiae baccalaureus*]; Bachelor of Theology [L *scientiae theologicae*

baccalaureus]
stbd. starboard
STC sensitivity-time control; Short-Title Catalogue; single-trip container
S.T.C. state teachers college
std. seated; standard; steward
STD sexually transmitted disease
S.T.D. Doctor of Sacred Theology [L *sacrae theologiae doctor*]
Ste. saint (female) [F *sainte*]
STEM scanning transmission electron microscope; scanning transmission electron microscopy
sten. stencil; stenographer; stenography
ster. sterilization; sterilizer; sterling
stev. stevedore
steve. stevedore
stf. staff; stiff
stg. staging; standing; sterling; storage
stge. storage
stgr. stringer
sth. south
STH somatotropic hormone

sthn. southern
stir. stirrup
stk stakes race
stk. sticky; stock; strake
stl. stall; steel; stile
STL studio transmitter link
S.T.L. Licentiate of Sacred Theology [NL *sacrae theologiae licentiatus*]
stlg. sterling
stm. storm
STM short-term memory
S.T.M. Master in Sacred Theology [L *sacrae theologiae magister*]
stmfr. steam fitter
stn. stainless; station
stnd. stained
sto. stoker; story
STO sea transport officer
STOL short takeoff and landing
stor. storage
STOVL short takeoff and vertical landing
stow. stowage
stp. stamp; stamped; stepping; stop; stopping
STP sewage treatment plant; standard temperature and pressure
stpd. stumped
STPP sodium tripolyphosphate
str. seater; steamer;

straight; strainer; strait;
stream; strength; stretch;
striking; string; stringed;
stroke; strophe; structural

STR submarine thermal
reactor

strd. strand

strep. streptococcus

string stringendo

strsph. stratosphere

struc. structure

struct. structure

STS serologic test for
syphillis; space
transportation system;
special treatment steel

stsm. statesman

stud. student

STV subscription
television

stwd. steward

stwy. stairway

SU service unit

S.U. sensation unit; set up;
Siemens's unit; Soviet
Union

sub. subaltern;
subcontractor;
sublieutenant; submerge;
submerged; subordinate;
subscriber; subsidiary;
subscription; subtract;
suburb; suburban; subway

SUB supplemental
unemployment benefits

subg. subgenus

subj. subject; subjective;
subjectively; subjunctive

subjv. subjunctive

subm. submarine;
submerge; submerged

subpar. subparagraph

sub-q subcutaneous

subs. subscription;
subsidiary; subsistence;
substantive; substitute

subsp. subspecies

subst. substantive;
substitute

substand. substandard

substd. substandard

suc. succeeded; successor;
suction

succ. succeeded; successor

S.U.C.L. set up in carloads

sucr. successor

suf. suffix

suff. sufficient; suffix

Suff. Suffolk

suffr. suffragan

sug. suggested; suggestion

sugg. suggested;
suggestion

S.U.L.C.L. set up in less
than carloads

sum. let him/her take [L
sumat]; take [L *sume*]; to
be taken [L *sumendum*]

Sun. Sunday

sund. sundries

sup superseded

sup. above [L *supra*];

superfine; superior;
superlative; supine;
supplement;
supplementary; supply;
support; supreme

supchgr. supercharger

super. superfine;
superheterodyne; superior

superl. superlative

supls. supplies

supp. supplement;
supplementary;
suppository

suppl. supplement;
supplementary

supr. supreme

Supr. superintendent

supsd. supersede

supt. superintendent;
support

supv. supervise

supvr. supervisor

sur. surcharged; surface;
surplus; surrendered

surg. surgeon; surgery;
surgical

surr. surrender;
surrendered; surrogate

surv. survey; surveying;
surveyor; surviving

susp. suspend

Suss. Sussex

sv saves

s.v. sailing vessel; spirit of
wine [L *spirit vini*]; under
the word [L *sub verbo* or

sub voce]

SV safety valve

S.V. sluice valve; stop
valve; Your Holiness [L
Sanctitas Vestra]

S/V surface vessel

svc. service

svce. service

svgs. savings

SVO subject-verb-object

SVP if you please [F *si'l
vous plaît*]

S.V.R. rectified spirit of
wine [L *spiritus vini
rectificatus*]

S.V.T. proof spirit of wine
[L *spiritus vini tenuis*]

svy. survey

sw. swatch; swell organ;
switch

s.w. sent wrong; specific
weight

s-w shortwave

Sw. Sweden; Swedish

SW salt water; seawater;
social work; southwest;
southwestern; station
wagon; stock width

S.W. senior warden;
shelter warden; shipper's
weight

S.W.A. South-West Africa

S. W. Af. South-West
Africa

SWAK sealed with a kiss

SWALK sealed with a

loving kiss
SWAPO South-West African People's Organization
SWAT Special Weapons and Tactics
Swazil. Swaziland
SWB short wheelbase
swbd. switchboard
SWC Southwest Conference
swchmn. switchman
swd sideward
swd. sewed
SWD sliding watertight door
Swed. Sweden; Swedish
swg. switching
S.W.G. standard wire gauge
S.W.I.F.T. Society of Worldwide Interbank Financial Telecommunication
Switz. Switzerland
s.w.l. sulfite waste liquor
SWP safe working pressure; Socialist Workers Party
SWR serum Wassermann reaction; standing wave ratio
swtg. switching
SWU separative work unit
sx simplex
sx. sacks

Sx symptoms
sxn. section
sy syrup
sy. sloppy; sticky; supply
SY square yard
S.Y. steam yacht
syl. syllable
syll. syllable
sym. symbol; symbolic; symmetrical; symphony
symph. symphony
syn. synchronize; synchronized; synchronizing; synergist; synonym; synonymous; synonymy; synthetic
sync. synchronism; synchronization; synchronize; synchronizing; synchronous
synch. synchronize; synchronized; synchronizing
synd. syndicate
synscp. synchroscope
SYNTOL Syntagmatic Organization Language
syr. syrup
Syr. Syria; Syrian
sys. system
SYSOP systems operator
syst. system
sz. size

T

t be silent [It *tace*]; tera; tertiary; thickness; troy; tutti

t. in the time of [L *tempore*]; table; taken; taper; tare; target; teaspoon; telephone; tempo; temporal; tense; terminal; tesla; times; ton; tooth; top; transit; transitive; trillo; trotter; tun; volume [L *tomus*]

T absolute temperature; octodecimo; tablespoon; tackle; teletype; temperature; tension; termination; thoracic; tied; time; total; trace; transformer; transverse; triple; tritium; tropical; true

T. territorial; territory; testament; thief; thread; Thursday; toe; town; township; tread; triangle; Trinity [LL *Trinitas*]; Tuesday; Turkish

t.a. let the acts show [L *testantibus actis*]

Ta tantalum

TA target area; teaching assistant; transactional analysis; transit authority

T.A. tax agent; technical analysis; telegraphic address; territorial army; traffic agent; traffic auditor

T/A table of allowances

tab. table; tablet; tabulate; tabulated

TABA The American Book Awards

TAC Tactical Air Command; The Athletics Congress

TACV tracked air-cushion vehicle

TAF tactical air force; tumor angiogenesis factor

TAG The Adjutant General

Tai. Taiwan

TAI International Atomic Time [F *Temps Atomique International*]

tan. tangent

T & A tits and ass

T and A tonsillectomy and adenoidectomy; tonsillitis and adenoiditis; tonsils and adenoids

T & E test and evaluation; travel and entertainment

T & G tongue and groove; tongued and grooved

t. & o. taken and offered

Tang. Tanganyika

TAP Trans-Alaska
Pipeline
Tas. Tasmania
TAS true air speed
Tasm. Tasmania
TAT thematic
apperception test; toxin-
antitoxin; true air
temperature
taut. tautological;
tautology
t.a.w. twice a week
taxon. taxonomic;
taxonomy
Tay. Tayside
tb. tablespoon;
tablespoonful
Tb terbium
TB technical bulletin;
thoroughbred; thymol
blue; times at bat; torpedo
boat; torpedo bomber;
torpedo bombing; total
bases; total bouts;
treasury bill; true
bearing; tubercle bacillus;
tuberculosis
T.B. tariff bureau;
telegraph bureau; time
base; traffic bureau
T/B trial balance
TBA to be announced; to
be assigned
TB & S top, bottom, and
sides
T.B.B. tenor, baritone, bass

TBG thyroid binding
globulin; thyroxine
binding globulin
T.B.L. through bill of
lading
T.B.M. temporary bench
mark
TBP true boiling point
tbs. tablespoon;
tablespoonful
TBS talk between ships;
tribromosalicylanilide
tbsp. tablespoon;
tablespoonful
TBT tax-benefit transfer
tc tierce
Tc technetium
TC tank corps; terra-cotta;
total chances; track
commander; true course;
turf course
T.C. teachers college;
technical college; town
clerk; town councillor;
traffic commissioner;
traffic consultant
T/C till countermanded
TCA trichloroacetic acid
TCAM
telecommunications access
method
TCB take care of business
TCC triclocarbon
TCDD dioxin
[trachlorodibenzo-*p*-dioxin]
TCE tetrachloroethylene;

tons of coal equivalent; trichloroethylene

tcf trillion cubic feet

tchg. teaching

tchr. teacher

TCID terminal computer identification

TCP tape conversion program; trichlorophenol; tricresyl phosphate

TCS terminal control system

TD tank destroyer; tardive dyskinesia; technical director; telegraph department; telephone department; temporary disability; temporary duty; territorial decoration; time deposit; touchdown; tracking dog; tractor-drawn; treasury decision; Treasury Department; Trinidad and Tobago

T.D. Member of Parliament [IrGael *Teachta Dala*]; traffic director

TDA tax deferred annuity

TDB Barycentric Dynamical Time [F *Temps Dynamique Barycentrique*]

TDDS television data display system

TDI temporary disability

insurance

TDIS Travel Document and Issuance System

tdm time division multiplexing

TDN total digestible nutrients

TDOS tape disk operating system

TDR time-domain reflectometry; transmit data register

t.d.s. to be taken three times a day [L *ter die sumendum*]

TDS time, distance, speed

TDT Terrestrial Dynamic Time

TDY temporary duty

Te tellurian; tetanus

TE tight end; trailing edge

T.E. topographical engineer

T/E table of equipment

TEA transversely excited atmospheric

tec. technical; technician; technology

tech. technical; technically; technician; technological; technology

technol. technological; technology

TEFL teaching English as a foreign language

t.e.g. top edges gilt

tel. telegram; telegraph; telegraphic; telegraphy; telephone; telephony
TEL tetraethyl lead
teleg. telegraphy
TEM transmission electron microscope; transmission electron microscopy
temp. in the time of [L *tempore*]; temperance; temperature; template; temporal; temporary
ten tenuto
ten. tenor
Tenn. Tennessee
TENS transcutaneous electrical nerve stimulation
TEPA triethyl-enephosphoramide
TEPP tetraethyl pyrophosphate
ter. terrace; terrazzo; territory; tertiary
term. terminal; termination
terr. territory
tert. tertiary
TESL teaching English as a second language
TESOL teachers of English to speakers of other languages
Test. Testament
TeV trillion electron volt

Tex. Texas
TF task force; teaching fellow
T.F. territorial force; till forbidden; to fill; to follow
TFE tetrafluoroethylene
TFN till further notice
tfr. transfer
TFX tactical fighter, experimental
tg. telegram; telegraph
t.g. type genus
TG task group; tollgate; transformational-generative; transformational grammar; tying goals
T.G.B. tongued, grooved, and beaded
TGC travel group charter
TGIF thank God it's Friday
tgt. target
th. threshold
Th thorium
Th. Thursday
TH thoroughbred; true heading
T.H. two hands
Thai. Thailand
Thail. Thailand
Th.B. Bachelor of Theology [L *theologiae baccalaureus*]
THC tetrahydrocannabinol
thd. thread; thunderhead

Th.D. Doctor of Theology [NL *theologiae doctor*]

THD total harmonic distortion

thdr. thunder

theat. theater; theatrical

theol. theologian; theological; theology

therm. thermometer

Thess. Thessalonians

THI temperature-humidity index; time handed in

Th.M. Master of Theology [NL *theologaie magister*]

thou. thousand

thp thrust horsepower

thr. their; there; through

3b third base; triple [3-base hit]

3-D three-dimensional

Thu. Thursday

Thur. Thursday

Thurs. Thursday

Ti titanium

TIA transient ischemic attack

t.i.d. three times a day [L *ter in die*]

T.I.H. Their Imperial Highnesses

Tim. Timothy

TIN taxpayer identification number

tinct. tincture

Tip. Tipperary

TIROS television and infrared observation satellite

tit. title; titular

Tit. Titus

tix ticket

tk. tank; truck

TKO technical knockout

tkt. ticket

t.l. total loss

Tl thallium

TL Texas League; thermoluminescence; throws left-handed; thrust line; tie line; trade-last; tubal ligation

T.L. truckload

T/L time loan

TLC tender loving care; thin-layer chromatography

TLD thermoluminescence dosimeter; thermoluminescence dosimetry

TLI total lymphoid irradiation

t.l.o. total loss only

tlr. tailor; trailer

TLR twin lens reflex

TLS typed letter signed

TLV threshold-limit value

tm true mean

Tm thulium

TM technical manual; technical memorandum; trademark; training

manual; Transcendental
Meditation

T.M. traffic manager;
trainmaster; trench
mortar

T/M tons per minute

TMG track made good

TMH tons per man-hour

TMJ temporomandibular
joint

tmkpr. timekeeper

TML three mile limit

T.M.O. telegraph money
order

tmp. temperature

TMV tobacco mosaic virus

tn. ton; town; train

TN telephone number;
Tennessee; thermonuclear;
true north

T.N. tariff number

TNF theater nuclear forces

tng. training

tnge. tonnage

tnpk. turnpike

TNT trinitrotoluene

TO table of organization;
technical order; tincture of
opium; transport officer

T.O. telegraph office;
telephone office;
traditional orthography;
turn over

TOA time of arrival

Tob. Tobit

TOEFL Test of English as
a Foreign Language

TOF time-of-flight

tol. tolerance

tonn. tonnage

TOP temporarily out of
print

topo. topographic;
topographical

topog. topography

tor. torpedo

TOS tape operating
system

tot. total

TOT time on target; tip of
the tongue

TOW tube-launched,
optically-tracked, wire-
guided

tox. toxicology

tp telephone

tp. township; troop

t.p. title page

TP target practice;
teaching practice;
technical paper;
teleprinter; teleprocessing;
total points; touchdowns
passing; transport pilot;
treaty port; triple play

T.P. at Easter time [L
tempore Paschale]

TPC thromboplastic
plasma component

tpd tons per day

tph tons per hour

tpi teeth per inch; threads

per inch; tons per inch;
tracks per inch; turns per
inch

tpk. turnpike

tpke. turnpike

t.p.m. title page mutilated

TPM total particulate
matter; trigger-price
mechanism

TPN triphosphopyridine
nucleotide

T.P.O. traveling post office

TPP thiamine
pyrophosphate

TPR teleprinter;
temperature, pulse,
respiration

tps tracks per second

tps. townships; troops

t.p.w. title page wanting

tpy tons per year

TQ three-quarter midget

TQM transport
quartermaster

tr treble

tr. tare; tincture; trace;
traced; track; trailer;
train; transaction;
transfer; transferred;
transit; transitive;
translated; translation;
translator; transom;
transport; transportation;
transpose; travel; tray;
tread; treasurer; trill;
troop; truss; trust; trustee

TR tape recorder;
technical regulation;
technical report; technical
representative; throws
right-handed; touchdowns
running; training
regulation; transmit-
receive

T.R. in the time of Kings
[L *tempore regis*]; tariff
reform; tons registered

T/R trust receipt

TRA Thoroughbred Racing
Association

trac. tractor

trad. tradition; traditional

traf. traffic

trag. tragedy; tragic

trans. transaction;
transfer; transferred;
transformer; transit;
transitional; transitive;
translated; translation;
translator; transmission;
transmitter; transparent;
transport; transportation;
transpose; transverse

transf. transfer;
transferred

transl. translated;
translation

transp. transparent;
transportation

transv. transverse

TRASOP Tax Reduction
Act Stock Ownership Plan

trav. travel; traveler

treas. treasurer; treasury

treasr. treasurer

trem. tremolo

tres. trestle

trf. tariff; transfer

TRF thyrotropin releasing factor; tuned radio frequency

trg. training

TRH thyrotropin releasing hormone

T.R.H. Their Royal Highnesses

trib. tribal; tribunal; tribune; tributary

trig. trigonometric; trigonometrical; trigonometry

Trin. Trinidad

trip. triple; triplicate

tripl. triplicate

trit. triturate

trk. track; truck; trunk

TRL Trail

trm. terminal

trml. terminal

tRNA transfer RNA

trop. tropic; tropical

trp. troop; tropical

TRPB Thoroughbred Racing Protective Bureau

trs. transfer; transpose

tru. trustee

trv. traverse

ts tensile strength

ts. teaspoon; teaspoonful

t.s. tub-sized

TS test solution; tool steel; topic statement; tough situation; transport and supply; transverse section; typescript

t-s time-sharing

TSD time, speed, and distance

T.Sgt. technical sergeant

TSH thyroid-stimulating hormone

T.S.H. Their Serene Highnesses

TSO time-sharing option

tsp. teaspoon; teaspoonful

TSP trisodium phosphate

tspn. teaspoon; teaspoonful

tspt. transport

T.S.R. traveling stock reserve

TSS toxic shock syndrome

T.S.S. twin-screw steamer

TSWE Test of Standard Written English

TT tablet triturate; teletype; teletypewriter; Tourist Trophy; tuberculin tested

T.T. teetotaler; telegraphic transfer; Trust Territories

TTL to take leave; transistor-transistor logic

T.T.P.I. Trust Territory of the Pacific Islands

TTS teletypesetter
TTY teletypewriter
Tu. Tuesday
TU toxic unit; tuition unit
T.U. thermal unit; trade union; traffic unit; transmission unit
TUC Trades Union Congress
Tue. Tuesday
Tues. Tuesday
Tun. Tunisia
turbt. turbulent
Turk. Turkey; Turkish
TV television; terminal velocity; transvestite
TVA tax value added [F *taxe sur la valeur ajoutée*]; Tennessee Valley Authority
TVI television interference
Tvl. Transvaal
TVP textured vegetable protein
tw terawatt
tw. twisted
Tw Twaddell (hydrometer)
twi. twilight
TWIMC to whom it may concern
2b double [2-base hit]; second base
2-D two-dimensional
2WD two-wheel drive
twp. township
twr. tower

TWS Test of Written Spelling
TWX teletypewriter exchange
tx. tax
TX Texas
txn. taxation
ty. territory; truly; type
typ. typical; typographer; typographic; typographical
Tyr. Tyrone

U

u eased up; unsymmetrical
u. and [Ger *und*]; under; unified; uniform; union; unit; united; universal; unpleasant; upper
U intrinsic energy; kosher certification [Union of Orthodox Hebrew Congregations]; uncirculated; unsatisfactory; upgraded; upper class; uranium; urology
U. uncle; unionist; university
UA ultra-audible; unauthorized absence
U/A underwriting account
UAE United Arab Emirates

UAM underwater-to-air missile

U. & O. use and occupancy

UAR United Arab Republic

UART Universal Asynchronous Receiver Transmitter

UAW United Automobile, Aerospace and Agricultural Implements Workers of America

u.b. under bark

UBV ultraviolet-blue-visual

u.c. uppercase

UC under construction; utility cargo

U/C undercarriage; undercharge

UCR usual, customary, or reasonable

Ucs unconscious

u.d. as directed [L *ut dictum*]

U.D. upper deck; urban district; utility dog

UDAG Urban Development Action Grant

UDC Universal Decimal Classification

U.D.C. urban district council

U.D.I. Unilateral Declaration of Independence

UDP uridine diphosphate

UDPG uridine diphosphate glucose

UDT underdeck tonnage; underwater demolition team

U.E. university extension

UFCT United Federation of College Teachers

UFD user file directory

UFO unidentified flying object

UFT United Federation of Teachers

UFW United Farm Workers

ugt. urgent

UH upper half

UHF ultrahigh frequency

UHT ultrahigh temperature

uhv ultrahigh vacuum

u.i. as below [L *ut infra*]

UI unemployment insurance

U/I unidentified

UIS Unemployment Insurance Service

UK United Kingdom

UL Underwriters Laboratories; upper left

ULC upper left center

ULCC ultra-large crude carrier

ULF ultralow frequency

ULMS underwater long-range missile system

ULSI ultra-large-scale-integrated

ult. ultimate; ultimately; ultimo

ULV ultralow-volume

um. unmarried

umb. umbilicus

Umbr. Umbrian

UMF ultramicrofiche

UMS universal military service

UMT universal military training

UMW United Mine Workers

un. unified; unifying; union; unit; united; university

UN United Nations

unan. unanimous

unb. unbound

unc. uncertain; uncirculated; uncut

UNCF United Negro College Fund

uncor. uncorrected

unct. uncut

undetd. undetermined

undsdg. undersigned

undtkr. undertaker

UNESCO United Nations Educational, Scientific, and Cultural Organization

ung. ointment [L *unguentum*]

Unh unnilhexium

UNICEF United Nations Children's Fund [United Nations International Children's Emergency Fund]

univ. universal; universally; universe; university

UNIVAC Universal Automatic Computer

unk. unknown

unkn. unknown

unl. unlimited

unm. unmarried

unop. unopened; unopposed

unp. unpaged

Unp unnilpentium

Unq unnilquadium

UNRWA United Nations Relief and Works Agency

uns. unsymmetrical

UNSC United Nations Security Council

unsgd. unsigned

unstdy. unsteady

unsym. unsymmetrical

unwmkd. unwatermarked

up. upper

UP underproof; Upper Peninsula (Mich.)

U.P. United Presbyterian

UPC Universal Product Code

uphlstg. upholstering
uphol. upholsterer;
   upholstering; upholstery
UPI United Press
   International
UPS ultraviolet
   photoemission
   spectroscopy;
   uninterruptible power
   system; United Parcel
   Service
UPU Universal Postal
   Union
ur. urinal; urine
Ur. Uruguay
UR unsatisfactory report;
   upper right
U.R. uniform regulations
URC upper right center
URD underground
   residential distribution;
   upper respiratory disease
URI upper respiratory
   infection
urol. urological; urologist;
   urology
Uru. Uruguay
u.s. as above [L *ut supra*];
   where above mentioned [L
   ubi supra]
US unconditioned
   stimulus; United States
U.S. undersecretary;
   united service
u/s unserviceable
USA United States Army;
   United States of America
USAAF United States
   Amateur Athletic
   Federation
USAC United States Auto
   Club
USAF United States Air
   Force
USAN United States
   Adopted Name
USASI United States of
   America Standards
   Institute
USB upper sideband
USC under separate cover
U.S.C. United States Code
USCC United States
   Catholic Conference
USCG United States Coast
   Guard
USCSC United States
   Collegiate Sports Council
USD United States
   Dispensatory
USDA United States
   Department of
   Agriculture
USES United States
   Employment Service
USGA United States Golf
   Association
USGS United States
   Geological Survey
USHL United States
   Hockey League
USIA United States

Information Agency
USIS United States
Information Service
USLTA United States
Lawn Tennis Association
USM underwater-to-
surface missile; United
States mail; United States
Marines
USMA United States
Military Academy
USMC United States
Marine Corps
USN United States Navy
USNA United States
Naval Academy
USNG United States
National Guard
USNR United States
Naval Reserve
USNS United States Navy
ship
USO United Service
Organizations
USOA United States
Olympic Association
USOC United States
Olympic Committee
USP unique selling
proposition; United States
Pharmacopeia
USPHS United States
Public Health Service
USPLTA United States
Professional Lawn Tennis
Association

USPO United States
Patent Office
USPS United States
Postal Service
USS United States ship;
United States standard
USSR Union of Soviet
Socialist Republics
USTA United States
Tennis Association;
United States Trademark
Association
USTFF United States
Track and Field
Federation
usu. usual; usually
u.s.w. and so forth [Ger
und so weiter]
USW ultrashort wave
USWF United States
Wrestling Federation
ut. utility
UT Universal time; Utah;
utility player
UTC Coordinated
Universal Time
ut dict. as directed [L *ut
dictum*]
UTI urinary tract infection
util. utility
UTM Universal
Transverse Mercator
UTP uridine triphosphate
UTS ultimate tensile
strength
UV ultraviolet

UV-A ultraviolet-long wave
UV-B ultraviolet-shortwave
UVICON ultraviolet image converter
UVM universal vendor marking
u/w underwater
U/w underwriter
UW underwater
ux. wife [L *uxor*]
UXB unexploded bomb

V

v velocity
v. turn [It *volti*]; turn over [L *verte*]; value; valve; van; vein; ventral; verb; verse; version; verso; versus; vertical; very; vicar; vide; village; violin; viscosity; vision; vocative; von; vowel
V electric potential; frequency; potential difference; vanadium; vector; versicle; vertex; vicinal; victory; virulence; visibility; visual acuity; volt; voltage; voltmeter; volume; volunteer
V. vacuum tube; vagabond

V vapor; variable
V. variation; venerable; vent; ventilator; virgin; viscount; voice
va volt-ampere
va. viola
v.a. he/she lived (a given number of) years [L *vixlt annas*]; verb active; verbal adjective
Va variance; visual acuity
Va. Virginia
VA Veterans Administration; vice admiral; Virginia; visual aid
V.A. vicar apostolic
V-A ventriculo-atrial
vac. vacant; vacation; vacuum
vacc. vaccination
VAD ventricular assist device
V.A.D. voluntary aid detachment
V.Adm. vice admiral
VADM vice admiral
val. valentine; valley; valuation; value; valued
valn. valuation
VAN value-added network; value-added networking
V. and M. virgin and martyr
V. and T. volume and

tension

var volt ampere reactive

var. variable; variant; variation; variegated; variety; variometer; various

VAR visual-aural radio range

var. lect. variant reading [L *varia lectio*]

VASCAR Visual Average Speed Computer and Recorder

VASSS Van Alen Simplified Scoring System

Vat. Vatican

VAT value-added tax

vb. verb; verbal

VB valve box; vertical beam

V.B. volunteer battalion

VBE vernacular black English

VBI vertical blanking interval

vbl. verbal

vc. violoncello

Vc vinylidene chloride

VC color vision [vision color]; valuation clause; veterinary corps; vice-chairman; vice-chancellor; vice-consul; Victoria Cross; Vietcong

V.C. valuable cargo; vigilance committee;

visible capacity; volunteer corps

VCM vinyl chloride monomer

VCR videocassette recorder

vct. victor

v.d. vapor density; various dates

VD veneral disease

VDA visual discriminatory acuity

VDH valvular disease of the heart

VDM vasodepressor material

VDRL venereal disease research laboratory

VDT video display terminal

VDU visual display unit

VE value engineer; vesicular exanthema

VEE Venezuelan equine encephalomyelitis

veg. vegetable

vel. vellum; velocity

vel sim. or similar [L *vel similis*]

VEM vasoexcitor material

Ven. venerable; Venezuela

vent. ventilate; ventilating; ventilation; ventilator

ver. verse; version; vertex

verb. sap. a word to the

wise is sufficient [L *verbum sapienti sat est*]

vers versed sine

vert. vertebra; vertebrate; vertical

ves. bladder [L *vesica*]; vesicular; vessel; vestry

vesic. blister [L *vesicula*]

vest. vestibule

vet. veterinarian; veterinary

v.f. very fair

VF vertical file; very fine; video frequency; vocal fremitus; voice frequency

V.F. vicar forane; visual field

VFD volunteer fire department

VFO variable frequency oscillator

VFR visual flight rules

VFW Veterans of Foreign Wars

v.g. for example [L *verbi gratia*]

VG very good

V.G. vertical grain; vicar-general

V.H.C. very highly commended

VHD video high density

VHF very high frequency

VHP very high performance

VHS video home system

VHSIC very high speed integrated circuit

v.i. see below [L *vide infra*]; verb intransitive

Vi virulent

V.I. Vancouver Island; vertical interval; Virgin Islands; viscosity index; volume indicator

vib. vibrate; vibration

vic. vicar; vicarage; vicinity

Vic. Victoria

vid. see [L *vide*]; video; widow [L *vidua*]

vil. village

vill. village

VIN vehicle identification number

viol. purple [L *violaceus*]

VIP vasoactive intestinal peptide; vasoactive intestinal polypeptide; very important person

vir. green [L *viridis*]

virg. virgin [L *virgo*]

vis. viscosity; visibility; visible; visiting; visual

Vis. viscount; viscountess

visc. viscosity

Visc. viscount; viscountess

VISTA Volunteers in Service to America

vit. vitamin; vitreous; vitrified

vitel. vitellus

viv vivace
viz. videlicet
VJ video jockey
vl. violin
v.l. variant reading [L *varia lectio*]
VL Vulgar Latin
vla. viola
VLA very large array; very low altitude
VLB very long baseline
VLBA very long baseline array
VLBI very long baseline interferometer; very long baseline interferometry
VLCC very large crude carrier
VLDL very low density lipoprotein
VLF very low frequency
Vlg village
VLH very lightly hinged
VLOL violating local option law
VLR very long range
VLSI very large scale integration
Vly valley
vm. voltmeter
v/m volts per meter
V.M.D. Doctor of Veterinary Medicine
Vmg velocity made good
VMT very many thanks
vn. violin

v.n. verb neuter
VNA Visiting Nurse Association
vo. verso
Vo vocalic
VO verbal order
V.O. very old
VOA Voice of America
voc. vocational; vocative
vocab. vocabulary
vol. volar; volcanic; volcano; volume; volumetric; voluntary; volunteer
VOLAR volunteer army
volc. volcanic; volcano
VOM volt ohm milliammeter
v.o.p. valued as in original policy
VOR very-high-frequency omnidirectional radio range
vou. voucher
VOX voice-actuated transmitter; voice operated transmitter
v.p. vapor pressure; various pagings; various places; verb passive; voting pool
VP variable pitch; verb phrase; vest pocket; vice president
V.P. vulnerable point
vpm volts per mil

V.P.M. vibrations per minute

V.P.P. value payable by post

v.p.s. vibrations per second

vr vulcanized rubber

v.r. variant reading; verb reflexive

VR vocal resonance; voltage regulator; voltage relay

V.R. vicar rural

vrbl. variable

vrg. veering

VRM variable rate mortgage

vs. verse; versus

v.s. see above [L *vide supra*]; turn quickly [It *volti subito*]; vibration seconds

VS visual signaling

V.S. vertical stripes; very superior; visible supply; volumetric solution

vsb. visible

vsby. visibility

V.S.E.P. very superior extra pale — used of brandy

VSF voice store and forward

vsn. vision

vso. verso

V.S.O. very superior old —

used of brandy

V.S.O.P. very superior old pale — used of brandy

vss. verses; versions

V/STOL vertical short takeoff and landing

vsw very shortwave

vt. voting

v.t. verb transitive

Vt. Vermont

VT vacuum tube; variable time; Vermont; voice tube

V.T.C. voting trust certificate; voting trust company

VTF vertical tracking force

VTO vertical takeoff

VTOC volume table of contents

VTOL vertical takeoff and landing

VTR video tape recorder; video tape recording

VTVM vacuum tube voltmeter

VU volume unit

Vulg. Vulgate

VUV vacuum ultraviolet

vv. verbs; verses; violins; volumes

v.v. vice versa

VV. venerables [L *venerabiles*]

vv. ll. variant readings [L *variae lectiones*]

V.V.O. very, very old —
used of brandy
V.V.S. very, very superior
— used of brandy
V.V.S.O.P. very, very
superior old pale — used
of brandy
V.W. very worshipful;
vessel wall
vy. very
v.y. various years

W

w base on balls [walk];
warm; watt; wins
w. wall; wanting; war;
warden; warehouse;
warehousing; waste;
water; weather; week;
weight; west; western;
wet; whip; white; wicket;
wide; widow; width; wife;
wind; wire; with; within;
wood; word; wrong
W energy; tungsten [Ger
Wolfram]; west; western;
withdrawal; won; work
W. Wednesday; Welsh
WA Washington
W.A. warm air; Western
Australia; with average
WAAC Women's Army
Auxiliary Corps

WAAF Women's Auxiliary
Air Force
WAC Women's Army
Corps
WADS Wide Area Data
Service
WAE when actually
employed
w.a.f. with all faults
WAF Women in the Air
Force
wag. wagon; wagoner
WAIS Wechsler Adult
Intelligence Scale
wal. walnut
w.a.l. wider all lengths
wam words a minute
WAN wide area network
W. & F. water and feed
W. & I. weighing and
inspection
W & R welfare and
recreation
W. & R. water and rail
W. & S. whiskey and soda
war. warrant
Warks. Warwickshire
warrtd. warranted
Wash. Washington
WASP White Anglo-Saxon
Protestant; Women's Air
Force Service Pilots
Wat. Waterford
WATS Wide-Area
Telecommunications
Service

W. Aust. Western Australia

WAVES Women Accepted for Volunteer Emergency Service

w.b. warehouse book; water ballast

Wb weber

WB wallboard; weather bureau; westbound; wet bulb; wheelbase

W.B. water board

W/B waybill

WBA World Boxing Association

WBC white blood cells; white blood count; World Boxing Council

WBF wood-burning fireplace

WBFP wood-burning fireplace

w.b.s. without benefit of salvage

wc wheelchair

w.c. water closet; without charge

WC will call; working capital

W.C. wood casing

WCT World Championship Tennis

WCTU Women's Christian Temperance Union

wd when distributed

wd. wind; window; wood; word; would; wound

WD war damage; War Department; wind direction

W.D. works department

wdg. winding; wording

wdr. wider

wdt. width

Wed. Wednesday

w.e.f. with effect from

Westm. Westmeath

Wex. Wexford

Westm Westmeath

Wex. Wexford

wf wrong font

WF wind force; wing forward; withdrawn failing

W.F. water finish; White Fathers

WFTU World Federation of Trade Unions

wg wing

w.g. weight guaranteed

W.G. West Germany; wire gauge

wgt. weight

wh watt-hour

wh. which; white

WH water heater

WHA World Hockey Association

whf. wharf

whfg. wharfage

whge. wharfage

whl. wheel

whm. weighmaster

whnsg. warehousing

WHO World Health Organization

whol. wholesale

whp water horsepower

whr watt-hour

whr. whether

whs. warehouse

whse. warehouse

whsle. wholesale

whsmn. warehouseman

wht. white

whvs. wharves

wi when issued

WI Wisconsin

W.I. West Indies; wrought iron

WIA wounded in action

WIC Women in Construction

Wick. Wicklow

wid. widow; widower

Wilts. Wiltshire

WIMC whom it may concern

WIN Work Incentive Program

Wis. Wisconsin

Wisc. Wisconsin

Wisd. Wisdom

wk. week; work

wkg. working

wkly. weekly

wkr. worker; wrecker

WL wavelength

W.L. waterline

wldr. welder

wm wattmeter

W.M. white metal

w/m watermark

W/M weight or measurement

wmk. watermark

wmkd. watermarked

wn. winch

wnd. wind

wng. warning

W.N.P. wire nonpayment

WNW west-northwest

w/o without

WO walkover; war office; warrant officer

W/O water-in-oil

W.O. wait order; wireless operator

w.o.b. washed overboard

WOC without compensation

W.O.G. with other goods

WOJG warrant officer junior grade

W.O.L. wharf owner's liability

WoO work without opus (number)

Wor. Worshipful

wp wild pitch

wp. waterproof; waterproofing

w.p. without prejudice

WP wastepaper;

weatherproof; wettable powder; white phosphorus; wild pitch; winning pitcher; withdrawn passing; word processing; word processor; working pressure

W.P. water packed; weather permitting; wire payment; working point

w.p.a. with particular average

WPA Works Progress Administration

wpc watts per candle

Wpfl. Worshipful

WPI wholesale price index

wpm words per minute

wpn. weapon

w.p.p. waterproof paper packing

wr. wreath; writing paper

w.r. war risk; with rights

Wr Wassermann reaction

WR wardroom; warehouse receipt; washroom

WRAC Women's Royal Army Corps

WRAF Women's Royal Air Force

wrfg. wharfage

W.R.I. war risk insurance

wrm. wardroom

WRNS Women's Royal Naval Service

wrnt. warrant

w.r.o. war risks only

wrps. wrappings

wrt. wrought

ws water-soluble; wetted surface

WS water supply; weather stripping; wingspread

W.S. weather station; writer to the signet

WSW west-southwest

wt. warrant; weight; without

w.t. with title

WT wartime; water tank; water tender

W.T. war tax; watertight

W/T wireless telegraphy; wireless telephony

wth. width

wthr. weather

wtr. waiter; winter; writer

Wtr waters

WV West Virginia

w/v weight/volume

W/V wind/vector; wind/velocity

W. Va. West Virginia

W.V.S. Women's Voluntary Services

WVTR water vapor transmission rate

w/w wall-to-wall

ww with warrants

WW water-white; waterworks; world war

W/W warehouse warrant

w.w.a. with the will annexed
WY Wyoming
Wyo. Wyoming

X

x abscissa; by; cross; crossed with; ex; extra; times
X admission limited to adults — used of a movie rating; experimental; power of magnification; reactance
x-c ex coupon
X-C cross-country
x-d ex dividend
x div. ex dividend
Xe xenon
XF extra fine
xg. crossing
x-i ex interest
x in. ex interest
Xing crossing
x int. ex interest
xl crystal; extra large
XL extra large; extra long
xlnt. excellent
Xn. Christian
x-n ex new
Xnty. Christianity
XO executive officer
XP Christ [fr. Gk XP, abbreviation for ΧΡΙΣΤΟΣ Christ]; extra person
XPS x-ray photoemission spectroscopy
x pt extra points
XQ cross-question
XR extended reponse
x-r ex rights
XRD x-ray diffraction
Xrds Cross Roads
xs extra small
XS extra small
Xt. Christ
xtal crystal
Xtian. Christian
xtry. extraordinary
Xty. Christianity
x.u. x unit
XUV extreme ultraviolet
xw ex warrant
XXL extra, extra large

Y

y ordinate
y. yard; year; yellow; yen; young; younger; youngest; your
Y admittance; yeoman; YMCA; yttrium
YA young adult
YAG yttrium aluminum garnet
YAVIS young, attractive,

verbal, intelligent, and
  successful
Yb ytterbium
Y.B. yearbook
YBP years before present
YC yacht club
yd. yard
yday. yesterday
ydg. yarding
yds. yards
y.e. yellow edges
yel. yellow
yeo. yeoman; yeomanry
yeom. yeomanry
yest. yesterday
yesty. yesterday
YH youth hostel
YHS Jesus [part
  transliteration of Gk IHΣ,
  abbreviation for IHΣOYΣ
  Jesus]
YHVH Yahweh
  [transliteration of the
  Hebrew]
YHWH Yahweh
  [transliteration of the
  Hebrew]
YIG yttrium iron garnet
yl. yellow
YL young lady
yld. yield
YMCA Young Men's
  Christian Association
YMHA Young Men's
  Hebrew Association
yo yarn over

YO year-old
YOB year of birth
Yorks. Yorkshire
YP yard patrol; young
  people
Y.P. yellow pine; yield
  point
yr. year; younger; your
YRA Yacht Racing
  Association
yrbk. yearbook
yrly. yearly
yrs. yours
y.s. yellow spot
Y.S. yield strength; young
  soldier
yst. youngest
Yt yttrium
Y.T. Yukon Territory
YTM yield to maturity
Yug. Yugoslavia
yumpie young upwardly
  mobile professional
yuppie young urban
  professional
YW Young Women's
  Christian Association
YWCA Young Women's
  Christian Association
YWHA Young Women's
  Hebrew Association

Z

z.   zero; zone
Z   atomic number; azimuth
   angle; impedance
Zach.   Zacharias
ZANU   Zimbabwe African
   National Union
ZAPU   Zimbabwe African
   People's Union
z.B.   for example [Ger *zum
   Beispiel*]
ZBA   zoning board of
   approval
ZBB   zero-based budgeting
ZD   zenith distance
Zech.   Zechariah

ZEG   zero economic growth
Zeph.   Zephaniah
ZF   zero frequency
Z/F   zone of fire
Z.G.   zoological garden
ZI   zone of interior
ZIP   Zone Improvement
   Plan
Zl.   zloty
Zn   azimuth [azimuth
   angle + north]; zinc
zool.   zoological; zoologist;
   zoology
ZPG   zero population
   growth
Zr   zirconium
Z.S.   zoological society
ZT   zone time
ZZZZ   snooze

Words and Phrases Commonly Abbreviated

A

abbess **Abb.**
abbey **abb.**
abbot **Ab.; Abb.**
abbreviated **abbr.; abbrev.**
abbreviation **abbr.; abbrev.**
abdomen **abd.; abdom.**
abdominal **abd.; abdom.**
A Better Chance **ABC**
ablative **abl.**
able-bodied seaman **AB; ABS**
abort **ab.**
abortion **ab.**
about **a.; ab.; abt.**
above **abv.; sup.**
above knee **AK**
above-named **a.n**
above proof **AP**
above sea level **a.s.l.**
above water **AW**
abridged **abr.**
abridger **abr.**
abridgment **abr.**
abscissa **x**
absent **a.; abs.**
absent over leave **AOL**
absent with leave **AWL**
absent without leave **AWOL**
absolute **a.; abs.**
absolute ceiling **A/C**
absolutely **abs.**
absolute temperature **T**
absolute zero **K**
absorbency **a.**
absorbent **a.**
absorbic acid factor **AAF**
abstract **ab.; abs.; abstr.**

abstracted **abstr.**
academic **acad.**
academician **a.**
academy **a.; acad.**
Academy of Certified Social
  Workers **ACSW**
accelerando **accel**
accelerated business collection
  and delivery **ABCD**
acceleration **a.**
acceleration of gravity **g**
acceptance **acc.; acce.; acpt.**
accepted **a.; acc.**
accommodation **a.**
accompanied **acc.**
accompaniment **acc.;
  accomp.; accpt.**
accomplishment quotient **AQ**
accordant **acc.**
according **acc.**
according to **ap.; sec.**
according to age
  pro rat. aet.
according to art **s.a.**
according to custom **a.u.**
according to law **sec. leg.;
  s.l.**
according to rule **sec. reg.**
according to the value
  ad val.; A/V
account **ac.; acc.; acct.**
accountant **acc.; acct.**
accountant general **AG**
account current **A/C**
account executive **A.E.**
account of **A/O**
account paid **AP**
account sales **A/S**
accounts payable **AP**

accounts receivable **AR**
accredited **accred.**
Accredited Record
  Technician **ART**
accrued **accrd.**
accusative **acc.; accus.**
ace **A**
acetum **a.**
acetylcholine **ACh**
acetylcholinesterase **AChE**
acetylsalicylic acid **ASA**
achievement age **A.A.**
achievement quotient **AQ**
acid **a.**
acid-fast bacillus **AFB**
acidity **a.**
acknowledge **ack.**
acknowledgment **ack.;
  ackgt.**
acknowledgment of receipt
  A.R.
acquired immunodeficiency
  syndrome **AIDS**
acre **a.; ac.**
acrylonitrile-butadiene-
  styrene **ABS**
act **a.**
actin **a.**
acting **a.; actg.**
acting appointment **AA**
actinium **Ac**
action **act.**
action potential **AP**
active **a.; act.**
active duty **AD**
active ingredient **AI**
activities of daily living
  ADL
activity **a.**
actor **act.**
actual **act.**

actual cash value **ACV**
actual weight **A/W**
actuary **act.**
actuating **actg.**
acute **ac.**
acute brain syndrome **ABS**
acute lymphoblastic
  leukemia **ALL**
acute myocardial infarction
  AMI
acute respiratory disease
  ARD
adagio **adag**
adaptation **adapt.**
adapted **ad.**
adapted by **adapt.**
add **add.**
addendum **add.**
addition **add.; addn.**
additional **add.; addnl.**
additional postscript **P.P.S.**
additional premium **AP**
address **add.**
adduction **add.**
adductor **add.**
adenine **A**
adenosine diphosphate **ADP**
adenosine monophosphate
  AMP
adenosine triphosphate **ATP**
adjacent **adj.**
adjective **a.; adj.**
adjourned **adj.**
adjourn in contemplation of
  dismissal **A.C.D.**
adjudged **adj.**
adjunct **adj.**
adjustable **adj.**
adjustable rate mortgage
  ARM
adjusted **adj.**

adjusted gross income **AGI**
adjustment **adj.**
adjutant **a.; Adj.; Adjt.**
adjutant general **AG**
adjutant general's office
  AGO
administration **a.; ad.;
  adm.; admin.**
Administration for Native
  Americans **ANA**
administrative **ad.; adm.**
administrative assistant **AA**
administrative law judge
  ALJ
administrative support **AS**
administrator **adm.;
  admor.; admr.; adms.;
  admstr.**
administratrix **admix.;
  admrx.; admx.**
admiral **Adm.; ADM;
  Adml.**
admiral of the fleet **AF**
admiralty **Adm.**
admission limited to adults —
  used of a movie rating **X**
Admissions Test for Graduate
  Study in Business **ATGSB**
Admissions Testing
  Program **ATP**
admit **adm.**
admittance **Y**
adrenocorticotropic hormone
  ACTH
adult **a.; ad.**
adult contemporary **AC**
advance **adv.**
advanced booking charter
  ABC
advanced graduate
  certificate **AGC**

Advanced Placement **AP**
advanced post **AP**
advantage **ad; advtg.**
advent **adv.**
adverb **ad.; adv.**
adverbial **adv.**
adverbially **adv.**
adversus **adv.**
advertisement **ad; adv.;
  advt.**
advertising **ad; adv.; advg.;
  advtg.**
advice **adv.**
advice of payment **AP**
advise **adv.**
advisory **adv.**
advocate **Adv.**
aeronautical **aero.**
Aeronautical Engineer **A.E.;
  Ae.E.**
aeronautics **aero.**
affairs **aff.**
affectionate **aff.**
affectionately **affly.**
affidavit **afft.**
affirmative **aff.**
affirmative action plan **AAP**
affix **Af**
afghani **Af.**
Afghanistan **Af.**
Africa **Afr.**
African **Afr.**
African Methodist Episcopal
  AME
after **a.**
after Christ **A.C.**
after date **A/d**
after meals **p.c.**
afternoon **a.; aft.; p; p.m.**
after receipt of order **ARO**
after sight **A/S**

again **agn.**

against **adv.; agst.; agt.; con.**

against all risks **a.a.r.**

against medical advice **AMA**

age **a.**

aged **a.; ae.; aet.; aetat.**

agency **agcy.**

Agency for International Development **AID**

agent **agt.**

agent-general **AG**

agglutination **agglut.**

aggregate **agg.**

agreed **agd.**

agreement **agt.**

agricultural **ag; agr.; agric.; agrl.**

Agricultural Adjustment Administration **AAA**

agricultural and mechnanical **A & M**

Agricultural Engineer **A.E.**

Agricultural Marketing Service **AMS**

agriculture **ag; agr.; agri.; agric.**

agronomist **agron.**

agronomy **agron.**

aide-de-camp **ADC**

aid to blind **AB**

Aid to Dependent Children **ADC**

Aid to Families with Dependent Children **AFDC**

air **a.**

airbase **AB**

airborne **AB; abn.**

airborne intercept **AI**

airborne warning and control

system **AWACS**

air-conditioning **A/C**

air corps **AC**

aircraft **a.; acft.**

aircraft interception **AI**

aircraftsman **AC**

aircraftswoman **ACW**

aircraft warning **AW**

air-cushion vehicle **ACV**

Air Defense Command **ADC**

air defense identification zone **ADIZ**

air-dried **AD**

air force **AF**

air force base **AFB**

air-launched cruise missile **ALCM**

air letter **AL**

airmail **AM**

airman **A; Amn.; AN**

airman basic **AB**

airman first class **A/1C**

air marshal **AM**

Air Medal **AM**

airplane **a.; AP**

airplane pilot **AP**

airport surveillance radar **ASR**

air position **AP**

air position indicator **API**

air-raid precautions **ARP**

air raid warden **ARW**

air route traffic control center **ARTCC**

air-sea rescue **ASR**

air service **A.S.**

airspeed **AS**

airspeed indicator **ASI**

air temperature **A.T.**

airtight **A.T.**

air-to-air missile **AAM**

air traffic control **ATC**
Alabama **AL; Ala.**
Alaska **AK; Alas.**
Alaska Hawaii standard
  time **AHST**
Albania **Alb.**
Albanian **Alb.**
Alberta **AB; Alba.; Alta.**
albumin **alb.**
alcohol **alc.**
Alcoholics Anonymous **AA**
alcohol on breath **AOB**
alderman **ald.; aldm.**
algebra **alg.**
alias **al.**
alicyclic **ac.**
alive and well **A & W**
alkaline **alk.**
alkaline phosphatase **AP**
alkalinity **alky.**
all but dissertation **ABD**
all correct **OK**
all edges gilt **a.e.g.**
allegro **allo**
allergist **a.**
allergy **a.**
alley **al.**
allied military government
  AMG
all lengths **a.l.**
allowance **allow.; alw.**
allowance race **alw.**
all points bulletin **APB**
all rail **A.R.**
all risks **A.R.**
all-terrain vehicle **ATV**
all water **AW**
all widths **a.w.**
almost uncirculated **A.U.**
alongside **AS**
alpha **a.**

alpha-naphthylthiourea
  ANTU
also known as **a.k.a.**
alter **alt.**
alteration **alt.; alter.; altn.**
altered states of
  consciousness **ASC**
alternate **alt.; altn.**
alternate captain **a**
alternate days **AD**
alternating **alt.**
alternating continuous wave
  ACW
alternating current **AC**
alternative **alt.**
altitude **alt.**
alto **a.; alt**
altocumulus **Ac**
altostratus **As**
aluminum **Al; alum.**
alumna **alum.**
alumnus **alum.**
alveolar **alv.**
always afloat **a.a.**
Alzheimer's disease **AD**
amateur **a.**
Amateur Athletic
  Association **AAA**
Amateur Athletic Union
  AAU
Amateur Bicycle League of
  America **ABLA**
Amateur Bicycling League
  ABL
Amateur Boxing
  Association **ABA**
Amateur Fencers League of
  America **AFLA**
Amateur Fencing
  Association **AFA**
Amateur Football

Alliance **AFA**
Amateur Football
Association **AFA**
Amateur Gymnastics
Association **AGA**
Amateur Hockey Association
of the United States
AHAUS
Amateur Skating Union of the
United States **ASUUS**
Amateur Softball
Association **ASA**
Amateur Trapshooting
Association **ATA**
ambassador **amb.**
ambulance **amb.**
ambulatory **amb.**
amendment **amdt.**
America **Am.; Amer.**
American **A.; Am.; Amer.**
American Academy of Arts
and Letters **AAAL**
American Academy of Family
Physicians **AAFP**
American Academy of
Pediatrics **AAP**
American Association for the
Advancement of Science
AAAS
American Association for the
Comparative Study of
Law **AACSL**
American Association of
Community and Junior
Colleges **AACJC**
American Association of
Retired Persons **AARP**
American Association of State
Colleges and Universities
AASCU
American Association of

University Professors
AAUP
American Association of
University Women **AAUW**
American Automobile
Association **AAA**
American Badminton
Association **ABA**
American Ballet Theatre
ABT
American Bankers
Association **ABA**
American Bar Association
ABA
American Basketball
Association **ABA**
American Bible Society **ABS**
American Board of Trial
Advocates **ABTA**
American Booksellers
Association **ABA**
American Bowling Congress
ABC
American Broadcasting
Company **ABC**
American Camping
Association **ACA**
American Cancer Society
ACS
American Canoe
Association **ACA**
American Casting
Association **ACA**
American Chemical Society
ACS
American Civil Liberties
Union **ACLU**
American College of Nurse-
Midwives **ACNM**
American College of
Obstetricians and

Gynecologists **ACOG**
American College of
Physicians **ACP**
American College of
Surgeons **ACS**
American College of Trial
Lawyers **ACTL**
American College Test **ACT**
American College Testing
ACT
American Conservative
Union **ACU**
American Council on
Education **ACE**
American Cycling Union
ACU
American Dental
Association **ADA**
American depositary receipt
ADR
American Dialect
Dictionary **ADD**
American Dietetic
Association **ADA**
American English **AmE**
American Expeditionary
Force **AEF**
American Federation of
Labor **AFL**
American Federation of Labor
and Congress of Industrial
Organizations **AFL-CIO**
American Federation of
Musicians **AFM**
American Federation of State,
County, and Municipal
Employees **AFSCME**
American Federation of
Teachers **AFT**
American Federation of
Television and Radio

Artists **AFTRA**
American Football Coaches
Association **AFCA**
American Football
Conference **AFC**
American Football League
AFL
American Foreign Law
Association **AFLA**
American Foxhound Club
AFC
American Hockey Coaches
Association **AHCA**
American Hockey League
AHL
American Hospital
Association **AHA**
American Hot Rod
Association **AHRA**
American Indian **AmerInd**
American Indian Movement
AIM
American Institute of
Architects **AIA**
American Institute of
Banking **AIB**
American Institute of
Certified Public
Accountants **AICPA**
American Junior Bowling
Congress **AJBC**
American Kennel Club **AKC**
American Labor Party **ALP**
American Law Institute **ALI**
American Lawn Bowling
Association **ALBA**
American Law Student
Association **ALSA**
American League **AL**
American Legion **AL**
American Library

Association **ALA**
American Medical
Association **AMA**
American Motorcyclist
Association **AMA**
American National Standards
Institute **ANSI**
American Newspaper
Association **ANA**
American Nurses
Association **ANA**
American Occupational
Therapy Association
AOTA
American Paddleball
Association **APA**
American Petroleum
Institute **API**
American plan **AP**
American Platform Tennis
Association **APTA**
American Power Boat
Association **APBA**
American Race Drivers
Club **ARDC**
American Red Cross **ARC**
American Registered
Respiratory Therapist
ARRT
American Registry of
Radiological Technologists
ARRT
American Revised Version
ARV
American Road Race of
Champions **ARRC**
American Roque League
ARL
American Safety Institute
A.S.I.
American Samoa **AS**

American Selling Price **ASP**
Americans for Democratic
Action **ADA**
American Shuffleboard
League **ASL**
American Sign Language
Ameslan; ASL
American Soccer League
ASL
American Society for Testing
and Materials **ASTM**
American Society for the
Prevention of Cruelty to
Animals **ASPCA**
American Society of Clinical
Pathologists **ASCP**
American Society of
Composers, Authors, and
Publishers **ASCAP**
American Society of
Mechanical Engineers
ASME
American Standard Code for
Information Interchange
ASCII
American Standards
Association **ASA**
American Standard Version
ASV
American Stock Exchange
Amex; ASE
American terms **A.T.**
American Trial Lawyers
Association **ATLA**
American Veterans of World
War II, Korea, Vietnam
AMVETS
American Veterinary Medical
Association **AVMA**
American Water Ski
Association **AWSA**

American wire gauge **AWG**
American Youth
  Congress **AYC**
American Youth for
  Democracy **AYD**
American Youth Hostels
  AYH
americium **Am**
aminolevulinic acid **ALA**
ammeter **am.**
ammunition **am.; amn.**
Amnesty International **AI**
among **amg.**
among other persons **int. al.**
among others **a.o.**
among other things **i.a.;**
  int. al.
amount **amt.**
amperage **amp**
ampere **A; amp**
ampere-hour **Ah; amp-hr**
ampere-turn **AT**
amphibian **a.; amph.**
amphibious **a.; amph.**
amplitude **a.; am.**
amplitude modulation **AM**
ampul **amp.**
amputation **amp.**
amyotrophic lateral
  sclerosis **ALS**
ana **A; aa; AA**
anagram **anag.**
analogous **anal.**
analog to digital **A/D**
analog-to-digital converter
  ADC
analogy **anal.**
analysis **anal.**
analytic **anal.**
analyze **anal.**
analyzed reagent **AR**

anatomic **anat.**
anatomical **anat.**
anatomy **anat.**
anaylsis of variance
  ANOVA
ancient **anc.; anct.**
ancient and modern
  A. and M.
Ancient Free and Accepted
  Masons **AFAM**
and **u.**
andante **and**
and elsewhere **et al.**
and others **a.o.; et al.**
and so forth **u.s.w.**
and the following one
  et seq.; f.
and the following ones
  et seq.; ff.
and wife **et ux.**
Anglican **Angl.**
Anglo-Saxon **AS**
Anglo-Saxon Protestant
  ASP
Angola **Ang.**
Angolan National Liberation
  Front **FNLA**
angstrom unit **A; AU**
angular **ang.**
angular momentum **J**
anhydrous **anhyd.**
animal **anl.**
animal protein factor **APF**
animate **an.**
ankle jerk **AJ**
anna **a.**
annals **ann.**
anneal **anl.**
annealed **ann.**
annual **ann.**
annual percentage rate **APR**

annual return **A.R.**
annuity **ann.**
anode **a.**
anonymous **a.; an.; anon.**
anonymously **anon.**
another **anor.; anr.**
answer **A; ans.**
answered **ans.**
Antarctica **Ant.**
ante **a.**
antenna **ant.**
anterior **a.**
anterior and posterior **A & P**
anterior axillary line **AAL**
anterior pituitary **A.P.**
anteroposterior **AP**
anthology **anth.**
anthropological **anthrop.**
anthropologist **anthro.**
anthropology **anthro.;
  anthrop.**
antiaircraft **AA**
antiaircraft artillery **AAA**
antiballistic missile **ABM**
anticipated **ant.**
Anti-Defamation League
  ADL
antidiuretic hormone **ADH**
antihemophilic factor **AHF**
antihemophilic globulin
  AHG
antihuman globulin **AHG**
antilymphocyte globulin
  ALG
antilymphocyte serum **ALS**
antilymphocytic globulin
  ALG
antilymphocytic serum **ALS**
antimony **Sb**
antipersonnel **AP**
antiquarian **ant.; antiq.**

antiquary **antiq.**
antiquity **ant.**
antireticular cytotoxic
  serum **ACS**
anti-satellite **ASAT**
antisubmarine **A/S**
antisubmarine warfare **ASW**
antitank **AT**
antitoxin unit **au**
antitrust law **ATL**
antonym **ant.**
Antrim **Ant.**
aorist **aor.**
aortic pressure **AP**
aortic stenosis **AS**
apartment **apt.**
Apocalypse **Apoc.**
Apocrypha **Apoc.**
apogee **apo.**
apostle **ap.**
apostrophe **apos.**
apothecaries' **ap.**
apparatus **app.**
apparent **app.**
apparently **app.**
appeal **app.; appl.**
appellate **app.**
appended **app.**
appendix **app.; appx.; apx.**
applicable **appl.**
application **appln.**
applied **app.; appl.**
applied science **AS**
appoint **appt.**
appointed **app.; appt.;
  apptd.**
appointment **appmt.;
  appnt.; appoint.; appt.**
appraised **app.**
apprentice **app.; appr.**
apprentice seaman **AS**

approbation **appro.**
approval **appro.**
approved **a.; appd.; appr.**
approved as amended **AAA**
approximate **approx.**
approximate absolute **A.A.**
approximately **app.; approx.**
April **Ap.; Apr.**
A Programming Language **APL**
aptitude **apt.**
aqua **a.**
aqueous **aq.**
Arabian **Arab.**
Arabic **Ar.; Arab.**
arbitrager **arb**
arbitrageur **arb**
arbitration **arb.; arbtrn.**
arbitrator **arb.**
arccosecant **arccse**
arccosine **arccos**
arccotangent **arccot**
archaic **arch.**
archbishop **Abp.; Arch.; Archbp.**
archdeacon **Archd.**
archduke **AD; Archd.**
archeology **archeol.**
archery **arch.**
archipelago **arch.**
architect **arch.; archt.**
architectural **arch.**
architecture **arch.; archit.**
archive **arch.**
arcsecant **arcsec**
arcsine **arcsin**
arctangent **arctan**
arctic **A**
are **a**
area **a.; ar**

area code **AC**
area of operation **AO**
area of outstanding natural beauty **AONB**
argent **arg.**
Argentina **Arg.**
argentum **AR**
argon **A; Ar**
Argyll **Arg.**
arithmetic **arith.**
arithmetical **arith.**
arithmetic logic unit **ALU**
arithmetic progression **A.P.**
Arizona **Ariz.; AZ**
Arkansas **AR; Ark.**
Armagh **Arm.**
armament **arm.**
armature **arm.**
Armenia **Arm.**
Armenian **Arm.**
armored **armd.**
armored personnel carrier **APC**
armor-piercing **AP**
Arms Control and Disarmament Agency **ACDA**
army **a.**
army corps **AC**
army-navy **AN**
Army of the Republic of Vietnam (South Vietnam) **ARVN**
Army of the United States **AUS**
Army post office **APO**
army regulation **AR**
Army Security Agency **ASA**
Army service number **ASN**
Army specialized training program **ASTP**

aromatic **ar**
arranged **arr.**
arrangement **arr.; arrgt.**
arranger **arr.**
arrival **ar.; arr.**
arrival notice **A.N.**
arrive **ar.; arr.; arv.**
arsenal **ars.**
arsenic **As**
arteriosclerosis **AS**
arteriosclerotic cardiovascular
   disease **ASCVD**
arteriosclerotic heart
   disease **ASHD**
arteriovenous **AV**
artery **a.**
article **a.; art.**
articles of war **AW**
artificial **art.**
artificial insemination **AI**
artificial insemination by
   donor **AID**
artificial insemination by
   husband **AIH**
artificial intelligence **AI**
artillery **a.; art.; arty.**
artist **art.**
artists and repertory **A & R**
arts and humanities **AH**
aryl **Ar**
as above **u.s.**
as below **u.i.**
asbestos **asb.**
as directed **u.d.; ut dict.**
Asian and Pacific Council
   ASPAC
asked **a.**
as loud as possible **fff**
as much as suffices **q.s.**
as much as you please **q.l.;
   q.p.; q.pl.**

as much as you will **q.v.**
as occasion arises **p.r.n.**
as often as needed **quot.**
aspirin, phenacetin, caffeine
   APC
as purchased **A.P.**
assay ton **AT**
assembly **asm.; ass.; assy.**
assembly district **AD**
assented **asstd.**
assertiveness training **AT**
assessed **assd.**
assessment **assmt.**
assessment paid **AP**
asset depreciation range
   ADR
assigned **asg.; asgd.; assd.**
assignment **asg.; asgmt.;
   assigt.**
assist **A**
assistant **ass.; asst.**
assistant director **AD**
assistant district attorney
   ADA
assistant division
   commander **ADC**
associate **a.; assoc.**
associated **assoc.; asstd.**
associate director **AD**
Associated Press **AP**
Associate in Applied Science
   A.A.S.
Associate in Arts **A.A.**
Associate in Engineering
   Technology **A.S.E.T.**
Associate in Science **A.S.**
associate justice **AJ**
associate member **AM**
association **a.; ass.; assn.;
   assoc.**
Association Football

Club **AFC**
Association Internationale de
  Boxe Amateur (boxing)
  AIBA
Association of American
  Publishers **AAP**
Association of Classroom
  Teachers **ACT**
Association of Colleges and
  Universities **AC and U**
Association of Cricket
  Umpires **ACU**
Association of Immigration
  and Nationality Lawyers
  AINL
Association of Intercollegiate
  Athletics for Women
  AIAW
Association of Southeast
  Asian Nations **ASEAN**
Association of State
  Colleges and Universities
  ASCU
Association of Tennis
  Professionals **ATP**
as soon as possible **ASAP**
assorted **asstd.**
assumed position **AP**
assurance **assce.**
assured **assd.**
Assyrian **Assyr.**
astatine **At**
astigmatism **as.**
as tolerated **as tol.**
astrologer **astrol.**
astrology **astrol.**
astronomer **astron.**
astronomical unit **A.U.**
astronomy **astron.**
asymmetric **a.**
asymmetry **a.**

at **a; a.**
at bats **AB**
at bedtime **h.s.**
at Easter time **T.P.**
athletic association **AA**
athletic club **AC**
athletic director **AD**
Atlantic **Atl.**
Atlantic Coast Conference
  ACC
Atlantic standard time **AST**
atmosphere **at.; atm.**
atmospheric **at.; atm.**
at night **n.**
atom **a.**
atomic **a.; at.**
atomic absorption **AA**
atomic, biological, and
  chemical **ABC**
atomic emission
  spectroscopy **AES**
Atomic Energy Commission
  AEC
atomic mass unit **a.m.u.**
atomic number **at. no.; Z**
atomic weight **a.; at. wt.**
at pleasure **ad lib.**
atrioventricular **AV**
at sight **AS**
attaché **att.**
attached **att.**
attempts **att.**
attendant **atdt.**
attention **att.; attn.**
at the beginning **ad init.**
at the end **ad fin.; a.f.**
at the place **ad loc.**
at the suit of **ad s.; ATS**
at this time **h.t.**
atto- **a**
attorney **at.; att.; atty.**

attorney general **AG;
att. gen.; atty. gen.**
attributive **attrib.**
attributively **attrib.**
audible **aud.**
audio frequency **AF**
audiovisual **AV**
audit **aud.**
Audit Bureau of
Circulations **ABC**
auditor **aud.**
augmentative **aug.**
augmented **aug.**
August **Ag; Aug.**
auricular fibrillation **AF**
aurum **aur.**
auscultation and percussion
A & P
Australia **Austral.**
Australia and New Zealand
Army Corps **ANZAC**
Australian **A.; Austral.**
Australian Broadcasting
Company **ABC**
Australian Capital
Territory **A.C.T.**
Australia, New Zealand,
United Kingdom **ANZUK**
Australia, New Zealand,
United States **ANZUS**
Austria **Aus.**
Austrian **Aus.**
authentic **auth.**
author **a.; auth.**
authoress **auth.**
authorities **auth.**
authority **auth.**
authority to pay **A/P**
authority to purchase **A/P**
authorized **auth.**
Authorized Version **AV**

authors **ss.**
author's alterations **AA**
author's correction **AC**
author's proof **A.P.**
autograph card signed **ACS**
autograph document **AD**
autograph document signed
ADS
autographed manuscript
Ams
autographed manuscript
signed **AMsS**
autographed presentation
copy **APC**
autograph letter **AL**
autograph letter signed **ALS**
autograph note signed **ANS**
Automated Biological
Laboratory **ABL**
automated teller machine
ATM
automatic **auto.**
automatic color control **ACC**
automatic data processing
ADP
automatic direction finder
ADF
automatic fine tuning **AFT**
automatic flight control **AFC**
automatic frequency control
AFC
automatic gain control **AGC**
automatic rifle **AR**
automatic teller machine
ATM
automatic transmission **AT**
automatic volume control
AVC
automatic volume expansion
AVE
automatic weapon **AW**

automobile   **a.**
automobile association   **A.A.**
automobile club   **AC**
Automobile Competition
  Committee for the United
  States   **ACCUS**
Automobile Legal
  Association   **ALA**
Automobile Racing Club of
  America   **ARCA**
autonomic nervous system
  ANS
autonomous republic   **AR**
Autonomous Soviet Socialist
  Republic   **ASSR**
auxiliary   **aux.; auxil.**
Ave Maria   **A.M.**
avenue   **av.; ave.**
average   **av.; avg.**
average daily attendance
  ADA
average daily gain   **ADG**
average deviation   **AD**
average goals against per
  period   **AGP**
average variability   **AV**
aviation   **av.; avn.**
aviation cadet   **AC**
avoirdupois   **av.; avdp.;
  avoir.**
axiom   **ax.**
axis   **ax.**
Ayrshire   **Ayr.**
azimuth   **Az; Zn**
azimuth angle   **Z**
azure   **az.**

B

Babe Ruth League   **BRL**
bachelor   **b.; B; bac.; bach.**
Bachelor of Aeronautical and
  Astronautical
  Engineering   **B.A.A.E.**
Bachelor of Aeronautical
  Engineering   **B.A.E.;
  B.Ae.E.**
Bachelor of Agricultural
  Engineering   **B.A.E.**
Bachelor of Agriculture
  B.Ag.
Bachelor of Applied Arts
  B.A.A.
Bachelor of Applied
  Mathematics   **B.A.M.**
Bachelor of Applied Science
  B.A.S.
Bachelor of Architectural
  Engineering   **B.A.E.**
Bachelor of Architecture
  B.Ar.
Bachelor of Art Education
  B.A.E.
Bachelor of Arts   **A.B.; B.A.**
Bachelor of Arts and
  Sciences   **B.A.S.**
Bachelor of Arts in
  Education   **B.A.E.;
  B.A.Ed.**
Bachelor of Arts in
  Elementary Education
  B.A.E.E.
Bachelor of Arts in Music
  B.A.M.
Bachelor of Arts in
  Teaching   **B.A.T.**
Bachelor of Business
  Administration   **B.B.A.**

Bachelor of Business
Education **B.B.E.**
Bachelor of Canon Law
**B.Can.L.; B.C.L.;
J.Can.B.; J.C.B.**
Bachelor of Chemical
Engineering **B.C.E.;
B.Ch.E.**
Bachelor of Chemical
Science **B.C.S.**
Bachelor of Chemistry **B.Ch.**
Bachelor of Civil
Engineering **B.C.E.**
Bachelor of Civil Law
B.C.L.; C.L.B.; J.C.B.
Bachelor of Commerce **B.C.**
Bachelor of Commercial
Law **B.C.L.**
Bachelor of Commercial
Science **B.C.S.**
Bachelor of Divinity **B.D.**
Bachelor of Domestic Arts
B.D.A.
Bachelor of Dramatic Art
B.D.A.
Bachelor of Education **B.E.;
B.Ed.; Ed.B.**
Bachelor of Electrical
Engineering **B.E.E.**
Bachelor of Engineering
B.E.; B.Engr.
Bachelor of Engineering of
Mines **B.E.M.**
Bachelor of Engineering
Science **B.Eng.S.; B.E.S.**
bachelor officers' quarters
BOQ
Bachelor of Fine Arts **B.F.A.**
Bachelor of Forestry **B.F.**
Bachelor of General Studies
B.G.S.

Bachelor of Hebrew Letters
B.H.L.
Bachelor of Hebrew
Literature **B.H.L.**
Bachelor of Industrial
Administration **B.I.A.**
Bachelor of Industrial Arts
B.I.A.
Bachelor of Industrial
Design **B.I.D.**
Bachelor of Industrial
Engineering **B.I.E.**
Bachelor of Journalism **B.J.**
Bachelor of Law **B.L.**
Bachelor of Laws **B.L.;
B.LL.; J.B.; LL.B.**
Bachelor of Letters **B.L.;
B.Lit.; B.Litt.; Lit.B.;
Litt.B.**
Bachelor of Liberal Studies
B.L.S.
Bachelor of Library Science
B.L.S.
Bachelor of Literature
**B.Lit.; B.Litt.; Lit.B.;
Litt.B.**
Bachelor of Marine Science
B.M.S.
Bachelor of Mechanical
Engineering **B.M.E.**
Bachelor of Medical
Technology **B.M.T.**
Bachelor of Medicine **B.M.;
M.B.**
Bachelor of Mining
Engineering **B.M.E.**
Bachelor of Music **B.M.;
Mus.B.**
Bachelor of Music
Education **B.M.E.;
B.M.Ed.**

Bachelor of Naval Science
B.N.S.

Bachelor of Nursing B.N.

Bachelor of Petroleum
Engineering B.P.E.

Bachelor of Pharmacy B.P.;
Phm.B.

Bachelor of Philosophy
B.Ph.; B.Phil.; Ph.B.

Bachelor of Physical
Education B.P.E.

Bachelor of Religious
Education B.R.E.

Bachelor of Sacred
Literature B.S.L.

Bachelor of Sacred Theology
S.T.B.

Bachelor of Science B.S.;
B.Sc.; S.B.; Sc.B.

Bachelor of Science in
Aeronautical Engineering
B.S.A.E.

Bachelor of Science in
Agricultural Engineering
B.S.A.E.

Bachelor of Science in
Agriculture B.S.A.;
B.S.Ag.

Bachelor of Science in Applied
Arts B.S.A.A.

Bachelor of Science in
Architectural Engineering
B.S.A.E.

Bachelor of Science in
Architecture B.S.Arch.

Bachelor of Science in
Business B.S.B.

Bachelor of Science in
Chemistry B.S.Ch.

Bachelor of Science
in Econom-
ics B.S.Ec.; B.S.Econ.

Bachelor of Science in
Education B.S.E.; B.S.Ed.

Bachelor of Science in
Electrical Engineering
B.S.E.E.

Bachelor of Science in
Elementary Education
B.S.E.E.

Bachelor of Science in
Engineering Technology
B.S.E.T.

Bachelor of Science in Foreign
Service B.S.F.S.

Bachelor of Science in
Forestry B.S.For.

Bachelor of Science in
Languages B.S.L.

Bachelor of Science in Law
B.S.L.

Bachelor of Science in Law
Enforcement B.S. in L.E.

Bachelor of Science in Library
Science B.S.L.S.

Bachelor of Science in
Linguistics B.S.L.

Bachelor of Science in
Mechanical Engineering
B.S.M.E.

Bachelor of Science in
Nursing B.Sc.N.; B.S.N.

Bachelor of Science in
Nursing Administration
B.S.N.A.

Bachelor of Science in
Nursing Education
B.S.N.E.

Bachelor of Science in
Pharmacy B.S.Ph.;
B.S.Phar.

Bachelor of Science in

Physical Therapy **B.S.P.T.**
Bachelor of Science in Public Health **B.S.P.H.**
Bachelor of Science in Public Health Nursing **B.S.P.H.N.**
Bachelor of Surgery **C.B.; Ch.B.**
Bachelor of Theology **S.T.B.; Th.B.**
Bach-Werke-Verzeichnis **BWV**
bacillary white diarrhea **BWD**
bacillus **b.**
bacillus Calmette-Guérin **BCG**
Bacillus thuringiensis **Bt**
back **b.**
back dividend **BD**
background **bg.; B.G.; bkgd.**
back order **BO**
backstrip **bks.**
backward **bwd.**
backwardation **back.; bk.**
backward edge **b.**
bacon, lettuce, and tomato **BLT**
bacteria **bact.**
bacterial **bact.**
bacteriological **bact.**
bacteriological warfare **BW**
bacteriology **bact.**
bacterium **bact.**
bad conduct discharge **BCD**
bag **b.; bg.**
baggage **bag.**
baht **B**
bail bond **B.B.**
bail court **BC**
bakery **bkry.**

balance **bal.; blc.**
balance sheet **BS**
balboa **B**
bale **b.; bl.**
balk **bk.**
ball **b.**
ballast **blst.**
ball bearing **B.B.**
ballistic missile defense **BMD**
ballistic missile early warning system **BMEWS**
ballistocardiogram **BCG**
Baltimore **Balt.; Balto.**
ban **b.**
band **b.; bd.; bnd.**
band elimination **BE**
band pass **BP**
bank **bk.**
bankbook **B.B.**
bank draft **BD**
Bank for International Settlement **BIS**
banking **bkg.**
bank note **B.N.**
bank post bill **BPB**
bank rate **BR**
bankrupt **bkpt.**
bankruptcy **bankr.; bkcy.**
bankruptcy cases **BC**
Baptist **Bap.; Bapt.**
baptized **bp**
bar **b.; B**
bare name **n.n.; nom. nud.**
barge **b.**
barium **Ba**
barium enema **BaE; BAE; BE**
bark **bar.; bk.**
barometer **bar.; brm.**
barometric **b.; bar.; brmc.**

baron **B.**; **Bn.**
baroness **Bnss.**
baronet **Bart.**; **Bt.**
barque **bar.**; **bq.**; **bque.**
barracks **bks.**
barrel **bar.**; **bbl.**; **bl.**; **brl.**
barrels **bbl.**
barrels of oil per day **BOPD**
barrels per day **b/d**; **bpd**
barrister **barr.**
Baruch **Bar.**
Barycentric Dynamical
   Time **TDB**
basal body temperature **BBT**
basal metabolic rate **BMR**
basal metabolism **BM**
base **b.**
base exchange **BX**
base hospital **BH**
baseline **BL**
basement **bsmt.**
base on balls **BB**; **w**
basic **bsc.**
basic airspeed **BAS**
basic air temperature **BAT**
Basic Assembly Language
   BAL
basic disk operating system
   BDOS
Basic Educational
   Opportunity Grant **BEOG**
basic input/output system
   BIOS
basic oxygen furnace **BOF**
basic pressure altitude **BPA**
basic telecommunications
   access method **BTAM**
basic training **BT**
basket **bkt.**; **bskt.**
Basle Nomina Anotomica
   BNA

basophil **baso.**
bass **b.**
basso **b**; **bas.**
bat **b.**
bath **b.**; **ba.**
bathroom privileges **BRP**
bats both right-handed and
   left-handed **BB**
bats left **BL**
bats left-handed **BL**
bats right **BR**
bats right-handed **BR**
battalion **batn.**; **batt.**; **bn.**;
   Bn.; **btn.**
batten **batt.**
battery **b.**; **batt.**; **btry.**; **bty.**
battery commander **BC**
batting average **BA**
batting practice **BP**
battle **b.**; **batt.**
battleship **BB**
Baumé **B**; **Bé**
Bavaria **Bav.**
Bavarian **Bav.**
bay **b.**
beacon **bcn.**; **bn.**
beam **bm.**
bearer bond **B.B.**
bearing **b.**; **brg.**
beat **bt.**
beat frequency **BF**
beat frequency oscillator
   BFO
beautiful people **BP**
bed-and-breakfast **B & B**
bed, breakfast, and bath **bbb**
Bedfordshire **Beds.**
bedroom **bdrm.**; **BR**
bedtime **BT**
been **bn.**
before **b.**; **bef.**

before Christ **A.C.; B.C.**
before meals **a.c.**
before noon **a; a.m.**
Before the Christian Era
  B.C.E.
Before the Common Era
  B.C.E.
before the day **A.D.**
before the present **BP**
begin **beg.**
Beginner's All-purpose
  Symbolic Instruction
  Code **BASIC**
beginning **beg.**
behavior **b.**
beige **bg.**
being **bg.**
bel **b**
Belgian **Belg.**
Belgium **Belg.**
below **bel.**
below elbow **BE**
below knee **BK**
below proof **BP**
bench **B**
bench mark **B.M.**
Benevolent and Protective
  Order of Elks **BPOE**
benign prostatic
  hypertrophy **BPH**
bent **bt.**
benzene hexachloride **BHC**
benzoyl **Bz**
bequest in trust **f.c.**
berkelium **Bk**
Berkshire **Berks.**
berth terms **BT**
Berwick **Berw.**
beryllium **Be**
be silent **t**
best **o.**

best in group **BIG**
best in match **BIM**
best in show **BIS**
best of breed **BB; BOB**
best practicable technology
  BPT
better **btr.**
Better Business Bureau
  BBB
between **bet.; btwn.**
beverage **bev.**
Bible **B.; Bib.**
biblical **bib.; bibl.**
bibliographer **bibliog.**
bibliography **bibl.; bibliog.**
biceps jerk **BJ**
bicycle club **BC**
bicycle motocross **BMX**
bid **b.; B**
big man on campus **BMOC**
bilirubin **bili.**
bill book **B.B.**
Billiard Congress of
  America **BCA**
billion **b.; bil**
billion cubic feet **bcf**
billion electron volts **BeV**
billion years **by; Byr**
bill of entry **BE**
bill of exchange **BE**
bill of health **BH**
bill of lading **B/L**
bill of material **BM**
bill of parcels **B/P**
bill of rights **BR**
bill of sale **B/S**
bill of sight **B/St**
bill of store **B/S**
bills discounted **BD**
bills payable **B/P**
bills receivable **B/R**

binary-coded decimal **BCD**
binary synchronous
  communication **BSC**
binding **bdg.**
biochemical oxygen
  demand **BOD**
biochemistry **biochem.**
biographer **biog.**
biographical **biog.**
biography **bio.; biog.**
biologic **biol.**
biological **biol.**
biological oxygen demand
  BOD
biological warfare **BW**
biologic false-positive **BFP**
biologist **biol.**
biology **biol.**
biopsy **Bx**
Birmingham wire gauge
  BWG
birthplace **bp; bpl.**
bisexual **bi**
bishop **B; bhp.; Bp.; Ep.;
  pont.**
bishop and martyr
  BM; E.M.
bishopric **bhpric.**
bishop suffragan **B.S.**
bismuth **Bi**
bissextile **bis.**
bitch **B**
bits per inch **bpi**
bits per second **bps**
black **b.; bk.; bl.; blk.**
black and white **B & W; BW**
black letter **BL**
blackout **BO**
bladder **ves.**
blank **blk.**
blend **b.**

Blessed **Bl.**
blessed **b.; BB.**
Blessed Mary the Virgin
  B.M.V.
Blessed Virgin **B.V.**
Blessed Virgin Mary **B.V.M.**
blinkers **b.**
blister **vesic.**
block **bk.; bl.; blk.**
blond **bld.**
blood **bld.**
blood alcohol **BA**
blood alcohol concentration
  BAC
blood alcohol level **BAL**
blood pressure **BP**
blood serological test **BST**
blood urea nitrogen **BUN**
blood Wassermann **BW**
blue **b.; bl.; bu.**
blue book **BB**
bluegrass **B.G.**
blueprint **BP**
B'nai B'rith **BB**
board **bd.; brd.**
board foot **bd.ft.; b.f.**
board measure **b.m.**
Board of Civil Service
  Examiners **BCSE**
board of control **B.C.**
board of education
  BE; B of E
board of health **B of H**
board of public works **BPW**
board of tax appeals **BTA**
board of trade **B of T;
  BOT; B.T.**
board of trade unit **BTU**
board of works **BW**
boat **bt.**
boat club **BC**

boatswain **b.**
body-centered cubic **BCC**
body odor **B.O.**
body weight **BW**
boiler **blr.**
boiling point **bp**
boiling water **aq. bull.**
boiling water reactor **BWR**
boils at **b.**
boldface **b.f.**
bolivar **B**
bombardier **bdr.; bom.**
bomb disposal **BD**
bomb disposal squad **BDS**
bomber **B**
bona fide occupational
 qualification **BFOQ**
bond **b.; B; bd.**
bondage and discipline
 B and D
bondage/domination **B/D**
bonded goods **BG**
bonded warehouse **BW**
bone **o.**
bonus points **BP**
book **b.; bk.; l.; lib.**
bookkeeper **bkpr.**
bookkeeping **bkg.; bkpg.**
bookplate **bkp.**
book value **BV**
born **b.; B; n.**
boron **B**
borough **bor.**
borough council **B.C.**
botanical **bot.; botan.**
botanist **bot.**
botany **bot.**
both dates included **b.d.i.**
both days inclusive **b.d.i.**
both eyes **O.U.**
bottle **bot.**

bottles per minute **bpm**
bottom **b.; bot.**
bottom settlings **BS**
bought **bght.; bgt.; bot.; bt.**
boulevard **blvd.**
bound **bd.; bnd.**
boundary **bd.; bdry.; bdy.**
bovine virus diarrhea **BVD**
bowel movement **BM**
bowel sounds **BS**
bowled **b.**
bowled out **b.**
bowler **b.**
bowling club **BC**
box **bx.**
boxed **bxd.**
box office **B.O.**
boyfriend **B.F.**
Boy Scouts of America **BSA**
bracket **bkt.**
braid **brd.**
Braille Institute of
 America **BIA**
brain tumor **BT**
brake **bk.**
brake horsepower **bhp**
brake mean effective
 pressure **BMEP**
branch **br.**
branch office **BO**
brand **br.**
brandy and soda **B and S**
brass **b.; br.; brs.**
Brazil **Braz.**
Brazilian **Braz.**
bread and water
 b and w; BW
breadth **b.**
breadth-length **BL**
breakage **bkg.**
break bulk **B.B.**

breaking and entering
B & E
breath sounds **BS**
Brecknockshire **Breck.**
breech-loading **BL**
breech-loading rifle **BLR**
breezing **b.**
brevet **bt.**
brick **b.**
bridge **br.; brg.**
brief **bf.; br.; brf.**
brig **br.**
brigade **bde.; br.; brig.**
brigade major **BM**
brigadier **bdr.; brig.**
brigadier general **BG;**
  B.Gen.; Brig.Gen.
brightness **B**
brilliant uncirculated **BU**
brindled **bd.**
Brinell hardness **BH**
Brinell hardness number
  BHN
bring your own **BYO**
bring your own booze **BYOB**
bring your own bottle **BYOB**
Britain **Br.; Brit.**
British **B.; Br.; Brit.**
British Amateur Athletic
  Board **BAAB**
British Broadcasting
  Corporation **BBC**
British Columbia **BC; B.C.**
British Cycling Federation
  BCF
British Empire Medal
  B.E.M.
British English **BrE**
British Expeditionary Force
  BEF
British Indian Ocean

Territory **BIOT**
British Museum **B.M.**
British Pharmacopoeia **BP**
British Railways **B.R.**
British Show Jumping
  Association **BSJA**
British standard **B.S.**
British Standards
  Institution **BSI**
British standard time **BST**
British thermal unit **B; Btu**
British thermal units per
  hour **Btuh**
British Virgin Islands **B.V.I.**
British West Indies **B.W.I.**
broadcast **b.; BC**
broadcast listener **BCL**
Broadcast Music
  Incorporated **BMI**
broché **br.**
broken **b.**
broker's order **BO**
bromine **Br**
bromocresol green **BCG**
bromodeoxyruidine **BUdR**
bronchial asthma **BA**
bronze **br.; bro.; brz.**
bronze medal **BM**
brook **bk.**
Brooklyn **Bklyn.**
brother **b.; br.; bro.; f.; Fr.**
brotherhood **b.**
brotherhood of man,
  fatherhood of God
  BOMFOG
brothers **bro.; bros.; FF**
Brothers of the Christian
  Schools **F.S.C.**
brought **brt.**
brought down **B/D**
brought forward **B/F**

brought over **BO**
brown **br.; brn.**
Browning automatic rifle **BAR**
brush **br.**
Buckinghamshire **Bucks.**
Buddhist Era **B.E.**
Buenos Aires **B.A.**
builder **bldr.**
builder's risk **BR**
building **bldg.**
building and loan **B and L**
building engineer **Bldg.E.**
building line **BL**
built **blt.**
bulb **B**
Bulgaria **Bulg.**
Bulgarian **Bulg.**
bulk **blk.**
bulkhead **bhd.; blkd.**
bulletin **b.; bu.; bull.**
bullshit **b.s.**
bunch **bch.**
bundle **bd.; bdl.; bdle.**
bundle branch block **BBB**
bureau **bu.; bur.**
Bureau of Alcohol, Tobacco, and Firearms **ATF**
Bureau of Economic Analysis **BEA**
Bureau of Employees' Compensation **BEC**
Bureau of Indian Affairs **BIA**
Bureau of Labor Statistics **BLS**
Bureau of Land Management **BLM**
Bureau of Narcotics **BN**
Bureau of Narcotics and Dangerous Drugs **BNDD**

burgomaster **BM**
buried **bur.; s.**
burlap **brlp.**
Burma **Bur.**
bushel **bsh.; bu.**
business **bus.**
business office must **BOM**
business reply envelope **BRE**
butterfly **bufly.**
butut **b.**
butylated hydroxyanisole **BHA**
butylated hydroxytoluene **BHT**
butylated hydrozyanisole **BTA**
buyer's option **BO**
by **p.; x**
by aid and counsel **o.c.**
bye **b.**
by mouth **p.o.**
bypass **byp.**
by proxy **per proc.; p.p.**
by reason of death **c.m.**
bytes per inch **bpi**
bytes per second **bps**
by the agency of **per proc.; p.p.**
by the decree of the Senate **S.C.**
by the grace of God **D.G.**
by the information of **ex rel.**
by the relation of **ex rel.**
by weight **pond.**

C

cabin **cab.**
cabinet **cab.; cabnt.; cbt.**
cable **ca.; cab.**

Cable Satellite Public Affairs
  Network **C-Span**
cable transfer **CT**
cab-over-engine **COE**
cadenza **cad.**
cadet **cad.**
cadmium **Cd**
cadmium sulfide **CdS**
cake **ck.**
calando **cal.**
calcium **Ca**
calculate **calc.**
calculated **calc.**
calculated date of
  confinement **CDC**
calculating **calc.**
calendar **cal.**
calendar year **CY**
calends **cal.; k.; kal.**
calf **cf.**
caliber **cal.**
calibrate **cal.**
calibrated air speed **CAS**
California **Ca.; CA; Cal.;
  Calif.**
californium **Cf**
calking **clkg.**
called **cld.**
call to quarters **CQ**
calm **c**
calorie **C; cal.**
Cambridgeshire **Cambs.**
camouflage **cam.**
Canada **Can.; Canad.**
Canadian **C.; Can.; Canad.;
  Cdn.**
Canadian Automobile Sports
  Club **CASC**
Canadian Broadcasting
  Corporation **CBC**
Canadian Football

League **CFL**
Canadian Standards
  Association **CSA**
canal **can.**
Canal Zone **CZ**
canceled **c.; can.; canc.**
canceled to order **c.t.o.**
canceling former order **CFO**
cancellation **can.; cancln.**
cancer **CA**
candela **cd**
candle **c; ca.; cd**
candlepower **c.p.; I**
canine parvo virus **CPV**
canned **cd.**
cannot find **CF**
canoe **c.**
canon **c.; can.; cn.**
Canticle of Canticles **Cant.**
canto **can.**
Cantonese **Cant.**
cantoris **can.**
capacitance **C**
capacitance electronic disc
  CED
capacity **C; cap.; capy.; cy.**
cape **c.**
Cape Province **CP**
capillary pressure **CP**
capital **cap.**
capital account **C/A**
capital and small capitals
  c. & s.c.
capitalize **cap.**
capitalized **cap.**
capitals **caps.**
capitals and lower case
  c. & l.c.
capital stock **C.S.**
capitulum **cap.**
capsule **caps.**

capsule communicator
  Capcom
captain **c.; cap.; Capt.; cpt.; Cpt.; CPT**
captain general **CG**
caput **c.; cap.**
carat **c.; car.; ct.**
carbine **cbn.**
carbohydrate **CHO; COH**
carbon **C**
carbon copy **cc**
carbon monoxide **CO**
carboy **cby.**
carcinoembryonic antigen
  CEA
carcinoma **CA**
card **cd.**
cardiac accelerator center
  CAC
cardiac arrest **CA**
Cardiac Care Registered
  Nurse **CCRN**
cardiac care unit **CCU**
cardiac enlargement **CE**
cardiac output **CO**
cardinal **Card.; cdl.**
cardiopulmonary
  resuscitation **CPR**
cardiorespiratory **CR**
cardiovascular **CV**
cardiovascular renal **CVR**
cardiovascular respiratory
  CVR
cards per second **CPS**
care of **c/o**
cargo **c.; car.; cgo.**
cargo's proportion of general
  average **C.G.A.**
Caribbean Basin Initiative
  CBI
carload **C.L.**

carload lot **C.L.**
Carlow **Car.**
carpenter **carp.; cptr.**
carriage **cge.**
carriage paid **CP**
carried down **C/D**
carried forward **C/F**
carried over **CO**
carrier route **CAR-RT**
carriers **carr.**
carrier's risk **C.R.**
cartage **ctg.; ctge.**
carting to shipside **C. to S.**
carton **ct.; ctn.**
carved **sculpt.**
case **c.; ca.; cs.**
case-hardened **C.H.**
case of need **CN**
cases **cs.**
cash before delivery **C.B.D.**
cashbook **CB**
cash credit **CC**
cash discount **CD**
cashier's check **CC**
cash letter **C/L**
cash on delivery **c.o.d.**
cash on delivery service
  CDS
cash on shipment **C.O.S.**
cash order **C/O**
cash with order **C.W.O.**
casing **cas.; csg.**
cask **ck.; csk.**
casting **cstg.**
cast iron **C.I.**
castle **c.; cas.**
casualty **cas.**
casualty clearing station
  CCS
catalog **cat.**
cataloged **cd.**

Cataloging in
  Publication **CIP**
catalyst **cat.**
cataplasm **cat.**
catcher **C**
catechism **cat.**
cathartic **cath.**
cathedral **cath.**
catheter **cath.**
cathodal opening clonus
  COCl
cathodal opening
  contraction **COC**
cathode **c.; ca.; cath.; k.; ka**
cathode ray **CR**
cathode-ray oscilloscope
  CRO
cathode-ray tube **CRT**
Catholic **C.; Cath.**
Catholic Youth
  Organization **CYO**
caught **c.; ct.**
caught out **c.**
causative **caus.**
cause **c.**
cavalier **cav.**
cavalry **cav.**
caveat **cav.**
cavity **cav.**
cedi **c**
ceiling **clg.**
ceiling and visibility
  unlimited **CAVU**
celluloid **cel**
Celsius **C; Cel.; Cels.**
cement **cem.**
cemetery **cem.**
census **cs.**
cent **c.; ct.**
cental **c.; cent.; ctl.**
centare **ca**

centavo **c.; ctvo.**
center **c.; cent.; cr.; ctr.**
center back **CB**
center field **CF**
Centers for Disease
  Control **CDC**
center forward **CF**
center halfback **CH; CHB**
center line **C.L.**
center matched **C.M.**
center of gravity **c.g.**
center of pressure **C.P.**
center to center **c. to c.**
centesimo **ctmo.**
centi- **c**
centiare **cent.**
centibar **cb**
centigrade **C; cent.**
centigrade heat unit **CHU**
centigrade thermal
  unit **CTU**
centigram **cg**
centiliter **cl**
centime **c.; cent.**
centimeter **c.; cm**
centimeter-gram-second **cgs**
centimo **ctmo.**
centipoise **cp.**
centistoke **cs**
central **cen.; cent.**
Central America **C.A.**
central business
  district **CBD**
central daylight time **CDT**
central excitatory state **CES**
central heating **CH**
Central Hockey
  League **CHL**
central information file **CIF**
Central Intelligence
  Agency **CIA**

Central Intercollegiate
Athletic Association **CIAA**
centralized traffic control
CTC
central nervous system **CNS**
central processing unit **CPU**
central standard time **CST**
central time **CT**
Central Treaty
Organization **CENTO**
central venous
pressure **CVP**
centrifugal force **c.f.**
cents **cts.**
centum **cent.; ct.**
centuries **cc.**
century **c.; cent.; saec.**
cephalic index **C.I.**
cerebral blood flow **CBF**
cerebral palsy **CP**
cerebrospinal fluid **CSF**
cerebrospinal
meningitis **CSM**
cerebrovascular
accident **CVA**
cerebrovascular
resistance **CVR**
cerium **Ce**
certificate **cert.; ctf.**
Certificated Master **C.M.**
Certificated Mistress **C.M.**
Certificated Teacher **CT**
Certificate in Data
Processing **CDP**
Certificate of Advanced
Graduate Study **C.A.G.S.**
Certificate of Advanced
Study **C.A.S.**
certificate of deposit **CD**
certificate of disability for
discharge **CDD**

certificate of insurance **C/I**
Certificate of Merit **C. of M.**
certificate of origin **C/O**
certificate of public
convenience and
necessity **C.P.C. & N.**
Certificate of Secondary
Education **C.S.E.**
certification **cert.**
certified **cert.**
Certified Financial
Planner **C.F.P.**
Certified Flight
Instructor **CFI**
Certified General
Accountant **CGA**
Certified Internal
Auditor **CIA**
Certified Laboratory
Assistant **CLA**
Certified Life
Underwriter **CLU**
Certified Medical
Assistant **CMA**
Certified Medical Assistant-
Administrative **CMA-A**
Certified Medical Assistant-
Administrative & Clinical
CMA-AC
Certified Medical Assistant-
Clinical **CMA-C**
Certified Medical
Electroencephalographic
Technician **CMET**
Certified Medical
Electroencephalographic
Technologist **CMET**
Certified Nurse
Midwife **CNM**
Certified Occupational
Therapy Assistant **COTA**

Certified Operating Room
Technician **CORT**

Certified Professional
Secretary **CPS**

Certified Prosthetist-
Orthotist **CPO**

Certified Public
Accountant **CPA**

Certified Registered Nurse
Anesthetist **CRNA**

Certified Respiratory Therapy
Technician **CRTT**

Certified Shorthand
Reporter **CSR**

Certified Social
Worker **CSW**

Certified Teacher **CT**

Certified Technician **CT**

certify **cert.**

certiorari **cert.**

cervical **c.; cerv.**

cesarean section **cs**

cesium **Cs**

chain **ch**

chairman **c.; ch.;
chm.; chmn.**

chaldron **ch.; chd.**

chalk **ck.**

chamber of commerce
CC; C. of C.

champion **ch.**

championship **chp.**

Championship Auto Racing
Teams **CART**

chancellor **c.; ch.; chanc.**

chancery **c.; ch.; chanc.**

change **chg.**

changed **chgd.**

change of rating **C/R**

channel **chan.**

channel electron multi-

plier **CEM**

chaplain **Ch.; Chap.**

chapter **c.; ch.; chap.**

chapters **cc.**

character **char.**

characteristic **char.**

characters per second **cps**

charge **chg.**

charge conjugation **C**

charge-conjugation/
parity **CP**

charge-coupled device **CCD**

charged **chgd.**

charge of quarters **CQ**

charity **char.**

charter **char.; chtr.**

chartered accountant **C.A.**

Chartered Financial
Analyst **CFA**

Chartered Life
Underwriter **CLU**

Chartered Property
and Casualty
Underwriter **CPCU**

Chartered Public
Accountant **CPA**

Chartered Stenographic
Reporter **CSR**

charterers pay dues **c.p.d.**

charter party **C.P.**

check **ch.; chk.; ck.**

checkered **ch.**

checkmate **chm.**

chemical **chem.**

chemical and biological
warfare **CBW**

chemical, bacteriological, and
radiological **CBR**

chemical, biological, and
radiological **CBR**

Chemical Engi-

neer **C.E.; Ch.E.**
chemically pure **C.P.**
chemical oxygen demand **COD**
chemical stimulation of the brain **CSB**
chemical warfare **CW**
chemist **chem.**
chemistry **chem.**
chemotherapeutic index **CI**
cheque **chq.**
chervonets **ch.**
Cheshire **Ches.**
chess club **CC**
chest **ch.**
chest and left arm **CL**
chest and right arm **CR**
chestnut **ch.; chstnt.**
chevalier **chev.**
chevron **chev.**
Chicago Board of Trade **CBT**
Chicago Board Options Exchange **CBOE**
chick cell agglutinating **CCA**
chief **c.; ch.; chf.**
chief accountant **C.A.**
chief administrative officer **CAO**
chief baron **CB**
chief clerk **CC**
chief complaint **CC**
chief counsel **CC**
chief executive officer **CEO**
chief flying instructor **CFI**
chief inspector **CI**
chief judge **C.J.**
chief justice **C.J.**
chief master sergeant **C.M.Sgt.**
chief of division **CD**

chief of general staff **CGS**
chief of naval operations **CNO**
chief of section **C. of S.; COS**
chief of staff **C. of S.; COS; CS**
chief petty officer **CPO**
chief value **c.v.**
chief warrant officer **CWO**
child **c.; ch.**
childhood disease **CHD**
children **ch.**
child welfare **CW**
chimney **chy.**
China, Burma, India **CBI**
Chinese **Chin.**
Chinese communist forces **CCF**
Chinese Communist Party **CCP**
chloride **Cl.**
chlorinated polyvinyl chloride **CPVC**
chlorine **Cl**
chloroacetophenone **CN**
chlorobenzamalonitrile **CS**
chlorofluorocarbon **CFC**
chlorofluoromethane **CFM**
chloroform **chl**
chlorpromazine **CPZ**
chlortetracycline **CTC**
chocolate-coated tablet **CCT**
choice **ch.**
choir organ **ch.**
choke **ch.**
cholecystokinin **CCK**
cholesterol **chol.**
cholinesterase **ChE**
chord **chd.**
chorionic gonadotropin **CG**

Christ **XP; Xt.**
Christian **Xn.; Xtian.**
Christian Era **C.E.**
Christianity **Xnty.; Xty.**
Christian Science
  practitioner **CS**
chromium **Cr**
chromogenic **ch.**
chronic **ch.; chr.**
chronic coronary
  insufficiency **CCI**
chronicle **chron.**
Chronicles **Chron.**
chronic lymphocytic
  leukemia **CLL**
chronic obstructive pulmonary
  disease **COPD**
chronic obstructive pulmonary
  emphysema **COPE**
chronic passive
  congestion **CPC**
chronic respiratory
  disease **CRD**
chronic ulcerative
  colitis **CUC**
chronological **chron.**
chronological age **CA**
chronology **chron.**
church **c.; ch.**
churchwarden **chwdn.; CW**
Cinncinnati **Cinn.**
circa **c.; ca.; cir.; circ.**
circiter **c.**
circle **cir.; circ.**
circuit **c.; cir.; circ.; ct.**
circuit court **CC**
circuit court of appeals **CCA**
circular **cir.; circ.; cr.**
circular error probable **CEP**
circular measure **CM**
circular mil **c.m.**

circular muscle **CM**
circular note **CN**
circulation **cir.; circ.**
circulation time **CT**
circum **c.**
circumference **C; cir.; circ.**
cirrocumulus **Cc**
cirrostratus **Cs**
cirrus **Ci**
citation **cit.**
cited **cit.**
citizen **cit.**
Citizens' Advice Bureau
  CAB
citizens band **CB**
citrate **cit.**
city council **CC**
civil **civ.**
Civil Aeronautics
  Board **CAB**
Civil Air Patrol **CAP**
civil air regulation **CAR**
civil cases **CC**
civil code **CC**
civil commotion **CC**
Civil Defense **CD**
Civil Engineer **C.E.**
civilian **civ.**
Civilian Conservation
  Corps **CCC**
Civilian Public Service **CPS**
civil law **C.L.**
civil liberties **CL**
civil power **CP**
civil procedure **CP**
civil rights **CR**
Civil Rights Commission
  CRC
Civil Service **CS**
Civil Service Commission
  CSC

claim **cl.**
claim agent **C.A.**
claimant **clt.**
claiming **cl.; clmg.**
claiming race **clm.**
clarinet **clar.**
class **cl.**
classical **cl.**
classification **cl.**
class rate **C.R.**
clause **cl.**
clavicle **cl.**
clean voided specimen **CVS**
clear **clr.**
clear-air turbulence **CAT**
clearance **c.; cl.; clr.**
cleared **cld.**
clearinghouse **CH**
clear to send **CTS**
clergyman **cl.**
clerical, administrative, and fiscal **CAF**
clerk **cl.; clk.**
clerk of the peace **CP**
Cleveland **Clev.**
clinic **cl.**
clinical **clin.**
clinical unit **CU**
clock **clk.**
clockwise **C; ckw.; CW**
clonus **c.**
close **cl**
closed bladder drainage **CBD**
closet **cl.**
close-up **CU**
closure **c.; cl.**
cloth **cl.**
clothing **clo.**
clot retraction **CR**
cloudy **c**

clove **cl.**
cluster bomb unit **CBU**
clutch **cl.**
coast artillery **CA**
coast defense **CD**
coast guard **CG**
coated tablet **CT**
cobalt **c.; Co**
cocaine **C**
code **cde.**
code of procedure **C.P.**
code telegram **CT**
codex **c.; cod.**
codices **codd.**
codicil **codl.**
cod-liver oil **CLO**
coefficient **c.; coef.; coeff.**
coefficient of drag **Cd**
coenzyme **Co**
cognate **c.; cog.**
coil **cl.**
cold **c.**
cold air **C.A.**
cold water **C.W.**
collated **col.; coll.**
collateral **clt.; col.; coll.; collat.**
colleague **col.; coll.**
collect **col.; coll.**
collected **col.; coll.**
collection **coll.**
collection and delivery **C. & D.**
collective **col.; coll.**
collect on delivery **c.o.d.**
collector **col.; coll.**
college **c.; col.; coll.**
college ability test **CAT**
College English Association **CEA**
College Football Asso-

ciation **CFA**
College Language
Association **CLA**
College Level Examination
Program **CLEP**
College Proficiency
Examination **CPE**
College Qualification
Test **CQT**
collegiate **col.; coll.**
collision avoidance system
CAS
colloidal **coll.**
colloquial **col.; coll.; colloq.**
colloquialism **col.; coll.**
collyrium **coll.**
cologarithm **colog**
Colombia **Col.**
colon **c.; co.**
colonel **Col.; COL**
colonial **col.**
colonial office **C.O.**
colony **col.**
colophon **col.; colo.**
color **c.; clr.; col.**
Colorado **Co.; CO;
Col.; Colo.**
colored **col.**
color index **C.I.**
Color Sequence with
Memory **SECAM**
color vision **VC**
Colossians **Col.**
colt **c.**
Columbia Valley
Authority **CVA**
columbium **Cb**
column **col.; coln.**
combat **c.**
combat command **CC**
combat group **CG**

combat team **CT**
combination **comb.**
combinatorial and algebraic
machine aided
computation **CAMAC**
combined **comb.**
combined chiefs of staff **CCS**
combining **comb.**
combustion **comb.**
comedy **com.**
comic **com.**
comma **com.**
command **cd.; cmd.;
comd.; comm.**
commandant **CDT;
comdt.; comm.**
commander **c.; Cdr.; CDR;
Cmdr.; com.; comd.;
comdr.; comm.; cr.**
Commander in Chief
CIC; C in C
Commander of the Order of
the British Empire **C.B.E.**
commanding **cdg.; cmdg.;
comd.; comdg.; comm.**
commanding general **CG**
commanding officer **CO**
command post **CP**
command sergeant
major **CSM**
command service
module **CSM**
comment **com.**
commentary **comm.**
commerce **com.; comm.**
commercial **cml.; com.;
coml.; comm.**
commercial agent **C.A.**
commercial dock **CD**
commercial quality **CQ**
commercial traveler **CT**

commercial weight **C.W.**
commissary **commy.**
commissary general **CG**
commission **comm.; commn.**
commission certified **CC**
commissioned **cd.; comd.; comm.**
commissioned warrant officer **CWO**
commissioner **com.; comm.; commr.; comr.; coms.**
commissioner for oaths **CO**
Commission Sportive Internationale **CSI**
committee **com.; comm.; cttee.**
Committee for Economic Development **CED**
Committee on Political Education **COPE**
Committee to Reelect the President **CREEP**
commodity rate **C.R.**
commodore **CDRE; Cmdre.; commo.**
common **com.; comm.**
common bench **C.B.**
common bile duct **CBD**
Common Business Oriented Language **COBOL**
common carrier **CC**
common council **CC**
commoner **com.; comm.**
Common Era **C.E.**
common law **C.L.**
common meter **c; C.M.**
common meter double **C.M.D.**
common particular meter **CPM**
common pleas **CP**

common pleas division **CPD**
common prayer **CP**
common time **c**
common version **C.V.**
commonwealth **com.; comm.**
commune **comm.**
communicable disease **CD**
communication **com.; comm.**
communications intelligence **comint**
communications officer **CO**
communications satellite **satcom**
Communications Workers of America **CWA**
communication with extraterrestrial intelligence **CETI**
communist **com.; comm.**
Communist Party **CP**
community **com.; comm.**
community antenna television **CATV**
community college **CC**
Community Development Block Grant **CDBG**
community mental health center **CMHC**
Community Services Administration **CSA**
companies **cos.**
companion **c.; comp.**
Companion of Honour **C.H.**
Companion of the Order of St. Michael and St. George **C.M.G.**
Companion of the Order of the Bath **C.B.**
company **Cía.; Cie.; co.; comp.; compy.; coy.**

company commander **CC**
company's risk **C.R.**
comparative **comp.; compar.**
compare **cf.; comp.; conf.; cp.**
compartment **compt.**
compass **comp.**
compass heading **CH**
compass north **CN**
compensation **comp.**
competitive protein binding **CPB**
compilation **comp.**
compiled **comp.**
compiler **comp.**
complains of **c/o**
complement **C; comp.**
complementary metal oxide semiconductor **CMOS**
complement fixation **c.f.**
complement fixation test **CFT**
complete **comp.; cpl.**
complete blood count **CBC**
complete games **CG**
completely **compl.**
completely denatured **CD**
completely knocked down **CKD**
completions **com.**
complex reaction time **CRT**
complier **comp.**
compline **cpl.**
composed **comp.**
composer **comp.**
composite **comp.**
composition **comp.**
compositor **comp.**
compound **comp.; compd.; cpd.**

compounded **comp.**
comprehensive **comp.**
Comprehensive Employment and Training Act **CETA**
compressed natural gas **CNG**
compressed tablet **C.T.**
comprising **comp.**
comptroller **comp.; compt.**
comptroller general **CG**
computed tomography **CT**
computer-aided design **CAD**
computer-aided design and drafting **CADD**
computer-aided engineering **CAE**
computer-aided instruction **CAI**
computer-aided manufacturing **CAM**
computer-assisted design **CAD**
computer-assisted instruction **CAI**
computer-assisted retrieval **CAR**
computer-based instruction **CBI**
computer-generated imagery **CGI**
computer-integrated manufacturing **CIM**
computerized axial tomography **CAT; CT**
computerized branch exchange **CBX**
computerized emission tomogram **CET**
computerized tomography **CT**
computer numerical

control **CNC**
computer output microfilm **COM**
computer output microfilmer **COM**
concentrate **conc.**
concentrated **conc.**
concentration **conc.; concn.**
concentric **conc.**
conceptual quotient **CQ**
concerning **conc.**
concerto **con.; cto.**
conchology **conch.; conchol.**
conclusion **C; con.**
concrete **conc.**
condemned **c.; cd.**
condensed **cond.**
condenser **cond.**
condition **cond.**
conditional **cond.**
conditioned emotional response **CER**
conditioned reflex **cond. ref.; CR**
conditioned response **cond. resp.; CR**
conditioned stimulus **CS**
conditioner **cond.**
conduct **cond.**
conductance **G**
conducted **cond.**
conductivity **cond.**
conductor **c.; cond.; condr.**
Confederate **Confed.**
Confederate States of America **C.S.A.**
confederation **conf.**
conference **conf.**
confessor **c.; conf.**
confidence **con**
confidential **c.; conf.**

confidential document **CD**
confined to barracks **CB**
confined to camp **CC**
confirmation of balance **C. of B.**
Confraternity of Christian Doctrine **CCD**
confused artificial insemination **CAI**
congenital **cong.**
congestive heart failure **CHF**
Congo red **CoR**
congregation **c.; cong.**
Congregation of the Holy Cross **C.S.C.**
Congregation of the Mission **C.M.**
Congregation of the Most Holy Redeemer **C.SS.R.**
Congregation of the Passion **C.P.**
congress **c.; cong.**
congressional **cong.**
congressional district **CD**
Congressional Research Service **CRS**
Congress of Industrial Organizations **CIO**
Congress of Racial Equality **CORE**
conic **con.**
conjugation **conj.**
conjunction **conj.**
conjunctive **conj.**
connected **conn.**
Connecticut **Conn.; CT**
connecting **con.**
connecting carrier **CC**
connecting line **CL**
connection **con.; conn.**

connotation **conn.**
connotative **conn.**
conscientious objector **CO**
consciousness **Cs**
consciousness-raising **CR**
consecrated **cons.**
conservative **c.; cons.**
consigned **cons.**
consignment **cons.; consgt.**
consignment note **C/N**
consol **con.; cons.**
console command processor **CCP**
consolidated **cn.; con.; cons.; consol.**
consonant **C; cons.**
consort **con.**
constable **c.; cons.**
constant **const.; K**
constant angular velocity **CAV**
constant drainage **CD**
constant linear velocity **CLV**
constant pressure **CP**
constituent **const.**
constitution **cons.; const.**
constitutional **const.; constl.**
constitutional psychopathic inferiority **CPI**
constitutional psychopathic state **CPS**
construction **cons.; const.; constr.**
construction and development **C & D**
construction battalion **CB**
Construction Specifications Institute **CSI**
constructive total loss **CTL**
consul **c.; con.; cons.; cos.; cs.**
consular declaration **CD**
consular invoice **C.I.**
consul general **CG**
consulship **cos.**
consulting **cons.**
consumer price index **CPI**
Consumer Product Safety Commission **CPSC**
Consumer Product Safety Corporation **CPSC**
consumption entry **C.E.**
contact **c.**
contact potential difference **CPD**
contagious disease **CD**
container **co.**
containing **cont.; contg.**
contango **cgo.**
contemporary **cont.**
contents **cont.**
contiguous fisheries zone **C.F.Z.**
continent **cont.**
continental **c; cont.; contl.**
continental plan **CP**
continuation **contn.**
continuation clause **C.C.**
continue **cont.**
continued **con.; cont.; contd.**
continuing education unit **CEU**
continuing medical education **CME**
continuous **cont.**
continuous negative pressure **CNP**
continuous positive airway pressure **CPAP**
continuous wave **CW**

contra **C.; con.**
contraband **contbd.**
contraband control **CBC**
contrabass **C.B.**
contra credit **CC**
contract **cont.; contr.**
contraction **c.; contr.**
contractor **contr.**
contralto **c; contr**
contrary **cont.; contr.**
contributing **contbg.**
contribution **contbn.; contrib.**
contributor **contbr.; contrib.**
control **cont.; contl.; contr.; CTR; CTRL**
controlled thermonuclear reactor **CTR**
controller **contr.**
controller of accounts **CA**
Control Program/ Microcomputers **CP/M**
convalescent **conv.**
convenient **conv.**
convent **conv.**
convention **conv.**
conventional **conv.**
conversation **conv.**
converted **conv.**
converter **conv.**
convertible **conv.; cv.; cvt.**
convex **cx.**
convict **conv.**
convocation **conv.**
convulsive disorder **CD**
convulsive shock therapy **CST**
cook **ck.**
Cooperative College Ability Test **CCAT**

Cooperative Commonwealth Federation (of Canada) **CCF**
Cooperative for American Relief to Everywhere **CARE**
cooperative society **CS**
Coordinated Universal Time **UTC**
coordination **coord.**
Coordinator of Inter-American Affairs **CIAA**
copies **cc.**
copper **c.; cop.; cpr.; Cu**
copper unit of pressure **c.u.p.**
Coptic **Cop.; Copt.**
copulative **cop.**
copy **c.; cop.**
copyright **c.; cop.; copr.**
coral **co.**
cord **c.; cd.**
cordoba **c.**
Corinthians **Cor.**
corner **cnr.; cor.**
cornerback **CB**
cornet **cor.**
Cornish **Corn.**
corn-soya-milk **CSM**
Cornwall **Corn.**
coronary artery disease **CAD**
coronary care unit **CCU**
coronary heart disease **CHD**
coronary intensive care unit **CICU**
coroner **cor.**
coronet **cor.**
corporal **Cpl.**
corporate **corp.**
corporate average fuel economy **CAFE**

corporation **AG; corp.; S.A.**
Corporation for Public
  Broadcasting **CPB**
corps **c.**
Corps of Engineers **C.E.**
cor pulmonale **CP**
corpus **cor.**
corpus luteum **CL**
correct **c.; cor.; corr.**
corrected **cor.; corr.**
correction **cor.; corr.**
correlation coefficient **r**
correlative **cor.; corr.**
correspondence **cor.; corr.**
correspondent **cor.; corr.**
corresponding **cor.; corr.**
corresponding fellow **CF;
  Corr. Fell.**
corresponding member **CM**
corrigendum **cor.; corr.**
corrugated **cor.; corr.**
corrupt **cor.; corr.**
corruption **cor.; corr.**
corticosteroid **cs**
cosecant **cosec; csc**
cosine **cos**
cost **c.**
cost accountant **C.A.**
cost and freight **C. & F.;
  C.F.**
cost and insurance **C. & I.**
Costa Rica **C.R.**
cost, assurance, and freight
  C.A.F.
cost-benefit ratio **CBR**
cost, freight, and insurance
  C.F.I.
cost, insurance, and freight
  c.i.f.
cost, insurance, freight, and
  commission **c.i.f. & c.**

cost, insurance, freight, and
  exchange **c.i.f. & e.**
cost, insurance, freight, and
  interest **c.i.f. & i.**
cost laid down **C.L.D.**
cost of living **COL**
cost-of-living adjustment
  COLA
cost of living index **CLI**
cost per thousand **CPM**
cost plus fixed fee **CPFF**
cotangent **cot; ctn**
could **cd.**
coulomb **c; coul**
council **conc.; coun.**
council accepted **C.A.**
Council for Mutual Economic
  Assistance **CMEA;
  COMECON**
councillor **cr.**
council of churches **CC**
Council of Economic
  Advisors **CEA**
Council on Environmental
  Quality **CEQ**
Council on Wage and Price
  Stability **COWPS**
counsel **col.; coun.**
count **c.; ct.**
counter **ctr.**
counterbalance **cbal.**
counterclockwise **CC; cckw.;
  CCW**
counter electromotive
  force **CEMF**
counterespionage **CE**
counterintelligence **CI**
countermark **CM**
countermarked **CM**
counterpoint **cpt.**
countersink **ck.; csk.**

countess **Ctss.**
counties **cos.**
country and western **C & W**
country club **CC**
counts per minute **cpm**
county **co.; ct.; cty.; cy.**
county council **CC**
county court **CC**
county seat **CS**
coupe **cpe.**
coupon **c.; cp.**
court **c.; crt.; ct.**
courthouse **C.H.**
court-martial **CM**
court of appeal **CA**
court of claims **CCLS; CTCLS**
court of claims reports **CCLSR**
court of common pleas **CCP**
court of customs and patent appeals **CCPA**
court of military appeals **CMA**
court of military review **CMR**
court of probate **CP**
court of sessions **CS**
cousin **c.**
cover note **C/N**
cover point **CP**
crafts, protective, custodial **CPC**
crate **cr.; crt.**
C-reactive protein **CRP**
cream **cr.**
creased **cr.**
created **c.; cr.**
creatine kinase **CK**
creatine phosphate **CrP**
creatine phosphokinase **CPK**

creatinine **Cr**
credit **cr.**
creditable record **CR**
credit account **CA**
credit note **C/N**
creditor **cr.**
creed **cr.**
creek **cr.**
crescendo **cr; cresc**
crew **cr.**
cricket club **CC**
criminal **crim.**
criminal cases **CC**
criminal conversation **crim. con.**
Criminal Investigation Department **CID**
Criminal Investigation Detachment **CID**
Criminal Investigation Division **CID**
criminologist **criminol.**
criminology **criminol.**
critical **crit.**
Critical Care Registered Nurse **CCRN**
critical care unit **CCU**
critical condition **CC**
critical list **CL**
critical path method **CPM**
critical ratio **CR**
criticism **crit.**
criticized **crit.**
crochet **cr.**
crocodile **croc.**
cross **x**
cross-country **X-C**
crossed with **x**
crossing **xg.; Xing**
cross-question **XQ**
cross reacting material **CRM**

crossroad **CR**
Cross Roads **Xrds**
crown **cr.**
crown agent **C.A.**
crown cases **C.C.**
crown colony **C.C.**
crowned **c.**
cruiser **cr.**
crutch walking **CW**
cruzeiro **cr.**
crystal **xl; xtal**
crystalline **cryst.**
crystallized **cryst.**
cubic **c.; cu.**
cubic centimeter **cc**
cubic contents **CC**
cubic feet per hour **cfh**
cubic feet per minute **cfm**
cubic feet per second **cfs**
cubic inch displacement **CID**
cultivar **cv.**
culture **cult.**
Cumbria **Cumb.**
cum dividend **C.D.**
cumulative **cm.; cu.; cum.**
Cumulative Book Index **CBI**
cumulonimbus **Cb**
cumulus **Cu**
cup **c.**
curative **cur.**
curative dose **CD**
curie **c; Ci**
curium **Cm**
currency **c.; cur.; cy.**
currency bond **CB**
currency regulation **CR**
currency transaction
  report **CTR**
current **c.; ct.; cur.; curt.**
current account **C/A**
current complaint **CC**

current cost **CC**
current density **C.D.**
current rate **C.R.**
current series **CS**
current strength **cs**
current transformer **CT**
curriculum vitae **CV**
customer **cust.**
customer's own material
  C.O.M.
customhouse **CH**
custom of port **C/P**
customs and excise **CE**
cut out **CO**
cyanide **cyn.**
cyanogen **Cy**
cycle **c.; cy.**
cycles per minute **cpm**
cycles per second **cps; c/s**
cyclic redundancy check
  CRC
cycling club **CC**
cyclonite **RDX**
cyclopedia **cyc.; cycl.**
cylinder **c.; cyl.**
cystic fibrosis **CF**
cytological **cytol.**
cytology **cytol.**
cytomegalovirus **CMV**
cytopathogenic effects **CPE**

D

daily **dly.**
dam **d.; DM**
damaged **dam.**
damage free **DF**
dame **d.**
Dame Commander of the
  Order of the British
  Empire **D.B.E.**

Dame Grand Cross Order of
the British Empire **G.B.E.**
damn **d.**
danger list **DL**
Daniel **Dan.**
Danish **Dan.**
dark **dk.**
data **D.**
data base **DB**
data base management
system **DBMS**
data interchange format **DIF**
data management system
DMS
data processing **DP**
data terminal equipment
DTE
date **d.**
dated **dd.**
dative **dat.**
daughter **d.; da.; dau.; dgt.**
Daughters of the American
Revolution **DAR**
day **d.; da.**
daybook **D.B.**
day letter **DL**
daylight saving time **DST**
daylight time **DT**
days after acceptance **D/A**
days after date **D/D**
days after delivery **D/D**
days after sight **D/S**
day's date **DD**
D day **D**
deacon **d.; dea.**
dead **d.**
dead air space **DS**
dead freight **d.f.**
dead heat **DH**
dead letter office **D.L.O.**
dead on arrival **D.O.A.**

dead reckoning **DR**
deadweight **d.w.**
deadweight capacity **dwc**
deadweight ton **dwt**
dead without issue **m.s.p.**
dean **d.**
debenture **db.; deb.**
debit **dr.**
debtor **dr.**
decade **dec.**
decani **dec.**
decayed, missing, and filled
teeth **DMF**
deceased **d.; dec.; decd.**
December **Dec.**
deci- **d**
decibel **db; dB**
deciduous **d.**
decigram **dg**
deciliter **dl**
decimal **dec.**
decimal classification **DC**
decimeter **dec; dm**
decistere **ds**
deck **dk.**
deckle edged **DE**
declaration **dec.**
declared **dec.; decd.**
declension **dec.**
declination **dec.**
decompose **dec.**
decorated **dec.**
decorative **dec.**
decrease **dec.**
decreased **decd.**
decrescendo **dec**
dedicated **ded.**
dedication **ded.**
deep **d.**
deep space network **DSN**
defeated **d.**

defecation **def.**
defendant **def.; deft.; dft.**
Defender of the Faith
 DF; F.D.
defense **D; def.**
defense counsel **DC**
Defense Intelligence
 Agency **DIA**
defense order **DO**
defensive end **DE**
defensive tackle **DT**
deferred **def.**
deficient **def.**
deficit **def.**
defined **def.**
definite **def.**
definition **def.**
degaussing **DG**
degeneration **deg.**
degree **d.; deg.**
degree of freedom **d.f.**
degree of polymerization
 D.P.
deka- **da**
dekagram **dag; dkg**
dekaliter **dal; dkl**
dekameter **dam; dkm**
dekastere **dks**
Delaware **DE; Del.**
delayed action **DA**
delayed action tablet **DAT**
delayed broadcast **DB**
delayed delivery **DD**
delayed weather **D.W.**
dele **d.**
delegate **del.**
delegation **del.**
delerium tremens **d.t.'s**
delete **d.; del.**
deliver **del.**
delivered **dd.; deld.; dld.**

delivered alongside
 ship **DAS**
delivered at docks **DD**
delivered free **fco**
delivery **del.; dely.;**
 dlvy.; dly.; dy.
delivery order **DO**
delivery room **DR**
delusion **del.**
demand deposit accounting
 DDA
demand draft **DD**
demand loan **DL**
demijohn **demj.**
demilitarized zone **DMZ**
Democrat **D.; Dem.**
Democratic **D.; Dem.**
Democratic National
 Committee **DNC**
demonstrative **dem.**
demurrage **dem.**
demy **dem.**
Denmark **Den.**
denotation **den.**
denotative **den.**
density **d.**
dental **dent.**
dentist **dent.**
dentistry **dent.**
deoxyribonuclease **DNase**
deoxyribonucleic acid **DNA**
depart **d.; dep.**
department **d.; dep.;**
 dept.; dpt.
Department of Defense **DOD**
Department of Energy **DOE**
Department of Health and
 Human Services **HHS**
Department of
 Health, Education, and
 Welfare **HEW**

Department of Housing and
Urban Development **HUD**
department of motor
vehicles **DMV**
Department of National
Defence **DND**
department of public health
DPH
department of public works
DPW
Department of State **DS**
Department of the Army **DA**
Department of
Transportation **DOT**
departure **d.; dep.**
deponent **dep.; dept.; dpt.**
deposed **dep.**
deposit **dep.**
deposit account **DA**
deposit passbook **DPB**
deposit receipt **DR**
depot **dep.**
depreciation **depr.**
depression **depr.**
depth **dpt.**
deputy **d.; dep.;
dept.; dpty.; Dy**
deputy assistant
director **DAD**
deputy chief **DC**
deputy director **DD**
deputy sheriff **DS**
Derbyshire **Derbys.**
derivation **der.; deriv.**
derivative **D.; der.; deriv.**
derived **der.**
dermatologist **derm.**
dermatology **derm.**
descendant **desc.**
deserted **d.; des.**
deserter **d.; des.**

desertion **des.**
design **des.**
designated hitter **DH**
designed **des.**
desired **des.**
despatch **desp.**
dessertspoon **dstspn.**
destination **destn.; dstn.**
destroyer **DD**
destroyer escort **DE**
detached **det.**
detached service **D.S.**
detachment **det.**
detail **det.**
detective **det.**
detention **detn.**
deterioration index **DI**
deterioration quotient **DQ**
determination **detn.**
determine **det.**
determined **detd.**
determiner **det.**
deuterium **D**
deuteron **d**
Deuteronomy **Deut.**
deutsche mark **DM**
develop **dev.**
developed **d.**
developer **dev.**
developing and printing
D. and P.
developing-out-paper **D.O.P.**
development **dev.; devel.**
developmental quotient **DQ**
deviation **d.; dev.**
deviation clause **DC**
Devonshire **Devon.**
Dewey Decimal
Classification **DDC**
dexter **d.**
diabetes insipidus **DI**

diabetes mellitus **DM**
diagnosis **Dx**
diagnosis undetermined **DU**
diagnostic center **DC**
diagonal **diag.**
diagram **diag.**
dialect **dial.**
dialectal **dial.**
dialectic **dial.**
dialectical **dial.**
dialectics **dial.**
dialogue **dial.**
diameter **d.; dia.; diam.**
diameter at breast height **d.b.h.**
diamine oxidase **DO**
diastolic murmur **DM**
diathermy **dia.**
dibromochloropropane **DBCP**
dichlorodiphenyl-
dichloroethane **DDD**
dichlorodiphenyl-
dichloroethylene **DDE**
dichlorodiphenyl-
trichloroethane **DDT**
dictaphone **dict.**
dictation **dict.**
dictator **dict.**
dictionary **dict.**
Dictionary of American
Biography **DAB**
Dictionary of American
English **DAE**
Dictionary of American
History **DAH**
Dictionary of
Americanisms **DA**
Dictionary of Canadian
Biography **DCB**
Dictionary of National

Biography **DNB**
did not finish **DNF**
did not play **DNP**
didymium **Di**
died **d.**
died without issue
d.s.p.; DWI
diethylstilbesterol **DES**
difference **dif.; diff.**
different **diff.**
differential **d.; diff.**
Differential Aptitude
Test **DAT**
differential rate **DR**
difluorodiphenyl-
trichloroethane **DFDT**
digest **dig.**
digital differential
analyzer **DDA**
digital to analog **D/A**
digital-to-analog
converter **DAC**
dihydroxyphenylalanine
dopa
diisopropyl fluorophosphate
DFP
dilatation **dilat.**
dilation and curettage
D & C
dilute **dil.**
dilute strength **DS**
dilute volume **DV**
dilution **dil.**
dime **d.**
dimension **dim.**
dimensional **d.**
dimercaprol **BAL**
dimethoxy methyl **DOM**
dimethyldichlorvinyl-
phosphate **DDVP**
dimethylsulfoxide **DMSO**

dimethyl terephthalate **DMT**
dimethyltryptamine **DMT**
diminished **dim.**
diminuendo **dim; dimin**
diminutive **dim.**
dinar **d.; din.**
dining room **DR**
dinitrobenzene **DNB**
dinitro-ortho-cresol **DNOC**
diopter **D**
dioptric strength **DS**
dioxin **TCDD**
diphenylamine **DPA**
diphosphopyridine
  nucleotide **DPN**
diphtheria **diph.**
diphtheria, pertussis,
  tetanus **DPT**
diphtheria, tetanus,
  pertussis **DTP**
diploma **dip.; dipl.; dpl.**
diplomacy **dipl.**
diplomat **dipl.; DPL**
diplomatic **dipl.; DPL**
diplomatic corps **C.D.**
direct action **DA**
direct broadcast satellite
  DBS
direct current **DC**
direct distance dialing **DDD**
directional gyro **D.G.**
direction finder **DF**
direction finding **DF**
direct memory access **DMA**
director **d.; dir.**
director general **D.G.**
director of religious
  education **D.R.E.**
Director of the Central
  Intelligence Agency **D.C.I.**
direct port **d.p.**

direct question **D.Q.**
direct random access
  memory **DRAM**
dirty book **d.b.**
disabled **dis.**
Disabled American
  Veterans **DAV**
discharge **dis.; disch.**
discharged **d.; dis.; disc.;
  disch.**
disciple **dis.**
discipline **dis.**
disc jockey **DJ**
disconnect **dis.; disc.**
discontinue **disc.**
discontinued **dis.; disc.**
discount **dis.; disc.; disct.**
discovered **disc.**
disease **d.**
diseased **dis.**
dishonorable discharge **DD**
disk operating system **DOS**
dispatch **disp.**
dispatcher **disp.**
dispatch loading only **d.l.o.**
dispensary **disp.**
dispenser **disp.**
displaced person **DP**
disqualified **d.; DQ**
dissertation **diss.**
dissolve **solv.**
dissolved **dissd.; solut.**
distance **d.; dis.; dist.; DX**
distance measuring
  equipment **DME**
distant early warning **DEW**
distillation **distn.**
distilled **dist.**
distilled water
  aq. dest.; D.W.
distinguished **dist.**

Distinguished Flying
Cross **DFC**
Distinguished Flying
Medal **DFM**
Distinguished Service
Cross **DSC**
Distinguished Service
Order **DSO**
distinguished visitor **DV**
distress signal **SOS**
distribute **dis.; distr.**
distributed data processing
DDP
distribution **distr.**
distributive **distr.**
distributor **distr.**
district **dist.**
district attorney
D.A.; dist. atty.
district court **DC**
district judge **D.J.**
District of Columbia
DC; D.C.
district officer **DO**
district registry **DR**
ditto **do.**
divergence **div.**
diversion **div.**
divide **div.**
divided **div.**
dividend **d.; div.; divd.**
divine **div.**
divinity **div.**
division **d.; div.**
divorced **d.; div.**
dock **dk.**
docket **dkt.**
dock receipt **DR**
dock warrant **D/W**
doctor **D.; doc.; Dr.**
Doctor of Arts **D.A.**

Doctor of Business
Administration **D.B.A.**
Doctor of Canon Law **D.C.L.;**
D.Cn.L.; J.Can.D.; J.C.D.
Doctor of Chemical
Engineering **D.Ch.E.**
Doctor of Chiropractic **D.C.**
Doctor of Civil Law **C.L.D.;**
D.C.L.; J.C.D.
Doctor of Commercial
Law **D.C.L.**
Doctor of Comparative
Law **D.Comp.L.**
Doctor of Comparative
Medicine **D.C.M.; M.C.D.**
Doctor of Dental Medicine
D.M.D.
Doctor of Dental Science
D.D.S.; D.D.Sc.
Doctor of Dental Surgery
D.D.S.
Doctor of Divinity **D.D.**
Doctor of Education **D.Ed.;**
Ed.D.
Doctor of Engineering **D.E.;**
D.Eng.
Doctor of Fine Arts **D.F.A.**
Doctor of Forestry **D.F.**
Doctor of Hebrew Letters
D.H.L.
Doctor of Hebrew Literature
D.H.L.
Doctor of Holy Scripture
D.S.S.
Doctor of Hospital
Administration **D.H.A.;**
D.H.Adm.
Doctor of Humane Letters
L.H.D.
Doctor of Humanities **D.H.;**
H.H.D.; L.H.D.

Doctor of Juridical Science **D.J.S.; D.Jur.Sc.; S.J.D.**

Doctor of Jurisprudence **D.J.; D.Jur.; J.D.**

Doctor of Law **D.L.; Dr.Jur.; J.D.**

Doctor of Laws **Dr.LL.; J.D.; LL.D.**

Doctor of Letters **D.Lit.; D.Litt.; Lit.D.; Litt.D.**

Doctor of Library Science **D.L.S.**

Doctor of Literature **D.Lit.; D.Litt.; Lit.D.; Litt.D.**

Doctor of Mechanical Engineering **D.M.E.**

Doctor of Medical Dentistry **D.M.D.**

Doctor of Medical Science **D.M.Sc.; Med.Sc.D.; M.Sc.D.; M.S.D.**

Doctor of Medicine **M.D.**

Doctor of Modern Languages **D.M.L.**

Doctor of Music **Mus.D.**

Doctor of Musical Arts **D.M.A.; Mus.A.D.**

Doctor of Nursing Science **D.N.Sc.**

Doctor of Optometry **O.D.; Opt.D.**

Doctor of Osteopathic Medicine and Surgery **D.O.**

Doctor of Osteopathy **D.O.**

Doctor of Pharmacy **Phar.D.; Pharm.D.**

Doctor of Philosophy **D.Ph.; D.Phil.; Ph.D.**

Doctor of Physical Education **D.P.E.**

Doctor of Podiatric Medicine **D.P.M.**

Doctor of Podiatry **D.P.; Pod.D.**

Doctor of Psychology **Psy.D.**

Doctor of Public Health **D.P.H.; Dr.P.H.**

Doctor of Religious Education **D.R.E.**

Doctor of Sacred Theology **D.S.T.; S.T.D.**

Doctor of Science **D.S.; D.Sc.; Sc.D.; S.D.**

Doctor of Science in Dentistry **D.Sc.D.**

Doctor of Social Science **D.S.Sc.**

Doctor of Social Welfare **D.S.W.**

Doctor of Surgical Chiropody **D.S.C.**

Doctor of Surgical Podiatry **D.S.P.**

Doctor of Theology **D.T.; D.Th.; Th.D.**

Doctor of Veterinary Medicine **D.V.M.; V.M.D.**

document **doc.**

documents against acceptance **D/A**

documents attached **DA**

documents for acceptance **D/A**

documents for payment **D.P.**

document signed **d.s.**

dog **d.**

doing business as **d/b/a**

do-it-yourself **DIY**

dollar **d.; D.; dol.**

Domesday Book **D.B.**

domestic **dom.**

domestic international sales corporation **DISC**
domestic prelate **D.P.**
dominant **dom.**
dominical letter **DL**
Dominican Republic **Dom. Rep.**
dominion **dom.**
dominus **d.; dnus.; dom.**
Donegal **Don.**
done in faith **a.f.**
don't answer **DA**
dorsal **d.**
Dorset **Dors.**
dosage **dos.**
dose **d.**
Douay Version **D.V.**
double **d.; dbl.; dble.; 2b**
double biased **d.b.**
double-breasted **d.b.**
double column **DC**
double crochet **d.c.**
double entry **DE**
double play **DP**
double pole **D.P.**
double pole, double throw **D.P.D.T.**
double pole, single throw **D.P.S.T.**
double stitch **ds.**
double strength **DS**
double throw **D.T.**
double time **D.T.**
double vibration **d.v.**
dowager **d.**
Dow Jones **D.J.**
Dow-Jones Industrial Average **DJIA**
down **dn.**
Down's syndrome **DS**
dozen **doz.; dz.**

drachma **d.; dr.**
draft **dft.**
drafting **dftg.**
dram **dr.**
dramatic **dram.**
dramatist **dram.**
draw **d.**
drawback **dbk.**
drawer **dr.**
drawing **dr.; drg.; dwg.**
drawn **dr.**
dressed and headed **D & H**
dressed and matched **D & M**
dressing **dr.**
drill instructor **DI**
drink **bib.**
drive **d.; Dr.**
driver **dvr.**
driving **d.**
driving under the influence **DUI**
driving while intoxicated **DWI**
drizzling **d.**
drop **gt.; gutt.**
drops **gtt.; gutt.**
drop zone **D.Z.**
Drug Enforcement Administration **DEA**
drum **dm.; dr.**
drunk and disorderly **D and D**
dry sterile dressing **DSD**
dual **du.**
dual in-line package **DIP**
Dublin **Dub.**
duchess **D.**
duchy **D.**
duck **dk.**
ducktail **DA**
due date **DD**

duel processing unit **DPU**
duke **D.; Du.**
Dumfries and Galloway
  Dumf. Gal.
dun **dn.**
duodecimo **D; duo**
duplex **dup.**
duplicate **dup.; dupl.**
durable press **DP**
duration **d.**
Durham **Dur.**
dust **consperg.**
dust jacket **d.j.**
dust wrapper **d.w.**
Dutch **D.; Du.**
duty **dy.**
duty officer **DO**
duty paid **DP**
Dvorak Simplified Keyboard
  DSK
dwelling **dwg.**
dynamic debugging
  tool **DDT**
dynamics **dynam.**
dynamic spatial
  reconstructor **DSR**
dyne **d**
dysprosium **Dy**

E

each **ea.**
each eye **O.U.**
earl marshall **E.M.**
earned run **ER**
earned run average **ERA**
earnings **e; earn.**
earnings from operations
  EFO
earnings per share **EPS**
ear, nose, and throat **ENT**

earth **e.**
earthen **fict.**
earth satellite vehicle **ESV**
eased up **u**
east **e.; E**
East African Community
  EAC
eastbound **E.B.**
East Caribbean **EC**
east central **EC**
easterly **e.**
eastern **e.**
Eastern Collegiate Athletic
  Conference **ECAC**
eastern daylight time **EDT**
eastern equine
  encephalomyelitis **EEE**
Eastern Hockey League
  EHL
eastern standard time **EST**
eastern time **ET**
Easter term **ET**
Easter time **P.T.**
East Indies **E.I.**
east-northeast **ENE**
east-southeast **ESE**
Ecclesiastes **Eccles.**
ecclesiastic **eccl.**
ecclesiastical **eccl.**
Ecclesiasticus **Ecclus.**
ecclesiology **eccl.**
echelon **ech.**
eclectic **ecl.**
eclogue **ecl.**
ecological **ecol.**
ecology **ecol.**
economic **econ.**
economic advisor **E.A.**
Economic Development
  Administration **EDA**
Economic Regulatory

Administration **ERA**
economics **ec.; econ.**
economist **econ.**
economy **econ.**
Ecuador **Ec.; Ecua.**
edge **e.**
edge grain **E.G.**
edited **ed.**
edition **ed.; edn.**
edition deluxe **EDL**
editor **ed.**
editor's presentation copy
EPC
educable mentally retarded
EMR
educated **ed.; educ.**
education **ed.; edn.; educ.**
educational **ednl.; educ.**
educational age **E.A.**
educationally subnormal
ESN
educational opportunity
grant **E.O.G.**
educational quotient **EQ**
educational television **ETV**
educational therapy **ET**
effect **eff.**
effective **eff.**
effective dose **ED**
effective horsepower **EHP**
effective renal plasma
flow **ERPF**
efficiency **eff.**
efficient **eff.**
Egypt **Eg.**
Egyptian **Eg.; Egypt.**
einsteinium **E; Es**
elapsed time **ET**
elder **eld.**
eldest **e.; el.; eld.**
elected **el.**

election district **ED**
electric **el.; elec.; elect.**
electrical **elec.; elect.**
electrical engineer **E.E.**
electrically alterable read-only
memory **EAROM**
electrically erasable
programmable read-only
memory **EEPROM**
electrically erasable read-only
memory **EEROM**
electrically programmable
read-only memory
EPROM
electrical stimulation of the
brain **ESB**
electrical transcription **ET**
electric current **I**
electric field **E**
electric horsepower **EHP**
electrician **elec.; elect.**
electricity **el.; elec.; elect.**
electric potential **V**
electric telegraph **ET**
electric vehicle **EV**
electrified **elec.; elect.**
electrocardiogram
ECG; EKG
electrocardiograph **EKG**
electroconvulsive therapy
ECT
electrodermal response **EDR**
electroencephalogram **EEG**
electroencephalograph **EEG**
electromagnetic **E.M.**
electromagnetic interference
EMI
electromagnetic pulse **EMP**
electromagnetic unit **emu**
electromotive force **E; emf**
electromyogram **EMG**

electromyograph **EMG**
electromyography **EMG**
electron-coupled oscillator **ECO**
electronic computer-originated mail **E-COM**
electronic countermeasures **ECM**
electronic data processing **EDP**
electronic funds transfer **EFT**
electronic funds transfer system **EFTS**
Electronic Information Exchange System **EIES**
electronic news gathering **ENG**
Electronic Numerical Integrator and Calculator **ENIAC**
electronic warfare **EW**
electron microscope **EM**
electron paramagnetic resonance **EPR**
electron spectroscopy for chemical analysis **ESCA**
electron spin resonance **ESR**
electron volt **eV**
electrooculogram **EOG**
electroplate **e.p.**
electroplated nickel silver **E.P.N.S.**
electroretinogram **ERG**
electroshock therapy **EST**
electrostatic **es**
electrostatic unit **esu**
electuary **elec.; elect.**
element **el.; elem.**
elementary **elem.**
elephant folio **el. fo.**

elevated **el.**
elevation **el.; elev.**
elite guard **S.S.**
elixir **elix.**
Elizabethan **Eliz.**
ell **e.**
El Salvador **El Salv.**
emanation **em.; Em**
embankment **emb.**
embargo **emb.**
embark **emb.**
embarkation **emb.**
embassy **emb.**
embossed **emb.**
embroidered **emb.; embr.**
embryo **emb.; embr.**
embryology **emb.; embr.; embryol.**
emergency **emer.**
emergency locator transmitter **ELT**
emergency maternity and infant care **EMIC**
emergency medical technician **EMT**
emergency room **ER**
emeritus **emer.**
eminence **em.**
emitter coupled logic **ECL**
emmetropia **E**
emperor **emp.; i.; imp.**
empire **emp.**
employee ownership plan **EOP**
Employee Retirement Income Security Act **ERISA**
employee stock ownership plan **ESOP**
employment **emp.**
Employment and Training Administration **ETA**

Employment Standards
  Administration **ESA**
empress **emp.; i.;**
  imp.; impx.
empty **e.; mt.**
emulsion **emul.**
enclosed **enc.; encl.**
enclosure **enc.; encl.**
encyclopedia **enc.;**
  ency.; encyc.
end **e.**
end matched **EM**
end of file **EOF**
end of month **EOM**
endoplasmic reticulum **ER**
endorsed **end.**
endorsement **end.**
endorsement irregular **E.I.**
endpaper **e.p.**
endpoint **e.p.**
enema **E**
enemy **en.**
enemy aircraft **EA**
energy **e.; E; W**
energy efficiency ratio **EER**
Energy Information
  Administration **EIA**
Energy Research
  and Development
  Administration **ERDA**
engine **eng.**
engineer **eng.; engr.**
engineering **eng.;**
  engg.; engin.
engineering change order
  ECO
Engineer of Mines **E.M.**
engine-sized **ES**
England **Eng.**
English **E.; Eng.**
English as a second

language **ESL**
English Dialect Dictionary
  EDD
English finish **E.F.**
English for students of other
  languages **ESOL**
English horn **c.a.**
English-Speaking Union
  E.S.U.
engraved **eng.; engr.;**
  inc.; sculpt.
engraver **eng.; engr.**
engraving **eng.; engr.**
enhanced oil recovery **EOR**
enlarged **enl.**
enlisted **enl.**
enlisted man **EM**
enlisted woman **EW**
enlistment **enl.**
ensign **Ens.; ENS**
entered **ent.; entd.**
entertainment **ent.**
enthalpy **H**
entomological
  entom.; entomol.
entomology **ent.;**
  entom.; entomol.
entrance **ent.**
entropy **S**
entropy unit **eu**
envelope **env.**
Environmental Protection
  Agency **EPA**
envoy **env.**
envoy extraordinary **EE**
enzyme **E**
eosinophil **eos.; eosin.**
ephemeris time **ET**
Ephesians **Eph.; Ephes.**
epilepsy **epil.**
epileptic **epil.**

epilogue **epil.**
Episcopal **Epis.; Episc.**
epistle **ep.**
epitaph **epit.**
epithelial **epith.**
epithelium **epith.**
epitome **epit.**
Epstein-Barr **EB**
equal **aeq.; eq.**
equal employment
  opportunity **EEO**
Equal Employment
  Opportunity Commission
  EEOC
equal opportunity employer
  EOE
equal parts **p. ae.;
  part. aeq.**
Equal Rights Amendment
  ERA
equation **eq.**
equator **eq.**
equatorial **eq.**
equerry **eq.**
equipment **eq.; eqpt.;
  equip.; equipt.**
equitable **eq.**
equity **eq.**
equivalency **equiv.**
equivalent **eq.; equiv.**
equivalent roentgen **ER**
erasable programmable read-
  only memory **EPROM**
erbium **Er**
erg **e.**
Erhard Seminars Training
  est
ermine **erm.**
erroneous **erron.**
error **e.**
error corrected **EC**

errors and omissions **E.O.**
errors and omissions
  excepted **E. and O.E.;
  E.O.E.**
errors excepted **E.E.**
erythema dose **ED**
erythrocyte sedimentation
  rate **ESR**
erythropoietic stimulating
  factor **ESF**
Esdras **Esd.**
Eskimo **Esk.**
especial **esp.**
especially **esp.**
esquire **Esq.; Esqr.; Esqre.**
essence **ess.**
establish **estab.**
established **estbd.; estd.**
established church **EC**
establishment **est.; estab.**
estate **est.; este.**
Esther **Esth.**
estimated **est.; estd.**
estimated position **E.P.**
estimated time of
  arrival **ETA**
estimated time of
  departure **ETD**
estrogen replacement
  theory **ERT**
estuary **est.**
et cetera **etc.; k.t.l.**
ether **eth.**
ethical **eth.**
ethics **eth.**
Ethiopia **Eth.**
ethnologist **ethnol.**
ethnology **ethnol.**
ethyl **Et**
ethylenediaminetetraacetic
  acid **EDTA**

ethylene dibromide **EDB**
ethylparanitrophenyl **EPN**
etymology **ety.**
Europe **Eur.**
European **Eur.**
European Atomic Energy
   Community **Euratom**
European Center for Nuclear
   Research **CERN**
European Coal and Steel
   Community **ECSC**
European Common Market
   ECM
European Community **EC**
European Currency
   Unit **ECU**
European Economic
   Community **EEC**
European Free Trade
   Association **EFTA**
European Monetary
   Union **EMU**
European plan **EP**
European theater of
   operations **ETO**
European Unit of
   Account **EUA**
europium **Eu**
evaluate **eval.**
evaluation **eval.**
evaluator **eval.**
evangelical **ev.**
evaporate **evap.**
evening **evg; evng.**
evening prayer **E.P.**
every **q.**
every day **o.d.; q.d.; quotid.**
every hour **omn. hor.; q.h.;**
   q.hr.; qq. hor.
every morning **o.m.;**
   omn. man.; q.m.

every night **omn. noct.;**
   o.n.; q.n.
every two hours **alt. hor.**
evidence **E**
ex **x**
examination **exam.**
examined **ex.; exd.**
examiner **exam.; exmr.**
example **ex.**
examples **exx.**
Excellency **Exc.**
excellent **e.; ex.; exc.; xlnt.**
except **exc.**
except as otherwise herein
   provided **EOHP**
except as otherwise
   noted **EAON**
excepted **exc.**
exception **ex.; exc.; excpt.**
exception noted **EN**
excess profits **E.P.**
excess profits duty **EPD**
excess-profits tax **EPT**
exchange **ex.; exc.; exch.**
exchanged **exch.**
exchequer **exch.**
exciter **exc.**
exclamation **excl.**
exclude **excl.**
excluding **ex.; excl.**
exclusive **excl.**
exclusive economic
   zone **EEZ**
ex coupon **x-c**
excursion **ex.**
excuse **exc.**
ex dividend **ED;**
   ex div.; x-d; x div.
executed **ex.; exec.**
execution **exec.**
executive **ex.; exec.**

executive officer **EO; XO**
executive order **EO**
executive secretary **ES**
executor **exec.; exor.; exr.**
executrix **exrx.; exx.**
exempt **ex.**
exercise **ex.**
exhibit **ex.**
exhibition **exhbn.**
ex interest **x-i; x in.; x int.**
ex new **x-n**
Exodus **Ex.; Exod.**
ex officio **e.o.**
expansion **exp.**
expected date of
  confinement **EDC**
expedition **expdn.**
expeditionary force **E.F.**
expense **exp.**
experience **exp.; exper.**
experienced **exper.**
experiment **exp.;
  exper.; expt.**
experimental **exp.; exper.;
  exptl.; X**
Experimental Prototype
  Community of Tomorrow
  EPCOT
experimental safety vehicle
  ESV
experimenter **E**
expert **expt.**
expiration **exp.; expn.**
expiration of term of
  service **ETS**
expired **exp.**
explosive **exp.**
exponent **exp.**
exponential **exp.**
export **ex.; exp.; expt.**
exported **exp.**

exporter **exptr.**
Export-Import Bank
  Eximbank
exposition **expn.**
exposure **exp.**
express **ex.; exp.**
expressway **expy.**
ex rights **x-r**
extended **ext.**
extended binary coded decimal
  interchange code **EBCDIC**
extended coverage
  endorsement **ECE**
extended play **EP**
extended release **ER**
extended reponse **XR**
extension **ext.**
exterior **ext.**
external **ext.; extl.**
externally **ext.**
extinct **ext.**
extinguisher **ext.**
extra **ex.; ext.; x**
extracelluar fluid **ECF**
extract **ex.; ext.**
extracting **extg.**
extra duty **ED**
extra, extra large **XXL**
extra fine **E.F.; XF**
extrahepatic blood
  flow **EHBF**
extra high tension **EHT**
extra high voltage **EHV**
extra large **xl; XL**
extra long **XL**
extraordinary **xtry.**
extraordinary and
  plenipotentiary **E. and P.**
extra person **XP**
extra points **x pt**
extrasensory perception **ESP**

extra series **ES**
extra small **xs; XS**
extraterrestrial intelligence **ETI**
extravehicular activity **EVA**
extravehicular life support system **ELSS**
extreme **ext.**
extremely **ext.**
extremely fine **E.F.**
extremely high frequency **EHF**
extremely low frequency **ELF**
extreme pressure **E.P.**
extreme ultraviolet **EUV; XUV**
extremity **ext.**
extruded **extr.**
extrusion **extr.**
ex warrant **xw**
eye **E; o.**
eye, ear, nose, and throat **EENT**
Ezechiel **Ezech.**
Ezekiel **Ezek.**
Ezra **Ez.; Ezr.**

F

fabricated **fab.**
face measurement **F.M.**
facing **fcg.**
facsimile **fac.; fs.**
factor **fac.**
factor VIII **AHF**
factor V **AcG**
factor of safety **f/s**
factory **fac.; fcty.**
faculty **fac.**
Fahrenheit **F; Fah.; Fahr.**

failure **f.**
fair **F**
fair average quality **FAQ**
Fair Employment Practices Act **FEPA**
Fair Employment Practices Commission **FEPC**
Fair Labor Standards Act **FLSA**
faithfully **ffy.**
Falkland Islands **F.I.**
falls **Fls**
false **F**
false reading **FL**
family **f.; fam.**
Family Viewing Time **FVT**
famous **fam.**
fancy **fcy.**
fan marker **FM**
farad **f**
faraday **F**
farm **fm.**
Farm Credit Administration **FCA**
Farmers Home Administration **FmHA**
Farm Security Administration **FSA**
far point **Pr**
farthing **f.; far.; q.**
fascicle **fasc.**
fast **fst.**
fast breeder reactor **fbr**
fast — used of a clock **a.**
father **f.; Fr.; p.**
Fathers **PP.**
fathom **f.; fath.; fm.; fth.; fthm.**
favorite **fav.**
fawn **f.**
feast **f.**

February **Feb.**
federal **fed.; fedl.**
Federal Accounting Standards Board **FASB**
Federal Aviation Administration **FAA**
Federal Bar Association **FBA**
Federal Bureau of Investigation **FBI**
Federal Communications Commission **FCC**
Federal Crop Insurance Corporation **FCIC**
Federal Deposit Insurance Corporation **FDIC**
Federal Election Commission **FEC**
Federal Emergency Management Agency **FEMA**
Federal Emergency Relief Administration **FERA**
Federal Excise Tax **FET**
Federal Financing Bank **FFB**
Federal Home Loan Bank Board **FHLBB**
Federal Housing Administration **FHA**
Federal Income Tax **FIT**
Federal Information Centers **FIC**
Federal Insurance Contributions Act **FICA**
Federal Licensing Examination **FLEX**
Federal Maritime Board **FMB**
Federal Mediation and Conciliation

Service **FMCS**
Federal National Mortgage Association **FNMA**
Federal Power Commission **FPC**
Federal Railroad Administration **FRA**
Federal Republic of Germany **FRG**
Federal Reserve Board **FRB**
Federal Reserve System **FRS**
Federal Savings and Loan Insurance Corporation **FSLIC**
federal tax included **FTI**
Federal Telecommunications System **FTS**
Federal Trade Commission **FTC**
federated **fed.**
federation **fed.; fedn.**
Fédération Equestrienne Internationale **FEI**
Fédération Internationale de Basketball Amateur **FIBA**
Fédération Internationale de Bobsleigh et de Tobogganing **FIBI**
Fédération Internationale de d'Escrime (fencing) **FIE**
Fédération Internationale de Football Association (soccer) **FIFA**
Fédération Internationale de Gymnastique **FIG**
Fédération Internationale de Handball **FIH**
Fédération Internationale de Hockey **FIH**
Fédération Internationale de

Judo **FIJ**

Fédération Internationale de Luge **FIL**

Fédération Internationale de Natation Amateur (swimming) **FINA**

Fédération Internationale de Rugby Amateur **FIRA**

Fédération Internationale des Echecs (chess) **FIDE**

Fédération Internationale de Ski **FIS**

Fédération Internationale des Societies d'Aviron (rowing) **FISA**

Fédération Internationale de Tennis de Table **FITT**

Fédération Internationale de Tir à l'Arc (archery) **FITA**

Fédération Internationale de Volleyball **FIVB**

Fédération Internationale Motorcycliste **FIM**

feet **ft.**

feet per minute **fpm**

feet per second **fps; f.s.**

fellow **F; s.**

Fellow of the American Academy of Pediatrics **FAAP**

Fellow of the American College of Anesthesiologists **FACA**

Fellow of the American College of Apothecaries **FACA**

Fellow of the American College of Cardiology **FACC**

Fellow of the American College of Chest Physicians **FCCP**

Fellow of the American College of Dentists **FACD**

Fellow of the American College of Obstetricians and Gynecologists **FACOG**

Fellow of the American College of Physicians **FACP**

Fellow of the American College of Radiologists **FACR**

Fellow of the American College of Surgeons **FACS**

Fellow of the American Medical Association **FAMA**

Fellow of the American Psychological Association **FAPA**

Fellow of the American Public Health Association **FAPHA**

Fellow of the College of American Pathologists **FCAP**

Fellow of the College of General Practitioners **FCGP**

Fellow of the College of Physicians and Surgeons **FCPS**

Fellow of the International College of Dentists **FICD**

Fellow of the International College of Surgeons **FICS**

Fellow of the Royal Society (British) **FRS**

Fellow of the Royal Society, Canada **FRSC**

felonious assault **FA**

female f.; fem.
feminine f.; fem.
femto- f
femur fem.
Fermanagh Ferm.
fermi f
Fermium Fm
ferry Fry; fy.
fever of undetermined
  origin FUO
fibrillation fib.
fibrous f.
fiction f.; fict.
fictitious fict.
fidelity fid.
fiduciary fid.
field f.; fd.; fld.
field artillery F.A.
field effect transistor FET
fielder's choice FC
field goal FG
field goal attempt FA
Field Hockey Association of
  America FHAA
fielding average FA
fielding position pos.
field manual FM
field marshall FM
field officer FO
field order FO
field post office FPO
field punishment F.P.
field service FS
fieri facias fi. fa.
fifth quint.
fighter f.; ftr.
figurative fig.
figuratively fig.
figure fig.
filament fil.
filial F

filial generation F
fillet fil.
fillister fil.
filly f.
film h.
Film Optical Sensing Device
  for Input to Computers
  FOSDIC
filter fil.
final common pathway FCP
final statement FS
finance f.; fin.
finance officer FO
financial f.; fin.
financial advisor FA
financial secretary
  fin. sec.; FS
fine f.
fine grain FG
fine measurement F.M.
fine paper F.P.
finis fin.
finish f.; fin.
finished fin.
finished with engines FWE
Finland Fin.
Finnish Fin.; Finn.
fire f.
fire brigade FB
fire control FC
fire controlman FC
fire department F.D.
fire direction center FDC
fire hydrant F.H.
fireplace f.p.; frpl.
fireplug F.P.
fireproof fprf.
fire resistent FR
fire retardant FR
fire risk on freight f.r.o.f.
firkin fir.

firm **f.**
firm offer **FO**
first aid **FA**
first-aid post **FAP**
first base **1b**
first-class certificate **FCC**
first day **F.D.**
first-day cover **F.D.C.**
First Families of Virginia **FFV**
first family **FF**
first in, first out **FIFO**
first open water **f.o.w.**
firsts and seconds **FAS**
fiscal **fis.; fisc.**
fiscal year **FY**
fish protein concentrate **FPC**
fitter **ftr.**
fixed **f.**
fixed focus **f.f.**
flag lieutenant **FL**
flag officer **FO**
flange **fl.; flg.**
flanker **fl.**
flash **fl.**
flashing **fl.**
flash point **F.P.**
flat **f.**
flat grain **F.G.**
flavin adenine dinucleotide **FAD**
flavin mononucleotide **FM; FMN**
fleet **f.; flt.**
fleet admiral **FADM**
fleet post office **FPO**
Flemish **Flem.**
fleur de coin **FDC**
flexible **flex.; flx.**
Flexible Loan Insurance Program **FLIP**

flight **flt.**
flight lieutenant **FL**
flight officer **FO**
Flintshire **Flint.; Flints.**
float **flt.**
floating **fltg.**
floating policy **F.P.**
flood **fl.**
flood control **FC**
floor **fl.; flr.**
flooring **flg.**
Florida **FL; Fla.**
florin **f.; fl.; flr.**
flotage **fltg.**
flour **fl.**
flourished **fl.; flou.**
flower **f.**
flowers **fl.**
fluid **f.; fl.; fld.**
fluidness **f.**
fluidounce **f; fl. oz.**
fluidram **fl. dr.**
fluorine **F**
flush **fl.**
flute **fl.**
flyaway factor **FAF**
flying boat **FB**
flying officer **FO**
focal distance **f.d.**
focal length **f; F; FL**
fog **f.**
Fog Investigation Dispersal Operations **FIDO**
folded and gathered **F & G**
folded flat **FF**
folio **f.; fo.; fol.**
folios **ff.**
follicle-stimulating hormone **FSH**
follow copy **f.c.**
following **fol.; foll.**

food **cib.**
Food and Agriculture
  Organization of the United
  Nations **FAO**
Food and Drug
  Administration **FDA**
Food and Nutrition
  Service **FNS**
food control **FC**
food stamp program **FSP**
foolscap **fcap.; fcp.**
foot **f.; ft.**
football association **F.A.**
football club **F.C.**
foot board measure **FBM**
footcandle **f.c.**
foot-lambert **fL**
footnote **fn.**
foot-pound **F.P.; ft-lb**
foot-pound second **fps**
for **f.; p.**
for a dose **pro dos.**
forage acre **FA**
force **f.**
forced **fd.**
ford **fd.**
fore and aft **f. and a.**
forecast **fcst.**
fore edges painted **FEP**
foreign **fgn.; for.**
Foreign Agricultural
  Service **FAS**
foreign airmail **FAM**
foreign body **FB**
foreign exchange **FX**
foreign freight agent **F.F.A.**
foreign general agent **F.G.A.**
foreign general average
  F.G.A.
foreign independent travel
  FIT

foreign individual travel **FIT**
foreign language **FL**
foreign medical graduate
  FMG
foreign mission **FM**
foreign office **FO**
Foreign Press Association
  FPA
foreign service **FS**
foreign service officer **FSO**
forel **for.**
forensic **for.**
forest **for.**
forestry **for.**
foreword **fwd.**
for example **e.g.; ex. gr.;**
  v.g.; z.B.
for external use
  ad us. exter; pro vs. ext.
for further assignment **FFA**
for further transfer **FFT**
forget it, I've got my orders
  FIGMO
for instance **f.i.**
forint **ft.**
fork **Fk.**
form **fm.**
forma **f.**
formed **fd.**
former **fmr.**
formula **f.**
formula translation
  FORTRAN
for orders **f.o.**
for private circulation **FPC**
fort **ft.**
forte **f**
for the emergency **p.r.n.**
for the intervening time
  ad int.; a.i.
for the plaintiff **pro quer.**

for the sake of honor **h.c.**
for the time being **pro tem.**
for this occasion **P.H.V.**
for this purpose **P.H.V.**
for this turn **P.H.V.**
fortification **fort.; ft.**
fortified **fort.; ft.; ftd.**
fortissimo **ff**
forward **f.; fwd.**
forward air controller **FAC**
forward-based systems **FBS**
forwarded **fwdd.**
forward-looking infrared **FLIR**
forward observer **FO**
for your information **FYI**
forzando **forz; fz**
foul **f.**
fouled up beyond all recognition **FUBAR**
found **fd.; fnd.**
foundation **fdn.; fndn.; found.**
foundation member **FM**
founded **fndd.**
founder **fndr.**
founding **fndg.**
foundry **fdry.**
four **quat.**
4/4 **c**
Fourier transform infrared **FTIR**
four times a day **q.d.; q.i.d.**
four-wheel brake **f.w.b.**
four-wheel drive **4WD; FWD**
foxed **fx.**
fractional **frl.**
fractional orbital bombardment system **FOBS**
fragile **f.**

fragment **fr.; frag.**
fragmentation **f.**
frame **fr.; frm.**
frames per second **fps**
framing **frm.**
franc **f.; fc.; fr.**
France **F.; Fr.**
francium **Fr**
Fraternal Order of Eagles **FOE**
free air delivered **FAD**
free alongside **FA; F.A.S.**
free astray **F/A**
free at quay **FAQ**
free church **F.C.**
free delivery **f.d.**
free discharge **f.d.**
free dispatch **f.d.**
free dock **f.d.**
Freedom of Information Act **F.O.I.A.**
free fatty acid **FFA**
free foreign agency **FFA**
free from alongside **f.f.a.**
free from average **f.f.a.**
free from infection **FFI**
free from marking **a.u.n.**
free in and out **FIO**
free into barge **f.i.b.**
free into bunker **f.i.b.**
free in truck **f.i.t.**
free in wagon **f.i.w.**
free of all average **FA; FAA**
free of capture and seizure **f.c. & s.**
free of charge **F.D.D.; f.o.c.**
free of damage **f.o.d.**
free of general average **F.G.A.**
free of income tax **f.i.t.**
free of knots **f.o.k.**

free of particular average **F.P.A.**

free of riot and civil commotion **f.r. and c.c**

free on board **f.o.b.**

free on car **f.o.c.**

free on quay **f.o.q.**

free on rail **FOR**

free on steamer **FOS**

free on truck **FOT**

free on wagon **f.o.w.**

free overside **f.o.**

free speech movement **FSM**

free throw **FT**

freeway **frwy.**

freezing point **fp**

freight **fgt.; frt.**

freight agent **F.A.**

freight and demurrage **f. & d.**

freight and passenger **F.P.**

freight bill **F.B.**

freight forwarder **FF**

freight release **F.R.**

French **F.; Fr.**

French fried **FF**

French West Indies **F.W.I.**

frequency **f; fqcy.; freq.; V**

frequency modulation **FM**

frequent **fqt.; fr.; freq.**

frequentative **freq.**

frequently **freq.**

freshwater **F.W.**

freshwater damage **f.w.d.**

friar **F.; Fr.**

friction glaze **FG**

Friday **F.; Fr.; Fri.**

from **f.; fm.; fr.; frm.**

from the beginning **ab init.; d.c.**

from the sign **d.s.**

from the year of the

founding of the city (of Rome) **A.U.C.**

front **fr.**

Front de Libération du Québec **FLQ**

frontispiece **front.; fspc.**

front-wheel drive **fwd**

fruit **fr.**

fuel **f.**

fuel gas **FG**

fuel oil **FO**

full **f.**

fullback **FB**

full-fashioned **FF**

full interest admitted **FIA**

full organ **FO**

full out **f.o.**

full rate **FR**

full terms **f.t.**

full-time equivalent **FTE**

full width at half maximum **fwhm**

fully good **FG**

fully paid **F.P.**

function **f.**

fund **fd.**

fundamental **fund.**

funding **fdg.**

furlong **f.; fur.**

furlough **fur.**

furnished **furn.**

furniture **furn.**

furniture and fixtures **F. & F.**

further **fur.**

fuselage **fus.**

fusilier **fus.**

fusion **fn.**

future **fut.**

Future Farmers of America **FFA**

G

gadolinium **Gd**
Gaelic **Gael.**
Galatians **Gal.**
gallbladder **GB**
gallery **gal.**
galley **gal.**
gallium **Ga**
gallium arsenide **GaAs**
gallon **C; cong.; gal.**
gallons per day **gpd**
gallons per hour **gph**
gallons per minute **GPM**
gallons per second **gps**
galvanic **galv.**
galvanic skin response **GSR**
galvanism **galv.**
galvanized **galv.**
galvanized iron **GI**
Gamblers Anonymous **GA**
game **g.**
games behind **GB**
games played **p**
gamma-aminobutyric acid
  GABA
gamma globulin **GG**
gamut **gam.**
garage **g.; gar.**
garbage in, garbage out
  GIGO
garden **gdn.**
gas chromatograph **GC**
gas chromatography **GC**
gas constant **R**
gaseous oxygen **gox**
gas-liquid chromatographic
  GLC
gas-liquid chromatography
  GLC
gas, oxygen, and ether **GOE**

gastroenterology **GE**
gastrointestinal **GI**
gate turn off **GTO**
gauge **g.; ga.**
gauss **g; gs**
gazette **gaz.**
gazetteer **gaz.**
Geiger-Müller **GM**
gelatinous **gel.**
gelding **g.**
Gemological Institute of
  America **GIA**
gender **g.; gen.**
general **g.; gen.; genl.; gn.**
General Accounting Office
  GAO
general adaptation
  syndrome **GAS**
general agent **GA**
General Agreement of Tariffs
  and Trade **GATT**
general assembly **GA**
general assistance **GA**
general average **G.A.**
general circular **G.C.**
general claim agent **GCA**
General Confederation of
  Labor **CGT**
general counsel **G.C.**
general court-martial **GCM**
general delivery **GD**
general duty **GD**
general educational
  development **G.E.D.**
general equivalency
  diploma **GED**
general freight average **GFA**
general headquarters **GHQ**
general issue **GI**
Generalized System of
  Preferences **GSP**

generally accepted accounting principles **GAAP**
generally recognized as safe **GRAS**
general manager **G.M.**
general medicine and surgery **GM & S**
general merchandise **GM**
general mortgage **GM**
General (movie rating) **G**
general obligation **G.O.**
general office **G.O.**
general officer **G.O.**
general officer commanding **G.O.C.**
general of the air force **Gen.A.F.**
general of the army **GA**
general order **G.O.**
general paralysis **G.P.**
general paralysis of the insane **GPI**
general paresis **G.P.**
general passenger agent **GPA**
general pause **GP**
general post office **GPO**
general practice **GP**
general practitioner **GP**
general purpose **G.P.**
general quarters **GQ**
general reconnaissance **GR**
general reserve **G.R.**
general rule **reg. gen.**
general rules **r.g.**
general schedule **GS**
general secretary **G.S.**
general semantics **GS**
general service **GS**
General Services Administration **GSA**

general sessions **G.S.**
general staff **GS**
general staff corps **GSC**
general staff officer **GSO**
general superintendent **G.S.**
general support **GS**
general traffic manager **GTM**
generation **gen.; s.**
generator **gen.**
generic **gen.**
Genesis **Gen.**
genetics **gen.**
genitive **g.; gen.**
genitourinary **GU**
gentleman rider **G.R.**
genus **gen.**
geographic **geog.**
geographical **geog.**
geographic position **GP**
geography **geog.**
geologic **geol.**
geological **geol.**
geology **geol.**
geometric **geom.**
geometrical **geom.**
geometric progression **G.P.**
geometry **geom.**
geopotential meter **GPM**
George Cross **G.C.**
Georgia **Ga.; GA**
geostationary operational environmental satellite **GOES**
germ **grm.**
German **G; Ger.**
German Democratic Republic **GDR**
Germanic **Gmc.**
germanium **Ge**
Germany **Ger.**

germination **grm.**
gerund **ger.**
gerundial **ger.**
gerundive **ger.**
Gibraltar **Gib.; Gibr.**
giga- **G**
gigacycle **GC**
giga-electron-volt **GeV**
gigahertz **GHz**
gigawatt **GW**
gilbert **g**
gill **gi.; gl.**
gilt **g.; glt.; gt.**
gilt edges **g.e.; GE**
gilt marble edges **GME**
gilt top **g.t.**
gilt top edge **GTE**
girder **gir.**
Girl Scouts of America **GSA**
girth breast height **g.b.h.**
glass **gl.**
glass-reinforced plastic **GRP**
glass-reinforced polyester **GRP**
glaze **gl.**
glide path **GP**
glider **g.**
Global Atmospheric Research Program **GARP**
gloom **g.**
gloria **gl.**
Glory be to the Father **G.P.**
gloss **gl.**
glossary **gl.; glos.; gloss.**
Gloucestershire **Glos.**
glutathione **GSH; GSSG**
goal **g.**
goalie **g.**
goalkeeper **GK**
goals against **a**
God willing **D.V.**

gold **Au; g.**
gold bond **GB**
golden number **GN**
gold medal **GM**
gold standard **GS**
gonadotropin releasing hormone **Gn.R.H.**
gonococcus **GC**
good **g.; gd.**
good delivery **GD**
good fair average **GFA**
goods **gds.**
good this month **GTM**
good this week **GTW**
good till canceled **GTC**
good till countermanded **GTC**
Gothic **Goth.**
Gothic letter **GL**
gourde **G; gde.**
government **g.; gov.; govt.**
governmental **gov.**
government furnished equipment **GFE**
government issue **GI**
Government National Mortgage Association **GNMA**
Government of American Samoa **GAS**
government-owned, contractor-operated **GOCO**
Government Printing Office **GPO**
government rubber styrene **GR-S**
government service **GS**
governor **gov.**
governor general **G.G.**
graceful **graz**
grade **gr.**

grade-point average **GPA**
gradient **grad.**
graduate **grad.**
graduate assistant **GA**
graduated **grad.**
graduated length method **GLM**
Graduated Payment Mortgage **GPM**
graduate grade-point average **GGPA**
Graduate in Law **G.L.**
Graduate in Pharmacy **Ph.G.; Phm.G.**
Graduate Management Admissions Test **GMAT**
Graduate Nurse **GN**
Graduate Realtors Institute **G.R.I.**
Graduate Record Examination **GRE**
graduate teaching assistant **G.T.A.**
graft versus host **GVH**
grain **g.; gr.**
gram **g.; gm; gr.**
grammar **gr.; gram.**
grammar school **GS**
grammatical **gr.; gram.**
gram-molecular volume **GMV**
gram-molecular weight **GMW**
Grampian **Gramp.**
grand **g.; gr.**
Grand Army of the Republic **GAR**
grand commander **G.C.**
grand cross **G.C.**
granddaughter **g.d.**
grand duchess **G.D.**

grand duchy **G.D.**
grand duke **G.D.**
grand jury **GJ**
Grand Lodge **G.L.**
grand master **G.M.**
grand old man **GOM**
Grand Old Party (Republican) **GOP**
grand organ **G.O.**
grand prix **GP**
grandson **g.s.**
grand theft auto **GTA**
grand touring car **GT**
grand unification theories **GUTS**
graphite **gr.**
gravel **gvl.**
gravid **grav.**
gravity **g; grav.**
gravity **gr.**
gray **gr.; gy.**
great **g.; gr.; gt.**
Great Books Foundation **GBF**
Great Britain **G.B.; Gr.Br.; Gt.Br.; Gt.Brit.**
great circle **G.C.**
Greater Manchester **Gtr. Man.**
greatest common divisor **GCD**
greatest common factor **GCF**
great gross **G.G.**
great organ **G.O.**
great primer **GP**
Greece **Gr.**
Greek **Gk.; Gr.**
green **g.; gn.; grn.; vir.**
Greenwich apparent time **GAT**
Greenwich civil time **GCT**

Greenwich hour angle **GHA**
Greenwich mean sidereal time **GMST**
Greenwich mean time **GMT**
Greenwich meridian **GM**
Greenwich sidereal time **GST**
Greenwich time **G**
grid **g.**
grid leak **GL**
grind **gr.; grd.**
grooved roofing **G.R.**
groschen **g.; gr.**
gross **g.; gr.; gro.**
gross domestic product **GDP**
gross national income **GNI**
gross national product **GNP**
gross ton **G.T.**
gross vehicle weight **GVW**
gross weight **gr. wt.**
ground **gd.; gnd.; grd.**
ground-controlled approach **GCA**
ground-controlled interception **GCI**
ground-controlled landing **GCL**
ground-effect machine **GEM**
ground fault circuit interrupter **GFCI**
ground fault interrupter **GFI**
ground-launched cruise missile **GLCM**
ground level **G.L.**
ground position indicator **GPI**
ground speed **GS**
ground-to-air pilotless aircraft **GAPA**
ground zero **GZ**
group **g.; gp.; gr.; gro.**

group captain **G.C.**
Group Inclusive Tour **GIT**
growing equity mortgage **GEM**
growth hormone **GH**
Guam **GU**
guanosine triphosphate **GTP**
guarantee **gu.; guar.**
guaranteed **grd.; gtd.; gu.; guar.**
guaranteed annual income **GAI**
guaranteed annual wage **GAW**
guaranteed retirement income **GRI**
guarantor **guar.**
guaranty **guar.**
guard **g.; gd.**
guardian **g.; gdn.**
guardsman **gdsm.**
Guatemala **Guat.**
guidance **guid.**
guide **g.**
guidebook **G.B.**
guided missile **GM**
guided space vehicle **GSV**
guilder **G; gld.**
Guild of Catholic Lawyers **GCL**
guinea **gn; gu.**
gulden **G**
gules **gu.**
gulf **G**
gun **gn.**
gunboat **GB**
gun control **G.C.**
gunlaying **GL**
gunmetal **GM**
gunner **gnr.**
gunnery sergeant **Gy.Sgt.**

guttural **gutt.**
Gwynedd **Gwyn.**
gynecologic **gyn.; gynecol.**
gynecological **gyn.; gynecol.**
gynecologist **gyn.; gynecol.**
gynecology **gyn.; gynecol.**

H

Habakkuk **Hab.**
habeas corpus **hab. corp.**
habitat **hab.**
hafnium **Hf**
Haggai **Hag.**
hail **h.**
haler **h.**
half **dim.; h.; hf.; m.**
half an hour **semih.**
halfback **HB**
half calf **HC**
half chest **HC**
half morocco **HM**
half pay **h.p.**
halfpenny **ob.**
half time **HT**
halftone **HT**
half-value layer **HVL**
hall **h.**
halt **hlt.**
Hamiltonian **H**
hamlet **hmlt.**
Hampshire **Hants**
hand **hd.; hnd.; m.**
handbook **handbk.;
   hdbk.; hndbk.**
hand control **HC**
handful **m.; man.**
handicap **hcap.; hcp.**
handily **h.**
handkerchief **hdkf.; hkf.**
handle **hdl.**

handling **hdlg.**
handmade **HM**
handmade paper **HMP; HP**
handpainted **h.p.**
hands high **hh**
Hansen's disease **HD**
harbor **h.; har.; Hbr.**
harbor defense **HD**
harbor master **HM**
hard **H; hrd.**
hard black **HB**
hard copy **HC**
hardness **h.**
hardtop **HT**
hardware **hdw.; hdwe.;
   hdwre.; hrdwre.**
hardwood **hdwd.**
harlequin **hlqn.**
harmonic mean **H.M.**
harpsicord **hps.**
have **hv**
haversine **hav**
Hawaii **HI**
Hawaiian standard time
   HST
Hawaii time **HT**
hazard **haz.**
haze **h.**
hazy **hzy.**
head **hd.**
head, heart, hands, and
   health **4-H**
heading per gyrocompass
   HPGC
headline **hdl.**
headmaster **h.m.**
headmistress **h.m.**
head office **H.O.**
headquarters **h.;
   hdqrs.; HQ**
Health Care Financing

Administration **HCFA**
health maintenance
  organization **HMO**
Health Opportunity for People
  Everywhere **HOPE**
Health Resources
  Administration **HRA**
Health Resources and Services
  Administration **HRSA**
hearing distance **HD**
heart **hrt.**
Heart and Lung
  Foundation **HLF**
heartwood **hrtwd.**
heat **h.; ht.**
heating **htg.**
heating, ventilation, and air
  conditioning **HVAC**
heavier than air **HTA**
heavy **hvy.; hy.**
heavy antiaircraft **HAA**
heavy artillery **H.A.**
heavy bomber **HB**
heavy-duty **HD**
heavy ion linear accelerator
  HILAC
heavy machine gun **HMG**
heavy mobile **HM**
Hebrew **Heb.**
Hebrews **Heb.**
hectare **ha**
hecto- **h**
hectogram **hg.; hgm**
hectoliter **hl**
hectometer **hm**
height **h.; hgt.; ht.**
height finding **HF**
height-length **HL**
height-range indicator **HRI**
heights **Hts.**
heir **h.; her.**

held covered **H.C.**
helicopter **h.**
heliogram **hg.**
helium **He**
heller **h.**
hemagglutination
  inhibition **HI**
hematocrit **hct.**
hemoglobin **Hb; Hgb**
hemstitched **HS**
hence **h.**
henry **h; H; Hy.**
heraldic **her.**
heraldry **her.**
Her Britannic Majesty **HBM**
herd test **HT**
here **hr.**
Hereford and Worcester
  Heref./Worcs.
here is buried **H.S.; HSE**
here lies **H.J.; i.h.**
here lies buried **h.j.s.**
here rests in peace **HRIP**
Her Exalted Highness **HEH**
Her Excellency **H.E.**
Her Grace **H.G.**
Her Highness **H.H.**
Her Imperial Highness **HIH**
Her Imperial Majesty **HIM**
Her Majesty **HM**
Her Majesty's **HM**
Her Majesty's Australian
  ship **HMAS**
Her Majesty's British
  ship **HMBS**
Her Majesty's Canadian
  ship **HMCS**
Her Majesty's Customs
  HMC
Her Majesty's Forces **HMF**
Her Majesty's

Government **HMG**
Her Majesty's Service **HMS**
Her Majesty's ship **HMS**
Her Majesty's Stationery
office **HMSO**
heroin **h.; H**
herpes simplex virus **HSV**
Herr **Hr.**
Her Royal Highness **HRH**
Her Serene Highness **HSH**
Her Serene Majesty **HSM**
Hertfordshire **Herts.; Hrt.**
hertz **Hz**
he/she carved it **sc.;
sculp.; sculpt.**
he/she designed **inv.; invt.**
he/she devised **inv.; invt.**
he/she did it
himself/herself **i.f.**
he/she died **ob.; obt.**
he/she died without
issue **o.s.p.**
he/she does not prosecute
non pros.
he/she drew it **del.; delin.**
he/she engraved it **exc.; sc.;
sculp.; sculpt.**
he/she erected this
monument **h.m.p.**
he/she gave and dedicated as
a gift **D.D.D.**
he/she gave as a gift **d.d.**
he/she gives, devotes, and
dedicates **D.D.D.**
he/she invented **inv.; invt.**
he/she lived (a given number
of) years **a.v.; v.a.**
he/she made it **f.; fec.**
he/she painted it **pinx.;
pnxt.; pxt.**
he/she reads **leg.**

he/she speaks **loq.**
he/she was not found **n.e.i.**
hexachlorobenzene **HCB**
hexachord **hex.**
hexaethyl tetraphosphate
HETP
hexagon **hex.**
hexagonal **hex.**
high **h.**
high-altitude bombing **HAB**
high-angle **H.A.**
high capacity **HC**
High Church **H.C.**
high commissioner **HC**
high-compression **HC**
high cost of living **HCL**
high definition television
HDTV
high density **HD**
high-density lipoprotein
HDL
high-density polyethylene
HDPE
high detergent **HD**
high efficiency **HE**
highest common factor **HCF**
highest possible frequency
HPF
high explosive **H.E.**
high explosive incendiary
HEI
high frequency **HF**
high-frequency current **HFC**
High German **HG**
high intensity **H.I.**
high intensity discharge
HID
high-level data link control
HDLC
high mobility multi-purpose
wheeled vehicle **HMMWV**

high-occupancy vehicle **HOV**
high oxygen pressure **HOP**
high-pass **HP**
high performance liquid
  chromatograph **HPLC**
high performance liquid
  chromatography **HPLC**
high power **HP**
high-power amplifier **HPA**
high power field **HPF**
high pressure **H.P.**
high-pressure nervous
  syndrome **HPNS**
high priest **H.P.**
high resistance **HR**
high-resolution mass
  spectrometry **HRMS**
high school **H.S.**
high speed **HS**
high-speed ground
  transport **HSGT**
high-speed launch **HSL**
high-temperature gas-cooled
  reactor **HTGR**
high-temperature reactor
  HTR
high tension **h.t.**
high-test hypochlorite **HTH**
high velocity **H.V.**
high-voltage **HV**
high water **H.W.**
high-water line **HWL**
high-water mark **HWM**
highway **hgwy.; hwy.**
highway post office **HPO**
Hindi **Hind.**
Hindustani **Hind.**
hire purchase **H.P.**
His Beatitude **H.B.**
His Blessedness **H.B.**
His Britannic Majesty **HBM**

His Eminence **H.E.**
His Exalted Highness **HEH**
His Excellency **H.E.**
His Grace **H.G.**
His Highness **H.H.**
His Holiness **H.H.**
His Imperial Highness **HIH**
His Imperial Majesty **HIM**
His Majesty **HM**
His Majesty's **HM**
His Majesty's Australian
  ship **HMAS**
His Majesty's British
  ship **HMBS**
His Majesty's Canadian
  ship **HMCS**
His Majesty's Customs **HMC**
His Majesty's Forces **HMF**
His Majesty's Government
  HMG
His Majesty's Service **HMS**
His Majesty's ship **HMS**
His Majesty's Stationery
  office **HMSO**
His Royal Highness **HRH**
His Serene Highness **HSH**
His Serene Majesty **HSM**
historian **hist.**
historical **hist.**
history **his.; hist.**
history of present
  illness **HPI**
hit **H**
Hittite **Hitt.**
hit wicket **HW**
hockey club **HC**
hogshead **hd.; hhd.**
hold **hld.**
hold covered **H.C.**
hold for money **HFM**
hollow **hol.**

hollow point **HP**
holmium **Ho**
holograph letter signed **HLS**
holy **h.; p.**
Holy Communion **HC**
holy day of obligation **H.O.**
Holy Name Society **HNS**
home **h.**
Home Box Office **HBO**
home defense **HD**
home fleet **H.F.**
home forces **H.F.**
home guard **H.G.**
home health aide **H.H.A.**
Home Missions **H.M.**
home office **H.O.**
home rule **H.R.**
home run **HR**
homiletics **hom.**
homily **hom.**
Honduras **Hon.; Hond.**
honey **hny.**
Hong Kong **H.K.**
honor **h.; hon.**
honorable **hon.; honble.**
honorary **hon.; hony.**
honorary secretary **HS**
honored **hon.**
horizon **h.; hor.; hrzn.**
horizontal **h.; hor.**
horizontal line **HL**
horizontal parallax **HP**
horn **h.**
horological **hor.**
horology **hor.; horol.**
horse **h.**
horse artillery **H.A.**
horse-drawn **HD**
horsepower **hp**
horsepower-hour **h.p.h.**
horticultural **hort.**

horticulture **hort.**
Hosea **Hos.**
hospital **hosp.**
hostilities only **H.O.**
hot **h.**
hot air **H.A.**
hot and cold **HC**
hot pressed **H.P.**
hot water **H.W.**
hour **h.; hr.**
hour and a half **sesquih.**
hour angle **HA**
house **h.; ho.; hse.**
House bill **HB**
household goods **HHG**
household pet **HHP**
House joint resolution **HJR**
House of Commons
 HC; H.C.
house of correction **H.C.**
House of Keys (Isle
 of Man) **H.K.**
House of Lords **H.L.**
House of Parliament **H.P.**
House of Representatives
 H.R.
house physician **HP**
House resolution **H.Res.**
house surgeon **H.S.**
House Un-American Activities
 Committee **HUAC**
housing **hsg.**
Housing and Home Finance
 Agency **HHFA**
how **hw.**
howitzer **how.**
Hubble constant **H**
human chorionic
 gonadotropin **HCG**
Human Development
 Services **HDS**

human growth hormone
    HGH
human intelligence
    HUMINT
humanities **hum.**
human leukocyte antigen
    HLA
human menopausal
    gonadotrophin **HMG**
Human Nutrition Information
    Service **HNIS**
human powered vehicle
    HPV
human serum albumin **HSA**
Humberside **Humber.**
humid **hmd.**
humidity **h.**
humidity index **HI**
humor **hum.**
humorous **hum.**
hundred **C; h.; hnd.; hun.**
hundredweight **cwt.**
Hungarian **Hung.**
Hungary **Hung.**
Huntington's disease **HD**
husband **h.**
hyaline membrane disease
    HMD
hybrid **hyb.**
hydrant **h.; hydt.**
hydraulic **hyd.**
hydraulic mean depth **HMD**
hydraulics **hyd.**
hydrocarbon **HC**
hydroelectric power **HEP**
hydroelectric unit **HEU**
hydrogen **H**
hydrographic **hyd.**
hydrography **hyd.**
hydrostatic **hyd.**
hydrostatics **hyd.**

hygiene **hyg.**
hyperbaric oxygenation
    HBO
hyperbolic secant **sech**
hyperbolic sine **sinh**
hypersonic transport **HST**
hyphenation and
    justification **H & J**
hypothesis **hyp.; hypoth.**
hypothetical **hyp.; hypoth.**

I

Iceland **Ice.**
Icelandic **Icel.**
ice point **IP**
ichthyology **ich.; ichth.**
iconography **icon.**
Idaho **ID**
identification **ID**
identification, friend or foe
    IFF
identified flying object **IFO**
idoxuridine **IDU**
if and only if **iff**
if occasion requires **s.o.s.**
if you please **SVP**
ignition **ign.**
illinium **Il**
Illinois **IL; Ill.**
illuminated **ill.**
illumination **ill.**
illustrated **il.; ill.;
    illus.; illust.**
illustration **il.; ill.;
    illus.; illust.**
illustrator **il.; ill.;
    illus.; illust.**
imaginary unit **i**
imitation **imit.**
imitative **imit.**

immature **im.**
immediate constituent **IC**
immediately **imdtly.;**
  immy.; stat.
immediate transportation **IT**
Immigration and
  Naturalization Service
  INS
immunity **immun.**
immunity test **IT**
immunization **immun.**
immunizing unit **IU**
immunoglobulin **Ig**
immunology **immunol.**
impedance **Z**
impedance angle **IA**
imperative **imp.; impv.; ipv.**
imperfect **imp.; imperf.;**
  impf.; ipf.
imperforate **imperf.**
imperial **i.; imp.; impl.**
imperial general staff **IGS**
imperial measure **IM**
imperial standard gallon
  i.s.g.
imperial standard wire
  gauge **ISWG**
implement **imp.; impl.**
import **imp.**
important **imp.; impt.**
imported **imp.**
importer **imp.; imptr.**
impression **imp.**
imprimatur **imp.**
imprint **imp.**
improve **ipv.**
improved **imp.; impr.**
Improved Order of Red
  Men **IORM**
improvement **imp.; impr.**
in arguing **arg.**

inboard **inbd.**
in bond **I.B.**
inbound **I.B.**
incendiary **i.**
incendiary bomb **IB**
incentive stock option **ISO**
inch **in.**
in charge **i/c**
inches **ins.**
inches per minute **ipm**
inches per revolution **ipr**
inches per second **ips**
inchoative **inch.**
inclosure **inc.; incl.**
included **inc.; incl.; incld.**
including **inc.; incl.**
including loading **IL**
including particular
  average **IPA**
inclusion **incln.**
inclusive **inc.; incl.**
Inclusive Tour Charter **ITC**
incognito **incog.**
income **inc.**
income tax **IT**
incoming **inc.**
incomplete **i.; inc.**
incorporated **inc.**
Incorporated Accountant **I.A.**
incorporation **inc.**
increase **inc.; incr.**
increased **incr.**
increased valve **i.v.**
increasing **incr.**
incumbent **inc.**
indefinite **indef.**
indemnity **indemy.**
indenture **indre.**
independence **ind.**
independent **i.; ind.**
Independent Bar

Association **IBA**
Independent Labour
 Party **ILP**
Independent Order of Odd
 Fellows **IOOF**
Independent Postal System of
 America **IPSA**
Independent Television **ITV**
index **ind.**
index correction **IC**
indexed **ind.**
indexed and paged **I and P**
indexed, paged, and
 titled **IPT**
indexed sequential-access
 method **ISAM**
index of refraction **n**
Indian **I.; Ind.**
Indiana **IN; Ind.**
Indian Claims Commission
 ICC
India paper **IP**
India paper proofs **IPP**
indicated **i.; ind.; indic.**
indicated airspeed **IAS**
indicated air temperature
 IAT
indicated horsepower
 i.h.p.; IHP
indicated pressure altitude
 IPA
indication **indn.**
indicative **i.; ind.; indic.**
indicator **ind.; indic.**
indigo **ind.**
indirect **ind.**
indium **In**
in divided parts **part. vic.**
individual **indiv.**
individualized education
 program **I.E.P.**

individual medley **IM**
individual package delivery
 IPD
individual practice
 association **IPA**
individual retirement
 account **IRA**
Indo-European **IE**
indoleacetic acid **IAA**
indolebutyric acid **IBA**
Indonesia **Indon.**
Indonesian **Indon.**
indorsement irregular **I/I**
inductance **L**
induction **ind.**
inductively coupled
 plasma **ICP**
industrial **i.; ind.;
 indsl.; indus.**
industrial design **ID**
industrial development
 bond **IDB**
Industrial Development
 Certificate **IDC**
industrial development
 revenue bond **IDR**
industrial engineer
 IE; Ind.E.
industrial revenue bond **IRB**
Industrial Workers of the
 World **IWW**
industry **ind.; indus.**
industry advisory committee
 IAC
infantry **i.; inf.**
infantry drill regulations
 IDR
infected area **IA**
infectious hepatitus **IH**
inferior **inf.**
infield **i.; inf.**

infielder **inf.**
infinitive **inf.; infin.**
infinity **inf.**
infirmary **inf.**
inflammable **infl.**
inflammation of connective
 tissue **ICT**
inflorescence **infl.**
influence **infl.**
influenced **infl.**
informant **inf.**
information **inf.; info.**
information and education
 I and E
information center **IC**
information circular **IC**
information officer **IO**
information requested
 in. req.
information retrieval **IR**
information technology **IT**
infra **inf.**
infrared **IR**
in full **IF**
infused **inf.**
infusion **inf.**
inhibitory **i.**
in his/her own person
 p.p.; pro. per.
in his/her proper person
 p.p.; pro. per.
initial **i.**
initial equipment **IE**
initial operating capability
 IOC
initial point **IP**
initial teaching alphabet
 ITA
initial velocity **i.v.**
initiative and referendum
 I and R

in its place **s.l.**
inject **inj.**
injection **inj.**
Inland Revenue **I.R.**
Inland Revenue Officer **I.R.O.**
inlet **in.**
in lieu of **i.l.o.**
inner **i.**
inner artillery zone **IAZ**
inner diameter **i.d.**
inner markov **IM**
inning **inn.**
innings pitched **IP**
in order **IO**
inorganic **inorg.**
inosine diphosphate **IDP**
inosinic acid **IMP**
in part **p.**
in passing **e.p.**
in proportion **p.r.**
input/output **I/O**
inquire **inq.; q.**
inscribed **ins.; insc.**
inside **i.; ins.**
inside diameter **i.d.**
inside dimensions **i.d.**
inside edge **I.E.**
inside height **i.h.**
inside left **IL**
inside length **i.l.**
inside width **i.w.**
insoluble **insol.**
insoluble residue **IR**
inspected **ins.**
inspected and condemned **IC**
inspecting order **IO**
inspection and security
 I and S
inspection and survey
 I and S
inspector **i.; ins.; insp.**

inspector general **Insp. Gen.**
inspector general **IG**
inspiratory capacity **IC**
installation **instl.**
installment **inst.**
installment paid **i.p.**
instant **inst.**
instantaneous **i.; inst.**
institute **i.; inst.**
Institute of High
  Fidelity **IHF**
Institute of Industrial
  Engineers **IIE**
Institute of Radio
  Engineers **IRE**
institution **i.; inst.; instn.**
institutional **inst.**
instruction **inst.; instn.;**
  instr.; instrn.
instructional television **ITV**
instructor **inst.; instr.**
instrument **inst.;**
  instmt.; instr.
instrumental **i.; inst.; instr.**
instrument approach and
  landing chart **IALC**
instrument flight rules **IFR**
instrument landing
  system **ILS**
insular **ins.**
insulated **ins.**
insulation **ins.**
insulin coma therapy **ICT**
insulin shock therapy **IST**
insurance **ince.; ins.; insce.**
integrated circuit **IC**
integrated data processing
  IDP
integrated-services digital
  networks **ISDN**
intelligence **i.; int.**

intelligence and
  reconnaissance **I and R**
intelligence branch **IB**
intelligence department **ID**
intelligence officer **IO**
intelligence quotient **IQ**
intelligence ratio **IR**
intensity **i.**
intensity of magnetic field **H**
intensive **intsv.**
intensive care unit **ICU**
intention **intn.**
Inter-American Defense
  Board **IADB**
Inter-American Development
  Bank **IADB**
Inter-American Foundation
  IAF
intercept **int.**
intercontinental ballistic
  missile **IBM; ICBM**
interest **i.; int.**
interferon **IF; IFN**
Inter-Governmental Maritime
  Consultative Organization
  IMCO
interim **int.**
interim report **IR**
interior **int.**
interior communications **IC**
interjection **int.; interj.**
interleaved **int.**
interline **I.L.**
intermediate **int.;**
  inter.; intmd.
intermediate frequency **IF**
intermediate power
  amplifier **IPA**
intermediate pressure **IP**
intermediate range ballistic
  missile **IRBM**

intermediate-range nuclear force **INF**
intermediate school **I.S.**
intermittent **intmt.**
intermittent commercial and amateur service **ICAS**
intermodulation distortion **IM**
internal **int.**
internal combustion **IC**
internal-combustion engine **ICE**
internal connection **IC**
internal diameter **i.d.**
Internal Revenue **I.R.**
Internal Revenue Officer **I.R.O.**
Internal Revenue Service **IRS**
internal thread **IT**
international **i.; int.; intl.; intnl.**
international airport **IAP**
International Air Transport Association **IATA**
International Amateur Athletic Federation **IAAF**
International Amateur Boxing Association **IABA**
international angstrom **IA**
International Association of Legal Science **IALS**
International Association of Machinists and Aerospace Workers **IAM**
International Association of Poets, Playwrights, Editors, Essayists and Novelists **PEN**
International Association of Universities **IAU**

International Astronomical Union **IAU**
International Atomic Energy Agency **IAEA**
International Atomic Time **TAI**
International Baccalaureate **I.B.**
International Bank for Reconstruction and Development **IBRD**
International Bar Association **IBA**
International Biological Year **IBY**
International Brotherhood of Electrical Workers **IBEW**
International Chamber of Commerce **ICC**
International Civil Aviation Organization **ICAO**
International Commission of Jurists **ICJ**
International Committee of the Red Cross **ICRC**
International Communication Agency **ICA**
International Confederation of Free Trade Unions **ICFTU**
International Cooperation Administration **ICA**
International Cooperative Alliance **ICA**
International Council of Nurses **ICN**
International Court of Justice **ICJ**
International Criminal Police Organization **Interpol**
International Cultural Exchange **ICE**

International Development
  Association **IDA**
international drawing
  rights **IDR**
international driving
  permit **IDP**
International Electronic
  Post **INTELPOST**
International Executive
  Service Corps **IESC**
International Finance
  Corporation **IFC**
International Geophysical
  Year **IGY**
International Hydrological
  Decade **IHD**
International Labor
  Organization **ILO**
International Ladies' Garment
  Workers' Union **ILGWU**
International Law
  Association **ILA**
International Legal Aid
  Association **ILAA**
International Longshoremen's
  Association **ILA**
International Match Point
  IMP
International Monetary
  Fund **IMF**
International Monetary
  Market **IMM**
International News Photo
  INP
international normal
  atmosphere **INA**
International Olympic
  Committee **IOC**
International Phonetic
  Alphabet **IPA**
International Planned

Parenthood Federation
  IPPF
International Practical
  Temperature Scale **IPTS**
International Quiet Sun
  Year **IQSY**
international radium unit
  IRU
International Red Cross **IRC**
International Scientific
  Vocabulary **ISV**
International Society of
  Christian Endeavor **CE**
International Standard Book
  Number **ISBN**
International Standard Serial
  Number **ISSN**
International Standards
  Organization **ISO**
international subscriber
  dialing **ISD**
International System of
  Units **SI**
International
  Telecommunications
  Satellite **Intelsat**
International
  Telecommunication Union
  ITU
international tolerance **IT**
International Trade
  Organization **ITO**
International Typographical
  Union **ITU**
international unit **I.U.**
interoffice memo **IOM**
interplanetary monitoring
  platform **IMP**
interpreter **int.;**
  interpr.; intpr.
interpupillary distance **PD**

interrogate **intg.**
interrogation prisoner of
war **IPW**
interrogative **inter.;
interrog.**
interrogator **intg.**
interrogator-responder **IR**
interrupted continuous
waves **ICW**
intersection **int.**
interservice **IS**
interstate **i.; I.S.**
interstate commerce **ISC**
Interstate Commerce
Commission **ICC**
interstitial-cell-stimulating
hormone **ICSH**
interval **int.**
interview **int.**
interview after combat **IAC**
in the first place **imp.**
in the following places **seqq.**
in the next month **prox.**
in the place **l.; loc.**
in the place cited **l.c.; l.l.;
loc. cit.**
in the place cited above **l.s.c.**
in the regions of
unbelievers **IPI**
in the same place **ib.; ibid.**
in the time of **t.; temp.**
in the time of Kings **T.R.**
in the work cited
o.c.; op. cit.
in the works of **ap.**
in the year **a.; an.**
in the year before Christ
A.A.C.
in the year from the founding
of the city (of Rome)
A.U.C.

in the year of Christ **A.C.**
in the year of light **A.L.**
in the year of our Lord **A.D.**
in the year of redemption
A.S.
in the year of the hegira
A.H.
in the year of the king's
reign **A.R.R.**
in the year of the queen's
reign **A.R.R.**
in the year of the reign **A.R.**
in the year of the world
A.M.
in this month **h.m.**
in this place **h.l.**
in this sense **h.s.**
in this year **h.a.**
intra-arterial **IA**
intracellular fluid **ICF**
intracranial self-stimulation
ICSS
intramural **IM**
intramuscular **i.m.**
intramuscularly **i.m.**
in transit **in trans.; i.t.**
intransitive **i.;
int.; intr.; intrans.**
intranuclear inclusion **INI**
intrauterine contraceptive
device **IUCD**
intrauterine device **IUD**
intravenous **IV**
intravenously **IV**
intrinsic energy **U**
introduced **intr.**
introducing **intr.**
introduction **intr.; introd.**
introductory **intr.**
invented **inv.**
invention **inv.**

inventor **inv.**
inventory **inv.; invt.**
inventory and inspection **I/I**
invertebrate **invert.**
investigational new drug **IND**
investment **inv.; invest.**
investment tax credit **ITC**
invitation **inv.**
invoice **inv.**
invoice book **I.B.**
invoice value **i.v.**
in what manner **qm.**
iodinated human serum albumin **IHSA**
iodine **I**
iodine value **IV**
ionium **Io**
Iowa **Ia.; IA**
I owe you **IOU**
Iraqi **I.**
Ireland **Ire.**
iridescent **irid.**
iridium **Ir**
Irish **Ir.**
Irish Republican Army **I.R.A.**
iron **Fe; i.**
iron pipe size **IPS**
irredeemable **irr.; irred.**
irregular **irr.; irreg.**
irregular route carrier **IRC**
Isaiah **Is.; Isa.**
island **i.; id.; is.; isl.**
isle **i.; is.**
Isle of Man **I.M.; I.O.M.**
Isle of Wight **I.O.W.; I.W.**
isolation **isoln.**
isoniazid **INH**
isotopic weight **IW**
Israel **Isr.**

Israeli **I.; Isr.**
issue **iss.**
isthmus **isth.**
Italian **It.; Ital.**
italic **ital.**
italicized **ital.**
Italy **It.**
item **it.**
it follows **seq.; sequ.**
itinerary **itin.**
it is not clear **n.l.**
it is not permitted **n.l.**

J

jack **j.**
Jamaica **Jam.**
James **Jas.**
January **J; Ja; Ja.; Jan.**
Japan **Jap.; Jpn.**
Japanese **Jap.; Jpn.**
Japanese vellum **JV**
Japanese vellum proofs **JVP**
Japan paper **JP**
Japan paper proofs **JPP**
Javanese **Jav.**
Jeremiah **Jer.**
Jeremias **Jer.**
Jesus **IHC; IHS; JHS; YHS**
Jesus Christ **J.C.**
Jesus, Mary, Joseph **J.M.J.**
Jesus of Nazareth, King of the Jews **INRI**
jet-assisted takeoff **JATO**
jet propellant **JP**
jet-propelled **JP**
jet propulsion **JP**
jettison and washing overboard **j. & w.o.**
jeweler **jwlr.**
job instruction training **JIT**

job methods training **JMT**
Job Opportunities in the
  Business Sector **JOBS**
jocose **joc.**
jocular **joc.**
Joel **Jl.; Jo.**
John **Jn.; Jno.**
John Birch Society **JBS**
join **j.; jn.**
joined **jd.**
joint **jnt.; jt.**
joint account **J/A**
joint agent **JA**
joint army-navy **JAN**
joint board **JB**
joint bond **JB**
Joint Chiefs of Staff **JCS**
Joint Commission
  on Accreditation of
  Hospitals **JCAH**
joint export agent **JEA**
joint industrial council **JIC**
joint intelligence committee
  JIC
jointly **jtly.**
joint operations center **JOC**
joint resolution **JR**
joint-stock company **JSC**
joint support **JS**
Joshua **Josh.**
joule **J**
journal **j.; jl.; jnl.; jour.; jr.**
journalism **j.**
journalist **jnlst.**
journey **jour.**
journeyman **jour.**
judge **j.; jud.**
judge advocate **JA**
Judge Advocate General
  JAG
Judges **Judg.**

judges **JJ**
judgment **jud.; judgt.**
judicature **jud.**
judicial **jud.**
judiciary **jud.**
Judith **Jud.**
Julian day **J.D.**
July **J; Jl.; Jul.; Jy.**
junction **jc.; jct.; jctn.;
  jn.; jnc.; junc.**
junction box **JB**
June **J; Je.; Ju.; Jun.**
Junior **Junr.**
junior **j.; jnr.; Jr.; jun.**
Junior Achievement **JA**
junior chamber of commerce
  JCC
junior college **JC; Juco**
junior college of business
  JCB
junior common room **JCR**
junior deacon **J.D.**
junior dean **J.D.**
junior grade **jg**
junior high school **J.H.S.**
junior military aviator **JMA**
junior officer **JO**
Junior Red Cross **JRC**
Junior Reserve Officers'
  Training Corps **JROTC**
junior training corps **JTC**
junior varsity **JV**
junior warden **J.W.**
juridical **jur.**
jurisconsult **J.C.**
jurisprudence **juris.; jurisp.**
jurist **jur.**
juror **jr.**
jury duty **J.D.**
jussive **juss.**
justice **j.; jus.; just.**

justice clerk **J.C.**
justice department **JD**
justice of the peace **J.P.**
justices **JJ**
just noticeable difference
 j.n.d.
juvenile **j.; juv.**
juvenile court **JC**
juvenile delinquent **JD**

K

Kansas **Kan.; Kans.; KS**
Kansas City **K.C.**
karat **K; kt**
keel **k.**
keep **cons.**
keep off **K.O.**
keep standing **K.S.**
keg **k.; kg.**
kelvin **K**
kennel club **K.C.**
Kentucky **Ky.; KY**
Kerry **Ker.**
key **k.**
keyboard send and receive
 KSR
keyword in context **KWIC**
keyword out of context
 KWOC
kicker **k.**
kidney, ureter, and bladder
 KUB
Kildare **Kild.**
kilderkin **kil; kild**
Kilkenny **Kilk.**
killed **kd.**
killed in action **KIA**
kiln-dried **KD**
kilo- **k**
kilobar **kb; kbar**

kilobase **kb**
kilobits per second **kbps**
kilobyte **K; KB**
kilocalorie **kcal**
kilocycle **kc**
kilocycles per second **kc/s**
kilo-electron volt **keV**
kilogauss **kG**
kilogram **k; kg**
kilogram calorie **kcal**
kilogram-meter **kg-m**
kilograms per second **kgps**
kilohertz **kHz**
kilojoule **kJ**
kiloliter **kl**
kilomegawatt **kmw**
kilomegawatt-hour **kmwh**
kilometer **klm; km**
kilometers per hour **kph**
kilometers per second **kmps**
kiloparsec **kpc**
kilopascal **kPa**
kiloton **kt**
kilovar **kvar**
kilovar-hour **kvarh**
kilovolt **kv; kV**
kilovolt-ampere **kva**
kilovolt-ampere-hour **kvah**
kilowatt **kw; kW**
kilowatt-hour **kwh;
 kWh; kw-hr**
kindergarten **k.; kind.**
kinetic energy **K.E.**
kinetic potential **L**
king **K; kg.; Ki.; R**
kingdom **kdm.; km.**
King James Version **KJV**
king of arms **K.A.**
king post **K.P.**
King's Bench **K.B.**
King's Counsel **K.C.**

king's messenger **K.M.**
King's Scholar **K.S.**
Kinross-shire **Kin.**
kips per square foot **ksf**
kips per square inch **ksi**
kitchen **k.; ki.; kit.**
kitchen and bathroom **K.B.**
kitchen police **KP**
kite balloon **K.B.**
kite balloon pilot **K.B.P.**
knee jerk **k.j.**
knight **k.; knt.; Kt.; N**
Knight Bachelor **K.B.**
Knight Commander **K.C.**
Knight Commander of the Order of St. Gregory **K.C.S.G.**
Knight Commander of the Order of St. Michael and St. George **K.C.M.G.**
Knight Commander of the Order of the Bath **K.C.B.**
Knight Commander of the Order of the British Empire **K.B.E.**
Knight Grand Commander **K.G.C.**
Knight Grand Cross of the Order of the Bath **G.C.B.**
Knight Grand Cross Order of the British Empire **G.B.E.**
Knight of the Grand Cross **K.G.C.**
Knight of the Order of the Garter **K.G.**
Knight of the Royal Guelphic Order of Hanover **K.H.**
Knights of Columbus **K.C.; K of C**
Knights of Pythias **K of P**
knit **k.**

knocked down **K.D.**
knocked down flat **K.D.F.**
knocked down, in carloads **K.D.C.L.**
knocked down, in less than carloads **K.D.L.C.L.**
knockout **KO**
knot **k.; kn.; kt.**
knotty pine **K.P.**
kopeck **k.**
Korea **Kor.**
Korean **Kor.**
koruna **Kčs**
kosher **K**
kosher certification **U**
kreuzer **kr.**
krona **Kr.**
krone **Kr.**
krypton **Kr**
Ku Klux Klan **KKK**
kurus **k.**
kwacha **K**
kyat **K**

L

label **sig.**
label clause **LC**
labor **lab.; lbr.**
labor exchange **LE**
Labrador **Lab.; LB**
lactate dehydrogenase **LDH**
lactic dehydrogenase **LDH**
lactobacillus bulgaricus factor **LBF**
Ladies Professional Golf Association **LPGA**
lady **l.; L.**
ladyship **ldp.; Lp.**
Lagrangian **L**
laid in this place **HLS**

lake L
lake and rail L and R
lambert L
Lamentations Lam.
laminated lam.
Lancashire Lancs.
lance lce.
lance corporal LC; LCpl
land l.; ld.
landed terms l.t.
landing l.; ldg.; lndg.
landing account L/A
landing barge LB
landing craft LC
landing craft air cushion
  LCAC
landing ground LG
landing ship LS
landing ship dock LSD
landing ship medium LSM
landing ship, tank LST
landing signal officer LSO
landing vehicle, tracked
  LVT
landing zone LZ
land mine LM
landplane l.; LP
land service LS
lane La.; ln.
langley ly
language lang.
language acquisition device
  LAD
lanthanide Ln
lanthanum La
laparotomy lap.
large l; L; lg.; lge.; lrg.
large calorie Cal.
large grain LG
large letter LL
large paper l.p.

large paper proofs LPP
large post LP
larger lgr.
large ring lr
large-scale integrated LSI
large-scale integration LSI
last la.
last in, first out LIFO
late l.
Late Latin LL
latent lat.
lateral lat.
Latin L; Lat.
latitude l.; lat.; latd.
latitude and longitude
  indicator LLI
Latter-day Saints LDS
Latvia Lat.
launch l.
launch telemetry station
  LTS
launch tracking system LTS
laundry ldry.
lava lv.
lavatory lav.
law j.; l.
law agent LA; L.A.
law courts LC
law efficiency LE
Law Enforcement Assistance
  Administration LEAA
Law Latin LL
Law of the Sea Treaty LOST
lawrencium Lr
laws ll.
Law School Admission
  Test LSAT
lawyer law.
layer upon layer s.s.s.
lead ld.; Pb
leader ldr.

leading **ldg.**
leading aircraftsman
  LA; LAC
leading aircraftswoman
  LACW
leading edge **LE**
leading seaman **LS**
leaf **l.; lf.**
leaflet **lf.; lft.**
league **l.; lea.**
League for Industrial
  Democracy **LID**
League of Women Voters
  LWV
leakage **lkg.**
learner **l.**
learning disability **LD**
learning disabled **LD**
lease **le.**
leased **lsd.**
least common denominator
  LCD
least common multiple **LCM**
least fatal dose **LFD**
least objectional program
  LOP
leather **l.; lea.; lthr.**
leave **l.; lea.; lv.; lve.**
leaves **ll.; lvs.**
Lebanese **Leb.**
Lebanon **Leb.**
lector **lect.**
lecture **lect.**
lecturer **lect.**
ledger **led.**
ledger folio **LF**
left **g.; l.; L; s.**
left center **LC**
left cornerback **LCB**
left defense **LD**
left end **LE**

left eye **O.L.; O.S.**
left field **LF**
left foot **LF**
left forward **LF**
left front **LF**
left fullback **LFB**
left guard **LG**
left halfback **LHB**
left hand **LH; MG; MS;
  sin.; S.M.**
left linebacker **LLB**
left on base **LB; LOB**
left rear **LR**
left side **l.s.**
left tackle **LT**
left wing **LW**
legal **leg.**
Legal Defense and
  Educational Fund **LDF**
legal scroll **L.S.**
Legal Services Corporation
  LSC
legal tender **LT**
legal volt **lv**
legate **leg.**
legation **leg.**
legato **leg.**
leg bye **l.b.**
legend **leg.**
Legion of Honor **L.H.**
Legion of Merit **LM**
legislation **leg.; legis.**
legislative **leg.; legis.**
legislative assembly **L.A.**
legislature **leg.; legis.**
legitimate **l.**
Leicestershire **Leics.**
Leitrim **Leit.**
lempira **L**
lending library **LL**
length **l.; lgth.**

length at waterline **L.W.L.**

length between
perpendiculars **LBP**

length, mass, time **LMT**

length of stay **LOS**

length over all **LOA**

less developed country **LDC**

less than carload **LCL**

less-than-carload lot **LCL**

less than truckload
LTL; LTT

lethal dose **LD**

let him/her take **cap.; sum.**

let it be added **add.**

let it be done **f.; ft.**

let it be labeled **sig.**

let it be made **f.; ft.**

let it be repeated **repet.**

letter **l.; ltr.**

letter box **lb**

lettering faded **LF**

letter of authority **L/A**

letter of credit **L/C**

letter signed **LS**

letter-sorting machine **LSM**

letter telegram **LT**

let the acts show **t.a.**

let the buyer beware **c.e.**

let them be added **add.**

leu **L**

leucine **leu**

leukocytosis-promoting
factor **LPF**

lev **Lv**

levant **lev.**

level crossing **LC**

leveraged buyout **LBO**

Leviticus **Lev.; Levit.**

levorotatory **L**

lewisite **L**

lexical **lex.**

lexicon **lex.**

liaison **l.**

liaison officer **LO**

Liberal **L**

liberal **lib.**

liberation **lib.**

librarian **lib.; libn.; libr.**

library **lib.**

library association **L.A.**

Library of Congress **LC**

library science **LS**

license **lic.**

licensed **lic.**

Licensed Practical Nurse
LPN

licensed victualler **L.V.**

Licensed Vocational Nurse
LVN

Licentiate **Lic.**

licentiate **L.**

Licentiate in Canon Law
J.C.L.

Licentiate in Theology **L.Th.**

Licentiate of Sacred
Scriptures **S.S.L.**

Licentiate of Sacred
Theology **S.T.L.**

Licentiate of the Royal
College of Physicians
L.R.C.P.

Licentiate of the Royal
College of Surgeons
L.R.C.S.

lien **ln.**

lieutenant **Lieut.; Lt.**

lieutenant colonel **LTC;
Lt.Col.**

lieutenant commander
LCDR; Lt.Comdr.

lieutenant general **LTG;
Lt.Gen.**

lieutenant governor **Lt.Gov.**
lieutenant, junior grade **Lt.(jg); LTJG**
Life Guards **L.G.**
life insurance policy **LIP**
lifesaving service **LSS**
lifesaving station **LSS**
life-support system **LSS**
lift **l.**
lifts not operating **no.**
lifts operating **opr.**
light **l.; lgt.; lt.**
light airborne multipurpose system **LAMPS**
light amplification by stimulated emission of radiation **laser**
light antiaircraft **LAA**
light bomber **LB**
light detection and ranging **lidar**
light-emitting diode **LED**
lightening **l.; ltg.; ltng.**
lightening arrester **LA**
lighter **ltr.**
lighter aboard ship **LASH**
lighterage **ltge.**
lighter than air **LA; LTA**
lightface **l.f.**
lighthouse **LH**
light infantry **L.I.**
lightly canceled **LC**
light machine gun **LMG**
light rail vehicle **LRV**
light transmission index **LTI**
light vessel **LV**
light water reactor **LWR**
Limerick **Lim.**
Limes **L**
limit **lim.; lmt.**
limited **ld.; lim.; ltd.; Ltd.**

limited duty officer **LDO**
limited liability **LL**
limiting nose dive **LND**
Lincolnshire **Lincs.**
line **l.**
lineal **lin.**
lineal feet **LF; L.F.**
linear **lin.**
linear energy transfer **LET**
linear predictive coding **LPC**
linear programming **LP**
lineman **LMN**
line of communication **LC**
line of communications **L of C**
line of dance **LOD**
line of direction **LOD**
line of duty **LD; LOD**
line of least resistance **LLR**
line of position **LOP**
line of scrimmage **LOS**
line of sight **LOS**
liner **l.**
lines **ll.**
lines of communication **LOC**
lines per minute **lpm**
line telegraphy **LT**
linguistic **ling.**
linguistics **ling.**
liniment **lin.**
lining **lng.**
link **l.; li.**
liquefied natural gas **LNG**
liquefied petroleum **LP**
liquefied petroleum gas **LPG**
liquid **l.; liq.**
liquid chromatography **LC**
liquid crystal display **LCD**
liquid crystal quartz **LCQ**
liquid oxygen **lox**
liquor **liq.**

lira L; Lit (Italy); Lt (Turkey)
lire L
listed securities LS
lit l.
liter l; L; lit.
literal lit.
literally lit.
literary lit.
literary criticism lit. crit.
literature lit.
lithium L; Li
lithographic lith.
lithography lith.; litho.
Lithuania Lith.
Lithuanian Lith.
little l.
little louder pf
live load L.L.
living and well L and W
living room LR
load ld.
load factor LF
loading ldg.
load waterline L.W.L.
load water plane L.W.P.
loan ln.
loans and discounts L and D
local lcl.; loc.
Local Access and Transport Area LATA
local agent L.A.
local apparent noon LAN
local apparent time LAT
local area digital transmission LADT
local area network LAN
local authority LA
local board L.B.
local civil time LCT
local delivery LD

local education authority LEA
local excitatory state LES
local freight agent LFA
local hour angle LHA
local mean time LMT
local naval commander LNC
local origination LO
local sidereal time LST
local standard time LST
local sunrise LSR
local sunset LS
local time LT
location loc.
locative loc.
locker lkr.
lock forward LF
lock rail L.R.
lodge l.
lodging ldg.
logarithm log
logarithmic mean temperature difference LMTD
logic log.
logical inferences per second LIPS
logistic log.
log run LR
London Lond.
Londonderry Lond.
long L; lg.
long-acting thyroid stimulator LATS
long delay LD
long distance LD
longer lgr.
Longford Long.
Long Island L.I.
longitude l.; lon.; long.
longitudinal longl.
longitudinal section LS

long meter **L.M.**
long meter double **L.M.D.**
long particular meter **LPM**
long picot **lp**
long play **LP**
long playing **LP**
long primer **l.p.**
long range **LR**
long-range navigation **LORAN**
long shot **LS**
long-term memory **LTM**
long ton **l.t.**
long wave **L.W.**
long wheelbase **LWB**
look for this **h.q.**
loose leaf **l.l.**
lord **l.; ld.; Lo.**
Lord **Ld.**
lord chamberlain **L.C.**
lord chancellor **L.C.**
lord chief justice **L.C.J.**
lord high admiral **L.H.A.**
lord high chancellor **L.H.C.**
lord high treasurer **L.H.T.**
Lord Justice **L.J.**
lord lieutenant **L.L.**
lord mayor **L.M.**
lord privy seal **L.P.S.**
lord provost **L.P.**
lordship **ldp.; Lp.**
Lords Justices **L.JJ.; LL.JJ.**
Los Angeles **L.A.**
loss and damage **L and D**
loss of coolant accident **LOCA**
loss of pay **LP**
lost **l.**
Lothian **Loth.**
lotion **lot.**
loudspeaker **LS**

loud, then soft **fp**
Louisiana **La.; LA**
Louth **Lou.**
low **l.**
low altitude **LA**
low altitude defense system **LOADS**
low-density lipoprotein **LDL**
low-energy electron diffraction **LEED**
lower **L**
lower case **l.c.**
lower dead center **LDC**
lower half **LH**
lower left **LL**
lower right **LR**
lowest common denominator **LCD**
lowest common multiple **LCM**
lowest required radiated power **l.r.r.p.**
lowest useful high frequency **LUHF**
low explosive **LE**
low frequency **LF**
low-frequency current **LFC**
Low German **LG**
low intensity **L.I.**
Low Latin **LL**
low pass **LP**
low point **L.P.**
low power television **LPTV**
low pressure **L.P.**
low speed **LS**
low tension **l.t.**
low voltage **LV**
low water **L.W.**
low-water mark **L.W.M.**
Loyal Order of Moose **LOOM**

lubricant **lub.**
lubricating **lub.**
lubricating oil **LO**
Luke **Lk.**
lumbar **L**
lumber **lbr.**
lumen **l.; lm; lu**
lumens per watt **LPW**
luminous flux **F**
lump sum **LS**
lunar excursion module **LEM**
lunar module **LM**
lunar roving vehicle **LRV**
lupus erythematosus **LE**
luteinizing hormone **LH**
luteinizing hormone-releasing factor **LRF**
luteinizing hormone-releasing hormone **LHRH**
luteotropic hormone **LTH**
lutetium **Lu**
Lutheran **Luth.**
lux **lx**
Luxembourg **Lux.**
lysergic acid diethylamide **LSD**

M

macadam **mac.**
Maccabees **Mac.; Macc.**
macerate **mac.**
Mach **M**
machine **mach.**
machine finish **M.F.**
machine-glazed **M.G.**
machine gun **MG**
machine-gun company **MGC**
machine-gun corps **MGC**
machine readable

cataloging **MARC**
machinery **mach.; machy.**
machinery certificate **MC**
machinery survey **MS**
machine translation **MT**
machining **mach.**
machinist **mach.**
machinist's mate **M.M.**
madam **Mdm.**
madame **Mdme.; Mme**
made merchantable **M.M.**
mademoiselle **Mdlle.; Mlle.**
mademoiselles **Mlles.**
Maelzel's metronome **M.M.**
magazine **mag.**
magistrate **m.**
magnesium **mag.; Mg**
magnet **mag.**
magnetic **m.; mag.; magn.**
magnetic airborne detector **MAD**
magnetic anomaly detector **MAD**
magnetic course **MC**
magnetic heading **MH**
magnetic induction **B**
magnetic ink character recognition **MICR**
magnetic levitation **maglev**
magnetic north **MN**
magnetism **mag.; magn.**
magneto **mag.; magn.**
magnetohydrodynamic **MHD**
magnetohydrodynamics **MHD**
magnetomotive force **mmf**
magnitude **mag.**
mahogany **mhg**
maiden **m.**
maiden over **m.**
mail **m.; ml.**

mail order **M.O.**
mail-order department **MOD**
mail payment **MP**
mail steamer **MS**
mail transfer **MT**
main dressing station **MDS**
Maine **Me.; ME**
main line of resistance **MLR**
main switch **MS**
maintain visual flight rules
  MVFR
maintenance **maint.; mntn.**
maintenance and supply
  M and S
maintenance, repair, and
  operation **MRO**
maintenance unit **M.U.**
main verb **MV**
Majesties **MM**
majesty **m.**
major **ma; Maj.**
major general
  Maj.Gen.; MG
major histocompatibility
  complex **MHC**
make **f.; m.**
make a draught **f.h.**
make good **MG**
Malachi **Mal.**
malacology **malac.**
male **m.**
male chauvinist pig **MCP**
maleic hydrazide **MH**
malleable cast iron **MCI**
malleable iron **MI**
management **mangt.;
  mgmt.; mgt.**
management and
  administration **M and A**
management by objective
  MBO

management information
  service **MIS**
management information
  systems **MIS**
manager **mgr.; mngr.**
managing **mng.**
managing director **MD**
managing editor **M.E.**
mandated territory **MT**
maneuverable reentry
  vehicle **MARV**
manganese **Mn**
manila **man.**
Manitoba **Man.; MB**
manned maneuvering
  unit **MMU**
manned orbiting
  laboratory **MOL**
manual **m.; man.**
manually operated **M.O.**
manual volume control
  MVC
manufacture **man.;
  manuf.; mf.; mfr.**
manufactured **mfd.**
manufacturer **manf.; mfr.**
manufacturing **manuf.; mfg.**
manuscript **MS**
manuscript on paper **MOP**
manuscript on vellum **MOV**
manuscripts **MSS**
map reference **MR**
marbled edges **m.e.**
marbled paper sides **MPS**
marcato **marc.**
March **M; Mar.**
marchioness **March.**
mare **m.**
margin **marg.; mg.**
marginal **marg.**
marginal credit **M/C**

margin of safety **MS**
marine **mar.**
marine corps **MC**
Marine Corps League **MCL**
marine insurance policy **MIP**
maritime **m.; mar.; mrtm.**
maritime administration **MA**
Mark **Mk.**
mark **m.; mk.**
marked **mkd.**
marked capacity **MC**
marker **m.; mrkr.**
market **mkt.**
marketing **mktg.**
market value **MV**
markka **mk.**
marksman **mkm.**
mark well **N.B.**
marquess **Marq.**
marquis **m.; Marq.**
married **m.; mar.**
martyr **m.; mart.**
martyrology **mart.**
martyrs **MM**
Maryknoll Missioners **M.M.**
Maryland **Md.; MD**
masculine **m.; mas.; masc.**
mass **m.**
Massachusetts **MA; Mass.**
mass number **A**
mass observation **M.O.**
mass spectrometry **MS**
master **M**
master **mstr.**
master antenna television **MATV**
master-at-arms **MAA**
master chief petty officer **CPOM; MCPO**

master gunnery sergeant **M.Gy.Sgt.**
Master in Pharmacy **Ph.M.**
Master in Sacred Theology **S.T.M.**
master mechanic **M.M.**
Master of Agricultural Business and Economics **M.A.B.E.**
Master of Applied Arts **M.A.A.**
Master of Arts **A.M.; M.A.**
Master of Arts in Education **M.A.E.; M.A.Ed.**
Master of Arts in Law and Diplomacy **M.A.L.D.**
Master of Arts in Liberal Studies **M.A.L.S.**
Master of Arts in Library Science **M.A.L.S.**
Master of Arts in Teaching **M.A.T.**
Master of Business Administration **M.B.A.**
master of ceremonies **MC**
Master of Civil Law **J.C.M.; M.C.L.**
Master of Commercial Science **M.C.S.**
Master of Comparative Jurisprudence **M.C.J.**
Master of Comparative Law **L.C.M.; M.C.L.; M.Comp.L.**
Master of Computer Science **M.C.S.**
Master of Dental Surgery **M.D.S.**
Master of Divinity **M.Div.**
Master of Education **Ed.M.; M.Ed.**

Master of Fine Arts **M.F.A.**
Master of Forestry **M.F.**
Master of Foxhounds **M.F.H.**
Master of Hospital
  Administration **M.H.A.**
Master of Jurisprudence
  Jur.M.
Master of Law **M.L.**
Master of Law and Taxation
  M.L.T.
Master of Laws **J.M.;**
  LL.M.; M.Laws
Master of Library Science
  M.L.S.
Master of Music **M.M.**
Master of Nursing **M.N.**
Master of Otterhounds
  M.O.H.
Master of Patent Law
  M.P.L.
Master of Public
  Administration **M.P.A.**
Master of Public and Private
  Management **M.P.P.M.**
Master of Public Health
  M.P.H.
Master of Science **M.S.;**
  M.Sc.; Sc.M.; S.M.
Master of Science in Civil
  Engineering **M.S.C.E.**
Master of Science in Criminal
  Justice **M.S.C.J.**
Master of Science in
  Education **M.S.Ed.**
Master of Science in Electrical
  Engineering **M.S.E.E.**
Master of Science in Library
  Science **M.S.L.S.**
Master of Science in
  Mechanical Engineering
  M.S.M.E.

Master of Science in
  Nursing **M.S.N.**
Master of Science in Public
  Health **M.S.P.H.**
Master of Science in Social
  Work **M.S.S.W.**
Master of Social Work
  M.S.W.
Master of Staghounds
  M.S.H.
Master of Surgery **C.M.;**
  M.C.; M.Ch.
Master of Theological
  Studies **M.T.S.**
Master of Theology **M.Th.;**
  Th.M.
Master of the Rolls **M.R.**
masters **MM**
master sergeant **MSG;**
  M.Sgt.
matched and beaded
  M and B
matches played **p**
mate **m.**
material **mat.; mtl.; mtrl.**
material requirements
  planning **MRP**
materials testing reactor
  MTR
material unaccounted for
  MUF
mate's receipt **MR**
mathematical **math.**
mathematician **math.**
mathematics **math.**
matinee **mat.**
matins **mat.**
matriculated **matric.**
matriculation **matric.**
Matthew **Matt.; Mt.**
maturity **mat.**

maximum **max.**
maximum allowable
  concentration **MAC**
maximum average price
  MAP
maximum effort **ME**
maximum except take-off
  METO
maximum permissible
  concentration **MPC**
maximum permissible dose
  MPD
maximum permissible level
  MPL
maximum stress **M.S.**
maximum sustainable yield
  MSY
maximum usable frequency
  MUF
maximum working pressure
  MWP
maxwell **m; Mx**
May **M; My.**
may he/she rest in peace
  R.I.P.
may he/she rest well **b.q.**
may they rest in peace
  R.I.P.
meal **cib.**
mean **m.**
mean corpuscular
  hemoglobin **MCH**
mean corpuscular hemoglobin
  concentration **MCHC**
mean corpuscular volume
  MCV
mean effective pressure **mep**
mean free path **MFP**
mean hemispherical
  candlepower **MHSCP**
mean high tide **MHT**

mean high water **MHW**
mean high water neaps
  MHWN
mean high water springs
  MHWS
mean horizontal
  candlepower **mhcp**
mean indicated pressure
  m.i.p.
meaning **mg.**
mean level **M.L.**
mean low tide **MLT**
mean low water **MLW**
mean low water neaps
  MLWN
mean low water springs
  MLWS
mean point of impact **mpi**
mean sea level **msl; MSL**
mean solar time **MST**
mean spherical candlepower
  mscp
mean square **MS**
mean temperature
  difference **MTD**
mean tidal level **MTL**
mean tide **MT**
mean time **MT**
mean variation **MV**
measure **m.; meas.**
measurement **mst.**
measurement ton **MT**
Meath **Mea.**
mechanic **mech.**
mechanical **m.; mech.**
mechanical aptitude test
  MAT
mechanical engineer **M.E.**
mechanical engineering
  M.E.
mechanical equivalent of

heat **J**
mechanical time fuse **MTF**
mechanical transport **MT**
mechanical transport corps **MTC**
mechanics **mech.**
mechanism **mech.**
mechanized **mech.**
medalist **med.**
medal of honor **MH**
median **med.**
median lethal dose **MLD**
mediator **med.**
medical **m.; med.**
medical advisory board **MAB**
medical aid post **MAP**
Medical Board **M.B.**
Medical College Admission Test **MCAT**
medical corps **MC**
medical department **MD**
medical examiner **M.E.**
medical inspection **MI**
Medical Laboratory Technician **MLT**
medical officer **M.O.**
medical officer of health **M.O.H.**
medical receiving station **MRS**
medical reserve corps **MRC**
Medical Technologist **MT**
medicine **med.**
medicine and duty **M and D**
medico-chirurgical **MC**
medieval **med.**
Mediterranean **Med.**
Mediterranean theater of operations **MTO**
medium **m; M; med.**

medium bomber **M.B.**
medium close-up **MCU**
medium frequency **MF**
medium range ballistic missile **MRBM**
medium-scale integration **MSI**
medium shot **MS**
medium steel **MS**
medium voltage **MV**
meeting **mtg.**
meeting point **M.P.**
mega- **M**
megabits per second **Mbps**
megabyte **MB**
megacurie **MCi**
megacycle **mc; Mc; meg**
megahertz **MHz**
megapascal **MPa**
megawatt **MW**
megawatt-hour **mwh**
megawatts electric **MWe**
megohm **meg**
melanocyte-stimulating hormone **MSH**
melting point **mp**
melts at **m.**
member **m.; mem.**
Member of Congress **M.C.**
Member of Council **M.C.**
Member of Parliament **M.P.; T.D.**
Member of Provincial Parliament **M.P.P.**
Member of the Legislative Assembly **MLA**
Member of the Order of the British Empire **M.B.E.**
Member of the Royal College of Physicians **M.R.C.P.**
Member of the Royal College

of Surgeons **M.R.C.S.**
memento **mem.**
memoir **mem.**
memorandum **m.; ɩnem.**
memorandum of deposit **M/D**
memorandum of partnership
M/P
memorial **mem.; meml.**
mendelevium **Md; Mv**
mental age **MA**
mental defective **MD**
mentally deficient **MD**
mentally retarded **MR**
mentioned **mentd.**
mercantile **merc.**
mercantile marine **M.M.**
mercaptobenzothiazole **MBT**
merchandise **mdse.**
merchant **mcht.**
merchantable **merch.**
merchant marine **M.M.**
merchant navy **M.N.**
merchant vessel **M.V.**
mercurial **merc.**
mercury **Hg; merc.**
meridian **m.; mer.**
meridional **mer.**
Merseyside **Mersey.**
meso- **ms**
message **msg.**
message dropping **MD**
messenger **msgr.; msngr.**
messenger RNA **mRNA**
messieurs **Messrs.; MM**
meta **m-**
meta-aminobenzoic acid
MABA
metabolic index **MI**
metabolizable energy **ME**
metal **m.; met.; mtl.**
metaling clause **MC**

metallurgical **met.; metal.;**
metall.
metallurgy **met.; metal.;**
metall.
metal-oxide semiconductor
MOS
metal-oxide-semiconductor
field-effect transistor
MOSFET
metal-semiconductor field-
effect transistor **MESFET**
metaphor **met.; metaph.**
metaphorical **met.; metaph.**
metaphysical **met.; metaph.**
metaphysics **met.; metaph.**
meteorological **met.;**
meteor.; metgl.
meteorology **met.**
meteorology **meteor.;**
meteorol.
meter **m.**
meter angle **MA**
meter-candle **MC**
meter-kilogram-second **mks**
meters per minute
mpm; MPM
meters per second
mps; MPS; M/S
methionine **Met**
method **meth.**
Methodist **Meth.**
methyl **Me**
methylated **meth.**
methylcyclopentadienyl
manganese tricarbonyl
MMT
methyl ethyl ketone **MEK**
methyl methacrylate **MM**
methyl tert-butyl ether
MTBE
methyl violet **MV**

metric carat **MC**
metric system **MS**
metric ton **MT**
metronome **met.**
metropolitan **m.; met.**
metropolitan police **M.P.**
Mexican **Mex.**
Mexico **Mex.**
mezza voce **mv**
mezzo forte **mf**
mezzo piano **mp**
Micah **Mic.**
Michigan **MI; Mich.**
micro- **m**
microanalytical reagent **MAR**
microfarad **mfd**
microfiche **MF**
microgram **mcg**
micromicrofarad **mmf; mmfd**
micromillimeter **mmm**
microwave amplification by stimulated emission of radiation **Maser**
microwave landing system **MLS**
middle **m.; mid.**
Middle Ages **MA**
Middle East Treaty Organization **METO**
Middle English **ME**
Middle French **MF**
Middle High German **MHG**
middle linebacker **MLB**
middle marker **MM**
middle of month **MOM**
middle of the road **MOR**
Middlesex **Middx.**
Mid Glamorgan **Mid Glam.**
midland **mid.**

midnight **mdnt.; mid.; midn.**
midshipman **mid.; midn.**
might **mt.**
mil **m.**
mild **mld.**
mild steel **MS**
mile **m.; mi.**
mileage **mi.; mil.**
milepost **M.P.**
miles in the hour **MIH**
miles per gallon **mpg**
miles per hour **mph**
miles per hour per second **mphps**
military **m.; mil.**
military academy **M.A.**
military aircraft types **MAT**
Military Airlift Command **MAC**
Military Air Transport Service **MATS**
military attaché **MA**
military aviator **MA**
military government **MG**
military government officer **MGO**
military intelligence **MI**
military intelligence department **MID**
military intelligence division **MID**
military judge **MJ**
military occupational specialty **MOS**
military police **MP**
military policeman **MP**
military post office **MPO**
military science **MS**
Military Sealift Command **MSC**

Military Sea Transportation
  Service **MSTS**
military training **MT**
militia **mil.**
mill **m.; mi.**
mill annealed **MA**
mill culls out **MCO**
milled in transit **MIT**
Miller Analogies Test **MAT**
mill finish **M.F.**
mill glazed **MG**
milli- **m**
milliampere **ma**
milliampere minute **MAM**
milliampere second **MAS**
milliangstrom **mA**
millibar **mb**
millicurie **mc; mC; mCi**
millicycle **mc**
millielectron volt **meV**
millieme **mil.**
milliequivalent **mEq**
millifarad **mf; mF**
milligal **mgal**
milligram **mg; mgm; mgrm**
milligrams per square
  decimeter per day **MDD**
millihenry **mh**
millilambert **mL**
milliliter **ml**
millimeter **mm**
millimole **mM; mmol;
  mmole**
milliner **mlnr.**
milling in transit **MIT**
million **m.; mil.; mill.**
million barrels per day **mbd**
million electron volts **MeV**
million floating point
  operations per second
  megaflop

million gallons per day **mgd**
million instructions per
  second **MIPS**
million volts **MV**
million years **my; Myr**
milliradion **mrad**
milliroentgen **mr**
millisecond **ms; msc; msec**
millivolt **mv; mV**
milliwatt **mw**
mill run **MR**
mimeograph **mim.**
mine **m.**
mine layer **M.L.**
mineral **min.**
mineralogical **min.**
mineralogy **min.; mineral.**
mineral rubber **MR**
mine-run **MR**
minesweeper **M.S.**
minim **m.; min.**
minimal brain dysfunction
  MBD
minimal effective dose **MED**
minimal infective dose **MID**
minimal inhibitory
  concentration **MIC**
minimum **min.**
minimum daily requirement
  MDR
minimum erythema dose
  MED
minimum fatal dose **MFD**
minimum hemolytic dose
  MHD
minimum identifiable odor
  MIO
minimum inhibitory
  concentration **MIC**
minimum lethal dose **MLD**
minimum reacting

dose **MRD**
mining **min.**
mining engineer **M.E.**
minister **min.**
minister plenipotentiary
  M.P.
minister residentiary **M.R.**
ministry **min.**
Ministry of Internal Affairs
  MVD
Ministry of State Security
  MGB
Minnesota **Minn.; MN**
Minnesota Multiphasic
  Personality Inventory
  MMPI
Minnesota Scholastic Aptitude
  Test **MSAT**
minor **m.; mi.; min.**
mint state **MS**
minute **m.; mi.; min.**
miscellaneous **m.; misc.;
  miscl.; msc**
miscellany **misc.; msc**
misnumbered **misn.**
miss **Ms.**
missile control system **MCS**
missile, experimental **MX**
missing in action **MIA**
missing persons bureau
  MPB
mission **miss.; msn.**
missionary **miss.; missy.**
missionary rector **MR**
Mississippi **Miss.; MS**
Missouri **MO**
Missouri Valley Authority
  MVA
mist **m.**
mister **Mr.**
mistress **Ms.**

mistress **Mrs.**
mix **M**
mixed **mxd.**
mixed grain **M.G.**
mixed lengths **m.l.**
mixed widths **m.w.**
mixture **m.; mist.; mixt.**
mobile **mbl.; mob.**
mobile army surgical
  hospital **MASH**
mobile home **MH**
mobile unit **M.U.**
mobilization **mob.**
mobilized **mob.**
model **m.; mod.**
model airplane club **MAC**
moderate **mdt.; mod.**
moderato **mod.**
moderator **mod.**
modern **mod.**
Modern Language
  Association **MLA**
modification **mod.; modif.**
modified **mod.**
modified American plan
  MAP
modify **mod.**
modulated continuous wave
  MCW
modulator **mod.**
modulo **mod.**
modulus **m.; mod.**
modus operandi **M.O.**
moisture **mstr.**
molal **m.**
molality **m.**
molar **m.**
molarity **m.**
mold **mld.**
molded **mld.**
molder **mldr.**

molding **mld.; mldg.**
mold line **M.L.**
mole **m.**
molecular **mol.**
molecular weight **mol.wt.**
molecule **mol.**
molybdenum **Mo**
moment **m.**
moment of inertia **I**
momentum of a particle **p**
Monaghan **Mon.**
monastery **mon.**
Monday **M; Mon.**
monetary **mon.**
money **moy.**
money allowance for
  quarters **MAQ**
money of account **ac.**
money order **M.O.**
money-order business **MOB**
money-order department
  MOD
monitor **mon.**
monoamine oxidase **MAO**
monoamine oxidase
  inhibitor **MAOI**
monoethanolamine **MEA**
mononitrotoluene **MNT**
mononucleosis **mono**
monophonic **mono**
monoplane **m.**
monosodium glutamate
  MSG
monseigneur **Mgr.;
  Mngr.; Msgr.**
monsieur **M.; Mon.; Mons.**
monsignor **Mgr.; Mngr.;
  Mon.; Msgr.**
monsoon **m.**
Montana **Mont.; MT**
month **m.; mo.; mth.**

monthly **mo.**
months **mos.**
months after date **M/D**
month's after sight **M/S**
month's date **M/D**
month's sight **M/S**
monument **mon.**
monumental inscription **M.I.**
moon **m.**
moral rearmament **MRA**
morendo **mor.**
more softly **pp**
morning **m.; mg.; mrng.**
morning prayer **M.P.**
morocco **mor.**
morphine **m.**
morphine sulfate **MS**
morphological **morph.**
morphology **morph.**
mortar **m.; mor.**
mortgage **m.; mtg.; mtge.**
mortgaged **mtgd.**
mortgagee **mtgee.**
mortgagor **mtgor.**
most **mt.**
most favored nation **MFN**
most holy **SS.**
Most Honorable **M.H.**
most illustrious **ill.; ilmo.**
most valuable player **MVP**
Most Worshipful **M.W.**
Most Worthy **M.W.**
mother **m.**
mother-of-pearl **mop**
motion picture **MP**
Motion Picture Association of
  America **M.P.A.A.**
motocross **MX**
motor **m.; mot.; mtr.**
motor boat **M.B.**
motor contact **M.C.**

motorcycle **M.C.**
motor freight **MF**
motor generator **M.G.**
motor gunboat **MGB**
motorized **mot.**
motor launch **M.L.**
motor ship **M/S**
motor torpedo boat **MTB**
motor transport **MT**
motor transport corps **MTC**
motor union **M.U.**
motor vessel **M.V.**
motor yacht **M.Y.**
mount **mt.**
mountain **m.; mt.; mtn.**
mountain artillery **M.A.**
mountain daylight time
  MDT
mountain standard time
  MST
mountain time **MT**
mounted **mtd.**
mounted police **M.P.**
mounting **mtg.**
mouthwash **collut.**
movement **mvt.**
movement control **MC**
moving target indicator **MTI**
mucilage **muc.**
mucoid **m.**
mud **m.**
muddy **my**
Muhammadan Era **ME**
mullion **mull.**
multilateral force **MLF**
multilateral trade
  negotiations **MTN**
multinational company
  MNC
multinational corporation
  MNC

multiple **mult.**
multiple contact **MC**
multiple independently
  targeted reentry vehicle
  MIRV
multiple mirror telescope
  MMT
multiple reentry vehicle
  MRV
multiple sclerosis **MS**
multiple systems operator
  MSO
multiple track radar **MTR**
multiple-unit steerable
  antenna **MUSA**
multiplex **MPX; MX**
multipoint distribution
  service **MDS**
multipoint distribution
  system **MDS**
multipole **MP**
Multiprogramming Control
  Program for
  Microprocessors **MP/M**
multipurpose meal **MPM**
multirole combat aircraft
  MRCA
municipal **mun.; munic.**
municipality **mun.; munic.**
municipal police **M.P.**
Municiple Assistance
  Corporation **MAC**
municiple borough **M.B.**
munitions **mun.; munic.**
munitions board **M.B.**
muscle **m.**
muscle shock factor **MSF**
muscular dystrophy **MD**
museum **mus.**
music **mus.**
musical **mus.**

musician **mus.**
music wire **MW**
music-wire gauge **MWG**
mustard gas **m.**
muster **m.**
mustered out **M.O.**
mustering-out pay **MOP**
mutilated **mut.**
mutual **mut.**
mutual assured destruction **MAD**
Mutual Broadcasting System **MBS**
muzzle-loading **M.L.**
muzzle-loading rifle **MLR**
muzzle velocity **MV**
my account **MA; MC**
mycology **myc.; mycol.**
mycoplasma **PPLO**
myocardial infarction **MI**
myopia **m.; my**
myriagram **myg**
myrialiter **myl**
myriameter **mym**
mythology **mythol.**

N

nacelle **naç.**
nadir **na.**
Nahum **Nah.**
nail **n.; na.**
naked weight **NW**
name **n.**
name of **NO**
names **nn.**
name unknown **n.u.**
nano- **n**
nanofared **nf**
nanogram **ng**
nanometer **nm**

nanosecond **ns; nsec**
narrow **nar.**
nasal **n.**
nasogastric **NG**
national **n.; nat.; natl.**
national academician **N.A.**
national academy **N.A.**
National Academy of Sciences **NAS**
national advisory committee **NAC**
national advisory council **NAC**
National Aeronautic Association **N.A.A.**
National Aeronautics and Space Administration **NASA**
national aircraft beacon **NAB**
National Archery Association **NAA**
national association **N.A.**
National Association for Mental Health **NAMH**
National Association for the Advancement of Colored People **NAACP**
National Association of Amateur Oarsmen **NAAO**
National Association of Broadcasters **NAB**
National Association of Businessmen **NAB**
National Association of Colleges and Universities **NACU**
National Association of Intercollegiate Athletes **NAIA**
National Association of

Securities Dealers **NASD**
National Association of
Securities Dealers
Automated Quotations
NASDAQ
National Association of Social
Workers **NASW**
National Association of Stock
Car Auto Racing
NASCAR
National Association of
Underwater Instructors
NAUI
National Automobile Dealers
Association **NADA**
National Basketball
Association **NBA**
National Basketball
Committee **NBC**
National Board for
Respiratory Therapy
NBRT
National Board for the
Promotion of Rifle
Practice **NBPRP**
National Boxing Association
NBA
National Broadcasting
Company **NBC**
National Bureau of
Standards **NBS**
National Cancer Institute
NCI
National Climbing
Classification System
NCCS
National Club Football
Association **NCFA**
National Collegiate Athletic
Association **NCAA**
National Collegiate Judo

Association **NCJA**
national debt **ND**
National Dental Association
NDA
National Education
Association **NEA**
National Educational
Television **NET**
National Educational
Television Film Service
NETFS
national emergency **NE**
National Endowment for the
Arts **NEA**
National Endowment for the
Humanities **NEH**
National Federation of
Business and Professional
Women's Clubs **NFBPWC**
National Fencing Coaches
Association of America
NFCAA
National Field Archery
Association **NFAA**
National Flying Club **NFC**
National Football
Conference **NFC**
National Football League
NFL
National Formulary **NF**
national guard **NG**
National Handball Club
NHC
National Health Insurance
N.H.I.
National Health Service
NHS
National Highway Traffic
Safety Administration
NHTSA
National Hockey

League **NHL**
National Horseshoe Pitchers
Association of America
NHPAA
National Hot Rod
Association **NHRA**
National Industrial Recovery
Act **NIRA**
National Institute of
Education **NIE**
National Institute of Mental
Health **NIMH**
National Institute of
Occupational Safety and
Health **NIOSH**
National Institutes of
Health **NIH**
National Intercollegiate
Fencing Association **NIFA**
National Intercollegiate
Women's Fencing
Association **NIWFA**
National Invitational
Tournament **NIT**
nationalist **n.; nat.**
National Junior College
Athletic Association
NJCAA
National Labor Relations
Board **NLRB**
National Lacrosse League
NLL
National League **NL**
National Liberation Front
FLN; NLF
National Library of
Medicine **NLM**
National Maritime Council
NMC
National Merit Scholarship
Qualifying Test **NMSQT**

National Muzzle Loading Rifle
Association **NMLRA**
National Oceanic and
Atmospheric
Administration **NOAA**
National Off Road Racing
Association **NORRA**
National Organization for
Women **NOW**
National Paddleball
Association **NPA**
National Public Radio **NPR**
National Recovery
Administration **NRA**
National Research Council
NRC
National Rifle Association
NRA
National Science
Foundation **NSF**
National Security Agency
NSA
National Security Council
NSC
National Shuffleboard
Association **NSA**
National Ski Association
NSA
National Ski Patrol System
NSPS
national special **NS**
National Squash Tennis
Association **NSTA**
National Standard Race
NASTAR
National Television System
Committee **NTSC**
National Tournament Golf
Association **NTGA**
National Transportation
Safety Board **NTSB**

national union **NU**
national wire gauge **NWG**
National Women's Football
  League **NWFL**
National Wrestling
  Confederation **NWC**
National Youth
  Administration **NYA**
native **nat.**
Nativity of the Virgin
  Mary **NVM**
natural **nat.**
naturalist **nat.**
naturalized **nat.**
natural logarithm **ln**
naturally **sec. nat.; s.n.**
natural order **NO**
nautical **naut.**
nautical almanac **NA**
nautical mile **n.m.; n. mi.**
naval **n.; nav.**
naval academy **NA**
naval air base **NAB**
naval aircraftsman **NAC**
naval air station **NAS**
naval architect **NA**
naval attaché **NA**
naval aviation pilot **NAP**
naval aviator **NA**
naval base **NB**
naval gun fire **NGF**
naval intelligence **NI**
Naval Intelligence
  Department **NID**
Naval Intelligence Division
  NID
naval liaison officer **NLO**
naval officer **NO**
naval officer in charge **NOIC**
naval operating base **NOB**
naval staff officer **NSO**

navigable **nav.**
navigate **n.; nav.**
navigating **n.**
navigation **n.; nav.**
navigator **nav.; navr.**
navy **n.; nav.**
navy department **ND**
navy standard part **NSP**
navy yard **NY**
N-channel metal oxide
  semiconductor **NMOS**
neap **np.**
near **nr.**
near face **NF**
near point **P.p.**
near side **NS**
Nebraska **NE; Neb.; Nebr.**
neck **nk.**
negative **neg.**
negative temperature
  coefficient **ntc**
negotiable **neg.**
negotiable order of
  withdrawal **NOW**
Negro **N**
Nehemiah **Neh.**
neodymium **Nd**
neologism **neol.**
neon **Ne**
nephew **n.**
neptunium **Np**
nerve growth factor **NGF**
nested **nstd.**
net **n.; nt.**
net control station **NCS**
Netherlands **Neth.**
net long ton **NLT**
net proceeds **NP**
net register **n.r.**
net register ton **n.r.t.**
net ton **NT**

net ton mile **ntm**
net weight **nt. wt.;
NW; n. wt.**
neurocirculatory asthenia
NCA
neurodevelopmental
treatment **NDT**
neurological **neurol.**
neurology **neurol.**
neuropsychiatric **NP**
neuropsychiatry **NP**
neuter **n.; neut.; nt.**
neutral **neut.**
neutron **n.**
neutron activation analysis
NAA
Nevada **Nev.; NV**
never hinged **NH**
new **n.**
New American Bible **NAB**
new and nonofficial drugs
NND
new and nonofficial
remedies **NNR**
newborn **NB**
New Brunswick **N.B.**
New Catholic Edition **NCE**
new charter **NC**
new crop **NC**
new drug application **NDA**
New Economic Policy **NEP**
new edition **NE**
New England **NE;
New Eng.**
New English Bible **NEB**
New English Dictionary
NED
Newfoundland **NF; Nfld.**
New Greek **NGk**
New Guinea **N.G.**
New Hampshire **NH; N.H.**

New Jersey **NJ; N.J.**
New Latin **NL**
new line **n.l.**
New Mexico **NM; N.M.; N.
Mex.**
new name **n.n.; nom. nov.**
new paragraph **n.p.**
new school **NS**
new series **NS**
new side **NS**
New South Wales **N.S.W.**
newspaper **n.**
new style **NS**
new terms **NT**
New Testament **NT**
newton **N**
new translation **NT**
new version **NV**
new year **NY**
New York **NY; N.Y.**
New York City **N.Y.C.**
New York Futures
Exchange **NYFE**
New York Stock Exchange
NYSE
New Zealand **N.Z.**
ngultrum **N**
nickel **Ni**
nickel-plated **NP**
nickel steel **NS**
nicotinamide adenine
dinucleotide **NAD**
nicotinamide adenine
dinucleotide phosphate
NADP
night **n.; ngt.; ni.; nt.**
night and morning
n. et m.; n.m.
night letter **NL; NLT**
night message **NM**
night stop **n.**

nimbostratus **Ns**
nimbus **Nb.**
niobium **Nb**
nitrilotriacetic acid **NTA**
nitrogen **N**
nitrogen oxide **NO$_x$**
nitroglycerin **NG**
no account **N/A**
no advice **NA**
no appreciable disease **NAD**
no ball **n.b.**
nobelium **No**
no bid **NB**
no change **NC**
no charge **NC**
no commercial value **NCV**
no commission until paid **NCUP**
no connection **NC**
no credit **NC**
no date **n.d.; N.D.**
no effects **N/E**
no fixed date **nfd**
no funds **NF**
no good **N.G.**
no mark **N/m**
nomen **n.**
nomenclature **nom.**
no middle initial **NMI**
nominal **nom.**
nominal horsepower **nhp**
nominative **n.; nom.**
nonacceptance **NA**
non-airline carrier **NAC**
noncollectible **NC**
noncommissioned officer **NCO**
nondirectional beacon **NDB**
none **n.**
nonessential **NE**
nonferrous **NF**

nonfundable **nf**
nongonococcal urethritis **NGU**
nongovernmental organization **NGO**
nonhygroscopic **NH**
nonofficial **NO**
nonparticipating **n.p.**
nonpersonal liability **NPL**
nonprotein nitrogen **NPN**
nonrapid-eye-movement **NREM**
non sequitur **non seq.**
nonspecific urethritis **NSU**
nonvolatile matter **NVM**
nonvolatile metal oxide semiconductor **NMOS**
nonvoting **NV**
noon **m.; n.**
no one contradicting **nem. con.**
no one dissenting **nem. diss.**
no orders **NO**
no pagination **n.p.**
no par value **NPV**
no place **n.p.**
no place or date **n.p. or d.**
no protest **NP**
no protest nonacceptance **NPNA**
nordihydroguaiaretic acid **NDGA**
Norfolk **Norf.**
no risk **n.r.**
no risk after discharge **n.r.a.d.**
normal **n.; nor.; norm.; nrml.**
normal boiling point **NBP**
normal pressure and temperature **NPT**

normal temperature and pressure **NTP**
north **N; no.; nor.**
North America **N.A.**
North American Air Defense Command **NORAD**
North American Hockey League **NAHL**
North American Soccer League **NASL**
Northamptonshire **Northants.**
North Atlantic Treaty Organization **NATO**
northbound **NB**
North Carolina **NC; N.C.**
North Dakota **ND; N.D.; N. Dak.**
northeast **NE**
northeastern **NE**
northern **N; no.; nor.; nthn.**
Northern Ireland **N.I.**
Northern Territory **NT; N.T.**
north latitude **N.L.**
north-northeast **NNE**
north-northwest **NNW**
north polar distance **NPD**
Northumberland **Nthmb.**
northwest **NW**
northwestern **NW**
Northwest Territories **NT; N.T.; NWT**
Norway **Nor.; Norw.**
Norwegian **Nor.; Norw.**
nose **no.; ns.**
not always afloat **n.a.a.**
not applicable **NA**
notary public **NP**
not available **NA**
not dated **n.d.**
note **n.; sch.**

not earlier than **n.e.t.**
not elsewhere included **n.e.i.**
not elsewhere indicated **n.e.i.**
not elsewhere mentioned **n.e.m.**
not elsewhere specified **n.e.s.**
notes **nn.**
not exceeding **n.e.**
not far **n.l.**
not fordable **nf**
not for sale **NFS**
not good **N.G.**
nothing abnormal discovered **NAD**
notice to airmen **NOTAM**
notify **ntfy.**
not invented here **NIH**
no title page **NTP**
not known **NK**
not later than **n.l.t.**
not less than **NLT**
not marked **N/m**
not more than **NMT**
not otherwise enumerated **N.O.E.**
not otherwise herein provided **N.O.H.P.**
not otherwise indexed by name **NOIBN**
not otherwise provided for **n.o.p.**
not otherwise specified **NOS**
not our publication **NOP**
not out **NO**
not provided for **n.p.f.**
not specifically provided for **NSPF**
not specified **N.S.**
not sufficient **N/S**
not sufficient funds **NSF**

not taken out **NTO**
Nottinghamshire **Notts.**
not to be noted **N/N**
not to be repeated **n.r.**
not to exceed **n.e.**
not to scale **NTS**
notwithstanding **non obs.;
    non obst.**
notwithstanding the verdict
    n.o.v.
not yet diagnosed **NYD**
not yet published **NYP**
not yet returned **NYR**
noun **n.**
noun phrase **NP**
nouns **nn.**
Nova Scotia **NS; N.S.**
novelist **nov.**
November **N; Nov.**
novice slope **n**
no voltage release **NVR**
no year **NY**
nuclear energy for propulsion
    of aircraft **NEPA**
nuclear magnetic resonance
    NMR
Nuclear Nonproliferation
    Treaty **NPT**
nuclear quadrupole
    resonance **NQR**
Nuclear Regulatory
    Commission **NRC**
nuclear ship **NS**
number **n.; no.; nr.; num.**
numbered **numb.**
Numbers **Num.; Numb.**
numbers **nos.**
number unobtainable **NU**
numeral **num.**
numerical aperture **N.A.**
numerical control **NC**

numismatic **numis.**
numismatical **numis.**
numismatics **numis.**
numismatic society **NS**
nurse corps **NC**
Nurse Practitioner **NP**
nurse's aide **NA**
nursing **Nsg.**
nursing auxiliary **NA**

O

Obadiah **Ob.; Obad.**
obbligato **obb.**
obedient **obdt.; obt.**
obiter **ob.**
object **o.; obj.**
objection **obj.**
objective **obj.**
oblast **o.**
Oblates of Mary
    Immaculate **O.M.I.**
obligation **obl.**
oblique **obl.**
oblong **ob.; obl.**
oboe **ob.**
obscure **obs.**
observation **o.; ob.;
    obs.; obsn.**
observation plane **OP**
observation post **OP**
observatory **obs.**
observed **obs.; obsd.**
observer **o.; obs.; obsr.**
obsolete **obs.**
obstacle **obs.**
obstetrical **OB; obstet.**
obstetrician **OB; OBS**
obstetrician-gynecologist
    OB-GYN
obstetrics **OB; OBS; obstet.**

obstetrics-gynecology **OB-GYN**
obstruction **obs.**
obtained **obtd.**
obverse **obv.**
occasion **occn.**
occasional **occ.**
occasionally **occ.; occas.**
Occident **O.**
Occidental **O.**
occipital-frontal **OF**
occiput anterior **OA**
occiput posterior **OP**
occulting **occ.**
occupation **occup.**
occupational **occup.**
occupational disease **OD**
occupational level **O.L.**
Occupational Safety and Health Administration **OSHA**
Occupational Therapist **OT**
Occupational Therapist, Registered **OTR**
occupational therapy **OT**
ocean **o.; oc.**
ocean and rail **O and R**
oceanography **oceanog.**
ocean thermal energy conversion **OTEC**
octamethylpyrophos-phoramide **OMPA**
octane number **O.N.**
octavo **O; oct.**
October **O.; Oct.**
octodecimo **T**
ocular hypertension indicator **OHI**
oersted **Oe**
of age **ae.; aet.; aetat.**
of blessed memory **B.M.**

of course **OC**
of death **m.**
of each **sing.**
off **o.**
off-Broadway **O.B.**
off center **OC**
offensive **off.**
offensive end **OE**
offensive guard **OG**
offensive tackle **OT**
offered **off.**
office **o.; ofc.; off.**
office copy **OC**
Office of Civil and Defense Mobilization **OCDM**
Office of Consumer Affairs **OCA**
Office of Economic Opportunity **OEO**
Office of International Trade **OIT**
Office of Management and Budget **OMB**
Office of Minority Business Enterprise **OMBE**
Office of Naval Intelligence **ONI**
Office of Strategic Services **OSS**
Office of Technology Assessment **OTA**
officer **o.; ofcr.; off.; offr.**
officer candidate **OC**
Officer Candidate School **OCS**
officer commanding **O.C.**
officer efficiency report **OER**
officer in charge **OC**
officer in tactical command **OTC**
officer of the day **OD**

officer of the deck OOD
officer of the guard O.G.
Officer of the Order of the
  British Empire O.B.E.
officer's cook OC
Officers' Reserve Corps ORC
officers' training camp OTC
officers' training corps OTC
Officers' Training School
  OTS
official o.; ofcl.; off.; offic.
official classification OC
official receiver O.R.
official referee O.R.
official test insecticide OTI
officinal off.
off-off-Broadway OOB
off-road vehicle ORV
off scene o.s.
offscreen o.s.
offstage o.s.
offtrack betting OTB
of medicine m.
of Oxford Oxon
of the goods not
  administered d.b.n.
of the order of o.
of this month h.m.
of this place h.l.
of this year h.a.
Ohio O.; OH
Ohio Improved Chester
  white OIC
ohm o
oil o.
oil-in-water O/W
oil of vitriol OV
oiltight O.T.
ointment oint.; ung.
Oklahoma OK; Okla.
old o.

old age OA
Old Age and Survivors
  Insurance OASI
old-age assistance OAA
old age pension O.A.P.
old age pensioner O.A.P.
Old Age, Survivors, and
  Disability Insurance
  OASDI
old charter OC
Old Church Slavonic OCS
old crop OC
Old English OE
Old French OF; OFr
Old High German OHG
Old Irish OIr
Old Latin OL
old man O.M.
old measurement O.M.
Old Norse ON
Old Persian OP
old prices OP
Old Saxon OS
old school O.S.
old series O.S.
old side O.S.
old style O.S.
old terms O/T
Old Testament O.T.
Old Tuberculin O.T.
Old Welsh OW
oleum ol
olive drab OD
omissions excepted o.e.
omnidirectional radio
  beacon ORB
on account o/a
on active service OAS
on behalf exp.
on center OC
on course OC

on demand **OD**
on duty **OD**
one half **sem.; ss.**
one side **O.S.**
one-stop tour charter **O.T.C.**
one-way **OW**
On Her Majesty's Service **OHMS**
On His Majesty's Service **OHMS**
Online Computer Library Center **OCLC**
only **o.**
only child **o.c.**
only son **o.s.**
on or about **o/a**
on order **oo**
on request **O/R**
on sale **OS**
on sample **OS**
on schedule **O.S.**
onset and course **O and C**
on sheet **O.S.**
on side **OS**
Ontario **ON; Ont.**
on the back of the page **f.v.**
on the back page of **f.v.**
on-the-job training **OJT**
on time **O.T.**
on track **O.T.**
on truck **o.t.**
ooze **oz.**
open account **o/a**
open charter **OC**
open-circuit television **OCTV**
open cover **OC**
open hearth **OH**
opening **o.; O; opg.; opng.**
opening of books **OB**
open policy **OP**

open race **opn.**
open systems interconnection **OSI**
open to buy **OTB**
opera **op.; opp.**
operate **opr.; opt.**
operating nursing procedure **ONP**
operating room **OR**
operating system **OS**
operation **o.; op.; OP; opn.**
operational amplifier **op-amp**
operational taxonomic unit **OTU**
operational training unit **OTU**
operations and maintenance **O & M**
operations research **OR**
operations room **OR**
operative **op.**
operator **op.; opr.**
ophthalmic **oph.**
ophthalmologic **oph.**
ophthalmologist **oph.**
ophthalmological **oph.**
ophthalmology, otology, laryngology, rhinology **OOLR**
ophthalmoscope **oph.**
ophthalmoscopy **oph.**
opinion **opn.**
opponent **opp.**
opponents' runs **OR**
opportunity **opp.; oppy.**
opposed **opp.**
opposite **op.; opp.**
opposite prompt **OP**
opposite prompter **OP**
optative **opt.**

optical **opt.**
optical character reader
  OCR
optical character recognition
  OCR
optical density **OD**
optician **opt.**
optics **opt.**
optimum working frequency
  OWF
option **opt.**
optional **opt.**
optional claiming race
  opt. clm.
opus **op.**
orally **p.o.**
oral polio vaccine **OPV**
Orange Free State **O.F.S.**
orange juice **OJ**
oratorio **ora.**
Orbiting Solar Observatory
  OSO
orchestra **orch.**
ordained **ord.**
order **o.; ord.**
order bill of lading **OBL**
order canceled **OC**
ordered back **OB**
ordered recorded **O.R.**
orderly **odly.; ord.**
orderly room **O.R.**
order notify **O/N**
order of **O/o**
order of battle **OB**
Order of Cistercians of
  the Strict Observance
  O.C.S.O.
Order of Friars Minor
  O.F.M.
order of merit **O.M.**
Order of Preachers **O.P.**

Order of St. Augustine
  O.S.A.
Order of St. Benedict **O.S.B.**
Order of the Eastern
  Star **OES**
order sheet **O.S.**
order to show cause **OSC**
ordinal **ord.**
ordinance **ord.**
ordinary **ord.**
ordinary least squares **OLS**
Ordinary National
  Certificate **ONC**
Ordinary National Diploma
  OND
ordinary seaman **OD; OS**
ordinary spring tides **o.s.t.**
ordinate **y**
ordnance **o.; ord.**
ordnance datum **OD**
ordnance office **OO**
ordnance officer **OO**
Oregon **OR; Ore.; Oreg.**
organic **org.**
organic acid soluble
  phosphorus **OASP**
organic heart disease **OHD**
organization **org.; orgn.**
organization development
  OD
Organization for Economic
  Cooperation and
  Development **OECD**
Organization of African
  Unity **OAU**
Organization of American
  States **OAS**
Organization of Petroleum
  Exporting Countries
  OPEC
Organization of the Secret

Army **OAS**
organized **org.**
Organized Reserve Corps **ORC**
oriental **o.; or.**
origin **orig.**
original **o.; or.; orig.**
original cover **OC**
original equipment
 manufacturer **OEM**
original gum **o.g.**
originally **orig.**
original series **O.S.**
origin and destination **OD**
originator **orig.**
Orkney **Ork.**
or nearest offer **o.n.o.**
ornithine carbamyl
 transferase **OCT**
ornithology **ornith.**
or similar **vel sim.**
orth- **o-**
ortho- **o-**
oscillate **osc.**
oscillating **osc.**
oscillator **osc.**
osmium **Os**
osmol **Osm**
osmotic pressure **OP**
osteoarthritis **OA**
osteogenesis imperfecta **O.I.**
osteopathic **ost.**
other ranks **O.R.**
other than psychotic **OP**
otherwise **orse.**
otherwise known as **o.k.a.**
ounce **oz.**
ounces **oz.**
our account **o/a**
Our Lord **N.S.**
Our Savior Jesus

Christ **NSIC; NSJC**
out **o.**
outboard **o/b; otdb.**
outer keel **OK**
outer marker **OM**
outfield **o.; OF**
outing club **OC**
outlet **o.**
out-of-body experience **OBE**
out of print **OP**
out of print at present **OPP**
out of stock **OS**
out-of-the-body **OOB**
outpatient **OP**
outpatient clinic **OPC**
outpatient department **OPD**
outpost **OP**
output per man shift **OMS**
outside **O.S.**
outside diameter **O.D.**
outside dimension **O.D.**
outside edge **o.**
outside guard **OG**
outside home **OH**
outside left forward **OL**
outside right forward **OR**
outside sentinel **O.S.**
outsize **O.S.**
outstanding **O/S**
out stealing **OS**
outward bound **OB**
ovation **O**
over **o.**
overall **OA**
overcast **o; ovo**
overcharge **OC**
overdose **OD**
overdraft **O/D**
overdrawn **O/D**
Overeaters Anonymous **OA**
overflow level **O.L.**

overhead **OH; ovhd.**
overhead camshaft **ohc**
overhead line **O.L.**
overhead valve **ohv**
overload **O.L.**
overprint **OP**
overproof **OP**
over, short, and damaged **O.S. & D.**
over the counter **O/C**
over-the-counter **OTC**
overtime **O.T.**
over voltage **OV**
ovum **ov.**
owned and operated **O & O**
owner **o.**
owners, landlords, and tenants **OL and T**
owner's risk **O.R.**
owner's risk of becoming wet **O.R.W.**
owner's risk of breakage **O.R.B.**
owner's risk of chafing **O.R.C.**
owner's risk of damage **O.R.D.**
owner's risk of fire **O.R.F.**
owner's risk of freezing **O.R.F.**
owner's risk of leakage **O.R.L.**
owner's risk of shifting **O.R.S.**
own recognizance **OR**
Oxford **Oxon**
Oxford Committee for Famine Relief **OXFAM**
Oxford English Dictionary **OED**
Oxfordshire **Oxon.**

oxidation-reduction **O-R; redox**
oxidizing flame **OF**
oxygen **O**
oxygen consumed **OC**
oxytetracycline **OTC**

P

pacer **p.**
Pacific **Pac.**
Pacific Coast Hockey League **PCHL**
Pacific Coast League **PCL**
Pacific daylight time **PDT**
Pacific standard time **PST**
Pacific time **PT**
pack **pk.**
package **pkg.; pkge.**
packed cell volume **PCV**
packed powder **pkd. pdr.**
packed weight **P.W.**
packer **pkr.**
packet **pkt.**
packing-house products **P.H.P.**
packmaster **pkm.**
page **p.; pg.**
pages **pp.**
paid **pd.**
painted **pntd.; ptd.**
painter **pntr.; ptr.**
pair **pr.**
Pakistan **Pak.**
paleontology **pal.; paleon.**
Palestine Liberation Organization **PLO**
palladium **Pd**
palmistry **palm.**
pamphlet **pam.; pph.**
Panama **Pan.**

Panama Canal **PC**
Pan American Union **PAU**
panel **pnl.**
paneled **pan.**
panorama **pan.**
paper **pa.; pap.**
paperback **P**
paper insulated **P.I.**
Papua New Guinea **P.N.G.**
papyrus **pap.**
para- **p-**
para-aminobenzoic acid
  PABA
para-aminohippurate **PAH**
para-aminohippuric
  acid **PAH**
para aminosalicylic
  acid **PAS**
para-aminosalicylic
  acid **PASA**
parabolic-aluminized
  reflector **PAB**
para-chlorophenylalanine
  PCPA
parachute **prcht.**
parachutist **prchst.**
paradichlorobenzene **PDB**
paradigm **pdg.**
paragraph **P; par.; para.**
Paraguay **Par.; Para.**
parallax **P; par.**
parallel **par.**
parathyroid hormone **PTH**
parcel **pcl.**
parcel airlift **PAL**
parcel post **PP**
parcel post insured **P.P.I.**
parental **P**
parental generation **P**
parental guidance (movie
  rating) **PG**

parent effectiveness
  training **PET**
parenthesis **par.**
parent-teacher association
  PTA
parent-teacher organization
  PTO
Paris granite **P.G.**
parish **par.**
parish priest **P.P.**
park **P; pk.; prk.**
parkway **pkwy.**
parliament **parl.**
parliamentary **parl.**
parliamentary cases **PC**
parliamentary private
  secretary **P.P.S.**
parliamentary report **P.R.**
parole officer **P.O.**
parsec **pc**
part **p.; pt.**
partial loss **P.L.**
participating **part.**
participial **part.**
participial adjective **p.a.**
participle **p.; part.; ppl.**
particular **part.**
particular average **P.A.**
Parti Québecois **PQ**
partition **partn.; Pn.**
partly soluble **P sol**
partner **part.**
part paid **P.P.**
parts per **pp**
parts per billion **ppb**
parts per million **ppm**
parts per million by volume
  ppmv
parts per thousand **ppt**
parts per trillion **ppt**
part-time **PT**

party **pty.**
par value **pv**
pascal **Pa**
pass **P**
passage **pass.**
passbook **PB**
passed **pd.**
passed ball **PB**
passenger **pass.; psgr.**
passenger agent **P.A.**
passenger steamer **P.S.**
passim **pass.**
passive **pass.**
pass slip stitch over **psso**
past **p.**
past commander **PC**
past due date **PDD**
paste **p.**
past master **P.M.**
pastor **P**
past participle **p.p.**
past tense **p.t.**
patent **pat.**
Patent and Trademark
  Office **PTO**
patent cases **PC**
patented **pat.**
pater **p.**
pathological **path.; pathol.**
pathologist **pathol.**
pathology **path.; pathol.**
patient **pt**
patrol **P; pat.**
patrol boat **PB**
patrol bomber **PB**
patrol craft **PC**
patrolman **Ptl.**
patrol torpedo **PT**
pattern **pat.; patt.**
patternmaker **ptrnmkr.**
patternmaking **patmkg.**

pawn **P**
payable on death **POD**
payable on receipt **POR**
pay as you earn **PAYE**
pay as you enter **PAYE**
paying guest **P.G.**
paymaster **payr.; PM**
paymaster general **PMG**
payment **payt.; pmt.;**
  pt.; pymt.
payment in kind **PIK**
pay on delivery **P.O.D.**
pay on return **POR**
pay-per-view **PPV**
payroll **P/R**
Peace Corps **PC**
peak **pk.**
peak to peak **PP**
peck **pk.**
pecky **pky.**
peculiar meter **P.M.**
pedal **ped.**
pedestal **ped.**
pedestrian **ped.**
Pediatric Nurse Practitioner
  PNP
pellagra preventive **PP**
pelvic inflammatory disease
  PID
penal code **PC**
penalities in minutes **pim**
penalty minutes **pm**
pence **d.; p.**
penetration **pen.**
peninsula **pen.; penin.**
penitent **pen.**
Pennsylvania **Pa.; PA;**
  Penn.; Penna.
penny **d.; p.**
penny nail **d**
pennyweight **dwt.; pwt.**

Pension Benefit Guaranty Corporation **PBGC**
pentachloronitrobenzene **PCNB**
pentachlorophenol **PCP**
pentaerythritol tetranitrate **PETN**
pentose nucleic acid **PNA**
people **p.**
People's Commissariat of Internal Affairs **NKVD**
People's Liberation Army **PLA**
People's Republic of China **PRC**
per **p.**
per annum **p.a.**
perceived noise decibel **PNdb**
percent **p.c.; pct.**
percentage **p.c.; pct.**
percentile **P**
perception of light **PL**
perch **p.**
percussion **perc.**
perdendosi **per.**
per diem **p.d.**
perennial **per.**
perfect **perf.; pf.**
perforate **perf.**
perforated **perf.**
perforation **P.; perf.**
performance **perf.; pfce.**
performed **perf.**
performer **perf.**
per gross ton **pgt**
perhaps **perh.**
perigee **peri.**
perimeter **p.**
perimeter acquisition radar **PAR**

per inquiry **PI**
period **p.; per.**
periodic acid-Schiff **PAS**
peripheral vascular disease **PVD**
perishable **P.; persh.**
permanent **perm.**
permanent bench mark **PBM**
permanent budget account **PBA**
permanent bunkers **P.B.**
permanent change of station **PCS**
permanent magnet **PM**
permanent secretary **P.S.**
per month **p.m.**
pernicious anemia **P.A.**
peroxyacetyl nitrate **PAN**
perpendicular **perp.**
perpetual **perp.**
perpetual curate **P.C.**
per power of attorney **p.p.a.**
Persia **Per.; Pers.**
Persian **Per.; Pers.**
person **per.; pers.**
personal **pers.**
personal appearance **PA**
personal computer **PC**
personal flotation device **PFD**
personal foul **pf**
personal identification number **PIN**
personality quotient **P.Q.**
personally **pers.**
personal property **PP**
personal rapid transit **PRT**
personal record **PR**
persona non grata **p.n.g.**
person in need of

supervision **PINS**
personnel **pers.**
personnel officer **PO**
person of the opposite sex
sharing living quarters
posslq
perspective **persp.**
per standard compass **psc**
pertaining **pert.**
per thousand **PM**
peseta **p.; pst.; pt.; pta.**
peso **p.**
pest control operator **PCO**
peta **P**
Peter **Pet.**
petite **p**
petition **petn.**
petrolatum **pet.**
petroleum **pet.**
petroleum engineer **P.E.**
petroleum, oil, and
lubricants **POL**
petty cash **P/C**
petty cashbook **PCB**
petty officer **PO**
pfennig **pf.; pfg.**
pharmaceutical **phar.;
pharm.**
pharmacist **phar.; pharm.**
pharmacopeia **P**
pharmacopoeia
P; ph.; phar.
pharmacy **phar.; pharm.**
phase **ph.**
phase line **PL**
phase-locked loop **PLL**
phase modulation **P.M.**
phencyclidine **PCP**
phenyl **Ph**
phenylketonuria **PKU**
phenylpropanolamine **PPA**

phenylthiocarbamide **PTC**
Phi Beta Kappa **PBK**
Philadelphia **Phila.**
Philemon **Philem.**
philharmonic **phil.**
Philippians **Phil.**
Philippine Islands **P.I.**
philological **phil.; philol.**
philologist **phil.; philol.**
philology **phil.; philol.**
philosopher **phil.; philos.**
philosophical **phil.**
philosophy **phi.; phil.;
philos.**
phone **ph.**
phonetically balanced **PB**
phonetics **phon.**
phonograph **phono.**
phonology **phon.**
phosphoenolpyruvate **PEP**
phosphor **ph.**
phosphorus **P**
phot **ph**
photoelectric **PE**
photoelectric cell **PEC**
photograph **phot.**
photographer **pho.; phot.**
photographic **phot.; photog.**
photographic intelligence
PHOTINT
photographic reconnaissance
unit **PRU**
photography **phot.; photog.**
photo interpretation **PI**
photo interpreter **PI**
photomultiplier tube **PMT**
photovoltaic **PV**
phrase **P; phr.**
phraseology **phr.**
phrase structure **PS**
physical **phys.**

physical education **PE; phy. ed.**

physical examination **PE**

physical fitness index **PFI**

physical therapist **PT**

physical therapy **PT**

physical training **PT**

physician **phys.**

physician's assistant **PA**

Physician's Assistant-Certified **PA-C**

Physicians' Desk Reference **PDR**

physics **phys.**

physiological **phys.**

physiologist **physiol.**

physiology **physiol.**

phytohemagglutinin **PHA**

pianissimo **pp**

pianississimo **ppp**

piano **p**

pianoforte **pf; pfte**

piaster **p.; pa.; pi.; pias.**

picked ports **p.p.**

pickup **PU**

pickup and delivery **P & D; P.U.D.**

pick your own **PYO**

pico- **p**

picofarad **pf**

picogram **pg**

picomole **pmol; pmole**

picopicogram **ppg**

picosecond **ps; psec**

picot **p**

pictorial **pict.**

picture **pic.**

picture postcard **PPC**

pie **p.**

piebald **p.b.**

piece **pc.; pce.**

pieces **ps.**

pigeon **pgn.**

pike **pk.**

pile **pl.**

pill **pil.**

pilot **pil.; plt.**

pilot direction indicator **PDI**

pilot officer **PO**

pinch hit **PH**

pinch hitter **PH**

pinion end **PE**

pint **O; p.; pt.**

pioneer **pnr.**

pipe **p**

pipe ventilated **PV**

pitch **p**

pitch circle **PC**

pitch diameter **PD**

pitcher **p**

pizzicato **pizz**

place **l.; pl.**

place of the seal **L.S.**

plain **pl.; pln.**

plainchant **C.F.**

plaintext **P**

plaintiff **plf.; pltf.**

Planck's constant **h**

planed **P**

Planned Parenthood **PP**

planning, programming, budgeting **PPB**

plan position indicator **PPI**

plaster **pl.**

plasterer **plstr.; plstrer.**

plastic **plstc.**

plate **P; pl.; plt.**

plateau **plat.**

platelet-activating factor **PAF**

platform **plat.**

plating **pltg.**

platinum **Pt**
platoon **pl.; plat.**
platoon sergeant **PSG**
pleasant **P**
please **pls.**
please exchange **P.X.**
please forward **f.s.**
please note **PN**
please reply **R.S.V.P.**
please reply at once
    R.V.S.V.P.
please turn over **PTO**
pleas of the crown **PC**
plebeian **pleb.**
plenipotentiary **plen.**
plug-compatible **PC**
plug-compatible maker **PCM**
plug-compatible
    manufacturer **PCM**
plumber **plbr.**
plumbing **plbg.; plmb.;
    plmg.**
plural **pl.; plu.**
plutonium **Pu**
pneumatic **pneu.; pneum.**
pneumothorax **Px**
pocket **pkt.**
pocket book **P.B.**
poet laureate **P.L.**
poetry **po.**
point **p.; po.; pt.**
point after touchdown **PAT**
point detonating **PD**
point detonating fuse **PDF**
pointed **ptd.**
point of purchase **P.O.P.**
point-of-sale **POS**
points **pts.**
points per game **PPG**
Poland **Pol.**
polar **P; pol.**

pole **p.; po.**
police commissioner **PC**
police constable **P.C.**
police department **P.D.**
police justice **P.J.**
police magistrate **PM**
police sergeant **P.S.**
policy proof of interest **p.p.i.**
Polish **Pol.**
polish **pol.**
polished **pol.**
political **pol.; polit.**
political action committee
    PAC
political code **PC**
politician **pol.**
politics **pol.**
Pollution Standard Index
    PSI
polonium **Po**
polyacrylonitrile **PAN**
polybrominated biphenyl
    PBB
polychlorinated biphenyl
    PCB
polycyclic aromatic
    hydrocarbon **PAH**
polyethylene **PE**
polyethylene terephthalate
    PET
polymethylmethacrylate
    PMMA
polymorphonuclear
    neutrophilic leukocyte
    PMN
polynuclear aromatic
    hydrocarbon **PAH**
polypropylene oxide **PPO**
polytechnic **poly.; polytech.**
polyunsaturated fatty acid
    PUFA

polyvinyl **PV**
polyvinyl acetate **PVA**
polyvinyl alcohol **PVA**
polyvinyl chloride **PVC**
polyvinylpyrrolidone **PVP**
pomposo **pomp**
pond **pd.**
Pontifex Maximus **P.M.**
pontoon **pon.; pont.**
poor skiing conditions **p**
pope **P; pp**
popular **pop.**
popularly **pop.**
population **P; pop.**
porcelain **porc.**
porch **pch.**
port **p.; pt.**
portable **port.; ptbl.**
portable life-support system **PLSS**
port dues **P.D.**
portfolio **port.**
portion **por.**
port of call **p.o.c.**
port of debarkation **PD**
port of embarkation **PE; POE**
port of entry **POE**
portrait **por.; port.**
Portugal **Pg.; Port.**
Portuguese **Pg.; Port.**
position **P; pn.; pns.; pos.**
position doubtful **PD**
positive **P; pos.**
positive crankcase ventilation **PCV**
positive end-expiratory pressure **PEEP**
positive square root of minus one **i**
positron-emission

tomography **PET**
positron emission transverse tomography **PETT**
possession **pos.; poss.; possn.**
possessive **pos.; poss.**
possible **poss.**
possibly **poss.**
post **p.**
post adjutant **PA**
postage **p.; pstg.**
postage and handling **p & h**
postage due **PD**
postage free **fco**
postal **post.**
postal district **PD**
postal order **PO**
Postal Rate Commission **PRC**
postal service center **PSC**
postal telegraph **p.t.**
postal telegraph cable **p.t.c.**
postal, telegraph, telephone **PTT**
postcard **p.c.**
post commander **PC**
postdated **P.D.**
posterior **P**
post exchange **PE; PX**
postgraduate **PG**
postgraduate year **PGY**
postmark **pmk.**
postmaster **PM**
postmaster general **PMG**
postmortem **PM**
post office **P.O.**
post office box **P.O.B.**
post office department **P.O.D.**
post office order **P.O.O.**
post office savings

bank **P.O.S.B.**
postpaid **P.P.; ppd.**
postpartum **PP**
post position **PP**
postscript **P.S.**
postscripts **P.SS.**
post town **p.t.**
post-traumatic stress
  disorder **PTSD**
post village **p.v.**
potassium **K**
potential **pot.**
potential difference **P.D.; V**
potentiometer **pot.**
potion **pot.**
pottery **pot.**
poultry **pltry.**
pound **l.; L; lb; lib.; pd.**
poundal **pdl.**
pounder **pdr.; pr.**
pounds force **lbf**
pounds per square foot **psf**
pounds per square inch **psi**
pounds per square inch
  absolute **psia**
pounds per square inch
  gauge **psig**
pounds pressure **p.p.**
pounds, shillings, pence **LSD**
powder **pdr.; pulv.; pwd.**
powder snow **pdr.**
power **P; pr.; pwr.**
power amplifier **PA**
power brakes **PB**
power factor **p.f.**
power of attorney **P/A**
power of magnification **X**
power plant **P.P.**
power play **pp**
power play goals **PPG**
power steering **PS**

power supply **PS**
power takeoff **PTO**
power window **PW**
practical **prac.**
practice **prac.**
practice cases **PC**
practitioners **prac.**
praise to God always **LDS**
praseodymium **Pr**
prayer **pr.**
prayer book **P.B.**
preacher's kid **PK**
prebend **preb.**
prebendary **preb.**
preceding **prec.**
precipitate **ppt.**
precipitation **pcpn.;
  ppn.; pptn.**
precision approach radar
  PAR
precision guided munitions
  PGM
preconscious **Pcs**
predicate **P; pred.**
predicative **pred.**
predicted drift angle **PDA**
preface **pref.**
prefatory **pref.**
prefect **pref.**
prefect apostolic **P.A.**
prefecture **pref.**
preference **pref.**
preferred **pf.; pfd.;
  pr.; pref.**
preferred provider
  organization **PPO**
prefix **pfx.; pref.**
pregnant mare serum **PMS**
preliminary **prelim.**
Preliminary Scholastic
  Aptitude Test **PSAT**

premature ventricular
  contraction **PVC**
premenstrual syndrome
  PMS
premier **prem.**
premium **pm.; prem.; prm.**
premolar **pm.**
prepaid **P.P.; ppd.**
preparation **prep.; prepn.**
preparatory **prep.**
prepare **prep.**
prepared **prepd.**
preparing **prepg.**
preposition **prep.**
prerequisite **prereq.**
presbyopia **pr**
Presbyterian **Presb.**
prescription **℞; Rx**
present **P; pr.; pres.; prs.**
presentation **pres.**
presentence investigation
  report **PSI**
present illness **PI**
present participle **pr. p.**
preserve **serv.**
presidency **pres.**
president **P; pres.**
presidential **pres.; presdl.**
presiding elder **P.E.**
presiding judge **P.J.**
press agent **P.A.**
press association **P.A.**
press feeder **prsfdr**
pressman **prsmn**
press release **PR**
pressure **P; pres.; press.**
pressure, volume,
  temperature **PVT**
pressurized water reactor
  PWR
presumptive **pres.**

preterit **pret.**
pretty damn quick **PDQ**
previous **prev.**
previously **prev.**
previous question **PQ**
price **pr.**
price current **P/C**
price/earnings **P/E**
price-level adjusted
  mortgage **PLAM**
price on request **POR**
priest **P; pr.**
priest vicar **p.v.**
primary **p.; pri.; prim.**
primary mental abilities
  PMA
primate **prim.**
prime minister **P.M.**
primitive **pr.; prim.**
prince **P; pr.**
Prince Edward Island
  PE; P.E.I.
principal **p; prin.; princ.**
principal clerk of session
  P.C.S.
principal, interest, taxes,
  insurance **PITI**
principally **prin.**
principal medical officer
  PMO
principle **prin.; princ.**
printed **pr.; ptd.**
printed circuit **PC**
printer **pr.; prntr.;
  prtr.; ptr.**
printer's error **PE**
printing **ptg.**
printing out paper **POP**
prior **pr.**
prior endorsement
  guaranteed **PEG**

prior to admission **PTA**
prism diopter **PD**
prison **pri.**
prisoner **pris.**
prisoner at large **PAL**
prisoner of war **POW; PW**
private **pr.; pri.;**
  priv.; Pte.; pvt.
private account **P/A**
private automatic branch
  exchange **PABX**
private automatic exchange
  PAX
private branch exchange
  PBX
private exchange **PX**
private first class **PFC**
private identification
  number **PIN**
private investigator **P.I.**
private line **P.L.**
privately **priv.**
privately bonded **P.B.**
privately printed **P.P.**
private secretary **P.S.**
private terms **p.t.**
privative **priv.**
privy council **P.C.**
privy councillor **P.C.**
privy seal **P.S.**
prize money **P.M.**
prize ring **P.R.**
pro **p**
probable **prob.**
probable error **PE**
probably **prob.**
probate **prob.**
probate judge **P.J.**
probation **prob.**
probation officer **P.O.**
problem **prob.**

problem oriented medical
  record **POMR**
procedures **proc.**
proceedings **proc.**
process **proc.**
proclamation **proc.**
proconsul **P**
proctor **proc.**
procurator fiscal **P.F.**
produce **prod.**
produced **prod.**
producer **prod.**
product **prod.**
production **prod.**
Production Credit
  Association **PCA**
production per man-hour
  PMH
profession **prof.**
professional **prof.**
professional association **PA**
Professional Bowlers
  Association **PBA**
Professional Corporation
  P.C.
professional engineer **P.E.**
Professional Golfers'
  Association **PGA**
professional standards review
  organization **PSRO**
Professional Women Bowlers
  Association **PWBA**
professor **Prof.**
profit and loss **P & L; P/L**
profit rate **PR**
profits/earnings **P/E**
pro forma **p.f.**
prognosis **Px**
program **pgm.; prog.**
program director **PD**
program evaluation and

review technique **PERT**
programmable logic array
  PLA
programmable logic
  controller **PLC**
programmable read only
  memory **PROM**
programmed instruction **PI**
programming language **PL**
progress **prog.**
progressive **pro.; prog.**
progressive multifocal
  leukoencephalopathy **PML**
project **proj.**
projector **proj.**
prologue **prol.**
promethium **Pm**
prominent **prom.**
promissory note **p.n.**
promontory **prom.**
promoted **prom.**
prompter **p**
prompt side **P.S.**
pronominal **pron.**
pronoun **pr.; pro.; pron.**
pronounced **pr.; pron.**
pronunciation **pr.; pron.**
proof **prf.**
proof spirit of wine **S.V.T.**
propeller **prop.**
proper **prop.**
properly **prop.**
property **prop.**
property damage **PD**
prop forward **PF**
proportion **propn.**
proportional **propl.**
proportional representation
  P.R.
proposed **prop.**
proposition **prop.**

proprietary **prop.; Pty.**
proprietor **prop.; propr.**
propyl **Pr**
prose **pr.**
prosecuting **pros.**
prosecutor **pros.**
prosody **pros.**
prostaglandin **PG**
prosthetic valve
  endocarditis **PVE**
protactinium **Pa**
protamine insulin **PI**
protamine zinc insulin **PZI**
protected **prot.**
protection **prot.**
protection and indemnity
  p. & i.
protectorate **prot.**
protein-bound iodine **PBI**
pro tempore **p.t.**
Protestant **Prot.**
Protestant Episcopal **PE**
prothonotary apostolic **P.A.**
proton **p**
proved **pr.**
proverb **prov.**
proverbial **prov.**
Proverbs **Prov.**
provided **prov.**
province **prov.**
Province of Quebec **P.Q.**
provincial **prov.**
proving ground **PG**
provision **prov.**
provisional **prov.**
provost **pro.; prov.**
provost marshal **P.M.**
provost marshal general
  PMG
Psalms **Ps.; Psa.**
pseudo **ps.**

pseudonym **ps.; pseud.**
pseudonymous **pseud.**
psychic **psych.**
psychical **psych.**
psychogalvanic response
  PGR
psychokinesis **PK**
psychological **psych.**
Psychological Stress
  Evaluator **PSE**
psychological warfare **PW**
psychologist **psych.;**
  psychol.
psychology **psych.; psychol.**
psychoneurotic **PN**
pteroylglutamic acid **PGA**
public **pub.; publ.**
public accountant **PA**
public address **PA**
public administration **PA**
public assistance **PA**
publication **pub.; publ.**
Public Broadcasting Service
  PBS
public domain **P.D.**
public gaol **P.G.**
public health **PH**
public health nurse **PHN**
Public Health Service **PHS**
Public Housing Agency
  PHA
public information office
  PIO
public information officer
  PIO
public interest research
  group **PIRG**
public law **PL**
Public Lending Right **P.L.R.**
public liability **PL**
public limited company **Plc.**

public records office **PRO**
public relations **PR**
public relations office **PRO**
public relations officer **PRO**
public sale **P/S**
public school **P.S.**
public service
  announcement **PSA**
public service commission
  P.S.C.
public stenographer **P.S.**
public television **PTV**
public utilities commission
  PUC
public utility district **PUD**
public works **PW**
Public Works
  Administration **PWA**
published **pub.; publ.**
publisher **pub.; publ.**
publishing **pub.; publ.**
Puerto Rican **P.R.**
Puerto Rico **P.R.**
pulley end **PE**
pulmonary capillary wedge
  pressure **PCWP**
pulse **P**
pulse-amplitude modulation
  PAM
pulse-code modulation **PCM**
pulse-duration modulation
  PDM
pulse position modulation
  PPM
pulse recurrence frequency
  PRF
pulse recurrence rate **PRR**
pulse repetition frequency
  PRF
pulse repetition rate **PRR**
pulses per second **pps**

pulse-time modulation **PTM**
pulverized **pulv.**
pulverizer **pulv.**
pumice **pm**
pump horsepower **p.h.p.**
puncheon **pun.**
punctuation **punc.**
punter **P**
pupil **P**
pupil teacher **p.t.**
purchase **pchs.; pur.**
purchase money **PM**
purchase order **PO**
purchaser **pur.**
purchasing **pur.**
purchasing agent **PA**
purification **pur.**
purl **p**
purple **viol.**
Purple Heart **PH**
pursuit **P; pur.**
push money **PM**
put and call **P & C**
put of more **P/M**
putout **po**
pyrexia of unknown
  origin **PUO**
pyrometric cone equivalent
  PCE
pyrotechnic **pyro.**
pyrotechnics **pyro.**

Q

quadrant **quad.**
quadrilateral **quad**
quadrillion **Q**
qualification **qual.**
qualified **qual.**
qualify **qual.**
qualitative **qual.**

quality **qlty.; qual.**
quality assurance **QA**
quality control **QC**
quality factor **Q**
quantitative **quant.**
quantity **q.; qt.; qty.**
quantity discount
  agreement **qda**
quantum chromodynamics
  QCD
quantum electrodynamics
  QED
quart **q.; qt.; qu.**
quarter **Q; qr.; qtr.;**
  qu.; quar.
quarterback **Q; QB**
quarterdeck **QD**
quartered **qtd.**
quarterfinals **QF**
quarterly **Q; qrly.; qrtly.;**
  qtly.; qtr.; qu.; quar.
quartermaster **Q; QM; Qmr.**
quartermaster corps
  QC; QMC
quartermaster general **QMG**
quartermaster sergeant
  QMS
quarters **qtrs.**
quarter section **QS**
quarter sessions **Q.S.**
quartile **Q**
quarto **Q; qto.**
quartz **qtz.; qz.**
quasi **q.; qu.**
quasi-stellar object **QSO**
quasi-stellar radio source
  quasar
Quebec **Que.**
queen **Q; qu.;**
Queen's Bench **Q.B.**
Queen's Counsel **Q.C.**

Queensland **Qld.**

query **q.; qu.; qy.**

question **q.; qn.; qu.; ques.**

question and answer
  Q-A; Q. and A.

questions **qq.**

quetzal **Q**

quick **q.**

quick-firing **Q.F.**

quiet **q.t.**

quiet takeoff and landing
  QTOL

quintal **q; ql**

quintuple **quint.**

quinuclidinyl benzilate
  QNB

quire **q.; qr.**

quotation **qn.; quot.**

R

rabbi **R.**

rabbinic **rabb.**

rabbinical supervision **RS**

racemic **r**

radar countermeasure **RCM**

radar intelligence **RADINT**

radarman **rdm.**

radar operator **RO**

radial **rad.**

radial keratotomy **RK**

radian **rad**

radiant **rad.**

radiant intensity **J**

radiation absorbed dose **rad**

radiator **rad.**

radical **rad.**

radical — used esp. of a
  univalent hydrocarbon
  radical **R**

radio **R; rad.; rdo.**

radioactinum **RdAc**

radioactive **RA**

radioallergosorbent test
  RAST

radiobeacon **RBn**

radio common carrier **RCC**

radio direction finder **RDF**

radio direction finding **RDF**

Radio Free Europe **RFE**

radio frequency **RF**

radio-frequency choke **RFC**

radio-frequency interference
  RFI

radioimmunoassay **RIA**

radiolocation **R/L**

radiological emergency
  medical team **REMT**

Radiological Technologist
  RT

radiological warfare **RW**

radio magnetic indicator
  RMI

radioman **RM**

radiopaque contrast
  material **ROM**

radiosonde observation **raob**

radio station **RS**

radio technician **RT**

radio telegraphy **R/T**

radiotelephone **R/T**

radiotelephone operator
  RTO

radiothorium **RdTh**

radium **Ra; rad.**

radium emanation **R.E.**

radius **R; rad.**

radix **rad.**

radon **Rn**

rail and canal **R. & C.**

rail and lake **R. & L.**

rail and ocean **R. & O.**

rail and water **R. & W.**
rail diesel car **RDC**
railhead **rhd.**
rail, lake, and rail **R.L. & R.**
railroad **r.; RR**
railroad transportation
    officer **RTO**
railway **r.; rly.; rwy.; Ry.**
Railway Express Agency
    REA
railway post office **RPO**
railway sorting office **R.S.O.**
railway suboffice **R.S.O.**
railway transportation
    officer **RTO**
rain **r.**
rallentando **rallo**
random **rdm.**
random access memory
    RAM
random lengths **r.l.**
random widths **r.w.**
range **R.; ra.; rng.**
range direction finding **RDF**
range finder **R.F.**
range-height indicator **RHI**
rank **R**
rank has its privileges
    RHIP
Rankine **R**
rapid **rap.**
rapid deployment force **RDF**
rapid eye movement **REM**
rapid fire **R.F.**
rapid-fire gun **R.F.G.**
rapid plasma reagin **RPR**
rappen **rp.**
rare **r.**
rare earth **RE**
rare earth element **REE**
rarity **r.; rty.**

rate of application **RA**
rate of energy loss **REL**
rate of exchange **RE**
ratio **r.**
rat unit **RU**
reactance **X**
reaction control system **RCS**
reaction injection molding
    RIM
reaction of degeneration **RD**
reactive kilovolt-ampere
    rkva
reactive volt-ampere **rva**
reading **rdg.**
reading test **R.T.**
read only **RO**
read-only memory **ROM**
read only storage **ROS**
ready-to-wear **rtw**
real **r**
real estate **RE**
real estate investment trust
    REIT
real-time analyzer **RTA**
Realtor **Rltr.**
ream **rm.**
reappointed **reaptd.**
rear **r.; rr**
rear admiral **RA;
    R.Adm.; RADM**
reasonable **reas.**
Reaumur **R**
rebounds **R; reb.**
rebounds per game **rpg**
receipt **rcpt.; rct.; rec.;
    recpt.; rect.; rept.**
receipt of goods **R.O.G.**
receive **rec.**
received **r.; rcd.; recd.**
Received Pronunciation **RP**
receiver **rcvr.; rec.; recr.**

receiving office **R.O.**
receptacle **rec.**
reception **rec.; recp.**
receptionist **recpst.**
recipe **R.; rec.; rp.**
recipient **recip.**
reciprocal **recip.**
reciprocal trade agreement
  RTA
reciprocate **recip.**
reciprocity **recip.**
recirculation **recirc.**
recitative **recit**
reclamation **rec.**
recommend **recm.**
recommended **rec.; recm.**
recommended daily
  allowance **RDA**
recommended dietary
  allowance **RDA**
reconnaissance **R; rcn.**
reconnaissance officer **RO**
record **rcd.; rec.**
recorded **rec.**
recorder **rec.**
recording **rec.**
recording secretary
  rec. sec.; R.S.
record of performance
  R.O.P.
record of production **R.O.P.**
recovery **rec.**
recovery room **RR**
recreation **rec.**
recreational therapy **RT**
recreational vehicle **RV**
recruit **rct.**
recruiting **rctg.**
recruiting center **RC**
recruiting officer **RO**
recruiting service **RS**

recruiting station **RS**
recrystallize **recryst.**
rectangle **rect.**
rectangular **rect.**
rectified **rect.**
rectified spirit of wine
  S.V.R.
rectifier **rect.**
recto **r.; ro.**
rector **r.; rect.**
rectory **rect.**
red **R.; rd.; rub.**
redactor **red.**
red blood cells **RBC**
red blood count **RBC**
Red Cross **RC**
reddish **r.**
red edges **r.e.**
red-green **RG**
red-green-blue **RGB**
reduce **rd.; red.**
reduced **rd.; red.**
reduced level **R.L.**
reducer **red.**
reducing **rdg.; red.**
reducing flame **R.F.**
reduction **rd.; red.**
reduction gear **RG**
reduction in force **RIF**
reduction of area **RA**
reentry vehicle **RV**
referee **ref.**
reference **re.; ref.**
references **reff.**
referred **ref.; refd.**
refer to acceptor **R/A**
refer to drawer **R.D.**
refilling point **R.P.**
refinery **ref.**
refining **ref.**
refining in transit **R.I.T.**

reflex **refl.**
reflexive **refl.**
reform **ref.**
reformation **ref.**
reformed **ref.; refd.**
reformed spelling **R.S.**
reformer **ref.**
refraction **R; refr.**
refractive index **R.I.**
refrain **ref.**
refrigerate **refr.**
refrigerating **refr.; refrig.**
refrigeration **ref.; refr.; refrig.**
refrigerator **r.; ref.**
refuel **rfl.**
refunding **ref.; rf; rf; rfg.**
regarding **re.**
regent **reg.; regt.**
regiment **reg.; regt.; rgt.**
regimental **regl.; regtl.**
regimental aid post **RAP**
regimental beachhead **RBH**
regimental combat team **RCT**
regimental court-martial **RCM**
regimental headquarters **RHQ**
regimental order **RO**
regimental sergeant major **R.S.M.**
regimental supply officer **RSO**
region **reg.**
regional director **R.D.**
register **reg.**
registered **r.; reg.; regd.**
Registered Cardiopulmonary Technologist **RCPT**
Registered Cardiovascular

Technologist **RCVT**
registered competitive market maker **RCMM**
Registered Diagnostic Medical Sonologist **RDMS**
Registered Dietitian **RD**
Registered Laboratory Technician **RLT**
Registered Medical Technologist **RMT**
Registered Nurse **RN**
Registered Occupational Therapist **ORT**
Registered Pharmacist **R.Ph.**
Registered Physical Therapist **RPT**
Registered Records Administrator **RRA**
Registered Records Librarian **RRL**
registered representative **RR**
Registered Respiratory Therapist **RRT**
registered trademark — often enclosed in a circle **R**
registered trade name **RTN**
Register of Merit **ROM**
register ton **RT**
registrar **reg.**
registration **reg.**
registry **reg.**
regius professor **R.P.**
regular **R; reg.**
regular army **RA**
regularly **reg.**
regular route carrier **RRC**
regulate **reg.**
regulating **R**
regulation **reg.**
regulator **reg.**

rehabilitation center **RC**
reichsmark **RM**
reichspfennig **rpf.**
reigned **r.**
reinforced concrete **R.C.**
reinsurance **R.I.**
rejoined **rejd.**
related **rel.**
relating **rel.**
relative **rel.**
relative bearing **RB**
relative biological
  effectiveness **RBE**
relative humidity **RH**
relatively **rel.**
relaxed pelvic floor **RPF**
relay **rel.**
release **rel.; rls.**
release clause **R.C.**
released **rel.**
released on own
  recognizance **R.O.R.**
released time **RT**
relics **rel.**
relief **rel.**
relief claim **R.C.**
relief pitcher **RP**
relieve **rel.**
relieved **rel.; reld.**
relieving **rel.**
religion **rel.; relig.**
religious **rel.**
remain **rem.**
remainder **rem.**
remark **rem.**
remit **rem.**
remittance **rem.**
remitted **rem.**
remote control **RC**
remotely operated vehicle
  ROV

remotely piloted vehicle
  RPV
remount **rmt.**
remove **rem.**
renal plasma flow **RPF**
renal tubular acidosis **RTA**
rendezvous **rdv.; R.V.**
repair **rep.; repr.**
repayable to either **R/E**
repeat **R; rep.; rpt.**
repeated **rptd.**
replace **repl.**
replacement **repl.**
replacement training center
  RTC
reply coupon **RC**
reply paid **RP**
reply paid postcard **RPP**
reply postcard **RPC**
report **rep.; rept.; rpt.**
reported **rep.; rpt.; rptd.**
reporter **rep.**
reporting **rpt.**
report of survey **R/S**
Report Program Generator
  RPG
represent **repr.**
representative **rep.; repr.**
representative fraction **RF**
represented **repr.**
representing **repr.**
reprint **repr.; RP**
reprinted **repr.; RP; rptd.**
reprinting **RP**
republic **R.; rep.; RP**
Republican **R.; Rep.**
Republican National
  Committee **RNC**
Republic of China **R.O.C.**
Republic of Korea **R.O.K.**
repulsion induction **RI**

request **req.**
request for proposal **RFP**
require **req.**
required **req.; reqd.**
requirement **reqmt.**
requisition **req.; rqn.**
rerun **r.; R**
resawed **res.**
research **res.**
research and development
   R & D
research safety vehicle **RSV**
reservation **res.**
reserve **res.**
reserve force **RF**
reserve officer candidate
   ROC
Reserve Officers' Training
   Corps **ROTC**
reserves **R**
reserve training corps **RTC**
reservoir **res.**
reside **r.**
residence **r.; res.**
residency **res.**
resident **r.; res.**
residential **res.**
resident magistrate **R.M.**
residue **res.**
resigned **res.**
resistance **R; res.**
resistance-capacitance **RC**
resistance transfer factor
   RTF
resistor **R; res.**
resolution **res.**
resorcylic acid lactone **RAL**
resort **res.**
resource interface module
   RIM
respective **resp.**

respectively **resp.**
respiration **R; resp.**
Respiration Therapist **RT**
respiratory **resp.**
respiratory distress
   syndrome **RDS**
respiratory quotient **R.Q.**
respiratory syncytial virus
   RSV
respiratory therapist **RT**
respiratory therapy **RT**
respond **R.**
respondent **R; resp.**
response **R.**
responsible **resp.**
rest and recreation **R & R**
rest and recuperation **R & R**
rest and rehabilitation
   R & R
restaurant **restr.**
restored **rest.**
restricted **R**
retain **ret.**
retained **retd.**
retainer **ret.; retnr.**
retaining **ret.**
retard **ret.**
reticuloendothelial **r.e.**
retired **r.; ret.; retd.; rtd.**
Retired Senior Volunteer
   Program **RSVP**
retirement income
   endowment **r.i.e.**
retracting **retrg.**
retree **R**
retrogression **retrog.**
retrogressive **retrog.**
retrolental fibroplasia **RLF**
return **ret.**
returned **ret.; retd.; rtd.**
returned letter office **R.L.O.**

returning **r**
return of post **R/P**
return on assets **ROA**
return on equity **ROE**
return on investment **ROI**
return premium **R.P.**
return ticket **RT**
Revelation **Rev.**
revenue **rev.**
reverberation-controlled
  gain **rcg**
reverend **Rev.; Revd.**
reverend father **R.P.**
reverse **rev.**
reverse annuity mortgage
  RAM
reversed **rev.**
reverse osmosis **RO**
reverse Polish notation **RPN**
reverse work **rw**
review **rev.**
reviewed **rev.**
revise **rev.**
revised **rev.**
Revised Standard Version
  RSV
revised statutes **Rev. St.;
  Rev. Stat.; R.S.**
Revised Version **R.V.**
revision **rev.**
revolution **rev.; revol.**
revolutions per minute **rpm**
revolutions per second **rps**
revolving **rev.**
Reynolds number **R; RN**
rhapsody **rhap.**
rhenium **Re**
rheostat **rheo.**
rhesus **Rh**
rhetoric **rhet.**
rheumatic fever **RF**

Rhode Island **RI; R.I.**
rhodium **Rh**
rhumb line **RL**
rhythm and blues **R & B**
ribonuclease **RNAase;
  RNase**
ribonucleic acid **RNA**
ribosomal RNA **rRNA**
ridge **rdg.**
ridgeling **rig.**
rifle **R**
rifle brigade **R.B.**
rifleman **rfn.**
right **r.; rt.**
right ascension **R.A.**
right back **RB**
right center **RC**
right cornerback **RCB**
right defense **RD**
right edge **R**
right end **RE**
Right Excellent **R.E.**
right eye **O.D.; RE**
right field **RF**
right foot **RF**
right forward **RF**
right front **RF**
right fullback **RB; RF; RFB**
right guard **RG**
right halfback **RH; RHB**
right hand **D.M.; MD; RH**
right-hand side **rhs**
Right Honorable **Rt. Hon.**
right line **RL**
right linebacker **RLB**
right lower quadrant **RLQ**
right of way **ROW; RW**
right rear **RR**
Right Reverend **R.R.;
  Rt. Rev.**
right safety **RS**

right side **r.s.**
right side up with care
  R.S.W.C.
right tackle **RT**
right upper extremity **RUE**
right upper quadrant **RUQ**
right wing **RW**
Right Worshipful **R.W.**
Right Worthy **R.W.**
rinforzando **rf; rfz**
ring **r**
ringer **rgr.**
riot and civil commotion
  r. & c.c.
ripieno **rip**
ripped **rip.**
riser **R.**
rises **r.**
ritardando **rit**
ritenuto **riten**
river **R.; riv.**
rix-dollar **rd.**
road **r.; rd.; ro.**
road junction **R.J.**
roan **ro.**
rock **rk.**
rock and roll **R and R**
rocket **rkt.**
rocket-assisted takeoff
  RATO
rocket launcher **RL**
Rockwell hardness **RH**
rocky **rky.**
rod **r.; rd**
Rodeo Cowboys Association
  RCA
roentgen **r**
roentgen equivalent
  physical **rep**
roentgen per hour at one
  meter **rhm**

roentgens per hour **r/hr**
rolled gold **R.G.**
Roman **R.; Rom.**
roman **rom.**
Roman Catholic **RC**
Romance **Rom.**
romance **rom.**
Romania **Rom.**
Romanian **Rom.**
Roman people **P.R.**
Romans **Rom.**
rood **r.; rd.; ro.**
roof **rf.**
roofer **rfr.**
roofing **rfg.**
rook **R**
room **rm.**
room temperature **RT**
root-mean-square **rms**
Roscommon **Ros.; Rosc.**
rotary **rot.**
rotary combustion **RC**
rotating **rot.**
rotation **rot.; rotn.**
rotor **R.**
rotten **rot.**
rough — used in
  bacteriology **R**
rough finish **rf**
roulette **roul.**
round **rd.; rnd.**
roundhouse **RH**
round trip **RT**
Rous sarcoma virus **RSV**
route **R.; rt.; rte.**
royal **R.**
Royal Academician **R.A.**
Royal Academy **R.A.**
Royal Academy of Dramatic
  Art **RADA**
Royal Air Force **RAF**

Royal Australian Air Force **RAAF**
Royal Automobile Club **RAC**
Royal Caledonia Curling Club **RCCC**
Royal Canadian Air Force **RCAF**
Royal Canadian Mounted Police **RCMP**
Royal Canadian Navy **RCN**
Royal Curling Club of Canada **RCCC**
royal dockyard **RDY**
Royal Highness **R.H.**
royal mail **R.M.**
Royal Mail Service **R.M.S.**
Royal Mail ship **R.M.S.**
Royal Mail steamer **R.M.S**
Royal Mail steamship **R.M.S**
Royal Military Academy **RMA**
Royal Military College **RMC**
Royal Navy **RN**
Royal New Zealand Air Force **RNZAF**
royal observatory **RO**
royal octavo **RO**
Royal Society **RS**
rubbed **rub.**
rubber **r.; rub.**
rubidium **Rb**
ruble **r.; rb.; rbl.; ro.**
rub together **conter.**
rudder **rud.**
rule **r.**
ruling case law **RCL**
Rumania **Rum.**
Rumanian **Rum.**
run **R**
runic **R.**

running back **RB**
running days **r.d.**
running-down clause **R.D.C.**
running title **RT**
run of kiln **R.K.**
run of mine **r.o.m.**
run-of-paper **ROP**
run-of-press **ROP**
runs **R**
runs batted in **RBI**
runway **rnwy.**
rupee **R; re.**
rupees **Rs.**
rupees, annas, pies **RAP**
rupiah **Rp.**
rupture **rupt.**
ruptured **rptd.**
rural dean **R.D.**
rural delivery **RD**
rural district **R.D.**
rural district council **R.D.C.**
rural electrification **RE**
Rural Electrification Administration **REA**
rural free delivery **RFD**
rural route **RR**
Russia **Russ.**
Russian **Russ.**
Russian Soviet Federated Socialist Republic **R.S.F.S.R.**
rust preventive **RP**
ruthenium **Ru**
rutherford **rd**
Rydberg **ry**
Rydberg constant **R**

S

sabbath **S.; Sab.**
Sabbath school **S.S.**
sable **sa.**
sack **sk.**
sacks **sx.**
sacral **S**
sacred **S.**
Sacred Scripture **S.S.**
sacrifice **S; sac.**
sacrifice fly **SF**
sacrifice hit **SH**
saddle **sdl.**
sadism and masochism
  S & M
sadist and masochist **S & M**
sadomasochism **S-M**
sadomasochist **S-M**
safety **S; saf.**
safety analysis report **SAR**
safety valve **SV**
safe working pressure **SWP**
Saharan Arab Democratic
  Republic **SADR**
said **sd.**
sailed **sld.**
sailing **slg.**
sailing vessel **s.v.**
saint **S.; St.; Sta.**
saint (female) **Ste.**
Saints **SS.**
salad **sal.**
salary **sal.**
sales book **S.B.**
salesman **slsmn.**
sales manager **slsmgr.**
salt added **SA**
Salt Lake City **S.L.C.**
salt water **SW**
salvage **salv.**

salvage charges **S.C.**
salvage loss **s.l.**
Salvation Army **SA**
samarium **Sa; Sm**
same case **SC**
same day **s.d.**
same size **s.s.**
Samuel **Sam.; Saml.**
sand **S; sd.**
Sandwich Islands **S.I.**
San Francisco **S.F.**
sanitary **san.; sanit.; sn.**
sanitary corps **SC**
sanitary engineer **S.E.**
sanitary engineering **S.E.**
sanitation **san.; sanit.; sn.**
Sanskrit **Skt.**
sap no defect **s.n.d.**
saponification **sapon.**
sapwood **sap.**
sash **sh.**
sash door **S.D.**
Saskatchewan **Sask.; SK**
satang **s.**
satellite **sat.**
satellite communications
  satcom
satellite master antenna TV
  SMATV
satellite positioning and
  tracking **SPOT**
saturable reactor **SR**
saturate **sat.**
saturated **sat.; satd.**
saturated solution **sat. sol.**
saturating **satg.**
saturation **sat.; satn.**
saturation deficit **s.d.**
Saturday **S; Sa.; Sat.**
saves **sv**
savings **sav.; savs.; svgs.**

savings and loan association
S & L
savings bank **S.B.**
scalar **S**
scale **sc.; scl.**
Scandinavia **Scand.**
Scandinavian **Scand.**
scandium **Sc**
scanning electron
microscope **SEM**
scanning electron
microscopy **SEM**
scanning transmission
electron microscope **STEM**
scanning transmission
electron microscopy **STEM**
scapula **Sc.**
scattered **sctd.**
scene **sc.**
schedule **scd.; sch.; sched.**
schilling **sch.**
scholar **sch.**
Scholastic Aptitude Test
SAT
school **s.; sch.; schl.**
School and College Ability
Test **SCAT**
school certificate **S.C.**
schoolhouse **sch.; S.H.**
schooner **sch.; schr.**
science **S; sc.; sci.**
science advisory board **SAB**
science and technology
S & T
science fiction **sf**
scientific **sc.; sci.**
Scotland **Scot.**
Scots **Sc.**
Scottish **Scot.**
scout **sct.**
screen **sc; scr.; scrn.**

Screen Actors Guild **SAG**
screen grid **SG**
screw **sc.; scr.**
screwed **scd.; scr.**
screw steamer **SS**
scribe **s.**
scrip **scp.; scr.**
script **scp.; scr.**
scriptural **scrip.; script.**
scripture **scrip.; script.**
scrum half **SH**
scruple **s; sc.; scr.**
sculptor **sculp.**
sculptural **sculp.**
sculpture **sculp.**
sea-damaged **S/D**
seal **sigill.**
sealed **sld.**
sealed with a kiss **SWAK**
sealed with a loving kiss
SWALK
sea level **SL**
seaman **S; sea.**
seaman apprentice **SA**
seaman recuit **SR**
seamless **smls.**
seamstress **smstrs.**
seaport **spt.**
sea post office **SPO**
search **S; srch.**
search and rescue **SAR**
Search for Extraterrestrial
Intelligence **SETI**
searchlight **SL; slt.**
seasonally adjusted **SA**
seasoned **sd.**
seat **s.**
seated **std.**
seater **str.**
sea transport officer **STO**
seawater **SW**

secant **sec**
second **s.; sec.**
secondary **s; sec.**
secondary ion mass
   spectrometry **SIMS**
Secondary School Admissions
   Test **SSAT**
second attack **SA**
second base **2b**
second defense **SD**
second entrance **s.e.**
second, Saybolt universal
   SSU
secretarial **sec'l**
secretariat **sec.**
secretary **s.; sec.;
   secty.; secy.**
secretary-general **S.G.**
Secretary of State **SS**
Secret Intelligence Service
   SIS
secret service **S.D.; SS**
section **s.; sec.; sect.; sxn.**
sectional **sect.**
sections **ss.**
sector **sctr.; sec.**
secured **sec.**
Securities and Exchange
   Commission **SEC**
security **sec.**
security council **SC**
sedan **sed.**
sediment **sed.**
sedimentation **sed.**
sedimentation rate **S.R.**
seditious libeler **S.L.**
see **s.; vid.**
see above **v.s.**
see below **v.i.**
see copy **SC**
seed **sd.**

seedling **sdl.**
seer **sr.**
see this **h.q.**
segment **seg.**
select **sel.**
select cases **SC**
selected **sel.**
selection **sel.**
selective service **SS**
Selective Service System
   SSS
selector **sel.**
selenium **Se**
self-addressed envelope **SAE**
self-addressed stamped
   envelope **SASE**
self-closing **S.C.**
self-contained **s.c.; SC**
self-contained underwater
   breathing apparatus
   scuba
self-inflicted wound **SIW**
self-propelled **SP**
self-propelled mount **SPM**
Self-Realization Fellowship
   SRF
self-rectifying **sr**
seller's option **SO**
seller's option to double **SOD**
semantic reaction **s.r.**
semble **sem.**
semen **sem.**
semester hour **SH**
semi- **s.**
semiannual **SA**
semi-armor-piercing **SAP**
semiautomatic **SA**
semiautomatic ground
   environment **SAGE**
semiautomatic rifle **SAR**
semicolon **sem.**

semidiameter **SD**
semifinals **S.F.**
semifinished **SF**
semimobile **sem.**
seminal **sem.**
seminal vesicle **sem. ves.**
seminar **sem.**
seminary **sem.**
semipostal **SP**
semisteel **SS**
Semitic **Sem.**
Semper Paratus **SPAR**
senate **S.; sen.**
senate bill **SB**
Senate Office Building **S.O.B.**
senate resolution **SR**
senator **sen.**
send **mit.**
sender **sdr.**
senile dementia of the Alzheimer's type **SDAT**
senior **sen.; snr.; Sr.**
senior chief petty officer **CPOS; SCPO**
senior common room **SCR**
senior deacon **S.D.**
Senior Executive Service **SES**
senior fellow **S.F.**
senior grade **SG**
senior magistrate **S.M.**
senior master sergeant **S.M.Sgt.**
senior medical officer **SMO**
senior naval officer **SNO**
senior navigation officer **SNO**
senior officer **SO**
senior officer present **SOP**
senior warden **S.W.**

señor **Sr.**
señora **Sra.**
señorita **Srita.; Srta.**
sensation unit **S.U.**
sensibility reciprocal **SR**
sensitivity-time control **STC**
sentence **S; sent.**
sentenced **sentd.**
sent wrong **s.w.**
sepal **sep.**
separate **div.; sep.**
separated **sep.; sepd.**
separately binned **S.B.**
separating **sepg.**
separation **sep.; sepn.**
separative work unit **SWU**
September **S.; Sep.; Sept.**
Septuagint **LXX**
sequel **seq.**
sequence **seq.; sq.**
Serbian **Serb.**
sergeant **Serg.; Sergt.; SG; Sgt.**
sergeant-at-law **S.L.**
sergeant first class **SFC**
sergeant major **Sgt.Maj.; SM; S.Maj.**
sergeant major of the army **SMA**
serial **ser.**
serial number **SN**
series **s.; ser.**
serine **Ser**
serjeant **Serj.; Serjt.; Sjt.**
sermon **ser.**
serologic test for syphillis **STS**
serous otitis media **SOM**
serum glutamic-oxaloacetic transminase **SGOT**
serum glutamic pyruvic

transminase **SGPT**
serum hepatitis **SH**
serum prothrombin conversion accelerator **SPCA**
serum Wassermann reaction **SWR**
servant **serv.; servt.**
serve **ser.**
service **ser.; serv.; svc.; svce.**
service ceiling **SC**
Service Corps of Retired Executives **SCORE**
service dress **SD**
service mark **sm**
service propulsion system **SPS**
service record **S/R**
services **serv.**
services no longer required **SNLR**
services of supply **SOS**
service unit **SU**
serving **ser.**
session **sess.**
session laws **SL**
set **s.**
set screw **SS**
set up **S.U.**
set up in carloads **S.U.C.L.**
set up in less than carloads **S.U.L.C.L.**
several **sev.; sevl.**
several dates **s.d.**
severe combined immune deficiency **SCID**
sewage treatment plant **STP**
sewed **sd.; swd.**
sewing **sewg.**
sexagesimo-quarto **Sf**
sex appeal **SA**

sex offender **SO**
sexually transmitted disease **STD**
sforzando **sf; sfz**
shaft **sft.**
shaft horsepower **shp**
shake before using **agit. a. us.**
Shakespeare **Shak.**
shake well **agit. bene**
shall **sh.**
shallow **shlw.**
shape memory alloy **SMA**
share **sh.; shr.**
shared appreciation mortgage **SAM**
shared equity mortgage **SEM**
sharp **S**
sheathing **shthg.**
sheep **sh.**
sheet **sh.; sht.**
shell **Sh; shl.**
shell-destroying tracer **SDT**
shelter **shltr.**
shelter warden **S.W.**
shergottites, nakhlites, chassignites **SNC**
Shetland **Shet.**
shield **shld.**
shilling **s.; sh.**
ship **s.**
shipfitter **SF**
shiplap **shlp.**
shipment **ship.; shipt.; shpmt.; shpt.**
shipowner's liability **SOL**
shipper and carrier **S. & C.**
shipper's load and count **S.L. & C.**
shipper's load and

tally **S.L. & T.**
shipper's weight **S.W.**
shipping **sh.; shg.; ship.; shpg.**
shipping and forwarding agent **S. & F.A.**
shipping board **S.B.**
shipping/handling **s/h**
shipping note **S/N**
shipping order **SO**
shipping receipt **S.R.**
shipping ticket **S.T.**
ship's cook **SC**
ship's heading **SH**
shipside **S.S.**
ship's option **SO**
shipwright **sh.**
shit out of luck **SOL**
shoal **shl.**
shock **sh.**
shop **sh.**
shop order **SO**
shore patrol **SP**
shore patrolman **SP**
shore police **SP**
short **sh.**
shortage **shtg.**
short bill **S.B.**
short delay **SD**
short delivery **sd**
shorthair **SH**
shorthanded goals **SHG**
short interest **s.i.**
short meter **S.M.**
shortness of breath **SOB**
short page **SP**
short particular meter **S.P.M.**
short-range attack missile **SRAM**
short rate **s.r.**

shortstop **SS**
short takeoff and landing **STOL**
short takeoff and vertical landing **STOVL**
short-term memory **STM**
Short-Title Catalogue **STC**
short ton **s.t.**
shortwave **s-w**
short wheelbase **SWB**
should **shd.**
should be **s/b**
shoulder **sh.; shld.**
show **sh.**
shower **sh.; shwr.**
shunt **sh.**
shut-off valve **SOV**
shutouts **SHO; SO**
sibling **sib.**
Sicily **Sic.**
sick **sk.**
side **s.**
side-looking airborne radar **SLAR**
side note **s.-n.**
sidereal hour angle **SHA**
side seam **S.S.**
sideward **swd**
siding **sdg.**
siemens **S**
Siemens's unit **S.U.**
sight draft **S/D**
sight draft, bill of lading attached **S.D.-B.L.**
sigma reaction **S.R.**
sign **s.**
signal **sig.**
signal boatswain **SB**
signal corps **SC**
signaler **sig.**
signal-frequency **SF**

signal intelligence **SIGINT**
signalman **sig.; SM**
signal to noise **S/N**
signal to noise ratio **SNR**
signature **s.; sig.**
signatures **sgg.; sigg.**
signed **s.; sd.; sg.; sgd.**
signifying **sig.**
Signing Essential English **SEE**
signor **S.; Sig.**
silence **sil.**
silent **si.**
silicate **S**
silicon **Si**
silicon-on-sapphire **SOS**
silicon photodiode **SPD**
silver **Ag; s.; sil.**
silver medal **SM**
silversmith **S.**
similar **sim.**
simile **sim.**
simple harmonic motion **S.H.M.**
simplex **s.; sx**
simplified employee pension **SEP**
simplified spelling **S.S.**
simultaneous broadcast **S.B.**
sine **s; sin**
single **1b; s.; S; sgl.; sing.**
single case **s.c.**
single-cell protein **SCP**
single column **S.C.**
single comb **SC**
single crochet **sc**
single deck **S.D.**
single entry **s.e.**
single lens reflex **SLR**
single line **S.L.**
single phase **S.P.**

single pole **S.P.**
single pole, double throw **S.P.D.T.**
single pole, single throw **S.P.S.T.**
single room occupancy **SRO**
single sideband **SS; SSB**
single throw **S.T.**
single-trip container **STC**
singular **s.; sg.; sing.**
sink **S.; sk.**
sinking **sk.**
sinking fund **S.F.**
sinoatrial **S-A**
sir **Sr.**
sire **S.**
sister **sist.; Sr.; Sr.**
Sisters of Charity **S.C.**
situation **sit.**
situation normal, all fouled up **snafu**
situation normal, all fucked up **snafu**
size **sz.**
sized and calendered **S. & C.**
sized and supercalendered **S. & S.C.**
Skate Sailing Association of America **SSAA**
sketch **sk.**
skewness **Sk**
skilled nursing facility **SNF**
skilled nursing home **SNH**
skin erythema dose **S.E.D.**
skip **sk**
slate **sl.**
Slavic **Slav.**
sleet **slt.**
sleeve **slv.**
slide **sl.**
sliding watertight door **SWD**

slightly **sl.**
Sligo **Slo.**
slip **s; sl.**
sloppy **sly; sy.**
slop sink **S.S.**
slow **S; sl.**
slow-moving vehicle **SMV**
slow reacting substance **SRS**
slow — used of a clock **R**
slugging average **SA**
sluice valve **S.V.**
small **s; S; sm.; sml.**
small arms **SA**
small arms ammunition **SAA**
small bonds **S.B.**
Small Business Administration **SBA**
small business investment company **SBIC**
small calorie **cal.**
small capitals **s.c.; sm. cap.**
smaller profit margin **SPM**
small packet **S.P.**
small paper **S.P.**
small pica **S.P.**
small profits, quick returns **S.P.Q.R.**
small ring **sr**
small-scale integration **SSI**
Smithsonian Institution **SI**
Smithsonian Institution Traveling Exhibition Service **SITES**
smoked **smkd.**
smokeless **smkls.**
smokeless powder **SP**
smooth **S**
snooze **ZZZZ**
snow **s; snw.**
soapsuds **s.s.**

social **soc.**
Social Democratic Party **SDP**
Social Democratic Party of Germany **SPD**
social history **SH**
socialist **s.; soc.**
socialist-revolutionary **S.R.**
Socialist Workers Party **SWP**
social science **SS**
Social Security **SS**
Social Security account number **SSAN**
Social Security Administration **SSA**
Social Security number **SSN**
social service **SS**
social work **SW**
society **s.; soc.; socy.**
Society for the Prevention of Cruelty to Animals **S.P.C.A.**
Society for the Prevention of Cruelty to Children **S.P.C.C.**
Society of Automotive Engineers **SAE**
Society of Jesus **S.J.**
Society of Mary **S.M.**
Society of Worldwide Interbank Financial Telecommunication **S.W.I.F.T.**
socioeconomic status **SES**
sociologist **sociol.**
sociology **soc.; sociol.**
socket **soc.**
sodium **Na; sod.**
sodium aluminum sulfate **SAS**

sodium dodecyl sulphate **SDS**

sodium tripolyphosphate **STPP**

soft **dol; S; sf; sft.**

soft capsule **cap. moll.**

soft drawn **S.D.**

softwood **sftwd.**

Soil Conservation Service **SCS**

soil pipe **S.P.**

sol **S**

solar neutrino unit **SNU**

solar power satellite **SPS**

sold **sld.**

solder **sld.**

soldier **sol.**

soldier's medal **SM**

solenoid **sol.**

solicitor **sol.; solr.**

solicitor-at-law **S.L.**

solicitor before the supreme court **S.S.C.**

solicitor general **SG**

solid **s**

solid drawn **s.d.**

solids not fat **S.N.F.**

solidus **s.**

solo **s.**

Solomon **Sol.**

solubility **s.; soly.**

soluble **sol.**

soluble nucleoprotein **SNP**

solution **sol.; soln.**

solvent **slv.**

somatotrophic hormone **SH**

somatotropic hormone **STH**

Somersetshire **Som.**

son **f.; s.**

sonata **son.**

song and dance **S and D**

son of a bitch **S.O.B.**

Sonora **Son.**

Sons of the American Revolution **SAR**

soon as possible **SAP**

sophomore **soph.**

soprano **s; sop.**

soprano, alto, baritone **S.A.B.**

soprano, alto, tenor, bass **S.A.T.B.**

sostenuto **sos**

sou **s.**

souls on board **S.O.B.**

sound **sd.; snd.**

sound fixing and ranging **SOFAR**

sounding tube **ST**

sound locator **S-L**

sound on film **SOF**

sound ranging **SR**

sounds **sds.**

Sound Surveillance System **SOSUS**

south **s.; S; so.; sou.; sth.**

South Africa **S.A.; S. Af.; S. Afr.; So. Afr.**

South African **S.A.; So. Afr.**

South African Republic **S.A.R.**

South America **S.A.; S. Am.; S. Amer.**

South American **S.A.**

South Australia **S.A.; S. Aust.**

South Australian **S.A.**

southbound **S.B.; sobnd.**

South Carolina **SC; S.C.**

South Dakota **SD; S.D.; S. Dak.**

southeast **SE**

Southeast Asia **SEA**
Southeast Asia Treaty
  Organization **SEATO**
southeastern **SE**
Southeastern Conference
  SEC
southerly **s.**
southern **s.; S.; so.;**
  son.; sou.; sthn.
Southern Christian
  Leadership Conference
  SCLC
Southern Hemisphere **SH**
Southern Hockey League
  SHL
south latitude **S.L.**
south-southeast **SSE**
south-southwest **SSW**
southwest **SW**
South-West Africa **S.W.A.;**
  S. W. Af.
South-West African People's
  Organization **SWAPO**
Southwest Conference **SWC**
southwestern **SW**
sovereign **sov.**
soviet **sov.**
Soviet Army Intelligence
  G.R.U.
Soviet Socialist Republic
  SSR
Soviet State Security
  Committee **KGB**
Soviet Union **S.U.**
space **sp.**
spacecraft **SC**
Space Detection and Tracking
  System **SPADATS**
space telescope **ST**
space transportation system
  STS

Spain **Sp.**
Spanish **Sp.; Span.**
spare **sp.**
speaker **spkr.**
special **S; sp.; spec.; spl.**
special air mission **SAM**
special care unit **SCU**
special circular **SC**
special constable **SC**
special delivery **SD**
special drawing rights **SDR**
special duty **SD**
special effects **SPFX**
Special Intelligence Service
  SIS
special interest group **SIG**
specialist **sp.; SP; spec.**
Specialist in Education
  Ed.S.
specialized common carrier
  SCC
Special Libraries
  Association **SLA**
specially denatured **SD**
special order **s.o.**
special public assistance
  SPA
special regulation **SR**
special session **S.S.**
special treatment steel **STS**
specialty **splty.**
Special Weapons and
  Tactics **SWAT**
species **s.; sp.; spec.; spp.**
specific **sp.; spec.; specif.**
specifically **spec.; specif.**
specification **spec.; specif.**
specific dynamic action **SDA**
specific gravity **sg; sp gr**
specific heat **sp. ht.**
specific inductive

capacity s.i.c.
specific soluble substance
   S.S.S.
specific weight s.w.
specified hours S.H.
specimen sp.; spec.; spn.
speck sp.
speckled spk.
spectacle spec.
spectacular spec.
spectrum spec.
speculation spec.
speech sp.
speech to noise ratio S/N
speed S; sp.; spd.
speed of relative movement
   SRM
spell sp.
spelled sp.
spelling sp.
sphere S; sph.
spherical s.; sph.
spherical candlepower scp
spina bifida SB
spinal sp.
spindle spdl.
spine sp.
spiral spir.
spirit sp.; spt.
spirit of wine s.v.
splash block SB
split end SE
sponge sp.; spg.
spontaneous spon.
spontaneous ignition
   temperature S.I.T.
spoon sp.
spoonful cochl.
sport sp.
Sports Car Club of
   America SCCA

sports information director
   SID
spot-faced SF
sprayed spd.
spreading coefficient S.C.
spring spg.; spr.
spring conditions sc
spring water aq. font.
sprinkle consperg.; spkl.
sprinkler spkr.
spurs s
squad sqd.
squad automatic weapon
   SAW
squadron sq.; sqdn.; sqn.;
   squad.
squadron gunnery officer
   SGO
squadron leader S.L.
squadron medical officer
   SMO
squadron sergeant major
   SSM
square sq.; sqr.
square foot SF
square yard SY
squire Sq.
staccato stac; stacc
staff s.; stf.
staff college SC
staff corps SC
staff officer SO
Staffordshire Staffs.
staff quartermaster
   sergeant SQMS
staff sergeant SSG; S.Sgt.
staff sergeant major SSM
staff surgeon S.S.
stage direction SD
stage manager S.M.
staging stg.

stain **st.**
stained **stnd.**
stainless **stn.**
stainless steel **s.s.**
stairway **stwy.**
stakes race **stk**
stall **stl.**
stamp **stp.**
stamped **st.; stp.**
stamped addressed envelope **SAE**
stanchion **stan.**
stand **st.**
standard **s.; stan.; std.**
standard average European **SAE**
standard bead **SB**
standard beam approach **SBA**
Standard Book Number **SBN**
standard calomel electrode **S.C.E.**
standard cubic feet **scf**
standard deviation **SD**
standard deviation of a sample **S**
Standard English **SE**
standard error **SE**
standard industrial classification **SIC**
standard inspection procedure **SIP**
standardized test **ST**
standard matched **SM**
standard metropolitan statistical area **SMSA**
standard operating procedure **SOP**
standard play **SP**
Standard & Poor's **S & P**
Standard Reference

Materials **SRM**
standard temperature and pressure **STP**
standard time **ST**
standard wire gauge **S.W.G.**
standing **stg.**
standing operating procedure **SOP**
standing order **S.O.**
standing room only **SRO**
standing wave ratio **SWR**
standpipe **SP**
Stanford-Binet intelligence test **SB**
stanza **st.**
staphylococcus **staph.**
starboard **stbd.**
starch equivalent **S.E.**
star route **SR**
start **st.**
starting line **st.**
starting point **S.P.**
starting price **S.P.**
state **st.**
State Certified Midwife **S.C.M.**
statement of billing **S/B**
statement of charges **S/C**
state militia **S.M.**
Staten Island (N.Y.) **S.I.**
state registered nurse **S.R.N.**
stateroom **SR**
statesman **stsm.**
state teachers college **S.T.C.**
static **stat.**
static no delivery **S.N.D.**
static pressure **SP**
static thrust **S.T.**
station **s.; sta.; stn.**
stationary **sta.; stat.; staty.**
stationer **sta.**

station headquarters **SHQ**
station master **S.M.**
station wagon **SW**
statistic **stat.**
statistical **stat.; statis.**
statistician **stat.**
stator **sta.**
statuary **stat.**
statue **stat.**
statute **s.; st.; sta.; stat.**
statute law **SL**
statutory rules and orders
     S.R. & O.
steam **st.**
steamboat **S.B.**
steamer **s.; str.**
steamer pays dues **s.p.d.**
steam fitter **stmfr.**
steamship **SS**
steam trawler **s.t.**
steam yacht **S.Y.**
steel **s.; st.; stl.**
steel casting **S.C.**
steel sash **S.S.**
steeplechase **s'chase**
stem **s.; st.**
stencil **sten.**
stenographer **sten.**
stenography **sten.**
step in place **SIP**
stepping **stp.**
steradian **sr**
stere **s; st**
sterile solution **SS**
sterilization **ster.**
sterilizer **ster.**
sterling **ster.; stg.; stlg.**
stern post **S.P.**
stet **st.**
stevedore **stev.; steve.**
steward **std.; stwd.**

sticky **stk.; sy.**
stiff **stf.**
stilb **sb**
stile **stl.**
stimulus **S; st.**
stimulus-organism-response
     S-O-R
stimulus-response **S-R**
stipendiary magistrate **S.M.**
stirrup **stir.**
stirrup pump **S.P.**
stitch **st**
stock **s.; st.; stk.**
stock appreciation rights
     SAR
stock exchange **SE**
stock length **SL**
stock width **SW**
stoker **sto.**
stolen base **S; SB**
stone **st.**
stop **stp.**
stop payment **S.P.**
stopping **stp.**
stopping in transit **S.I.T.**
stop valve **S.V.**
storage **stg.; stge.; stor.**
storage in transit **S.I.T.**
storage room **S.R.**
store door delivery **S.D.D.**
storekeeper **SK**
storm **stm.**
stormtroopers **S.A.**
story **sto.**
stotinka **st.**
stowage **stow.**
strabismus **Sb**
straight **s.; st.; str.**
straight duty **SD**
straight-line capacitance **slc**
straight-line wavelength **slw**

strainer **str.**
strait **st.; str.**
strake **stk.**
strand **strd.**
strapped, corded, and sealed
  S.C. & S.
Strategic Air Command
  SAC
strategic air force **SAF**
Strategic Arms Limitation
  Talks **SALT**
Strategic Arms Reduction
  Talks **START**
strategic business unit **SBU**
strategic integrated
  operational plan **SIOP**
stratocumulus **Sc**
stratosphere **strsph.**
stratus **St**
stream **str.**
streamline **S/L**
street **st.**
strength **str.**
streptococcus **strep.**
streptomycin **SM**
stretch **str.**
stretcher bearer **S.B.**
stretcher party **S.P.**
strikeout **K**
strikeouts **SO**
strikes, riots, and civil
  commotions **SR & CC**
striking **str.**
string **str.**
stringed **str.**
stringendo **string**
stringer **stgr.**
stroke **str.**
strokes per minute **spm**
strong safety **SS**
strong soap solution **SSS**

strontium **Sr**
strophe **st.; str.**
structural **str.**
structure **struc.; struct.**
student **stud.**
Student Nonviolent
  Coordinating Committee
  SNCC
student of the civil law **SCL**
Students for a Democratic
  Society **SDS**
studio transmitter link **STL**
stuffing box **SB**
stumped **st.; stpd.**
styrene acrylonitrile **SAN**
styrene-butadiene rubber
  SBR
subacute sclerosing
  panencephalitis **SSPE**
subaltern **sub.**
subarachnoid hemorrhage
  SAH
subcontractor **sub.**
subcutaneous **sc.; s.c.; sub-q**
subcutaneously **s.c.**
subgenus **subg.**
subito **s**
subject **S; subj.**
subjective **subj.**
subjectively **subj.**
subject ratio **SR**
subject to approval **s/a**
subject to approval, no risk
  s.a.n.r.
subject to particular
  average **s.p.a.**
subject-verb-object **SVO**
subjunctive **sbj.;
  subj.; subjv.**
sublieutenant **S.L.; sub.**
submachine gun **SMG**

submarine S; subm.
submarine chaser SC
submarine-launched ballistic
  missile SLBM
submarine-launched cruise
  missile SLCM
submarine patrol SP
submarine thermal reactor
  STR
submerge sub.; subm.
submerged sub.; subm.
suboffice S.O.
subordinate sub.
subparagraph subpar.
subprofessional SP
subscriber sub.
subscription sub.; subs. •
subscription television STV
subsidiary sub.; subs.
subsistence subs.
subspecies ssp; subsp.
substandard substand.;
  substd.
substantive s.; sb.; subs.;
  subst.
substitute subs.; subst.
substitute natural gas SNG
subtract sub.
suburb sub.
suburban sub.
subway sub.
succeeded s.; suc.; succ.
successor suc.; succ.; sucr.
succinic dehydrogenase
  activity SDA
sucre S/
sucrose polyester SPE
suction suc.
sudden infant death SID
sudden infant death
  syndrome SIDS

sudden ionospheric
  disturbance SID
sufficient suff.
suffix suf.; suff.
Suffolk Suff.
suffragan suffr.
sugar, acetone, diacetic acid
  SAD
sugar coated SC
suggested sug.; sugg.
suggestion sug.; sugg.
sulfite waste liquor s.w.l.
sulfo-ricinoleic acid SRA
sulfur S
sulfur oxide SO_x
summary smry.
summary court SC
summary court-martial SCM
sun s.
Sunday S.; Sun.
Sundays and holidays
  S. & H.
Sunday school S.S.
sundries sund.
sun protection factor SPF
superb S
supercalendered s.c.
supercharger supchgr.
superconducting quantum
  interference device
  SQUID
superfine sup.; super.
superheterodyne super.
superhigh frequency SHF
superimposed current SC
superintendent Supr.; supt.
superintendent of car
  service S.C.S.
superintendent of
  transportation S.T.
superior S; sup.; super.

superlative **sup.; superl.**
super long play **SLP**
supersede **supsd.**
superseded **sup**
supersized and calendered **S.S. & C.**
supersonic commercial air transport **SCAT**
supersonic transport **SST**
supervise **supv.**
supervisor **supvr.**
supine **sup.**
supplement **sup.; supp.; suppl.**
supplemental retirement annuity **SRA**
Supplemental Security Income **SSI**
supplemental unemployment benefits **SUB**
supplementary **sup.; supp.; suppl.**
supplementary regulation **SR**
supplies **supls.**
supply **sup.; sy.**
supply and transport **S. & T.**
supply corps **SC**
supply department **SD**
supply depot **SD**
supply officer **SO**
support **spt.; sup.; supt.**
suppository **supp.**
supraprotest **S.P.**
supreme **sup.; supr.**
supreme court **SC**
Supreme Judicial Court **SJC**
surcharged **sur.**
surface **sur.**
surface area **SA**
surfaced **S**

surface feet per minute **sfm; sfpm**
surface foot **sf**
surface ground zero **SGZ**
surface measure **s.m.**
surface tension **S.T.**
surface-to-air missile **SAM**
surface-to-surface missile **SSM**
surface vessel **S/V**
surgeon **S.; sg.; surg.**
surgeon general **SG**
surgeon general's office **SGO**
surgeon major **S.M.**
surgery **surg.**
surgical **surg.**
surplus **s.; sur.**
surrender **surr.**
surrendered **sur.; surr.**
surrogate **surr.**
survey **s.; surv.; svy.**
surveying **surv.**
surveyor **surv.**
survival dose **S.D.**
surviving **surv.**
suspend **susp.**
suspended sentence **SS**
Sussex **Suss.**
svedberg **S**
swatch **sw.**
Swaziland **Swazil.**
Sweden **Sw.; Swed.**
Swedish **Sw.; Swed.**
swell organ **sw.**
swimming club **SC**
Swiss franc **SF**
switch **S; sw.**
switchboard **Sb; swbd.**
switching **swg.; swtg.**
switchman **swchmn.**
Switzerland **Switz.**

sworn statement **s.s.**
syllable **syl.; syll.**
Symbionese Liberation
    Army **SLA**
symbol **sym.**
symbolic **sym.**
symmetrical **s; sym.**
symphony **sym.; symph.**
symptoms **Sx**
synchronism **sync.**
synchronization **sync.**
synchronize **syn.; sync.;
    synch.**
synchronized **syn.; synch.**
synchronizing **syn.; sync.;
    synch.**
synchronous **sync.**
synchronous data link
    control **SDLC**
synchroscope **synscp.**
syndicate **synd.**
synergist **syn.**
synonym **syn.**
synonymous **syn.**
synonymy **syn.**
Syntagmatic Organization
    Language **SYNTOL**
synthetic **syn.**
synthetic-aperture radar
    SAR
synthetic natural gas **SNG**
Syria **Syr.**
Syrian **Syr.**
syrup **sy; syr.**
system **sys.; syst.**
systematic assertiveness
    training **S.A.T.**
systemic lupus
    erythematosus **SLE**
system network architecture
    SNA

systems engineer **SE**
Systems for Nuclear Auxiliary
    Power **SNAP**
systems operator **SYSOP**

T

table **t.; tab.**
table of allowances **T/A**
table of equipment **T/E**
table of organization **TO**
tablespoon **T; tb.; tbs.; tbsp.**
tablespoonful **tb.; tbs.; tbsp.**
tablet **tab.**
tablet triturate **TT**
tabulate **tab.**
tabulated **tab.**
tackle **T**
Tactical Air Command **TAC**
tactical air force **TAF**
tactical fighter,
    experimental **TFX**
tailor **tlr.**
Taiwan **Tai.**
take **sum.**
take care of business **TCB**
taken **t.**
taken and offered **t. & o.**
talk between ships **TBS**
Tanganyika **Tang.**
tangent **tan.**
tank **tk.**
tank corps **TC**
tank destroyer **TD**
tantalum **Ta**
tape conversion program
    TCP
tape disk operating system
    TDOS
tape operating system **TOS**
taper **t.**

tape recorder **TR**
tardive dyskinesia **TD**
tare **t.; tr.**
target **t.; tgt.**
target area **TA**
target practice **TP**
tariff **trf.**
tariff bureau **T.B.**
tariff number **T.N.**
tariff reform **T.R.**
task force **TF**
task group **TG**
Tasmania **Tas.; Tasm.**
tautological **taut.**
tautology **taut.**
tax **tx.**
tax agent **T.A.**
taxation **txn.**
tax-benefit transfer **TBT**
tax deferred annuity **TDA**
taxonomic **taxon.**
taxonomy **taxon.**
taxpayer identification
number **TIN**
Tax Reduction Act Stock
Ownership Plan **TRASOP**
tax value added **TVA**
Tayside **Tay.**
teacher **tchr.**
teachers college **T.C.**
teachers of English to
speakers of other
languages **TESOL**
teaching **tchg.**
teaching assistant **TA**
teaching English as a foreign
language **TEFL**
teaching English as a second
language **TESL**
teaching fellow **TF**
teaching practice **TP**

teaspoon **t.; ts.; tsp.; tspn.**
teaspoonful **ts.; tsp.; tspn.**
technetium **Tc**
technical **tec.; tech.**
technical analysis **T.A.**
technical bulletin **TB**
technical college **T.C.**
technical director **TD**
technical knockout **TKO**
technically **tech.**
technical manual **TM**
technical memorandum **TM**
technical order **TO**
technical paper **TP**
technical regulation **TR**
technical report **TR**
technical representative **TR**
technical sergeant **T.Sgt.**
technician **tec.; tech.**
technological **tech.; technol.**
technology **tec.; tech.;
technol.**
teeth per inch **tpi**
teetotaler **T.T.**
telecommunications access
method **TCAM**
telegram **tel.; tg.**
telegraph **tel.; tg.**
telegraph bureau **T.B.**
telegraph department **TD**
telegraphic **tel.**
telegraphic address **T.A.**
telegraphic transfer **T.T.**
telegraph money order
T.M.O.
telegraph office **T.O.**
telegraphy **tel.; teleg.**
telephone **t.; tel.; tp**
telephone department **TD**
telephone number **TN**
telephone office **T.O.**

telephony **tel.**
teleprinter **TP; TPR**
teleprocessing **TP**
teletype **T; TT**
teletypesetter **TTS**
teletypewriter **TT; TTY**
teletypewriter exchange **TWX**
television **TV**
television and infrared observation satellite **TIROS**
television data display system **TDDS**
television interference **TVI**
tellurian **Te**
temperance **temp.**
temperature **T; temp.; tmp.**
temperature-humidity index **THI**
temperature, pulse, respiration **TPR**
template **temp.**
tempo **t.**
temporal **t.; temp.**
temporarily out of print **TOP**
temporary **temp.**
temporary bench mark **T.B.M.**
temporary disability **TD**
temporary disability insurance **TDI**
temporary duty **TD; TDY**
temporomandibular joint **TMJ**
tender loving care **TLC**
Tennessee **Tenn.; TN**
Tennessee Valley Authority **TVA**
tenor **ten.**

tenor, baritone, bass **T.B.B.**
tense **t.**
tensile strength **ts**
tension **T**
tens of rupees **Rx**
tenuto **ten**
tera **t**
terawatt **tw**
terbium **Tb**
terminal **t.; term.; trm.; trml.**
terminal computer identification **TCID**
terminal control system **TCS**
terminal velocity **TV**
termination **T; term.**
terrace **ter.**
terra-cotta **TC**
terrazzo **ter.**
Terrestrial Dynamic Time **TDT**
territorial **T.**
territorial army **T.A.**
territorial decoration **TD**
territorial force **T.F.**
territory **T.; ter.; terr.; ty.**
tertiary **t; ter.; tert.**
tesla **t.**
Testament **Test.**
testament **T.**
test and evaluation **T & E**
Test of English as a Foreign Language **TOEFL**
Test of Standard Written English **TSWE**
Test of Written Spelling **TWS**
test solution **TS**
tetanus **Te**
tetrachloroethylene **TCE**
tetraethyl lead **TEL**

tetraethyl pyrophosphate
TEPP
tetrafluoroethylene **TFE**
tetrahydrocannabinol **THC**
Texas **Tex.; TX**
Texas League **TL**
textured vegetable protein
TVP
Thailand **Thai.; Thail.**
thallium **Tl**
thank God it's Friday **TGIF**
thanks to God **D.G.**
that **i.**
that is **h.e.; i.e.**
that is to say **sc.; scil.**
that which is to be
proved **IQED**
The Adjutant General **TAG**
The American Book Awards
TABA
theater **theat.**
theater nuclear forces **TNF**
The Athletics Congress **TAC**
theatrical **theat.**
the court wishes to consider
c.a.v.
the defendant being absent
abs. re.
the following **seq.; sq.**
the following ones
seqq.; sqq.
their **thr.**
Their Imperial Highnesses
T.I.H.
Their Royal Highnesses
T.R.H.
Their Serene Highnesses
T.S.H.
thematic apperception test
TAT
theologian **theol.**

theological **theol.**
theology **theol.**
the public good **b.p.**
there **thr.**
thermal unit **T.U.**
thermoluminescence **TL**
thermoluminescence
dosimeter **TLD**
thermoluminescence
dosimetry **TLD**
thermometer **therm.**
thermonuclear **TN**
the same **ead.; id.**
the same as **i.q.**
the senate and the people of
Rome **SPQR**
Thessalonians **Thess.**
the work cited from **op. cit.**
they made it **ff.**
they read **leg.**
thiamine pyrophosphate
TPP
thick fog **FF**
thickness **t**
thief **T.**
thin-layer chromatography
TLC
third base **3b**
this is **h.e.**
thoracic **T**
thorium **Th**
thorough bass **bc**
thoroughbred **TB; TH**
Thoroughbred Racing
Association **TRA**
Thoroughbred Racing
Protective Bureau **TRPB**
thousand **k; m.; thou.**
thousand board feet **M.B.F.**
thousand cubic feet **Mcf**
thousand feet board

measure **MBM; M.F.B.M.**
thousand feet surface
  measure **MSM**
thread **T.; thd.**
threads per inch **tpi**
three-dimensional **3-D**
three mile limit **TML**
three-quarter midget **TQ**
three times a day **t.i.d.**
threshold **th.**
threshold-limit value **TLV**
thromboplastic plasma
  component **TPC**
through **thr.**
through bill of lading **T.B.L.**
throws left-handed **TL**
throws right-handed **TR**
thrust horsepower **thp**
thrust line **TL**
thulium **Tm**
thunder **thdr.**
thunderhead **thd.**
Thursday **T.; Th.; Thu.;
  Thur.; Thurs.**
thymol blue **TB**
thyroid binding globulin
  TBG
thyroid-stimulating
  hormone **TSH**
thyrotropin releasing factor
  TRF
thyrotropin releasing
  hormone **TRH**
thyroxine binding globulin
  TBG
ticket **tix; tkt.**
tied **T**
tie line **TL**
tierce **tc**
tight end **TE**
till countermanded **T/C**

till forbidden **T.F.**
till further notice **TFN**
time **T**
time base **T.B.**
time deposit **TD**
time, distance, speed **TDS**
time division multiplexing
  tdm
time-domain reflectometry
  TDR
time handed in **THI**
timekeeper **tmkpr.**
time loan **T/L**
time of arrival **TOA**
time-of-flight **TOF**
time on target **TOT**
times **t.; x**
times at bat **TB**
time-sharing **t-s**
time-sharing option **TSO**
time, speed, and distance
  TSD
Timothy **Tim.**
tin **Sn**
tincture **tinct.; tr.**
tincture of opium **TO**
tip of the tongue **TOT**
Tipperary **Tip.**
titanium **Ti**
title **tit.**
title page **t.p.**
title page mutilated **t.p.m.**
title page wanting **t.p.w.**
tits and ass **T & A**
titular **tit.**
Titus **Tit.**
to **a**
tobacco mosaic virus **TMV**
to be announced **TBA**
to be assigned **TBA**
to be taken **sum.**

to be taken three times a
day **t.d.s.**
to be unwilling to prosecute
nol. pros.
Tobit **Tob.**
toe **T.**
to fill **T.F.**
to follow **T.F.**
to God, the best and
greatest **D.O.M.**
to infinity **ad inf.**
tolerance **tol.**
tollgate **TG**
ton **t.; tn.**
tongue and groove **T & G**
tongued and grooved **T & G**
tongued, grooved, and
beaded **T.G.B.**
tonnage **tnge.; tonn.**
tonsillectomy and
adenoidectomy **T and A**
tonsillitis and adenoiditis
T and A
tonsils and adenoids
T and A
tons of coal equivalent **TCE**
tons per day **tpd**
tons per hour **tph**
tons per inch **tpi**
tons per man-hour **TMH**
tons per minute **T/M**
tons per year **tpy**
tons registered **T.R.**
tool steel **TS**
tooth **t.**
top **t.**
top, bottom, and sides
TB & S
top edges gilt **t.e.g.**
topic statement **TS**
topographic **topo.**

topographical **topo.**
topographical engineer **T.E.**
topography **topog.**
torpedo **tor.**
torpedo boat **TB**
torpedo bomber **TB**
torpedo bombing **TB**
to saturation **ad sat.**
to take leave **P.P.C.; TTL**
total **T; tot.**
total bases **TB**
total bouts **TB**
total chances **TC**
total digestible nutrients
TDN
total harmonic distortion
THD
total loss **t.l.**
total loss only **t.l.o.**
total lymphoid irradiation
TLI
total particulate matter
TPM
total points **TP**
to the end **ad fin.; a.f.**
to the greater glory of God
A.M.D.G.
to the place **ad loc.**
touchdown **TD**
touchdowns passing **TP**
touchdowns running **TR**
tough shit **TS**
Tourist Trophy **TT**
toward the end **s.f.**
tower **twr.**
to whom it may concern
TWIMC
to wit **ss**
town **T.; tn.**
town clerk **T.C.**
town councillor **T.C.**

township   T.; tp.; twp.
townships   tps.
toxicology   tox.
toxic shock syndrome   TSS
toxic unit   TU
toxin-antitoxin   TAT
trace   T; tr.
traced   tr.
track   tr.; trk.
track commander   TC
tracked air-cushion vehicle   TACV
tracking dog   TD
track made good   TMG
tracks per inch   tpi
tracks per second   tps
tractor   trac.
tractor-drawn   TD
trade-last   TL
trademark   TM
Trades Union Congress   TUC
trade union   T.U.
tradition   trad.
traditional   trad.
traditional orthography   T.O.
traffic   traf.
traffic agent   T.A.
traffic auditor   T.A.
traffic bureau   T.B.
traffic commissioner   T.C.
traffic consultant   T.C.
traffic director   T.D.
traffic manager   T.M.
traffic unit   T.U.
tragedy   trag.
tragic   trag.
Trail   TRL
trailer   tlr.; tr.
trailing edge   TE
train   tn.; tr.
training   tng.; trg.

training manual   TM
training regulation   TR
trainmaster   T.M.
transaction   tr.; trans.
transactional analysis   TA
Trans-Alaska Pipeline   TAP
Transcendental Meditation   TM
transcutaneous electrical nerve stimulation   TENS
transfer   tfr.; tr.; trans.; transf.; trf.; trs.
transferred   tr.; trans.; transf.
transfer RNA   sRNA; tRNA
transformational-generative   TG
transformational grammar   TG
transformer   T; trans.
transient ischemic attack   TIA
transistor-transistor logic   TTL
transit   t.; tr.; trans.
transit authority   TA
transitional   trans.
transitive   t.; tr.; trans.
translated   tr.; trans.; transl.
translation   tr.; trans.; transl.
translator   tr.; trans.
transmission   trans.
transmission electron microscope   TEM
transmission electron microscopy   TEM
transmission unit   T.U.
transmit data register   TDR
transmit-receive   TR

transmitter **trans.**
transom **tr.**
transparent **trans.; transp.**
transport **tr.; trans.; tspt.**
transport and supply **TS**
transportation **tr.; trans.; transp.**
transport officer **TO**
transport pilot **TP**
transport quartermaster **TQM**
transpose **tr.; trans.; trs.**
Transvaal **Tvl.**
transverse **T; trans.; transv.**
transversely excited atmospheric **TEA**
transverse section **TS**
transvestite **TV**
travel **tr.; trav.**
travel and entertainment **T & E**
Travel Document and Issuance System **TDIS**
traveler **trav.**
travel group charter **TGC**
traveling post office **T.P.O.**
traveling stock reserve **T.S.R.**
traverse **trv.**
tray **tr.**
tread **T.; tr.**
treasurer **tr.; treas.; treasr.**
treasury **treas.**
treasury bill **TB**
treasury decision **TD**
Treasury Department **TD**
treaty port **TP**
treble **tr**
tremolo **trem.**
trench mortar **T.M.**

trestle **tres.**
trial balance **T/B**
triangle **T.**
tribal **trib.**
tribromosalicylanilide **TBS**
tribunal **trib.**
tribune **trib.**
tributary **trib.**
trichloroacetic acid **TCA**
trichloroethylene **TCE**
trichlorophenol **TCP**
triclocarbon **TCC**
tricresyl phosphate **TCP**
triethylenephosphoramide **TEPA**
trigger-price mechanism **TPM**
trigonometric **trig.**
trigonometrical **trig.**
trigonometry **trig.**
trill **tr.**
trillion cubic feet **tcf**
trillion electron volt **TeV**
trillo **t.**
Trinidad **Trin.**
Trinidad and Tobago **TD**
trinitrotoluene **TNT**
Trinity **T.**
triphosphopyridine nucleotide **TPN**
triple **T; 3b; trip.**
triple play **TP**
triplicate **trip.; tripl.**
trisodium phosphate **TSP**
tritium **T**
triturate **trit.**
troop **tp.; tr.; trp.**
troops **tps.**
tropic **trop.**
tropical **T; trop.; trp.**
trotter **t.**

troy **t**
truck **tk.; trk.**
truckload **T.L.**
true **T**
true air speed **TAS**
true air temperature **TAT**
true bearing **TB**
true boiling point **TBP**
true course **TC**
true heading **TH**
true mean **tm**
true north **TN**
truly **ty.**
trunk **trk.**
truss **tr.**
trust **tr.**
trustee **tr.; tru.**
trust receipt **T/R**
Trust Territories **T.T.**
Trust Territory of the Pacific
  Islands **T.T.P.I.**
tubal ligation **TL**
tube-launched, optically-
  tracked, wire-guided **TOW**
tubercle bacillus **TB**
tuberculin tested **TT**
tuberculosis **TB**
tub-sized **t.s.**
Tuesday **T.; Tu.;**
  Tue.; Tues.
tuition unit **TU**
tumor angiogenesis factor
  TAF
tun **t.**
tuned radio frequency **TRF**
tungsten **W**
Tunisia **Tun.**
turbulent **turbt.**
turf course **TC**
Turkey **Turk.**
Turkish **T.; Turk.**

turn **v.**
turn over **T.O.; v.**
turnpike **tnpk.; tpk.; tpke.**
turn quickly **v.s.**
turns per inch **tpi**
tutti **t**
Twaddell (hydrometer) **Tw**
twice a day **b.d.; b.i.d.**
twice a week **t.a.w.**
twilight **twi.**
twin lens reflex **TLR**
twin-screw steamer **T.S.S.**
twisted **tw.**
two-dimensional **2-D**
two hands **T.H.**
two-wheel drive **2WD**
tying goals **TG**
type **ty.**
typed letter signed **TLS**
type genus **t.g.**
typescript **TS**
typical **typ.**
typographer **typ.**
typographic **typ.**
typographical **typ.**
Tyrone **Tyr.**

U

ultimate **ult.**
ultimately **ult.**
ultimate tensile strength
  UTS
ultimo **ult.**
ultra-audible **UA**
ultrahigh frequency **UHF**
ultrahigh temperature **UHT**
ultrahigh vacuum **uhv**
ultra-large crude carrier
  ULCC
ultra-large-scale-

integrated **ULSI**
ultralow frequency **ULF**
ultralow-volume **ULV**
ultramicrofiche **UMF**
ultrashort wave **USW**
ultraviolet **UV**
ultraviolet-blue-visual **UBV**
ultraviolet image converter
UVICON
ultraviolet-long wave **UV-A**
ultraviolet photoemission
spectroscopy **UPS**
ultraviolet-shortwave **UV-B**
umbilicus **umb.**
Umbrian **Umbr.**
unanimous **unan.**
unauthorized absence **UA**
unbound **unb.**
uncertain **unc.**
uncirculated **U; unc.**
uncle **U.**
unconditioned stimulus **US**
unconscious **Ucs**
uncorrected **uncor.**
uncut **unc.; unct.**
under **u.**
under bark **u.b.**
undercarriage **U/C**
undercharge **U/C**
under consideration **s.j.**
under construction **UC**
underdeck tonnage **UDT**
underground residential
distribution **URD**
underproof **UP**
undersecretary **U.S.**
under separate cover **USC**
undersigned **undsdg.**
undertaker **undtkr.**
under the word **i.v.; s.v.**
under the year **s.a.**

under this title **h.t.**
under this word **s.h.v.**
underwater **u/w; UW**
underwater demolition team
UDT
underwater long-range missile
system **ULMS**
underwater-to-air missile
UAM
underwater-to-surface
missile **USM**
underwriter **U/w**
Underwriters Laboratories
UL
underwriting account **U/A**
undetermined **undetd.**
unemployment insurance **UI**
Unemployment Insurance
Service **UIS**
unexploded bomb **UXB**
unfit for military service **4-F**
unidentified **U/I**
unidentified flying object
UFO
unified **u.; un.**
uniform **u.; un.**
uniform regulations **U.R.**
unifying **un.**
Unilateral Declaration of
Independence **U.D.I.**
uninterruptible power
system **UPS**
union **u.; un.**
unionist **U.**
Union of Soviet Socialist
Republics **USSR**
unique selling proposition
USP
unit **u.; un.**
united **u.; un.**
United Arab Emirates **UAE**

United Arab Republic **UAR**
United Automobile, Aerospace and Agricultural Implements Workers of America **UAW**
United Farm Workers **UFW**
United Federation of College Teachers **UFCT**
United Federation of Teachers **UFT**
United Kingdom **UK**
United Mine Workers **UMW**
United Nations **UN**
United Nations Children's Fund **UNICEF**
United Nations Educational, Scientific, and Cultural Organization **UNESCO**
United Nations Relief and Works Agency **UNRWA**
United Nations Security Council **UNSC**
United Negro College Fund **UNCF**
United Parcel Service **UPS**
United Presbyterian **U.P.**
United Press International **UPI**
united service **U.S.**
United Service Organizations **USO**
United States **US**
United States Adopted Name **USAN**
United States Air Force **USAF**
United States Amateur Athletic Federation **USAAF**
United States Army **USA**
United States Auto

Club **USAC**
United States Catholic Conference **USCC**
United States Coast Guard **USCG**
United States Code **U.S.C.**
United States Collegiate Sports Council **USCSC**
United States Department of Agriculture **USDA**
United States Dispensatory **USD**
United States Employment Service **USES**
United States Geological Survey **USGS**
United States Golf Association **USGA**
United States Hockey League **USHL**
United States Information Agency **USIA**
United States Information Service **USIS**
United States Lawn Tennis Association **USLTA**
United States mail **USM**
United States Marine Corps **USMC**
United States Marines **USM**
United States Military Academy **USMA**
United States National Guard **USNG**
United States Naval Academy **USNA**
United States Naval Reserve **USNR**
United States Navy **USN**
United States Navy ship **USNS**

United States of America
USA
United States of America
Standards Institute
USASI
United States Olympic
Association **USOA**
United States Olympic
Committee **USOC**
United States Patent Office
USPO
United States Pharmacopeia
USP
United States Postal Service
USPS
United States Professional
Lawn Tennis Association
USPLTA
United States Public Health
Service **USPHS**
United States ship **USS**
United States standard **USS**
United States Tennis
Association **USTA**
United States Track and Field
Federation **USTFF**
United States Trademark
Association **USTA**
United States Wrestling
Federation **USWF**
universal **u.; univ.**
Universal Asynchronous
Receiver Transmitter
UART
Universal Automatic
Computer **UNIVAC**
Universal Decimal
Classification **UDC**
universally **univ.**
universal military service
UMS

universal military training
UMT
Universal Postal Union
UPU
Universal Product Code
UPC
Universal time **UT**
Universal Transverse
Mercator **UTM**
universal vendor marking
UVM
universe **univ.**
university **U.; un.; univ.**
university extension **U.E.**
unknown **ign.; unk.; unkn.**
unless before **ni. pr.;**
ni. pri.; n.p.
unless otherwise noted
n.a.n.
unlimited **unl.**
unmarried **um.; unm.**
unnilhexium **Unh**
unnilpentium **Unp**
unnilquadium **Unq**
unopened **unop.**
unopposed **unop.**
unpaged **unp.**
unpleasant **u.**
unsatisfactory **U**
unsatisfactory report **UR**
unserviceable **u/s**
unsigned **unsgd.**
unsteady **unstdy.**
unsymmetrical **u;**
uns.; unsym.
unwatermarked **unwmkd.**
upgraded **U**
upholsterer **uphol.**
upholstering **uphlstg.;**
uphol.
upholstery **uphol.**

upper **u.; up.**
uppercase **u.c.**
upper class **U**
upper deck **U.D.**
upper half **UH**
upper left **UL**
upper left center **ULC**
Upper Peninsula (Mich.) **UP**
upper respiratory disease **URD**
upper respiratory infection **URI**
upper right **UR**
upper right center **URC**
upper sideband **USB**
uranium **U**
Urban Development Action Grant **UDAG**
urban district **U.D.**
urban district council **U.D.C.**
urgent **ugt.**
uridine diphosphate **UDP**
uridine diphosphate glucose **UDPG**
uridine triphosphate **UTP**
urinal **ur.**
urinary tract infection **UTI**
urine **ur.**
urological **urol.**
urologist **urol.**
urology **U; urol.**
Uruguay **Ur.; Uru.**
us **n.**
use and occupancy **U. & O.**
user file directory **UFD**
usual **usu.**
usual, customary, or reasonable **UCR**
usually **usu.**
Utah **UT**
utility **ut.; util.**

utility cargo **UC**
utility dog **U.D.**
utility player **UT**

V

vacant **vac.**
vacation **vac.**
vaccination **vacc.**
vacuum **vac.**
vacuum tube **V.; VT**
vacuum tube voltmeter **VTVM**
vacuum ultraviolet **VUV**
vagabond **V.**
valentine **val.**
valley **val.; Vly**
valuable cargo **V.C.**
valuation **val.; valn.**
valuation clause **VC**
value **v.; val.**
value-added network **VAN**
value-added networking **VAN**
value-added tax **VAT**
valued **val.**
valued as in original policy **v.o.p.**
value engineer **VE**
value payable by post **V.P.P.**
valve **v.**
valve box **VB**
valvular disease of the heart **VDH**
van **v.**
vanadium **V**
Van Alen Simplified Scoring System **VASSS**
Vancouver Island **V.I.**
vapor **V**
vapor density **v.d.**

vapor pressure v.p.
variable V; var.; vrbl.
variable frequency oscillator
  VFO
variable pitch VP
variable rate mortgage
  VRM
variable time VT
variance Va
variant var.
variant reading var. lect.;
  v.l.; v.r.
variant readings vv. ll.
variation V.; var.
variegated var.
variety var.
variometer var.
various var.
various dates v.d.
various pagings v.p.
various places v.p.
various years v.y.
vasoactive intestinal peptide
  VIP
vasoactive intestinal
  polypeptide VIP
vasodepressor material
  VDM
vasoexcitor material VEM
Vatican Vat.
vector V
veering vrg.
vegetable veg.
vehicle identification
  number VIN
vein v.
vellum vel.
velocity v; vel.
velocity made good Vmg
velocity of light c
venerable V.; Ven.

venerables VV.
venereal disease VD
venereal disease research
  laboratory VDRL
Venezuela Ven.
Venezuelan equine
  encephalomyelitis VEE
vent V.
ventilate vent.
ventilating vent.
ventilation vent.
ventilator V.; vent.
ventral v.
ventricular assist device
  VAD
ventriculo-atrial V-A
verb v.; vb.
verb active v.a.
verbal vb.; vbl.
verbal adjective v.a.
verbal order VO
verb intransitive v.i.
verb neuter v.n.
verb passive v.p.
verb phrase VP
verb reflexive v.r.
verbs vv.
verb transitive v.t.
Vermont Vt.; VT
vernacular black English
  VBE
verse v.; ver.; vs.
versed sine vers
verses vss.; vv.
versicle V
version v.; ver.
versions vss.
verso v.; vo.; vso.
versus v.; vs.
vertebra vert.
vertebrate vert.

vertex **V; ver.**
vertical **v.; vert.**
vertical beam **VB**
vertical blanking interval **VBI**
vertical file **VF**
vertical grain **V.G.**
vertical interval **V.I.**
vertical short takeoff and landing **V/STOL**
vertical stripes **V.S.**
vertical takeoff **VTO**
vertical takeoff and landing **VTOL**
vertical tracking force **VTF**
very **v.; vy.**
very fair **v.f.**
very fine **VF**
very good **VG**
very high frequency **VHF**
very-high-frequency omnidirectional radio range **VOR**
very highly commended **V.H.C.**
very high performance **VHP**
very high speed integrated circuit **VHSIC**
very important person **VIP**
very large array **VLA**
very large crude carrier **VLCC**
very large scale integration **VLSI**
very lightly hinged **VLH**
very long baseline **VLB**
very long baseline array **VLBA**
very long baseline interferometer **VLBI**
very long baseline

interferometry **VLBI**
very long range **VLR**
very low altitude **VLA**
very low density lipoprotein **VLDL**
very low frequency **VLF**
very many thanks **VMT**
very old **V.O.**
very rarely **rr.**
Very Reverend **R.A.**
very shortwave **vsw**
very superior **V.S.**
very superior extra pale — used of brandy **V.S.E.P.**
very superior old — used of brandy **V.S.O.**
very superior old pale — used of brandy **V.S.O.P.**
very, very old — used of brandy **V.V.O.**
very, very superior — used of brandy **V.V.S.**
very, very superior old pale — used of brandy **V.V.S.O.P.**
very worshipful **V.W.**
vesicular **ves.**
vesicular exanthema **VE**
vessel **ves.**
vessel wall **V.W.**
vestibule **vest.**
vest pocket **VP**
vestry **ves.**
Veterans Administration **VA**
Veterans of Foreign Wars **VFW**
veterinarian **vet.**
veterinary **vet.**
veterinary corps **VC**
vibrate **vib.**
vibration **vib.**
vibration seconds **v.s.**

vibrations per minute
V.P.M.
vibrations per second **v.p.s.**
vicar **v.; vic.**
vicarage **vic.**
vicar apostolic **V.A.**
vicar forane **V.F.**
vicar-general **V.G.**
vicar rural **V.R.**
vice admiral **VA;
V.Adm.; VADM**
vice-chairman **VC**
vice-chancellor **VC**
vice-consul **VC**
vice president **VP**
vice versa **v.v.**
vicinal **V**
vicinity **vic.**
victor **vct.**
Victoria **Vic.**
Victoria Cross **VC**
victory **V**
vide **v.**
videlicet **viz.**
video **vid.**
videocassette recorder **VCR**
video display terminal **VDT**
video frequency **VF**
video high density **VHD**
video home system **VHS**
video jockey **VJ**
video tape recorder **VTR**
video tape recording **VTR**
Vietcong **VC**
vigilance committee **V.C.**
village **v.; vil.; vill.; Vlg**
vinyl chloride monomer
VCM
vinylidene chloride **Vc**
viola **va.; vla.**
violating local option

law **VLOL**
violin **v.; vl; vn.**
violins **vv.**
violoncello **vc.**
virgin **V.; virg.**
virgin and martyr
V. and M.
Virginia **Va.; VA**
Virgin Islands **V.I.**
virulence **V**
virulent **Vi**
viscosity **v.; vis.; visc.**
viscosity index **V.I.**
viscount **V.; Vis.; Visc.**
viscountess **Vis.; Visc.**
visibility **V; vis.; vsby.**
visible **vis.; vsb.**
visible capacity **V.C.**
visible supply **V.S.**
vision **v.; vsn.**
visiting **vis.**
Visiting Nurse Association
VNA
visual **vis.**
visual acuity **V; Va**
visual aid **VA**
visual-aural radio range
VAR
Visual Average Speed
Computer and Recorder
VASCAR
visual discriminatory acuity
VDA
visual display unit **VDU**
visual field **V.F.**
visual flight rules **VFR**
visual signaling **VS**
vitamin **vit.**
vitellus **vitel.**
vitreous **vit.**
vitrified **vit.**

vivace **viv**
vocabulary **vocab.**
vocal fremitus **VF**
vocalic **Vo**
vocal resonance **VR**
vocational **voc.**
vocative **v.; voc.**
voice **V.**
voice-actuated transmitter **VOX**
voice frequency **VF**
Voice of America **VOA**
voice operated transmitter **VOX**
voice store and forward **VSF**
voice tube **VT**
volar **vol.**
volcanic **vol.; volc.**
volcano **vol.; volc.**
volt **V**
voltage **V**
voltage regulator **VR**
voltage relay **VR**
volt-ampere **va**
volt ampere reactive **var**
voltmeter **V; vm.**
volt ohm milliammeter **VOM**
volts per meter **v/m**
volts per mil **vpm**
volume **t.; V; vol.**
volume and tension **V. and T.**
volume indicator **V.I.**
volumes **vv.**
volume table of contents **VTOC**
volumetric **vol.**
volumetric solution **V.S.**
volume unit **VU**
voluntary **vol.**

voluntary aid detachment **V.A.D.**
volunteer **V; vol.**
volunteer army **VOLAR**
volunteer battalion **V.B.**
volunteer corps **V.C.**
volunteer fire department **VFD**
Volunteers in Service to America **VISTA**
von **v.**
voting **vt.**
voting pool **v.p.**
voting trust certificate **V.T.C.**
voting trust company **V.T.C.**
voucher **vou.**
vowel **v.**
vulcanized rubber **vr**
Vulgar Latin **VL**
Vulgate **Vulg.**
vulnerable point **V.P.**

W

wagon **wag.**
wagoner **wag.**
waiter **wtr.**
wait order **W.O.**
walkover **WO**
wall **w.**
wallboard **WB**
wall-to-wall **w/w**
walnut **wal.**
wanting **w.**
war **w.**
war damage **WD**
warden **w.**
War Department **WD**
wardroom **WR; wrm.**
warehouse **w.; whs.; whse.**

warehouse book w.b.
warehouseman whsmn.
warehouse receipt WR
warehouse warrant W/W
warehousing w.; whnsg.
warm w
warm air W.A.
warm water aq. ferv.
warning wng.
war office WO
warrant war.; wrnt.; wt.
warranted warrtd.
warrant officer WO
warrant officer junior grade
  WOJG
war risk w.r.
war risk insurance W.R.I.
war risks only w.r.o.
war tax W.T.
wartime WT
Warwickshire Warks.
washed overboard w.o.b.
Washington WA; Wash.
washroom WR
Wassermann reaction Wr
waste w.
wastepaper WP
water aq.; w.
water and feed W. & F.
water and rail W. & R.
water ballast w.b.
water board W.B.
water closet w.c.
water finish W.F.
Waterford Wat.
water heater WH
water horsepower whp
water-in-oil W/O
waterline W.L.
watermark w/m; wmk.
watermarked wmkd.

water packed W.P.
waterproof wp.
waterproofing wp.
waterproof paper packing
  w.p.p.
waters Wtr
water-soluble ws
water supply WS
water tank WT
water tender WT
watertight W.T.
water vapor transmission
  rate WVTR
water-white WW
waterworks WW
watt w
watt-hour wh; whr
wattmeter wm
watts per candle wpc
wavelength WL
waybill W/B
we n.
weapon wpn.
weather w.; wea.; wthr.
weather bureau WB
weather permitting W.P.
weatherproof WP
weather station W.S.
weather stripping WS
weber Wb
Wechsler Adult Intelligence
  Scale WAIS
Wednesday W.; We; Wed.
week w.; wk.
weekly wkly.
weighing and inspection
  W. & I.
weighmaster whm.
weight P; w.; wgt.; wt.
weight guaranteed w.g.
weight or measurement W/M

weight/volume **w/v**
welder **wldr.**
welfare and recreation **W & R**
Welsh **W.**
west **w.; W**
westbound **WB**
western **w.; W**
Western Australia **W.A.; W. Aust.**
West Germany **W.G.**
West Indies **W.I.**
Westmeath **Westm.**
west-northwest **WNW**
west-southwest **WSW**
West Virginia **WV; W. Va.**
wet **w.**
wet bulb **WB**
wettable powder **WP**
wetted surface **ws**
Wexford **Wex.**
wharf **whf.**
wharfage **whfg.; whge.; wrfg.**
wharf owner's liability **W.O.L.**
wharves **whvs.**
wheel **whl.**
wheelbase **WB**
wheelchair **wc**
when actually employed **WAE**
when distributed **wd**
when issued **wi**
where above mentioned **u.s.**
whether **whr.**
which **wh.**
which is **q.e.**
which see **qq.v.; q.v.**
which was to be demonstrated **Q.E.D.**
which was to be done **Q.E.F.**
which was to be found out **Q.E.I.**
whip **w.**
whiskey and soda **W. & S.**
white **w.; wh.; wht.**
White Anglo-Saxon Protestant **WASP**
white blood cells **WBC**
white blood count **WBC**
White Fathers **W.F.**
white metal **W.M.**
white phosphorus **WP**
wholesale **whol.; whsle.**
wholesale price index **WPI**
whom it may concern **WIMC**
wicket **w.**
Wicklow **Wick.**
wide **w.**
Wide Area Data Service **WADS**
wide area network **WAN**
Wide-Area Telecommunications Service **WATS**
wider **wdr.**
wider all lengths **w.a.l.**
widow **vid.; w.; wid.**
widower **wid.**
width **w.; wdt.; wth.**
wife **ux.; w.**
wild pitch **wp; WP**
will call **WC**
Wiltshire **Wilts.**
winch **wn.**
wind **w.; wd.; wnd.**
wind direction **WD**
wind force **WF**
winding **wdg.**
window **wd.**
wind/vector **W/V**

wind/velocity **W/V**
wing **wg.**
wing forward **WF**
wingspread **WS**
winning pitcher **WP**
wins **w**
winter **wtr.**
wire **w.**
wire gauge **W.G.**
wireless operator **W.O.**
wireless telegraphy **W/T**
wireless telephony **W/T**
wire nonpayment **W.N.P.**
wire payment **W.P.**
Wisconsin **WI; Wis.; Wisc.**
Wisdom **Wisd.**
with **c.; w.**
with all faults **w.a.f.**
with average **W.A.**
withdrawal **W**
withdrawn failing **WF**
withdrawn passing **WP**
with effect from **w.e.f.**
with expression **esp**
within **w.**
with other goods **W.O.G.**
without **s.; sen;
  sn.; w/o; wt.**
without benefit of salvage
  w.b.s.
without charge **w.c.**
without compensation **WOC**
without date **s.a.; s.d.**
without day **s.d.**
without issue **s.p.**
without lawful issue **s.l.p.**
without legitimate issue
  s.p.l.
without male issue **s.m.p.;
  s.p.m.**
without mutes **ss**

without name **s.n.**
without place **s.l.**
without place, year, or
  name **s.l.a.n.**
without prejudice **w.p.**
without regard to time **st**
without surviving issue
  s.p.s.
without thymonucleic acid
  SAT
with particular average
  w.p.a.
with rights **w.r.**
with the bass **cb**
with the bow **ca**
with the left hand **cs**
with the necessary changes
  having been made **m.m.**
with the respective differences
  having been considered
  m.m.
with the right hand **cd**
with the solo part **cp**
with the voice **cv**
with the will annexed
  c.t.a.; w.w.a.
with title **w.t.**
with warrants **ww**
Women Accepted for
  Volunteer Emergency
  Service **WAVES**
Women in Construction **WIC**
Women in the Air Force
  WAF
Women's Air Force Service
  Pilots **WASP**
Women's Army Auxiliary
  Corps **WAAC**
Women's Army Corps **WAC**
Women's Auxiliary Air
  Force **WAAF**

Women's Christian
  Temperance Union **WCTU**
Women's Royal Air Force
  WRAF
Women's Royal Army Corps
  WRAC
Women's Royal Naval
  Service **WRNS**
Women's Voluntary
  Services **W.V.S.**
won **W**
wood **w.; wd.**
wood-burning fireplace
  WBF; WBFP
wood casing **W.C.**
word **w.; wd.**
wording **wdg.**
word processing **WP**
word processor **WP**
words a minute **wam**
words per minute **wpm**
word to the wise is
  sufficient **verb. sap.**
work **W; wk.**
worker **wkr.**
Work Incentive Program
  WIN
working **wkg.**
working capital **WC**
working point **W.P.**
working pressure **WP**
works department **W.D.**
Works Progress
  Administration **WPA**
work without opus (number)
  WoO
World Boxing Association
  WBA
World Boxing Council **WBC**
World Championship Tennis
  WCT

World Federation of Trade
  Unions **WFTU**
World Health Organization
  WHO
World Hockey Association
  WHA
world war **WW**
Worshipful **Wor.; Wpfl.**
would **wd.**
wound **wd.**
wounded in action **WIA**
wrappings **wrps.**
wreath **wr.**
wrecker **wkr.**
write on label **s.**
writer **wtr.**
writer to the signet **W.S.**
writing paper **wr.**
written above **s.s.**
wrong **w.**
wrong font **wf**
wrought **wrt.**
wrought iron **W.I.**
Wyoming **WY; Wyo.**

X

xenon **Xe**
x-ray diffraction **XRD**
x-ray photoemission
  spectroscopy **XPS**
x unit **x.u.**

Y

yacht club **YC**
Yacht Racing Association
  YRA
Yahweh **YHVH; YHWH**
yard **y.; yd.**
yarding **ydg.**

yard patrol **YP**
yards **yds.**
yarn over **yo**
year **a.; an.; y.; yr.**
yearbook **Y.B.; yrbk.**
yearly **yrly.**
year of birth **YOB**
year-old **YO**
years **ann.**
years before present **YBP**
yellow **y.; yel.; yl.**
yellow edges **y.e.**
yellow pine **Y.P.**
yellow spot **y.s.**
yen **y.**
yeoman **Y; yeo.**
yeomanry **yeo.; yeom.**
yesterday **yday.; yest.; yesty.**
yield **yld.**
yield point **Y.P.**
yield strength **Y.S.**
yield to maturity **YTM**
YMCA **Y**
Yorkshire **Yorks.**
young **juv.; y.**
young adult **YA**
young, attractive, verbal, intelligent, and successful **YAVIS**
younger **y.; yr.**
youngest **y.; yst.**
young lady **YL**
Young Men's Christian Association **YMCA**
Young Men's Hebrew Association **YMHA**
young people **YP**
young soldier **Y.S.**
young upwardly mobile professional **yumpie**

young urban professional **yuppie**
Young Women's Christian Association **YW; YWCA**
Young Women's Hebrew Association **YWHA**
your **y.; yr.**
Your Holiness **S.V.**
yours **yrs.**
youth hostel **YH**
ytterbium **Yb**
yttrium **Y; Yt**
yttrium aluminum garnet **YAG**
yttrium iron garnet **YIG**
Yugoslavia **Yug.**
Yukon Territory **Y.T.**

Z

Zacharias **Zach.**
Zechariah **Zech.**
zenith distance **ZD**
Zephaniah **Zeph.**
zero **z.**
zero-based budgeting **ZBB**
zero economic growth **ZEG**
zero frequency **ZF**
zero population growth **ZPG**
Zimbabwe African National Union **ZANU**
Zimbabwe African People's Union **ZAPU**
zinc **Zn**
zirconium **Zr**
zloty **Zl.**
zone **z.**
Zone Improvement Plan **ZIP**
zone of fire **Z/F**
zone of interior **ZI**
zone time **ZT**

zoning board of approval
    ZBA
zoological **zool.**
zoological garden **Z.G.**

zoological society **Z.S.**
zoologist **zool.**
zoology **zool.**